331 BOU

BOUNDARIES AND FRONTIERS OF LABOUR LAW

Labour law has always been preoccupied with boundaries. One can either be an 'employee' or not, an 'employer' or not, and the answer dictates who comes within the scope of labour law, for better or worse. But such divisions have always been difficult, and in recent years their shortcomings have become ever more pronounced. The proliferation of new work arrangements and heightened global competition have exposed a world-wide crisis in the regulation of work. It is therefore timely to re-assess the idea of labour law, and the concepts, in particular the age-old distinctions—that are used to delimit the field. This collection of essays, by leading experts from around the world, explores the frontiers of our understanding of labour law itself. Contributors: Harry Arthurs, Paul Benjamin, Hugh Collins, Guy Davidov, Paul Davies, Simon Deakin, Mark Freedland, Judy Fudge, Adrián Goldin, Alan Hyde, Jean-Claude Javillier, Csilla Kollonay Lehoczky, Brian Langille, Enrique Marín, Kamala Sankaran, Silvana Sciarra, Katherine Stone and Anne Trebilcock.

Boundaries and Frontiers of Labour Law

Goals and Means in the Regulation of Work

Edited by

Guy Davidov and Brian Langille

International Institute for Labour Studies

·HART·
PUBLISHING

OXFORD AND PORTLAND, OREGON
2006

Published in North America (US and Canada) by
Hart Publishing
c/o International Specialized Book Services
920 NE 58th Avenue, Suite 300
Portland, OR 97213-3786
USA
Tel: +1 503 287 3093 or toll-free: (1) 800 944 6190
Fax: +1 503 280 8832
E-mail: orders@isbs.com
Website: www.isbs.com

Hart Publishing, 16c Worcester Place Oxford, OX1 2JW
Telephone: +44 (0)1865 517530 Fax: +44 (0) 1865 510710
E-mail: mail@hartpub.co.uk
Website: http://www.hartpub.co.uk

British Library Cataloguing in Publication Data
Data Available

ISBN-13: 978-1-84113-595-3 (hardback)
ISBN-10: 1-84113-595-X (hardback)

Typeset by Compuscript Ltd, Shannon
Printed and bound in Great Britain by
Biddles Ltd, King's Lynn, Norfolk

Acknowledgements

Our first and greatest debt is to the extraordinary group of distinguished scholars who responded to our call to convene with a view to reflecting upon the state of the discipline of labour law, and its basic conceptual 'building blocks' of 'employee' and 'employer', in this era of globalisation. This meeting took place in May 2005 at the Bellagio Study and Conference Centre, on Lake Como in Northern Italy. We are extremely grateful for the magnificent support of the Rockefeller Foundation in inviting us to hold our workshop at this spectacular venue, which has a long and distinguished history of hosting scholars working in a wide range of disciplines. The contributors to this book all prepared their papers in advance of the workshop and the opportunity to discuss these papers during three full days, in a closed, exceptionally welcoming, and inspiring environment, contributed immensely to the final product before you. Our warm thanks go to the very professional and dedicated staff of the Rockefeller Foundation, both at Bellagio and at the New York office, in particular to Susan Garfield, Nadia Gilardoni and Gianna Celli.

The workshop also enjoyed the collaboration and generous financial support of the International Institute for Labour Studies, Geneva. We wish to convey our deep thanks to the Institute, and in particular to Jean-Pierre Laviec, who, as Acting Director, responded warmly to our request for support, and to Gerry Rodgers, current Director of the Institute.

We are also indebted to Benjamin Aaron, Bob Hepple and Silvana Sciarra, who supported the project as evaluators of our initial proposal; to Harry Arthurs, Paul Benjamin and Mark Freedland, who agreed to assist us by serving as an informal 'organizing committee'; to Pnina Alon-Shenker who provided excellent research assistance; to Einat Geva for administrative assistance; to Annette Henry at the Faculty of Law, University of Toronto, for handling the finances so skilfully; and to Richard Hart for overseeing the publication of this book in such a friendly and professional way.

It has been a very real privilege to be able to draw upon all of these resources—intellectual, material, professional, and personal—in our efforts to make a contribution to the discipline of labour law which, we believe, can only fulfill its destiny through constant critical reflection upon its basic goals and the means for achieving them in the world as we know it.

Guy Davidov and Brian Langille

Contents

List of Contributors

Harry Arthurs is President Emeritus and University Professor of Law and Political Science at York University, Toronto, Canada.

Paul Benjamin is Director of Cheadle, Thompson & Haysom Inc, Cape Town, and Adjunct Professor at the Institute of Development and Labour Law, University of Cape Town, South Africa.

Hugh Collins is Professor of English Law at the Law Department of the London School of Economics and Political Science.

Guy Davidov is a Lecturer at the Faculty of Law of the University of Haifa, Israel.

Paul Davies is Cassel Professor of Commercial Law at the Law Department of the London School of Economics and Political Science.

Simon Deakin is Robert Monks Professor of Corporate Governance at the University of Cambridge.

Mark Freedland is Professor of Employment Law at the Faculty of Law of the University of Oxford.

Judy Fudge is a Law Professor at Osgoode Hall Law School of York University, Toronto, Canada.

Adrián Goldin is Professor Plenario at the Unversidad de San Andrés, Victoria, Argentina.

Alan Hyde is Professor of Law and Sidney Reitman Scholar at Rutgers University in New Jersey, USA.

Jean-Claude Javiller is a Senior Adviser at the International Institute for Labour Studies of the International Labour Office, Geneva, Switzerland.

Csilla Kollonay Lehoczky is Professor of Law at the Central European University, Budapest, Hungary.

Brian Langille is Professor of Law at the Faculty of Law, University of Toronto, Canada.

Enrique Marín is a Labour Law Specialist at the International Labor Office, Geneva, Switzerland.

Kamala Sankaran is a Reader at the Faculty of Law of the University of Delhi, India.

Silvana Sciarra is Jean Monnet Professor of European Labour and Social Law at the University of Florence, Italy.

Katherine Van Wezel Stone is Professor of Law at UCLA School of Law, California, USA.

Anne Trebilcock is a Legal Adviser and Director of the Office of Legal Services at the International Labour Office, Geneva, Switzerland.

Table of Cases

Australia

Canada

Europe

Table of Legislation

International (For ILO Conventions see separately below)

ILO Conventions

1

Introduction: Goals and Means in the Regulation of Work

GUY DAVIDOV AND BRIAN LANGILLE

THE LAWS REGULATING and protecting people at work are in crisis. One dimension and cause of this dramatic situation is changes in the empirical reality of the world of work which result in millions of workers throughout the world finding themselves outside the scope of labour law.[1] This is perhaps one of the most profound results of the shift in our times towards the reign of 'free markets', and with it we are witnessing the return of some of the harsh consequences that brought about the enactment of labour regulations in the early years of the twentieth century. Not that many governments in the world explicitly decided to accept such extreme deregulation. It is rather the result of inaction in light of two separate (though inter-related) developments: the growth of the so-called 'informal economy',[2] and the proliferation of new forms of work relations that fall outside the definition of 'employee', which continues to be the basis for most labour protections. The former phenomenon is more dominant in developing economies, while the latter presents a greater challenge to developed ones. But both problems arise for similar reasons, and both can be found, to different degrees, throughout the world, as the International Labour Organisation (ILO) recently recognised.[3]

While total exclusion from the scope of labour law is prevalent, partial exclusion is similarly troubling. By using triangular employment relationships and other atypical work arrangements, employers around the world

---

[1] A note to our North-American readers: the term 'labour law' is used here to denote employment law as well.

[2] *Decent Work and the Informal Economy* (Geneva, International Labour Office, 2002), available at: http://www.ilo.org/public/english/standards/relm/ilc/ilc90/pdf/rep-vi.pdf.

[3] *Report of the Committee on the Informal Economy* (90th Session of the General Conference, Geneva, International Labour Office, 2002), available at: http://www.ilo.org/public/english/standards/relm/ilc/ilc90/pdf/pr-25.pdf; *Provisional Record No 21: Report of the Committee on the Employment Relationship* (International Labour Conference, 91st Session, Geneva, International Labour Office, 2003), available at: http://www.ilo.org/public/english/standards/relm/ilc/ilc91/pdf/pr-21.pdf.

have been successful in avoiding specific responsibilities, even for workers who are considered 'employees'. Such employees may come within the scope of labour law, in the sense that minimum wage laws and other protective regulations apply to them. But they often do not enjoy collective agreements that apply to others in the same workplace; nor the security and other entitlements that come with the 'traditional' jobs for the same employer. Risk is being shifted to the most vulnerable.[4] The crisis which results from these changes in the world of work clearly makes necessary an inquiry into possible adjustments of the boundaries of labour law.

But there is a second, difficult, and important dimension to our crisis, one that is not empirical but conceptual. It is difficult to get a grip upon precisely because it brings into question the very idea and category of labour law itself. Simply put the question is whether, in light of the stress being placed upon the basic conceptual building blocks—'employee', 'employer', 'the contract of employment', and so on—the familiar edifice of labour law can remain standing. Or as some of our authors put it, the question is not simply 'what are the boundaries of labour law?'. The question is also 'what is labour law?'.

This two-dimensional crisis in labour law has many significant consequences. Obviously a failure in the delivery of workers' protection has grave distributive consequences, but this is not the *only* reason that it urgently needs to be addressed. Labour laws are not just about ensuring that workers 'in need of protection' are getting their fair share of the pie. There is a growing understanding in recent years that regulation can play a crucial role in promoting productivity, efficiency and competitiveness as well.[5] Other societal goals and values surely play a role here as well, as will be discussed shortly. As a result of the current crisis in labour law, these values—distributive justice, efficiency and others—are all being compromised. This worldwide problem requires urgent in-depth discussion and analysis. The aim of this book is to contribute to these important tasks by confronting the fundamental questions at the heart of labour law; by rethinking its goals as well as the means (legal concepts and techniques) that can best achieve them.

---

[4] See, eg, P. Cappelli, L. Bassi and H. Katz, *Change at Work* (New York, Oxford University Press, 1997); K.V.W. Stone, *From Widgets to Digits: Employment Regulation for the Changing Workplace* (Cambridge, Cambridge University Press, 2004).

[5] See, eg, S. Deakin and F. Wilkinson, 'Labour Law and Economic Theory: A Reappraisal' in H. Collins, P. Davies and R. Rideout (eds.), *Legal Regulation of the Employment Relation* (London, Kluwer Law International, 2000) 29; H. Collins, 'Regulating the Employment Relation for Competitiveness' (2001) 30 *ILJ* 17.

1. THE VERY IDEA OF LABOUR LAW

Our basic approach is purposive. Labour laws should be designed—and interpreted—in light of their goals. The failure of current regulatory techniques is therefore a good opportunity to ponder about the purpose—indeed the very idea—of labour law. According to the traditional view of labour law, employees are in need of protection because they suffer from inequality of bargaining power *vis-à-vis* their employers.[6] Most of the contributors to this volume seem to believe—even if, for the most part, implicitly—that this traditional view remains valid.[7]

This traditional view is provocatively challenged by two of the contributors. **Brian Langille** and **Alan Hyde** both believe that it is no longer helpful to focus on the distributive or 'protective' aspects of labour law. They both feel that labour law should be re-conceptualised and re-formulated around its advantages to society and to employers. They part ways, however, in the definition of such advantages. Langille follows Amartia Sen in focusing on broad non-pecuniary advantages that are important to society as a whole, such as enhancing human freedom and mobilising human capital. He argues that, rather than being a 'zero-sum game', or an 'afterthought', labour laws should be seen as both the aim and an instrument for human development and a positive factor in the maximisation of societal welfare. Their narrowing scope should therefore worry not just the workers themselves, but governments of all persuasions.

Hyde, on the other hand, puts the emphasis on the role of labour laws in correcting market failures. The view that labour laws can sometimes promote efficiency is hardly new, as already noted. But Hyde argues provocatively that for all practical matters we should disregard all other values and purposes, and focus on the correction of market failures *alone*. His aim is to broaden the scope of labour law to every relationship in which such market failures are prevalent and labour law techniques could be useful. At the same time, however, his approach could arguably lead to a significant narrowing of labour law, by excluding those regulations that are designed mostly for purpose of redistribution or the promotion of other non-market values.

The same topic is attacked from a different angle by **Anne Trebilcock** in her chapter on the 'informal economy'. Trebilcock argues that our discussion of informal labour markets can benefit from development theories; when we ask ourselves whether we should bring workers from the 'informal' realm to the 'protected' one, and how, it is useful to consider three

---

[6] For a classic account see P. Davies and M. Freedland, *Kahn-Freund's Labour and the Law* (3rd edn, London, Stevens, 1983), ch 1.

[7] For *explicit* affirmations of the traditional view, although not necessarily by reference to 'inequality of bargaining power', see the chapters by Davidov, Goldin, Javillier and Sciarra in this volume.

approaches from the rich literature dealing with development. These approaches—one focusing on sustainable livelihood, another on human capabilities and the third on empowerment—can be seen as offering specific content to the debate on the purpose of labour law. The human capabilities approach fits well with Langille's chapter. The other two approaches put the emphasis on some additional goals that can be seen as explaining and justifying labour laws. They can also assist in determining its scope *vis-à-vis* the realm of 'informality'.

2. THE EMPLOYMENT RELATIONSHIP AS A VEHICLE FOR THE DELIVERY OF RIGHTS AND ENTITLEMENTS

As a matter of positive law, numerous rights are currently tied to the employment relationship throughout the world. One must be considered an 'employee' to enjoy protective employment standards, the right to bargain collectively with other employees, and often also rights concerning health and safety, equality at work, and various welfare entitlements. Recent years have seen growing scepticism regarding the wisdom of this tie. It was perhaps useful and reasonable, at least in developed economies, as long as the post-war model of employment persisted. But as the paradigm changed— and the long-term, full-time, secure, family-wage employment for males in industry ceased to be the norm—experts begun to come to the realisation that it serves to exclude significant parts of the population. Indeed, an influential report for the European Commission[8] and a significant number of academics have argued for the extension of different rights to other groups as well. Thus, for example, there seems to be no reason for the exclusion of independent contractors from health care schemes, health and safety regulations, the right to equal treatment at work, or from protection against sexual harassment. Some scholars went further and argued that the concept of 'employee'—and the legal distinction between employees, independent contractors, and others—should be completely dissolved.[9] But so far such ideas and their implications have not been fully explored.

The problem is not merely a conceptual one. It is rather a fundamental question of finding the best means for the delivery of workers' protection as well as various welfare entitlements. Any solution must be based on identifying the exact deficiencies in current models, both in terms of their distributive consequences and in terms of their miscalculation of the benefits

---

[8] European Commission, *Transformation of Labour and Future of Labour Law in Europe: Final Report* (Brussels, European Commission, 1999) (also published as A. Supiot, *Beyond Employment: Changes in Work and the Future of Labour Law in Europe* (Oxford, Oxford University Press, 2001)).

[9] For references see Davidov, this volume.

of labour laws for society as a whole. Is it still justified to maintain the distinction between employees and independent contractors, on the one hand, and between employees and unpaid workers (especially women working at home) on the other? Otherwise put, to what extent is there still a need for 'labour law' separated from 'welfare law' or, more broadly, 'social law'? In what contexts could such distinctions be useful and in what contexts are they archaic and harmful? More generally, what could be an alternative platform for the delivery of work-related and other rights? And how can we ensure continuity for those who frequently change employers or even status (employee, independent contractor, unemployed etc.)?[10]

Many of these timely questions are addressed, both directly and indirectly, by the contributors to this volume. **Simon Deakin** provides an historical account of the contract of employment—indeed the concept of an employer–employee relationship—in the United Kingdom and in continental Europe. This historical comparison leads him to some interesting conclusions about the evolution of labour law, which he argues is closely tied with the timing of industrialisation and the form taken by the welfare state as a whole. More specifically to the concept of the contract of employment, Deakin argues that it serves important functions in a market-based economy, and is unlikely to be replaced by any radically different model. At the same time, he acknowledges that the *existing form* of the contract of employment is losing its force as a device of classification.

The diminishing usefulness of current concepts and tests is further explored by **Adrián Goldin**. In his chapter, Goldin argues that the concept of 'legal subordination', which is understood in civil-law systems to form the basis of employment relationships, is losing its efficacy. As long as the large majority of work relations fell either clearly within or outside the boundaries of this concept, it was useful and effective; but, as a result of the changes in the world of work, this is no longer the case. Moreover, Goldin argues that the power of direction, expressed in the juridical notion of subordination, no longer necessarily coincides with the predominance of the employer, against which labour laws are designed to protect. Legal subordination should be replaced by the broader notion of contractual inequality to ensure that labour law covers new forms of exercising power.

In a somewhat similar vein, **Guy Davidov** also believes that changes are necessary in the way we use our legal techniques (means) in order to achieve societal goals. He points to four different ways in which the use of current tests and definitions should be changed. He goes on to argue, however, in line with Deakin, that the concept of 'employee' is here to stay. While Deakin observed the endurance of the employment relationship model based on an historical comparison, Davidov makes the normative argument

---

[10] For preliminary suggestions see European Commission, above n 8.

that 'employees' are different from other groups in need of protection, and therefore require special protection (labour law). So subject to some adjustments—adjustments that are not minor, but not impossible either—he argues that the continued use of the concept of employee is justified.

3. BRINGING ATYPICAL WORK ARRANGEMENTS INTO THE SCOPE OF LABOUR LAW

There is broad agreement among scholars that the realities of work relations have changed. It is much less clear how these changes affect labour law. In Part 3 of the book, five contributors from very different backgrounds rely on experience from their own countries to make some general arguments about the possible expansion of labour law. In different ways, they all discuss various means that were used in their own countries—or call for the adoption of other means—to bring into the scope of labour law workers that were unjustly (partially or wholly) excluded.

A far-reaching reform is proposed by **Katharine Stone**, who argues that American labour law has been built on the assumption of long-term attachment to a specific employer, an assumption which is no longer valid. She explains that there are currently new risks for 'regular' employees (like job insecurity, wage uncertainty and skills devaluation), alongside complete or partial exclusion from labour law for 'atypical' workers. She goes on to suggest a number of ways in which labour law could be expanded and improved, to provide protection against those new risks.

Stone devotes particular attention to the creation of 'transition assistance'. This theme is also taken up by **Paul Benjamin**.[11] Benjamin describes changes in the South African labour market, which resulted in the exclusion of numerous workers from the scope of labour law. He goes on to describe some attempts by the legislature and the courts to alleviate the problem, and to suggest the use of international law—the ratified ILO conventions— as a means of pressing towards expanding labour law's scope. He also argues in favour of legislative schemes that will bridge the current division between labour law, unemployment insurance and skills development programmes to ensure effective protection during transition periods.

Benjamin devotes some specific attention to the unique difficulties of developing economies. The same difficulties are also considered by **Kamala Sankaran**, who describes the enormous informal labour market in India, as well as some unique attempts that were made to protect casual workers there. Interestingly, she discusses two opposite shifts between a bilateral and a tripartite model of employment, both directed at the same end of ensuring protection for atypical workers. On the one hand there are state-created

---

[11] For additional discussion of this issue see Goldin, this volume.

'boards' in specific sectors, which serve as intermediaries between casual workers and their short-term employers (a technique that is also being considered for the creation of industry-specific social insurance schemes for workers, including the self-employed). At the same time, Indian courts were willing to look beyond formally commercial arrangements, and find an employment relationship between workers producing cigarettes at home and the buyer who also supplied the materials; Sankaran argues that the same logic can be extended to consider other family members, working together with the aforementioned employee at home, as directly employed by the same buyer.

An entirely different legal regime, but with similar problems, is discussed by **Csilla Kollonay Lehoczky** in a contribution from a Hungarian perspective. She describes the transformation of post-socialist states—with the increased contractual (and market) freedom and unbounded flexibility—as a necessary background to more recent attempts to ensure protection to workers. Legislation and case law have legitimised, but also regulated, new forms of employment; attempted to prevent false self-employment; and extended some basic protection to the self-employed. Kollonay Lehoczky concludes by offering some thoughts on the goals of labour law and its possible extension. She argues that an employment contract is an exchange that has to be fair. The relationships between work and learning, work and family, risk and control must all be taken into account when considering the 'fair price' of labour.

Like Kollonay Lehoczky, **Silvana Sciarra** also combines a discussion of the legal regulation of atypical workers with comments on the very idea of labour law. While describing a wide array of developments in European countries as well as the European Union, Sciarra lends support to various legal techniques aimed at ensuring protection—in particular regarding 'fundamental rights' or 'core principles'—to non-standard workers. Such efforts are explained by her articulation of the purpose of labour law as achieving an equilibrium of bargaining power, as well as supporting mechanisms that will empower the weaker parties to emerge from their state of dependency.

4. IDENTIFYING THE EMPLOYER AND DETERMINING ITS RESPONSIBILITIES

For many years, case law and scholarship dealing with the scope of labour law have focused entirely on the side of the employee. The proliferation of triangular work relations in recent years necessitated the shift of much attention to the employer's side as well. The next part of the book is dedicated to the question who should be considered the employer, and, more generally, what responsibilities should be borne by the *user* of labour.

The traditional view assumes a relationship between an employee and a single employer. But this unitary conception of the 'employer' is losing ground, as **Paul Davies** and **Mark Freedland** explain in their joint chapter. It is challenged from within the enterprise, when managerial (employer) powers are exercised by dual-role employees; and, at the same time, it is challenged from the outside, by the proliferation of multi-agency structures or networks. Both phenomena are becoming more significant in recent years, according to Davies and Freedland, as a result of the trend towards vertical disintegration. They go on to discuss the (limited) response of UK labour law to these challenges, and conclude that an understating of the employing organisation has become the most important factor in re-drawing the boundaries of the field.

The legal boundaries of the 'employer' are also the subject of **Judy Fudge**'s contribution. Fudge argues that the equation of the legal employer with the corporate form ignores the way contemporary employment functions are organised. As a result, firms are able to externalise risks and responsibilities concerning workers. She uses Canadian examples to show the difficulties in determining the identity of the employer in practice, and concludes by calling for a functional approach to ensure that precarious workers are included within the scope of labour law.

One specific and dominant problem related to the identification of the employer concerns comparative fairness (or non-discrimination) claims, as explained by **Hugh Collins** in his chapter. Claims for equal treatment guaranteed by European Community law—for example claims by part-time or fixed-term employees—create considerable difficulties in situations of different employing entities. Most significantly, temporary agency workers have been unable to succeed in comparative fairness claims, because of the 'single source' doctrine developed by the European Court of Justice. The result is unjustified, argues Collins, and creates incentives for employers' use of segmentation involving multi-employers. He suggests the adoption of a network concept of an integrated workforce, in which comparisons can be made regardless of the identity of the immediate employer.

5. INTERNATIONAL AND INSTITUTIONAL SOLUTIONS

Upon consideration of the first four parts of this book, readers may well be struck by the universality of problems concerning the scope of labour law and, indeed, the similarity of the difficulties faced in different parts of world. Our contributors—coming from different continents, from diverse legal systems, from developed as well as developing economies—have all described and considered very similar problems. These issues, therefore, quite clearly invite comparative analyses and a consideration of possible international responses. This task is undertaken in the next part by two ILO specialists, **Enrique Marín** and **Jean-Claude Javillier**.

Marin draws on extensive comparative work done at the ILO to describe the employment relationship's 'lack of focus', as well as recent attempts that have been made in different countries to 're-focus' it. Marin notes that, although problems are very similar, there are also differences of legal tradition, as well as differences in social and economic conditions. He goes on to consider the possibility of adopting an international standard on the subject, with the assumption that, because of those differences, it would have to be supple (a Recommendation), with the main goal being guidance and orientation.

This discussion is complemented by Javillier's contribution, which in a sense provides the theoretical and methodological foundations for the ILO work on this subject. Javillier stresses the importance of an empirical investigation—to ensure that policy makers have a real picture of the labour market—and a sociological perspective to understand it. He then poses the questions we face in terms of legal techniques—in particular the need to adapt current definitions—and argues that we can find answers in the long-standing vision of the ILO for this purpose.

International institutions can certainly play a vital role in rethinking and resetting the scope of labour law. But the responsibility for performing this crucial task—and the power to do so—lies first and foremost within each legal system. In most countries this task is assigned to the courts; the role of other institutions, like Departments of Labour, has often been neglected. **Harry Arthurs** gives a number of explanations for the declining power of these bodies of government, and calls for their resurrection as advocacy agencies, that will seek to ensure the consideration of workers' interests as part of the calculus, in every relevant public policy decision. He is quick to declare his scepticism about the feasibility of this idea, though, given the trend towards neo-liberalism.

Arthurs' chapter is dedicated, for the most part, to a consideration of *means* in the regulation of work. But by looking beyond concrete legal techniques, he also takes us back to where we began—the attempts to redefine our *goals*. Arthurs sees effective advocacy, or representation—and the empowerment of labour representatives—as most important, and attempts to redraw definitive boundaries as futile. Indeed, contentions and indeterminacies will surely remain. But boundaries will always remain an indispensable part of the law. Arthurs simply provides additional insights into the goals that should guide us in this necessary (even if not always easy and politically feasible) line-drawing.

* * *

This is not a book that aims to provide definitive and detailed suggestions and solutions. Our aim is simply to contribute to the debate about the very idea, and the scope, of labour law. Each chapter provides, in its own way, a significant contribution to this debate. But there is also one crucial cumulative contribution. All the chapters can be seen to share the same commitment—whether explicitly or implicitly—to an open, critical and *purposive* approach. None of the contributors has taken a formalistic-doctrinal view of the employment relationship. We all agree that terms like employer and employee—and the boundaries they create—have a purpose. Our task is to understand and define this purpose, indeed the *goal,* and thus the very idea, of labour law—and to develop the best *means* (conceptual boundaries and other legal techniques) to achieve it. Indeed, failure to attend to our true goals is a common human, and legal, failing. It often results in our means becoming detached from the ends they were originally constructed to serve, and taking on an arbitrary life of their own. If we succeed in re-defining the terms of the debate along the purposive lines we suggest, this may well be our greatest achievement.

I

The Very Idea of Labour Law

2

Labour Law's Back Pages

BRIAN LANGILLE*

For Sinzheimer labour law was 'the guardian of human beings in an age of unconstrained materialism'. His vision of labour law was as a force to counteract inequality.

> Sir Bob Hepple, Sinzheimer Lecture (2002).

Equality, I spoke the word as if a wedding vow, Ah, but I was so much older then, I'm younger than that now.

> Bob Dylan, 'My Back Pages' (1964).

The difficulty lies not in the new ideas, but in escaping from the old ones, which ramify, for those brought up as most of us have been, into every corner of our minds.

> Keynes, Preface to The General Theory (1931).

I. INTRODUCTION: OUR TRUE QUESTION

THE FOUNDING FATHER of Canadian labour law is Bora Laskin. Laskin was a Professor of Labour Law at the University of Toronto who later became Chief Justice of the Supreme Court of Canada. In 1947 Bora Laskin created what I believe to be the first labour law 'casebook', that is a set of teaching materials, for the first law school labour law course offered in Canada. In his preface to that casebook he wrote:

The 'maturing' of labour law as a subject worthy of an independent place on a Canadian law school curriculum is an eloquent commentary on the impact of economic factors on the traditional categories of the common law. 'Labour relations' as a matter for legal study has outgrown any confinement to a section

---

* Professor of Law, Faculty of Law, University of Toronto, Toronto, Canada.

of the law of torts or to a corner of the criminal law. Similarly, and from another standpoint, it has burst the narrow bounds of the law of master and servant.[1]

These remarks are of great interest to me. They may seem at first blush to be simply a bit of promotional and prefatory puffery aimed at selling the idea of a new and unfamiliar course. But to regard them as such is, in my view, a mistake. They are better understood as articulating a profound point about the nature of labour law, a point to which we are well advised to return in these times. But it is a difficult and often overlooked point. What does it mean to say that labour law has 'outgrown' tort, criminal law and the law of master of servant and that it deserves its own place in the law school curriculum, or that it needs to be recognised as a subject of study and inquiry on its own? Why is labour law a suitable subject for treatment in a single text, or inclusion as a separate course in a law school curricula, or as a way of organising specialised law firms? Why was it an appropriate category around which to build domestic departments of labour? Or international organisations, such as the ILO? If the snappy response is that it no longer is, then my question simply becomes, why was it ever? And if the response is that it never was, then my belief is that that is wrong, as a similar comment about family law or trade law would be, and in just the same way. And my task would be to show why this is so.

In what follows I try to show how subject matters such as labour law work, ie can be subject matters. I then draw attention to inherent risks in the construction of such subjects. In part 4 I actually articulate what I take to be the dominant and received account of (Canadian?) labour law. Then I make the obvious point that the inherent risks are indeed threatening that account of our discipline. My central point can be put as follows—if all this is true, then the result is not simply that we are forced to redraw the 'boundaries' of labour law. Our problem is that we need first to ask the question 'the boundaries of what?'. That is, as I see it, we need nothing short of a new account of our discipline. In other words, our first question is not 'what are the boundaries of labour law?'. It is 'what is labour law?'.

That is a large and important question. It is also a difficult one to answer, for reasons which I will now explore.

2. THE IDEA OF A CONSTITUTING NARRATIVE

One way of approaching these questions about labour law as a separate legal subject matter is to think along the following lines. If one examines the

---

[1] B. Laskin, *Labour Materials* (Toronto, Law Society of Upper Canada, Osgoode Hall Law School, Unpublished, 1947).

typical North American law school curriculum it is not hard to see that it reveals a basic structure based upon some very basic legal distinctions which can be easily mapped. We start with the familiar if controversial division between public law (state–citizen relationships) and private law (citizen–citizen relationships). Thus criminal law and constitutional law fall on the public side, and tort, contract and property on the private law side. And within private law we have other familiar distinctions—the law of property (what people own) and the law of obligations (what people owe each other). And within the law of obligations we have the distinction between obligations voluntarily assumed (contract) and those involuntarily imposed (tort). And so on. But there is another truth revealed in the structure of the standard curriculum. This is that law school courses are considered to be suitable for singling out as separate subject matters because they have a coherence and severability from the rest of law. This coherence is often in virtue of the rationality given to their subject matter not simply by the logic of the conceptual map just outlined, and upon which they can be located, but in virtue of the conceptual coherence, or basic grammar, of individual legal concepts themselves. So, the coherence of tort law, for example, is provided with the inner logic or rationality of the legal concept of tort itself. This is what makes tort law tort law, provides its internal organisational structure, and its distinctiveness from the rest of the law— something separate from contract, or unjust enrichment, or tax law for that matter. And the fundamental normative (that is, moral) underpinnings appropriate to tort (say, corrective justice) give it a claim to our resources, intellectual and otherwise.

But it will be quickly observed that while this can be said of some of the law's categories it is not true of all. Many other topics in the law school curriculum—say family law and labour law, but also trade law and environmental law—do not have whatever coherence they have in virtue of a defining legal concept. Their claim to coherence must be and is based upon another mode of thinking, one which is at once also intuitively obvious but also more complex, difficult, and controversial. Rather than start with the law or a legal concept (as with tort or contract—or trusts, by way of another example) these other sorts of subject matters start with reality, ie by looking out of the window and seeing what goes on in the real world. Subjects like labour law take a dimension (a chunk, a slice) of human life such as work, or the family, or trade between nations, and then draw together all of the law which applies to that aspect of life. But while this may be a useful and necessary intellectual game to play it is also a dangerous one, for how is one to know whether one has carved up reality 'at the joint' as it were. How do we know we have a coherent and appropriate subject if we obtain it by simply looking at life without a guiding legal framework to tell us where to carve? On this approach one could (and some actually have) come up with categories such as 'swimming pool law'. (I apologise for this homely example which is famous in our faculty as a way of explaining to graduate students what a thesis is not.) The thinking is—here is a part of reality, swimming pools, and we should draw together all of the law which applies to them (people can be injured in them, they can be bought and sold, they raise planning and environmental issues) and write a text, or offer a course, to satisfy our need to address all of these issues comprehensively. But there is the rub—what would it mean to address these issues 'comprehensively', that is beyond merely listing, comprehensively, other legal categories which may bear upon this aspect of reality? This is a good and difficult question. It is precisely the question Laskin believed he had an answer to when making his claim on behalf of the autonomy of Canadian labour law. But in what does, and did, Laskin's claim actually consist? What must be true of our chunk of reality and the law which applies to it, for us to be able to say we have good reason to carve here? Comprehensiveness is not enough. We could, I assume, make comprehensive lists of all the laws applying to anything or any action we see when we look out the window. But that would take a very long time and at some point we would end up asking 'is it really useful to carve reality here?'. But this leads to the obvious questions—When will it be the case that we have hit upon a useful category? What informs our judgement of 'usefulness'?

It must be something more than comprehensiveness—it must be some notion of 'coherence'. But, as we have noted, coherence here cannot mean what it means in the case of tort or contract law. There is no single defining and embracing legal logic in play here. With labour law it is simply true that contract and tort and property and crime and administrative law and constitutional law and much else will be in play. But then what separates labour law from a useless category such as swimming pool law? It must be a different idea of coherence, and I believe that our notion of coherence has two dimensions. First, it must be the case that there is something compelling, or deeply interesting, about this particular part of reality, something which makes it normatively salient and not simply another grain of sand on a very large empirical beach. It must be, in a word, important. Secondly, it must also be the case that when we carve reality at this point and address all the law applicable, the whole is greater than the sum of the parts. That is, it must be the case that in studying all of the various aspects of law which bear upon, inform, structure this part of our lives, we see them as part of a larger structure. That is we see in each aspect of the law something which would be missed if we did not see them as connected to the other parts of a larger whole. In short, there must be a benefit to be obtained from an overview of all of the law which bears upon our chosen category in the form of insight which would be lost if we did not carve reality here and if we did not attempt to provide a surview or account of it as a whole. This is not to say that there is only one way to carve reality. Rather it is to say, by way of an example, that while the contract of employment may usefully be seen as part of contract law, it is also usefully seen as a key part of labour law because something is gained when it is seen as a building block of this cross-cutting category, that is, when it is seen in the light of the other legal elements of the package of law regulating, say for now, work. To put it another way, there is a package here which needs to be seen and understood as a package.

There is a positive way of putting this. In order to say that we have found an appropriate subject matter of the sort in which coherence is generated in this way, it must be true that we are able to construct a compelling story (or narrative), both conceptually and normatively, of all the law appropriate to this subject matter as a subject matter, that is, of what it is (and is not), why it is important, and therefore why we should worry about it. If such a constituting narrative is available and compelling then we have a viable subject matter—and not something to be relegated to the garbage can along with swimming pool law. Such a narrative provides the organising conceptual structure and framework for the field (revealing connections, allowing us to see common dilemmas, providing an account of an evolving and interlinked history, and so on) as well as an account of its normative importance. When such narratives are successful, as labour law's has been, they are not so much what people have in mind when they think about the question 'what is labour law?' as the background condition that makes that question possible. It tells us that there is such a subject which one can worry about. So, such frameworks are often implicit and unarticulated, but are understood and deployed by every well-educated labour lawyer—in the most mundane of activities (answering questions such as 'should I read this case?', 'is it of relevance to my field?') to the construction of the most complicated legal arguments (this labour arbitration case about 'management rights' under a collective agreement has to be understood against the backdrop of the common law case on constructive dismissal involving variation of contracts of employment). Yet, while able to deploy these arguments and operate intelligently within the field of labour law, many labour lawyers may not be able to spell out the narrative with which they are so intimately familiar. This is because what the narrative makes available is basic—it is what competent labour lawyers do not have to worry about.

3. INHERENT RISKS

As we shall see, I do believe that labour law has such a constituting narrative and I set it out below. But first I wish to draw attention to what is, at least upon some reflection, a very real issue with subject matters which are constructed and defended in the manner I have just described. The nature of this sort of test for coherence means that such claims to coherence for subject matters such as labour law will always be, in the nature of things, more contestable than with subject matters which are delineated in other ways. This is because construction of narratives is different from conceptual analysis. Moreover, and this is a critical point for the current project, any and all such successful accounts will always be subject to change and challenge over time precisely because they are answerable to the real world and its phenomena, and not some noumenal world of concepts. The world outside our window changes and the story line must keep up, it must make sense of that world.

But there is a further problem which is important to keep an eye on. Once a constituting narrative becomes familiar, once a subject matter becomes established (through the work of a Laskin, say), once the curriculum becomes set, once the teaching and journals become specialised, once the wisdom of the constituting narrative becomes not insightful but merely obvious, once there is a critical mass of former students who have received the mother's milk of the organisation of thought which allows us to make sense of labour law, and so on . . . it is very hard to get rid of, even when well past its intellectual due date. This is Keynes' point. But it is a difficult point. It is not merely that we may be intellectually lazy or complacent, or that we do not have time to think about these things in the normal run of our professional or intellectual lives. It is not even simply that any entrenched understanding will favour some over others and that change will come at a cost to those whose investments and expertise will be threatened by any reconsideration. Important as all of these points are, our problem with rethinking our familiar terrain is a deeper problem than all of that.

Let me try to explain this deeper point as follows. Wittgenstein famously wrote: 'What is you aim in philosophy?—to show the fly the way out of the flybottle'.[2] The image here is important to grasp—a fly inside a bottle. A fly inside a bottle keeps bumping up against the glass barrier. It bumps up against the invisible outer limits of its world. In Wittgenstein's view, many problems of philosophy are generated in just the same way. People ask, and answer, questions which seem to make sense, but which really don't if you investigate them. The way they ask questions, and use the concepts they deploy not only to ask but answer them, constitute a bottle that they run up against. But like the fly they cannot see that—they too do not know they are in a bottle. The questions are the only ones that make sense to them. They construct a conceptual bell jar which is just as confining intellectually as the fly's is physically. This is the deepest of our problems—that we learn and teach and think within a particular constituting narrative such that we do not and often cannot think of the world but in those terms, even when

---

[2] L. Wittgenstein, *Philosophical Investigations* (2nd edn, Oxford, Blackwell, 1968), para 309.

the world and true critical thinking about it have moved well beyond those confines. The time scale over which this happens is medium to long term. It takes several generations, at least, for a paradigm of understanding of a field to be successful and dominant enough potentially to create this sort of problem. But one of the ironic truths about successful constituting narratives is that the more successful they are, the more difficult real critical thinking about them becomes.

The view I take is that Laskin was right in his claim about the emergence of labour law and its claim to both coherence (of the sort discussed above) and normative salience. In fact labour law is one of the great 'success stories'—a demonstration that creative thinking can overcome obstacles, of many kinds, resulting in a new conceptualisation, a new intellectual map, a more appropriate and really useful and fruitful way to categorise and understand our law. The problem now is whether we can rise to the same sort of challenges. Or will we, like our fly in the bottle, not even see we have a problem and simply accept the limits to our world which the narrative constructs?

In what follows I wish to set out as completely as I can what I think is the best version of the received wisdom which Laskin initially put his finger on. It has developed and matured and deepened and even radically expanded over the decades. The result of all of this refining and thinking has been to construct a truly powerful constituting narrative which has a story line, a chronology and a morality, all of which tells labour lawyers what they intuitively know—what labour law is and what is not, and why we have it, that is, why it is a matter of import. This received wisdom both frames and justifies the field. The initial insight and subsequent elaboration result in a story with both a conceptual and normative dimension and purpose. I think it is probably true that some labour lawyers could not tell the story very well simply because it is too natural, too basic, and because it is what makes things make sense and therefore does not need, in our daily lives, its own justification. Such lawyers are like completely competent speakers of a natural language who often cannot articulate the rules of grammar of that language of which they are complete masters. Others will have been taught by teachers who have explicitly organised their thinking around an explicit attempt to have them see the framework as vital to understanding any individual part of it. And the theory is both explicit and implicit in the structure of the basic teaching materials used in Canadian law school labour courses. But what both sorts of labour lawyers share is a framework which lets them see the subject matter as, obviously, a coherent one, that is, the result of an intelligent and very useful carving of reality at an important joint. But of course it is the theory which sheds the light which not simply lets us see the joint but rather makes available the idea of a joint being present or useful at this particular spot to begin with. The theory is at once answerable to reality but autonomous from it. It has to rest upon a claim that a certain dimension of real life is to be profitably carved off for intellectual study and also at the same time provide us the way of seeing things which makes that so. It is precisely because of this dual aspect that there is the real risk of the theory detaching from reality and at the same time making it very hard to see that this is indeed the state of intellectual play.

I should also point out one other feature of this account. This account of the content and purpose of domestic labour law 'drives' and 'leads', that is, makes both necessary and available a certain account of international labour law which functions, just as does the domestic version, to articulate both the domain of, and justification for, that enterprise.

But the point of all this is not simply to explore the nature of and then set out our best account of our subject. The real point is that we are at a fluid moment in which reality in labour law's neck of the woods, both domestically and internationally, both empirically and normatively, is increasingly perceived to be changing, and dramatically so. The issue is whether our received, dominant, and traditional account of labour law, both nationally and at the global level, has kept up. The answer is, I believe, no. This of course leads to another question—'what is labour law, now?'.

4. THE RECEIVED WISDOM

For Canadian labour lawyers the story of labour law, the narrative which both delineates and justifies the field, has evolved over time since Laskin first introduced labour law into the law school curriculum. But it has been reasonably secure for the past 25 or 30 years. Many very distinguished Canadian labour law academics, of whom Harry Arthurs would be the acknowledged Dean, have spent much of the last decade or so pointing out the threat which 'globalisation' poses for the system constructed and held together by this narrative. But there is no doubt that the system so constructed is the system under threat.

For Laskin and those who immediately followed him, the subject matter of labour law was collective labour relations, that is, the relationship between firms and unions. It subsequently became much broader. Laskin studied law in Toronto but pursued his graduate work at Harvard in the late 1930s. This was in the immediate glow of the New Deal in general and the passing of the Wagner Act in particular. Laskin's return to Canada from Harvard was soon followed by the importation of the Wagner Act model, with some very important local innovations, into Canada. These were heady days. The common law was hostile to collective worker action, and in its normal analysis of working relations still did not blink in using the labels of a dead social order, 'master' and 'servant', to describe them. The break with this common law past offered by the new legislative and administrative regime was radical and must have been truly exhilarating.

Moreover this new system of labour law was given coherence and content by the comprehensive statutory scheme itself, which started at the beginning, defining the eligible players (employees, employers, unions etc.), then constructing a chronology, and, implicitly, a narrative about life for those players in the new world of labour law. The chronology begins with the right to organise and legal protection thereof ('unfair labour practices'), then how to convert union organisation into union recognition via the new 'certification' process. Next, how this leads to the imposition of a 'duty to bargain in good faith' upon employers and unions following certification, then to the law of strikes and lockouts when negotiations fail, and finally to the law of 'labour arbitration' when a collective agreement is reached and the law is applied in the daily life of a functioning collective agreement. Then the statute shows how the system repeats itself, possibly *ad infinitum*. All of this administered by new tripartite entities, such as the labour relations and labour arbitration boards, which were specifically not courts and which administered a world from which the common law contact of employment was banished. This was the world of labour law in which I grew up as a law student in the 1970s.

But by then there were changes underway. Law faculties, following Innis Christie's lead,[3] began to offer courses in what became called 'employment law'. The subject matter here is somewhat more difficult to describe, but we would say now that it is all of the rest of labour law lying outside collective bargaining law. This has two components—the common law of the employment relationship (most critically the law of the contract of employment and of 'wrongful dismissal') and the vast and expanding world of statutory regulation of the contract of employment including health and safety laws, human rights codes, employment standards legislation (meaning minimum wage, maximum hours, holiday and vacation regulation, etc.), pension regulation, and so on. In the United States this turn to employment law was also a turn away from collective labour law driven by the radical decline in the union density rates and the de-centring of collective bargaining in that country. In Canada this was not the motivation. The initial interest in employment law is best explained by simply the existence, and in the case of most of the statutes recent creation, of much new law which applied to many people. But there was a problem in giving a meaningful account of employment law. The common but erroneous account was that collective bargaining law was for organised workers and employment law for the unorganised. This was commonly said, but clearly wrong, for most of the statutory component of employment law applies across the board to all

---

[3] Professor Innis Christie at Dalhousie Law School was a leader in introducing a course in 'Employment Law' into Canadian law schools.

workers. This problem of how to give a meaningful account of employment law could be, and was, resolved only when employment law and labour law were seen as one coherent system of law organised around not simply the comprehensive set of statutory novelties which dominated the emergence and account of labour law as collective bargaining law which Laskin offered, nor (poorly) organised around the idea of labour law for the unorganised on the other, but on a reading of the two as parts of a whole greater than the simple sum of these two parts. This was achieved gradually and finally explicitly around 25 years ago. And the narrative which stitches these subject matters together is the narrative we are after. It is labour law's foundational framing and justificatory account of itself.

There are many dimensions of, and possible routes into, this compelling story, but let me start with the idea of contract. The labour law narrative takes the category of contract law as prior and primitive. In one way the entire story can be seen as a story of the 'real life of contract law', as opposed to the abstract and general rules of general contract law. It is what happens when the rubber of contract law hits the real and hard road of the working life. Part of the reasoning here is 'historical'. (A word of caution here—the history revealed here is not meant to be taken as accurate, although some or even all of it might be. The claim to accuracy is, rather, about the structure of the narrative.) Labour lawyers know that contract is a relatively modern category of legal thinking. They know that productive activity is possibly, and was long, organised on other lines. And labour lawyers, as are all lawyers, are familiar with Sir Henry Maine's famous dictum that

The movement of all progressive societies is one from status to contract.[4]

I am also quite certain that our labour lawyer will be very familiar with many pronouncements of which the following from the Supreme Court of Canada is merely representative:

The common law views mutually agreed upon employment relationships through the lens of contract . . .[5]

But our modern labour lawyer will not actually need to know any specific milestones on the road to modern labour law because a very general history suffices to underwrite what follows. Nonetheless this idea of the emergence

---

[4] H. Sumner Maine, *Ancient Law: Its Connection with the Early History of Society, and its Relation to Modern Ideas* (London, John Murray, 1861), 170.

[5] *Attorney General of Quebec v Labrecque* [1980] 2 SCR 107 (Supreme Court of Canada). See also the reaffirmation in *Wells v Newfoundland* [1999] 3 SCR 199 (Supreme Court of Canada).

of contract, of a chronology, is of importance to the credibility of the received wisdom. The entire narrative makes its way in the world by taking this idea of historical development and seeing the emergence of our current law as a reaction to it, combined with a justificatory account of why these developments are important. At its core this account is one of law constraining, or humanising, or softening, or resisting contract in the name of justice, democracy, fairness, and equality. It is an account of justice against, or as resistance to, markets.

How does the constituting narrative construct itself upon this foundation of the emergence of contract as the dominant legal category relevant to labour law? As we have noted, labour lawyers understand that productive relations can be organised, and historically have been organised, by different principles. Nonetheless they accept that the overwhelmingly important mode of engaging in productive relations in modern society, at least in North America, is through the mechanism of contract and specifically the contract of employment. On this view employees and employers are seen as participants in the labour market, and they are engaged in the exercise of contracting, that is, the formation of individual contracts of employment. Here, all of the conceptual apparatus appropriate to private market ordering is understood to apply. Nonetheless, labour lawyers see the development of labour law, certainly within recent memory, as one of the elaboration and remedying of a series of disenchantments with this contractual reality. Labour law is thus primarily conceived as a set of interventions in the labour market, that is, in the negotiation process for contracts of employment. The point of all this is, of course, 'justice' in this part of our lives, that is, in employment relationships. The idea of justice does not need, for most labour lawyers, a complete theoretical account. The more sophisticated will likely be able to draw upon ideas elaborated by John Rawls or Ronald Dworkin about a liberal theory of justice containing two elements, sometimes expressed as, 'concern' and 'respect'. Others may now draw upon the human development approach elaborated by Sen. But the core normative claim which the received wisdom makes is that justice for employees will never be completely secured as long as the relationship is analysed in purely (common law) contractual terms. (As a result the very idea of a contract of employment separates out those who are employees from those who are simply independent commercial contractors—those who need protection from those who do not.) When employees negotiate contracts of employment they suffer from an 'inequality of bargaining power'. As a result, they will not obtain just outcomes. We should pause to note that the claim about 'inequality of bargaining power' is famously controversial. From the point of view of economic theory, any discussion of 'inequality of bargaining power' can be viewed as a form of economic nonsense. This is not a point which dismays many labour lawyers. But it does call for some clarification. It may well be that on certain views of economic theory a discussion of 'inequality of bargaining power' in the labour market is a form of economic nonsense. This may indeed be at least partly true if it is meant to be understood as a comment within economic theory (because the idea is meant to go beyond correcting for market failures). But I think the best understanding of the idea of 'inequality of bargaining power' is that it is not meant to be taken as a comment from within economic theory. Rather, it is meant to offer a critique external to that theory. It has the form of another famous slogan: 'property is theft'. When Proudhon offered this remark he did not intend it to be taken as a comment 'within' the legal theory of property. Rather, it was meant to be an external critique of the idea of property. An interesting feature of the slogan, and whence it derives its rhetorical force, is, as John Searle has pointed out, that it uses concepts from within the theory being criticised in order to make a criticism of the theory.[6]

Labour law then continues its self-constituting narrative in the following way. If our aim is to secure justice for employees, and employees will not secure justice because the employment relationship is a contractual one and employees suffer from inequality of bargaining power in the contracting process, then there are two possible responses. These two responses are two possible modes of 'consumer protection'. Labour law is to be understood on a par with other interventions in other market places in the name of defending 'weaker parties'.[7] The law protects those in need of protection in the market place. The first mode of intervention is procedural. If the problem is that we are not securing justice for employees through this contractual bargaining relationship, because of inequality of bargaining power on the part of employees, then we must simply adopt the procedural device of turning up the bargaining power on the side of the employee. Our primary mechanism for achieving this is through the device of collective bargaining. Here we permit workers to secure whatever additional substantive rights and benefits they can in the contracting process by making available to them whatever increases in bargaining power will accrue through collective representation by unions. This approach is, at least in theory, purely procedural. There is no guarantee that employees will be able to secure much benefit by acting collectively. The essence of collective bargaining law is to remove legal obstacles to collective action and to compel the employer to deal with the union as the collective representative of the employees. The accepted wisdom is that collective bargaining is entirely

---

[6] See B. Langille, 'Fair Trade is Free Trade's Destiny' in J.N. Bhagwati and R. Hudec (eds), *Fair Trade and Harmonization: Prerequisites for Free Trade?* (Boston, Mass, MIT Press, 1996), 231.

[7] B. Laskin, 'The Protection of Interests by Statute and the Problem of "Contracting Out"' (1938) 16 *Canadian Bar Review* 669.

procedural in the sense that the substance of the bargain to be is still left open to the parties to determine through the exercise of their now restructured bargaining power relationship. The employer's freedom *to* contract with whom it wishes is taken away, and it is compelled to bargain with the collective representative. But the employer's freedom *of* contract is maintained.

Most labour lawyers acknowledge that this is a deeply problematic condition to sustain.[8] But the important point is that collective bargaining guarantees no substantial results. It is the device of procedural justice. If employees are located in labour markets such that collective action does improve their bargaining position, then they will achieve results. But for other employees collective bargaining may be no guarantee at all of any improvement in their substantive conditions of work.

But labour law consists in more than simply procedural intervention through collective bargaining. There is a second response to our problem of securing justice in employment relationships. This second response is substantive in nature. The logic here is as follows. If our problem is that we will not secure justice in employment relationships because these relationships are analysed in contractual terms, and employees suffer from inequality of bargaining power in the negotiation of such contracts, then we should simply rewrite the resulting bargain. This we do via human rights codes, employment standards legislation, occupational health and safety regulation, and so on.

Thus at the end of the day labour law ends up being constituted by three legal regimes—the 'original' common law of the contract of employment, collective bargaining, and what we can refer to as 'direct statutory intervention'—all organised by the story we have just told. There are many places where the Supreme Court of Canada has articulated this narrative, often piecemeal. But a very comprehensive rendition of the whole narrative can be found in the following words of Madame Justice Wilson:

> Collective bargaining is a mechanism by which individual employees come together and form a union to represent their interests. The whole purpose of unionization is to strengthen the position of these employees in order to offset the countervailing power of employers. Rather than simply enacting legislation aimed solely at protecting individual workers by controlling employer abuses (eg minimum wage, occupational health and safety, and workers' compensation legislation), government established our current regime of collective bargaining. The purpose of this system is also to curb the excesses of the common law of the employment relationship and to thereby assuage industrial tensions.

---

[8] B. Langille and P. Macklem, '"Beyond Belief": Labour Law's Duty to Bargain' (1988) 13 *Queens Law Journal* 62.

This is achieved, not through legislative protectionism, but rather through the promotion of the self-advancement of working people. Thus, these two systems differ in respect of the mechanisms they adopt to achieve their ends, but both individual employment law and collective employment law aim to advance the interests of a vulnerable group, the individual employees.[9]

Although not in perfect order, almost all of the elements of the package which is the received wisdom are nicely stated here.

It will be apparent that every element of the received wisdom is contestable and controversial. But the point of the narrative is not so much that it resolves our controversies, or generates a consensus about them, but rather that it gives us a way of understanding and ordering those controversies as being the very controversies which constitute labour law. At its heart, of course, is the central dilemma of its claims about 'justice' or lack thereof in market ordering. Labour lawyers may actually disagree among themselves as to whether the claims made by labour law, along the lines just outlined, actually do advance the cause of justice, in whole or in part. But they will be in agreement that this is the way that labour law, that is the law that we actually do have, is to be understood. (It may be wrongheaded, but this is what labour law is.) The result is a unified account of all of our labour law, that is, all three legal régimes, including the previously bifurcated subjects of labour law and employment law. Part of the narrative's value added, from the normative and pedagogical points of view, is precisely that it opens up the different sets of normative underpinnings of each of the three constituting legal approaches. The normative underpinnings of procedural intervention, that is, of collective bargaining ('self advancement of working people') are to be distinguished from the paternalistic normative underpinnings of much substantive legal intervention ('legislative protectionism'). And both substantial and procedural re-regulation of the bargaining relationship stand in sharp contrast to the values underlying common law market ordering (with its 'excesses'). What is opened up to us is the possibility of seeing common problems 'solved' in different ways by the three different legal approaches. So too there is much value added in our ability to see the normative tensions played out in decision-making under each of the three separate regimes. There is, in addition, much detailed legal controversy about the proper institutional, let alone the substantive, relationships between the three regimes. But the great achievement of the constituting narrative is that it provides a chronology, a justification, and a delineation of the field in a concise and compelling manner.

---

[9] Wilson J in *Lavigne v Ontario Public Service Employees Union* [1991] 2 SCR 211 (Supreme Court of Canada).

5. THE CHASM WHICH YAWNS BETWEEN OUR NARRATIVE AND OUR REALITY

I do not here seek to establish but rather simply remind the reader of what many authors in this volume have been instrumental in observing and chronicling—that the real world of the labour market has moved on, both in the developed and the developing worlds.

I have tried to summarise elsewhere some of the changes in the developed world as follows:

> The core assumption of the narrative is the idea of the contract of employment—something to which someone called an employee and someone called in employer are parties. Furthermore, the core assumption is that the contract of employment was 'available' as a 'platform' for intervention. It seemed the obvious way to think about things. Our problem was simply a problem of regulating the contract. We did so in the name of people (employees) 'in need of protection'. . . . The contract of employment was available for substantive and procedural regulation. Re-regulation of that contract could reallocate risks, cure market defects, subsidize bargaining power, and be the platform for reallocation of broader social risks in terms of unemployment, pensions, etc.

> This received wisdom of labour lawyers did not evolve in some formal legalistic realm. It cohered with and was made possible by the real world of the North American economy for much of the twentieth century. The real world of that 'old' economy provided the context, melded with, made necessary, made possible, and made available all of this is a way of thinking.

> Coase's theory of the firm as a nexus of contracts explains that it is transaction costs that lead firms to decide to 'build' rather than to 'buy'. That is, Coasean economics explains that sometimes firms will hire employees within the firm subject to managerial direction and subordination, rather than contracting at arm's length with 'independent contractors'. In the last century, the transaction costs of the time (combined with the then dominant management theory),[sic] led to Taylorist modes of production which involved vertical integration, the hiring of a large number of employees on long-term contracts, the construction of 'internal labour markets', and the rise of the basic understanding of the trade-offs that employees, as opposed independent contractors, make. The basic trade-off was that those who are party to an employment contract—employees—receive security and stability in employment through a long-term contract, in return for subordination to the control, rules, and directives of the firm; while the self-employed independent entrepreneur foregoes security in return for the chance of profit, subsidized in part by the tax system. This workplace reality was supplemented by a social reality in family life that, from the modern perspective, is extremely striking. In 1960 more than 70 percent of Canadian families had two parents with the father in full-time, long-term employment, and the mother at home raising the children. In 1990 fewer than 20 percent of Canadian families had this structure.

> In this context, it was 'natural' that labour law would focus upon regulation of the long-term contract of employment in the name of employees conceived of

as those in need of protection, because of inequality of bargaining power, in the ongoing negotiation of those long-term contracts of employment. The contract of employment was the obvious 'platform' for regulation and for the delivery of a social safety net that insured against both employment risks and wider social risks, for both the worker and the family.[10]

In addition, others can and will document the difficulty of mapping our received wisdom onto a world of 'informality'. There is also the reality, which I discuss below, that the received wisdom concerning the role of international labour law is under similar stress.[11] The point is simply that with time there is change. There are these real world changes which all of those who are interested in labour markets and labour law know so well. The world which our constituting narrative has to make sense of has indeed not stood still. But, as we shall see, there is more—our best economic and normative thinking has evolved too. There are also new data on labour law's connection to successful economies which have required a rethinking of the relationship of the economic and the social dimensions. Our task is to come to grips with these developments. But if my account of labour law's structure is right, then the narrative is 'all that there is'. There is therefore no escaping the conclusion that we need a new narrative.

6. IS A NEW NARRATIVE POSSIBLE?

Let us begin with a note of optimism. The ILO is the ILO, not the IEO—that is, it is the International Labour Organisation not the International Employment Organisation. And the ILO's current organising mantra is 'Decent Work', not 'Decent Employment'. Harry Arthurs has noted the evolution in the naming of what used to be ministries of labour.[12] All of this could signal an ability on the part of our narrative to change with the times. Or, on the other hand it could, as Harry points out, simply be a sort of public last nail in the coffin of our subject, a particularly brash and insensitive 'rubbing in' and celebration of the end of our discipline which only reconfirms how desperate it all is.

How will we decide? I think the answer lies where it is always to be found with subject matters such as ours. It is a matter of 'looking and seeing'—of

---

[10] B. Langille, 'Labour Policy in Canada—New Platform, New Paradigm' (2002) 28 *Canadian Public Policy* 133, at 137.

[11] B. Langille, 'Re-reading the 1919 ILO Constitution in Light of Recent Evidence on Foreign Direct Investment and Workers Rights' (2003) 42 *Columbia Journal of Transnational Law* 101; B. Langille, 'What Is International Labour Law For?' (The ILO Governing Body Public Lecture, Geneva, International Labour Office, March 2005), available at: http://www.ilo.org/public/english/bureau/inst/download/langille.pdf.

[12] Arthurs, this volume.

looking out of our windows at the new world. The question is, as always, whether we can see a way of carving that new reality in a way which will make available a coherent and normatively compelling account of a subject matter which we could recognise as our own. Such an account will again be answerable to our new reality but also autonomous from it. It must shed the light that enables us to map our new terrain, while at once simply organising it into a whole which is greater than the sum of its parts, and also showing why it is normatively important. My suggestion is that this requires a look at the evolution of realities not only in the developed world, but also in the developing world. Of changes not only in domestic but also in international law. And it is obviously not only an empirical but also a normative quest. This need not mean that all of the detail of what we once knew as labour law has to be jettisoned. Rather it may be a new way of seeing the true nature and point of much of what we have known and studied. Also, possibly, much more as well.

Our starting point must be a belief that our new realities really do force us to this point. For me this is clearly the case at the level of domestic labour law. First, it is evident that employment, and adjusting for power inequalities in the negotiation of contracts of employment, cannot do all of the heavy lifting required to address the phenomenon of 'informality'. Secondly, many at this meeting have made the case that in the developed world changes in the model of employment have created a new reality which our existing modes of thinking have failed to keep step with. The ideas in the Supiot report, for example that we need to re-think our attachment to the contract of employment as our central mechanism (or 'platform'), and employees and employers as our conceptual 'building blocks', are correct. We need to shake off the grip of the idea that it is deficiencies in the negotiation of the contract of employment which provide the central rationale for labour law, and that the contract of employment is our central focus and platform for delivering labour law. Always knowing that, as Keynes said, this is difficult because these ideas really do 'ramify into every corner of our minds'. Thirdly, for me there is evident conceptual confusion all around us, at least in Canada. We actually have law reform proposals, and realities, based on ideas such as 'independent employee' and 'collective bargaining for independent contractors'. This really is just like saying 'property is theft' and *meaning it* as a comment within property theory. These are signals of conceptual stress. They are dead canaries down our disciplinary mine. Finally there is also the pretty obvious fact that the narrative's central mechanisms of unionisation and collective bargaining are, in a word, de-centred. What all of this amounts to is that our narrative no longer describes, or deals with, our world. Something needs to be done.

At the same time, and resting their case upon the same perceived realities, others will claim that any such effort, if futile, and that the economic forces of globalisation, along with what Harry Arthurs has called 'globalisation of the mind',[13] make all of this an exercise in self-delusion. If we were honest we would simply lament the passing of both the world which our subject once commanded, and our subject itself, and be content with writing a good obituary for it.

But at a basic level this cannot be right. There will always be labour law in the sense that, as long as productive human beings exist, some law will regulate their productive efforts, whether in their capacity as share-holders, or their status as holders of their own human capital. So the issue is the death not of labour law, but of one possible account of it. But should we despair or not? Again that depends on what we come up with as we try to make sense of our current world.

One seemingly optimistic starting point is that in our world there is something contradictory about lamenting the passing of labour law. Those who are worried are very comfortable with a familiar account of globalisation. Basically what worries them is that we have an increasingly integrated world in which global chains of investment, production and consumption are made possible by new laws, institutions, processes and technologies. In this world most factors of production, especially goods and capital but also ideas and processes, are 'mobile', but labour, ie human beings, are not. We see the triumph of capital as it escapes the fetters of the nation state. But there is an obvious paradox here. If 'everything' but labour is mobile, then is it not obvious that 'labour policy' is the one domestic policy lever over which states retain control? As a result should not labour law be at the centre of national economic policy and, rather than marginalised, more important than ever?

To this there is a familiar rejoinder. It is pointed out that this potential source of optimism is undermined by another familiar aspect of our modern world. Our old idea was that labour was being treated as a commodity by capitalists and that labour law was required to address this very problem. (This is the one sentence version of the received wisdom.) The problem now is that mobile capital is able to treat that very labour law as a commodity.[14] This is because states are 'forced' to bid down their labour standards in competition with other states seeking to attract or retain mobile investment resulting in what we all now know to call a prisoners' dilemma/race to the bottom type of collective action problem. Labour law, ministries of labour, the ILO *are* marginalised on the current model.

This gloomy observation is then followed by a further and equally familiar discussion of international labour law along the following lines. The idea is

[13] H. Arthurs, 'Globalization of the Mind: Canadian Elites and the Restructuring of Legal fields' (1998) 12 *Canadian Journal of Law and Society* 219.

[14] B. Langille, 'Labour Law is Not a Commodity' (1998) 19 *The Industrial Law Journal* (South Africa) 1002.

that we need to have international labour law to prevent this race to the bottom by providing the required remedies for all such prisoners' dilemmas. These are binding and enforceable contracts or laws in which states undertake or are forced not to bid below a common floor. This is what most people think ILO conventions are for. The problem is that ILO conventions are neither binding nor enforceable. Hence the need for a WTO 'social clause'. But no such luck there either. (In large part because of the developing world's opposition. My question is basically, why not?, given the dominant theory's account of what is being done to them.) Thus, at the end of the day, capital both gains and retains the upper hand. We are back where we started, with Sinzheimer and Laskin, but this time without the ability to do anything about it.

We should note just how compelling a package this set of views about international labour law really is. It is dominant. It is dominant because it fits with our (dominant) received wisdom about domestic labour law. This is the sense in which our dominant account 'drives' and makes both available and inevitable a certain account of international labour law. The ideas which our familiar account of labour law makes available to this story of international labour law are that labour law is about equalising bargaining power, about redistribution, of constraining market activity, that justice comes at a price—in a word, that labour law can be best viewed as a tax, which mobile capital would rather not pay and which states in our new world find it more and more difficult to impose. It is this idea which generates our whole understanding of both the need for international labour law and its failure to deliver. What this amounts to is that our received wisdom is not only increasingly irrelevant to the real world (see above), but that it instructs us to do impossible things about it.

Unfortunately there is more. The real problems in the world are big ones. There are 6 billion persons on the planet, and of these 3 billion live on less than $2 a day, and 1.2 billion in 'absolute poverty' of less than $1 a day. Labour law needs to raise its sights, and when it does so needs to ask the question, how can it be part of the solution to this global problem? Labour law will never be part of the solution on the old narrative. This is because, as we have noted, globalisation is simply a threat to labour law. Rather than seeing globalisation as a driver of just societies it will see it as a destroyer of them. This results in a politics of (rational, necessary) protectionism which will make it much more difficult to see progress on our big problems, which require a global investment in and support for the developing world—including market access and foreign direct investment (FDI). It also makes, as we have seen, the task of the ILO an impossible one. Worse, it makes international labour law part of the problem—for it is conceived as being charged with preventing states acting rationally in their own economic self-interest—rather than helping them identify and achieve it. It imposes a tax on the developing world. No wonder we do not have a social clause at the WTO. On our current view the developing world is right to resist it. We also get international law, to the extent that we have it at all, which is drafted and 'enforced' on an unhelpful model, that is, a 'constraining self interest and enforcement model'.

So, to sum up, there is a breakdown, in both the developing and developed world, of the basic conceptual building blocks of the reality our received wisdom takes for granted and seeks to make sense of. We are furthermore, at least in Canada, in conceptual disarray as we try to adjust our existing categories to a world which has left them behind. Labour law and labour ministries are marginalised. Even though they deal with the non-mobile factor of production, and should be seen as the central policy issues and players, globalisation has rendered them useless. From this fate international labour law, as currently understood, cannot rescue us. To top it all off, labour law is part of the problem, not part of the solution, when it comes to our really significant global problems. And that is why we need a new account of our discipline.

7. SOME NEW STARTING POINTS

Labour law's back pages do not have to dominate out thinking. In fact it is pretty obvious that they cannot. But there is more at hand than just the desperation which this necessity visits upon us.

Here is a sketch of some possible starting points for labour law's future self-understanding. We can begin by noting that there is an increasingly large body of empirical literature which, crude as it is, all points in one direction, suggesting that we need to revisit our account of international labour law. The data refuse to play ball with the theory.[15] It seems that there is no empirical evidence for the existence of a race to the bottom which our dominant theory makes inevitable. Investment is not attracted, nor is trade performance improved, by lower labour rights protection. This is startling, at least on the received wisdom's account of things. This not only suggests that we need to rethink the purposes and design of international labour law,[16] but has other implications as well. Because of the rational link between the international and the domestic there is a feedback effect here. If the common rationality does not hold for international law it will not for domestic law.

---

[15] See the sources cited in Langille, 'Re-reading', above n 11 and A. Hyde, 'A Stag Hunt Account and Defence of Transnational Labour Standards—A Preliminary Look at the Problem' in J. Craig and M. Lynk (eds.), *Globalization and Transnational Labour Law* (Cambridge, Cambridge University Press, 2006).

[16] Langille, 'What Is', above n 11.

Secondly, we do have new theoretical insights which help us understand why the old account of labour law does not satisfy our best normative thinking. Sen's placing of real human freedom as both our goal and a chief means to achieve it has radical implications. So do his ideas about the complex interactions of various kinds of human freedoms—economic, political and social. Only such a view can explain the data we see at the international level. The basic idea is that social justice and economic development are not locked in a zero sum game, but that human freedom is both the goal of and the necessary precondition to the construction of just and durable economies and societies. States are not acting irrationally in enforcing labour rights. There is no prisoners' dilemma. The role of the ILO is not an impossible one. Labour law has a contribution to make to the real and large problems of the world. It does not have to be seen merely as part of the problem, a role made inevitable by the received wisdom's account of the world.

Moreover, only such a theory could lay the groundwork for a 'post-Washington consensus', 'integrated' theory of development precisely because at its base it rejects the segregation and sequencing of the (prior) economic and the (subsequent, if desired) political and social dimensions. In fact, it turns out that the reason our dominant and received view of labour law is morally impoverished is that it is exactly a Washington consensus view of the world. It sees the world the same way (there is a big trade-off between justice and economic progress (it is a tax) and merely votes for a different outcome (we think we should, as decent people, pay it).

What are we to make of our new modes of production and the breakdown of our familiar building block of the contract of employment? The fact that familiar modes of organising production are evolving, with old ones breaking down and new ones opening up, should not surprise or deflect us on this view. It may be that some of this is just 'bad employment' which needs to be fixed. But much of it may not be. It is driven by our new realities (of family life for example) new technologies, new values, or be a function of different levels of development. To attach eternal significance to ephemeral forms is obviously a mistake. These new forms have no impact upon our purposes. They merely provide new design challenges for delivering on our goals. But we still need a coherent account of what we are doing, of our purposes and how 'labour law' advances them. Our reason for being interested in contracts of employment is no longer simply an idea of justice or fairness which demands that we need to equalise bargaining power in a certain type of contract. Our new idea of human freedom provides an overarching framework for organising much of what is not currently central to labour law, such as education, family care (including child care), training and active labour market policies, intellectual property, and so on, as well as much of what is currently central to labour law's familiar categories, such as employment standards (hours, notice provisions, leaves), collective bargaining, health and safety, human rights etc.

The perspective of human freedom also makes better sense of the idea of labour law as being central precisely because it deals with the non-mobile factor of production. The key to economic growth can be simply stated. At the end of the day it is labour productivity, which at the end of the day is importantly a matter of human capital. Growth is achieved by putting more people to work and then by increasing the productivity of each. There is a natural limit to the number of workers a state can put to work—full employment, however defined. But there is no *a priori* limit to the productivity of each. Productivity is a matter of the efficiency of public capital (infrastructure), private capital, and human capital. In our world human capital policy is a critical margin. In knowledge-based economies human beings, and their minds, are what counts. This is, it will be noted, basic to the idea of human freedom. This is a matter of creation of human capital, ie education, and then the productive use of that human capital. That is what labour law is about. Contrary to our current starting point, much of what our subject is about is not only protecting humans, it is liberating them, ie removing obstacles to the realisation of their human capital. So, hours of work, portable pensions, notice periods, education and other leaves, information sharing, intellectual property rules, child care, active labour market policies, should all be seen in this light. So too, non-discrimination, and so on. Recall that this is not shifting to an instrumental account of what we once considered a matter of 'rights' (worth paying for) but the result of our clearly thinking about what our true goals, as opposed to our means for achieving them, really are. But it also turns out that our goal (human freedom—ie the real capacity to lead lives we have reason to value) is also instrumentally critical in advancing its own cause. From this perspective the words of Wilson J in describing collective bargaining in terms of 'self advancement' of working people take on fresh meaning. Both substantive and procedural labour law will have to find new techniques and platforms of operation to do the required work.

On this view any particular mode of human productive activity, such as employment, is not the focal point. Our goals are at once broader and deeper than any notion of justice as remedying inequality of bargaining power in any particular configuration of human productive interactions could be. These categories are not conceptually basic, no longer building blocks of the theory, but simply one possible site of deployment of an intelligent 'labour law' policy. (What should we call our subject on this new view? 'Work law?'—too narrow. 'Human development law?'—too broad, but closer to the mark.)

As we have noted, our new view also makes international labour law's task possible. It is no longer allocated the role of constraining a state's self-interest without the tools to do so, but of promoting that self-interest in the first place. One effect will be to unblock the current ILO/WTO stalemate in which labour law is an obstacle to solving the large development problems which the world faces.

This is not a view which is naïve about inequality of bargaining power. It is a view which sees and claims that we have even better reason, and techniques available, for doing something about it. It is also a view which does not blind us to what we know is true, that states do in fact trade off labour rights for investment. The question is whether we believe, as the received wisdom would have us do, that there is a prisoners' dilemma here. This requires that the choice to lower standards be dominant and that there be only one possible equilibrium, at the bottom. But, as Alan Hyde has argued, this is not the only 'game' in town.[17] Sen's ideas claim, and the evidence shows, that we face a much different collective action problem where there are two possible equilibria, with higher outcomes for all states through cooperation on a 'high road' policy. On this account the problem is not one of changing the rational motivations of states, but of assisting states to understand them clearly and to achieve them.

There appears, then, to be the possibility of an outline of a new account of our discipline, but much remains to be done. My point here has been to show the true and limiting nature of labour law's back pages, and then simply to suggest what it will take to rewrite our future. That rewriting is a task which still lies ahead.

* * *

Hirschman wrote that the true problems of development lie where 'all difficulties of human action begin and belong: in the mind'.[18] Stiglitz, picking up on this idea 40 years later in his writings about the comprehensive development theory (which owes in turn a lot to Sen), wrote:

> Development represents a *transformation* of society, a movement from traditional relations, traditional ways of thinking, traditional ways of dealing with health and education, traditional methods of production, to more 'modern' ways. For instance, a characteristic of traditional societies is the acceptance of the world as it is; the modern perspective recognizes change, it recognizes that we, as individuals and societies, can take actions . . . [19]

He sums this up by noting that this 'change in mindset is at the center of development'.[20] This is ultimately a change in self-conception from one of passivity to one of human agency, an idea which is the idea at the core of Sen's human development approach. Stiglitz further notes that the prior dominant

---

[17] Hyde, above n 15.

[18] A.O. Hirschman, *A Strategy of Economic Development* (New Haven, Conn, Yale University Press, 1958), 11.

[19] J.E. Stiglitz, 'Participation and Development: Perspectives from the Comprehensive Development Paradigm' (2002) 6 *Review of Development Economics* 163, at 164.

[20] Ibid., at 165.

theory of development focussed exclusively and more narrowly upon economic issues, and that the comprehensive development theory's accomplishment was to broaden the focus in the way just set out. In a way labour law's problem is just the mirror image of that of development theory. Labour law has been too narrowly focused as well, but in the opposite direction (on remedying unfairness in bargaining). It, too, needs to broaden its focus, re-think its basic goals, take into account new realities, and tell itself a new story about what it is and why it is important that that be so. At the centre of that account will be new ways of seeing our world including our 'new realities' and a richer set of reasons for being concerned with them. It will also require liberation from labour law's 'back pages' which now hinder our efforts to see our world clearly and to deal with it in a way that advances our true aims.

3

What is Labour Law?

ALAN HYDE*

T O BE A scholar or practitioner of labour or employment law in the early years of the twenty-first century is to be confronted, not occasionally, but on a daily basis, with legal relationships that might or might not be characterised as relationships or contracts of employment—and will appear anomalous however characterised. Here are only six examples, chosen more or less at random from documents on my desk. Each can serve as a paradigm of the difficult problems of classification that one takes on when one speaks of defining labour law or expanding its boundaries:

—a tenant who pays a portion of his earnings as rent;
—the relationship of a garment sewer to the clothing manufacturer who has contracted actual production to a contractor;
—the relationship of a janitor to the owner of the building she cleans;
—the relationship of a physician to the insurance company that reimburses her for her services;
—the relationship of a farm worker to the restaurant chain that buys the produce;
—the unquestionable employees, who choose for strategic reasons to characterise their relationship with their employer (say, a restaurant) as something other than a contract of employment.

All of these raise difficult legal issues. Discussing them will also introduce the reader to some of the most dynamic worker advocacy organisations in the United States. It is no coincidence that these vital, movement-like

* Professor of Law and Sidney Reitman Scholar, Rutgers University School of Law, Newark, NJ, USA.

organisations operate precisely on the margins of the traditional definition of our subject.[1]

Part 1 of this chapter presents these six paradigmatic cases on the boundaries of labour and employment law. Part 2 discusses and criticises the normal legal analysis of these cases in every legal system: a multi-factor analysis to determine the resemblance of each to a core stereotype of employment or subordinate labour. In brief, in an economy that generates novel relationships such as those discussed above, an analysis in terms of traditional employment is an infallible method for generating nonsensical distinctions and unfairness. Part 3 thus broadens the debate by trying to determine why the traditional relation of subordinate employment has been the defining case for labour and employment law. It discusses two self-justifying narratives of labour law that generalise from the core case of subordinate employment. The first explains labour law as the home of values that are not realised in a competitive labour market. The second explains labour law as largely an exercise in the control of social conflict.

I shall argue that, while all these accounts contain important insights into labour law, none is adequate to answer even our six paradigm cases. I will therefore offer in Part 4 a revised definition of labour or employment law that locates its distinctiveness in its techniques for overcoming collective action problems that will produce sub-optimum contracts in markets that do not permit the formation of organisations and similar collective devices. On this view, there is no necessary connection between labour law and the contract of employment, merely a historic relationship. The techniques and practices that constitute labour law were first developed in an era when the employment relationship was, always and simultaneously, the locus of the greatest social oppression, inequality, and conflict. Now that this is no longer the case, there is no reason for labour law to shrink or retreat. Rather, its practices continue to apply to any market in which atomisation of legal personality will produce sub-optimum contracts. On this view, most or all of the six problematic paradigm cases should be seen as cases of labour and employment law.

1. SIX HARD CASES

A. Lessee Paying a Percentage of Revenue

Mr and Mrs Starkey leased for 10 years an Australian hotel which they managed themselves. The lease, anticipating development of the area that never took place, included an escalator clause that soon outpaced revenues

[1] In general, the collective, organisational aspect of labour law is conspicuous by its absence from this volume. All the papers equate labour law with benefits and minimum terms for employment contracts.

and forced the Starkeys to operate at a loss. The Starkeys applied to the Industrial Relations Commission under a statute permitting it to avoid or vary 'any contract whereby a person performs work in any industry if the Commission finds that the contract is an unfair contract'.[2] That Commission found the contract unfair, reduced the rent, and ordered the owner to renew the lease, but the state Court of Appeal reversed.[3]

Is a contract in which I operate your hotel, paying you rent, a contract 'whereby a person performs work in an[] industry'? Earlier decisions in New South Wales had found this language to include share farming,[4] and an agreement between a petroleum company and a service station operator.[5] So it was too late to argue that a contract involving an interest in land could not also be a contract of employment. These decisions applied what might be termed a culinary approach: they asked whether the transaction had the necessary 'industrial colour or flavour'. Judged by this almost entirely indeterminate standard, the Court of Appeal concluded that the hotel lease lacked the necessary 'industrial colour or flavour'. Of course the lease contemplated that the Starkeys would work, and they did work. But, held the Court, they might also have hired others to run the hotel. To treat this lease as a contract of employment would, said the Court, bring all commercial contracts before the Industrial Relations Commission since every contract contemplates effort by a human being. Of course, the Court's reasoning is equally circular: genuine employment doesn't stop being employment in situations in which the employee can hire a helper.

Although the Court does not articulate the multiple factors that some other common law courts use to define employment, the basic reasoning process appears similar: reasoning by prototype. In the best-known example, people in Europe or North America asked to think of a bird usually picture a robin or bluebird, not an ostrich. Similarly, people know what kind of relationship is the prototype for employment. As has often been pointed out, our prototype for employment is regular work for wages by one with nothing to sell but his labour power who thus places himself under the daily direction of one with capital.[6] When faced with a slightly different relationship, courts and industrial tribunals have but one technique: they ask whether the relationship before them is, or is not, like the prototype. For example, here the Starkeys contributed financial as well as human capital and were compensated out of enterprise earnings. These factors may distinguish

---

[2] *Industrial Relations Act* 1996, §106, NSW Consol.Acts. 'Industry' in turn is defined: 'industry includes . . . any trade, manufacture, business, project or occupation in which persons work' (§7).
[3] *Mitchforce v Industrial Relations Commission* [2003] NSWCA 151.
[4] *Stevenson v Barham* (1977) 136 CLR 190.
[5] *Caltex Oil (Australia) Pty Ltd v Feenan* [1981] 1 NSWLR 169; *Majik Markets Pty Ltd v Brake and Service Centre Drummoyne Pty Ltd* (1992) 28 NSWLR 443.
[6] Use of the gendered pronoun is intentional.

them from the prototype case of factory labour. Of course, they are shared with other relationships which might be analysed as employment relationships even though the individual contributes financial capital and is compensated largely through bonuses or stock. Examples might include partners in law or accounting partnerships or the workforce of a high-tech start-up.

Analyses of this type are always unsatisfactory. The disputed relationship will resemble the prototype employment relationship in some ways (or we wouldn't be having the discussion), but not in others (or we wouldn't be having the discussion). The analyst is quickly left speechless when asked whether a different relationship is, or is not, like the prototype of subordinate employment, because we have no agreed-on story of exactly why the prototype is singled out for special legal treatment.

B. Triangular Relationship: Garment Worker/Contractor/Manufacturer

We often use the concept of employment to identify, not merely relations of employment, but the rather different question who is the employer. For example, consider the common case of a garment 'manufacturer' (Hugo Boss, Donna Karan) who directly employs (that is, has on its payroll) no individuals who sew garments. Instead, work is contracted to small contractors who employ garment workers. The garment workers are normally employees of, at the least, the contractor, and treated as such in most legal systems, so far as I know. That is not surprising. They fit the classic prototype in which they sell labour power and work under the direction of one with capital.

It might also follow that such individuals are jointly employed by the manufacturer and the contractor, with each liable for wage payments and other compliance with employment laws. This is in fact the conclusion reached in two recent US cases applying the federal Fair Labour Standards Act.[7] The Court of Appeals cautioned, however, that not every garment manufacturer is now a joint employer with its contractors. The manufacturer is only a joint employer when it exercises control over the workplace in 'reality', and this requires careful examination of multiple factors which need not detain us for present purposes. A district court in the same circuit has held, examining actual control, that delivery personnel for supermarkets are employed jointly by the supermarket and the agency that nominally refers them.[8] The same Court

---

[7] *Zheng v Liberty Apparel Co., Inc.* 355 F 3d 61 (2d Cir, 2003); *Liu v Donna Karan International, Inc.*, 2000 US Dist LEXIS 18847 (SDNY 2001).

[8] *Ansoumana v Gristede's Operating Corp.*, 255 F Supp 2d 184 (SDNY 2003). I discuss the relationship among the multiple organisations purporting to speak for the delivery workers in A. Hyde, 'Who Speaks for the Working Poor?: A Preliminary Look at the Emerging Tetralogy of Representation of Low-Wage Service Workers' (2004) 13 *Cornell Journal of Law & Public Policy* 599, at 607–9. The delivery workers, mostly immigrants from west Africa, held demonstrations outside stores and eventually came to be represented by a legal advocacy group and the state Attorney General. Labour unions played no part in their representation.

of Appeals has held that recipients of public assistance, required to work for the city as a condition of their grant, are employees of the city.[9] These decisions would be obvious if the purpose of the labour standards legislation was understood as preventing labour exploitation and guaranteeing payment of compensation. However, it would seem that such liability should then attach to the more powerful party: the garment manufacturer, supermarket, and city—simply as the solvent party. It is not clear why this *economic* liability should instead turn on the manufacturer's involvement in *supervision* of the employee. In these American cases, the court did not adopt this purposive approach. The relationship of sewer to garment manufacturer, delivery personnel to supermarket, and welfare recipient to city are employment relationships because of their resemblance to the prototype, and not because of any general commitment to wage regulation, or preference for inclusion.

To define these problems as problems of classification, in which the factors constituting employment are individually examined, is thus to beg the question. They are rather problems of defining the purpose of the relevant legislation. The concept of employment becomes the alibi for not conducting this purposive analysis.

C. Janitor/Building Owner

However, if (as seems to be true in the US) the garment manufacturer normally jointly employs the garment worker together with the contractor, it would seem obvious that a building owner jointly employs the maintenance crews hired by contractors. Even on the assumption, which I am resisting, that the relevant question is the control of the worker, it is surely impossible to imagine building maintenance that is delegated to the unfettered discretion of the maintenance contractor. In Canada, allegedly employing the same multi-factor analysis used by US courts, building owners are sometimes, but by no means always, held to be the employers of maintenance workers also employed by a maintenance contractor.[10] In the US no case so holds, though this might seem the next step from the cases discussed in the last section. Successful union organising among janitors in the US in recent

---

[9] *US v City of New York (Colon v City of New York)*, 359 F 3d 83 (2d Cir, 2004) (city liable for sexual harassment of worker by city supervisor). See also *Stone v McGowan*, 308 F Supp 2d 79 (NDNY 2004) (city liable to pay minimum wage to welfare recipients in Work Experience Programme).

[10] *Labourers' International Union Local 183 v York Condominium Corp. No. 46*, 1977 OLRB Rep Oct 645; J. Sack, QC, C.M. Mitchell and S. Price, *Ontario Labour Relations Board Law and Practice* (3rd edn, Toronto: Butterworths, 1997), paras 2.6-2.12; D.A. Wright, 'Agency Workers and Collective Bargaining Law in Canada' (unpublished, seminar paper, 2000).

years has found ways to place economic pressure on building owners, but always within the bounds that limit economic pressure on neutral parties in labour disputes, surely an odd way to think about the owner of the building being cleaned.[11]

D. Physician/Insurance Company

The same concept of employment that prevents janitors in the US from bargaining with or pressuring building owners also prevents physicians from forming organisations to negotiate with insurance companies. Dentists who sent individual letters as a group, to dental insurance plans, requesting higher fees were criminally convicted of a conspiracy to fix prices under the antitrust laws.[12] Of course, employees are protected by labour law when they demand higher wages and refuse to work for less, and this labour law protection also grants employees immunity from antitrust liability. However, physicians and dentists in private practice are self-employed, or employees of their own companies. Since they are not employed by insurance companies, they cannot negotiate with them as a group.[13]

E. Farmworker/Produce Consumer

A remarkable achievement for some of the US's least powerful workers is the recent agreement between the Coalition of Immokalee Workers and the large fast-food chain Taco Bell. Taco Bell agreed to pay more for Florida tomatoes and cut off any grower with abusive labour conditions.[14] This agreement falls completely outside the field of labour law. The Coalition represents no employees of Taco Bell. Agricultural workers are excluded from the National Labour Relations Act. The Coalition is not a traditional

---

[11] On the Justice for Janitors campaign, see H. Wial, 'The Emerging Organizational Structure of Unionism in Low-Wage Services' (1993) 45 *Rutgers Law Review* 671, at 693–8; C.L. Erickson, C. Fisk, R. Milkman, D.J.B. Mitchell and K. Wong, 'Justice for Janitors in Los Angeles and Beyond: A New Form of Unionism in the Twenty-first Century?' in P.V. Wunnava (ed.), *The Changing Role of Unions: New Forms of Representation* (Armonk, NY, ME Sharpe, 2004) 22. US law is criticised in A. Hyde, 'The Story of *First National Maintenance Corp. v. NLRB*: Eliminating Bargaining for Low-Wage Service Workers' in L.J. Cooper and C.L. Fisk (eds.), *Labor Law Stories* (New York, Foundation Press, 2005), 311.

[12] *US v A. Lanoy Alston, D.M.D., P.C.,* 974 F 2d 1206 (9th Cir, 1992).

[13] A group of physicians may alert its members to defects in an insurance plan's standard agreement so long as the members are individually free to refuse to sign it: *International Healthcare Mgt. v Hawaii Coalition for Health,* 332 F 3d 600 (9th Cir, 2003).

[14] E. Leary, 'Immokalee Workers Take Down Taco Bell' (2005) 57 *Monthly Review* 11, available at: http://www.monthlyreview.org/1005leary.htm.

union. It is probably not a statutory labour organisation, if it represents only agricultural workers. Its members are mainly Guatemalan and Mexican.

The Coalition has achieved something that already is better than a collective bargaining agreement under the US system of labour law. While an employer has a statutory duty to bargain with the union representing its employees, it has no duty to negotiate the price it will pay for components (such as tomatoes), or the labour relations of outside contractors. Yet surely if this remarkable, exciting agreement falls outside labour law, that is so much the worse for labour law. The Taco Bell story shows the power of social movements to achieve gains for workers that are beyond the reach of unions, unless those unions themselves become social movements, using techniques of publicity and consumer pressure.

F. Union Choosing to Function as a Movement

It is tempting to describe the agreement between Taco Bell and the Coalition of Immokalee Workers as somehow suited or fitted to workers on the outside or margins or boundaries of labour law. So we must close the circle by pointing out that staying outside the system of labour law may appeal, for strategic reasons, to workers who are unquestionably statutory employees, and organisations that might as well choose to call themselves unions.

Consider Restaurant Opportunities Center New York (ROC–NY), a spin-off of Local 100, Hotel and Restaurant Employees. ROC seeks to represent the overwhelming majority (95 per cent) of New York City restaurant workers who do not have formal union representation.[15]

ROC was originally founded after the destruction of the World Trade Center on 11 September 2001 to coordinate social services to the surviving staff of the Windows on the World restaurant. With charitable donations coming in, the union found it convenient to create a separate entity, organised, not as a labour organisation, but a non-profit charity. However, such a nonunion soon proved potentially useful as an organising vehicle, particularly after the hiring of executive director Saru Jayaraman, who formerly worked at the Workplace Project, a successful organising project among Latin American immigrant workers on Long Island, New York.[16]

---

[15] An estimated 165,000 people work in New York City restaurants, of whom only 5% or so are members of the Hotel and Restaurant Employees (HERE): seminar presentation, Saru Jayaraman, Rutgers University School of Law, 5 Apr. 2005.

[16] K. Kulkarni, 'Fighting for Justice: Organizing for Immigrant Workers' Rights, an interview with Saru Jayaraman' (27 February 2004), available at: www.nyu.edu/gallatin/communitylearning/writings. On the Workplace Project, see the memoir by its founder, Jennifer Gordon, *Suburban Sweatshops: The Fight for Immigrant Rights* (Cambridge, Mass, Harvard University Press, 2005).

ROC has now engaged in six successful organising campaigns at groups of fancy, 'white tablecloth' restaurants in New York City. These campaigns culminate in the signing of a contract, enforceable not as a collective bargaining agreement (since ROC claims not to be a statutory 'labour organisation'), but as a contract under common law. The employers commit to increases in wages and benefits, settle claims that they have discriminated or failed to pay minimum wage or overtime, and pledge job security, including a pledge not to discharge employees without notice to ROC.[17] These contracts have followed lengthy campaigns marked by public demonstrations, 'dinner theatre' performances by actors who gain admission to the restaurant as patrons, and similar media events.[18]

I asked Saru Jayaraman why, in light of this success, it was important for ROC that it not be a 'labour organisation', since these employers might well have recognised HERE as an exclusive representative. She mentioned four legal advantages that ROC believes that it gains from being a charity rather than a labour organisation. (There may well be others.) First, ROC does not service contracts. It does not arbitrate grievances or owe a duty of fair representation. Secondly, ROC does not file the increasingly extensive financial reporting forms that unions must file under the Labour–Management Reporting and Disclosure Act (LMRDA).[19] Thirdly, ROC's public organising activities have lasted as long as six or nine months. Labour organisations, by contrast, may engage in organisational picketing of a non-union establishment for only 30 days, unless they then request an election from the National Labour Relations Board.[20] Fourthly, ROC opened a worker-owned restaurant in Greenwich Village in Autumn 2005. Although unions

---

[17] S. Greenhouse, 'Two Restaurants to Pay Workers $164,000', *New York Times* (12 January 2005) at B3, col 1. A crucial moment in the growth of any alternative worker organisation in New York is its first appearance in an article by Steven Greenhouse in the *New York Times*. See, eg, S. Greenhouse, 'Gristede's Deliverymen to Share in $3.2 Million Wage Settlement', *New York Times* (18 December 2003) at B2; S. Greenhouse, 'Korean Grocers Agree to Double Pay and Improve Workplace Conditions', *New York Times* (18 September 2002) at B1. See generally Hyde, above n 8.

[18] Jayaraman, above n 15.

[19] *Labour-Management Reporting and Disclosure Act* ss 201–210, 29 USC ss 431–440. Union financial disclosure has recently been made considerably more onerous: see 68 Fed Reg 58374 (9 Oct. 2003).

[20] *National Labour Relations Act* s 8(b)(7)(C), 29 USC s 158(b)(7)(C). One restaurant, subjected to a lengthy campaign of demonstrations, did file charges with the Board. ROC responded by ending the demonstrations, so there was no determination whether ROC is or is not indeed a statutory 'labour organisation'. In more recent campaigns, ROC does not picket restaurants, but restricts itself to handbilling: Jayaraman, above n 15. Such handbilling of consumers falls outside the statute regulating organisational picketing. (That is, the statute in terms reaches only picketing, and the Supreme Court has held, construing a different statutory section, that the distinction between picketing and handbilling is of constitutional importance: *Edward J. DeBartolo Corp. v Florida Gulf Coast Bldg. & Constr. Trades Council* 485 US 568 (1988)(NLRA s 8(b)(4)(ii), 29 usc, s 158(b)(4)(ii) construed to reach only picketing, in order to avoid constitutional problems that would arise if it were applied to consumer handbilling).

have helped organise employee trusts to own companies, the legal picture is not entirely clear, and Jayaraman thinks that it is possible that an organisation that is not a labour organisation might have more freedom to own a business or facilitate such employee ownership.[21] (A possible offsetting drawback in ROC's not being a labour organisation might be that unions have greater freedom of political action under federal law than do charities.)[22] ROC also litigates claims for restaurant workers under employment statutes, lobbies and advocates for restaurant workers, and provides classes on immigration rights and other subjects. Apart from its intrinsic interest, I tell its story here to emphasise that, so long as there is an 'inside' and an 'outside' to labour law, that boundary will be available as a site of strategic intervention, not only by employers, but by workers and their organisations.

2. THE FAILING PARADIGM OF SUBORDINATE LABOUR

How do, and how should, labour tribunals around the world decide whether to take jurisdiction of agreements like the Starkeys' with the hotel they rent, physician or dentist negotiation with insurance companies, farm worker organisations with Taco Bell, or self-styled movements of restaurant employees with those restaurants?

In a series of able articles (including one in this collection), Guy Davidov has shown that, around the world, the analysis of such questions is remarkably similar, although sometimes lines are drawn in different places.[23] Decision makers start with what I have been calling a paradigm of subordinate employment: an individual sells his labour power to someone who pays for it and supervises the details of his work. They approach problematic cases by asking a greater or lesser series of questions designed to probe its similarity to, or difference from the paradigm case of subordinate labour.

---

[21] In this paragraph, I am reporting what Saru Jayaraman told me about why ROC has attempted to be a charity, rather than a labour organisation. I do not entirely agree with her analysis. There is no legal impediment to union involvement in employee ownership. See generally A. Hyde and C. Harnett Livingston, 'Employee Takeovers' (1987) 41 *Rutgers Law Review* 1131 (discussing union-led takeovers of 1980s). I am also not so confident as she that ROC has achieved its goal of avoiding 'labour organisation' status. See A. Hyde, 'New Institutions for Worker Representation in the United States: Some Theoretical Issues', *New York Law School Law Review* (forthcoming 2006) 68 at nn 68–77. Failure of a labour organisation to file necessary reports is punishable with fines or a year in prison: LMRDA s 209, 29 USC s 439.

[22] Email communication, Saru Jayaraman, 6 Apr. 2005. I cannot explore the complexities of regulation of campaign contributions and expenditures here.

[23] G. Davidov, 'Who is a Worker?' (2005) 34 *Industrial Law Journal* 57; G. Davidov, 'Joint Employer Status in Triangular Employment Relationships' (2005) 42 *British Journal of Industrial Relations* 727; G. Davidov, 'The Three Axes of Employment Relationships: A Characterization of Workers in Need of Protection' (2002) 52 *University of Toronto Law Journal* 357; Davidov, this volume.

This approach comes naturally to any scholar of the field.[24] It has, however, in my opinion, nothing to recommend it absent some explanation of why the paradigm case should continue to define the boundaries of the subject. The construction of such an explanation is a conspicuous task, and equally conspicuous failing, of this volume.

Davidov is unquestionably correct that *if* the question has already been defined as the resemblance or not of a particular arrangement to employment, there is probably no alternative to the multi-factor analysis of similarities and differences. But as far as I am concerned, this just begs the question. *Why* should the ability of the Starkeys to get relief from their lease, or the ability of doctors to send letters as a group to an insurance company, or the ability of the restaurant workers to organise for nine months, turn on their resemblance to employment, traditionally understood? The demand that labour law extend 'beyond employment' is by now not exactly novel.[25]

This is not the place for a history of the concept of employment.[26] I think, however, that the following story is roughly true, though subject to refinement.

The question, why is the employment relationship deserving of special legal treatment would not have occurred to the generation that founded the subject. Labour and employment law grew up against a universal assumption that the relationship of work or employment was simultaneously the site of: (1) the greatest social oppression, (2) the greatest inequality of bargaining power, (3) the most revolting excesses of power, and (4) the greatest social conflict. On these four assumptions, special legal institutions, to provide floors of protection, permit collectivised bargaining, restrict employer power and mediate conflict, obviously are well-targeted at the employment relationship, though of course the forms and force of such legal interventions will always be controversial. On the assumption that the employment relationship is the site of the greatest need for legal intervention,

---

[24] Indeed, at the oral presentation of this chapter, Paul Benjamin immediately reacted to my posing the question of physician organisations to negotiate with insurance companies by saying that this was a 'peripheral' concern of labour law. Benjamin has written eloquently of the need to expand the scope of labour protection to some individuals who fall outside it: P. Benjamin, 'Who Needs Labour Law? Defining the Scope of Labour Protection' in J. Conaghan, R.M. Fischl and K. Klare (eds.), *Labour Law in an Era of Globalization: Transformative Practices and Possibilities* (Oxford, Oxford University Press, 2002), 75. Yet at bottom this argument is still based on their similarities to a core or paradigm case of employment. It is that assumption that I wish to draw into question.

[25] A. Supiot, *Au-delà de l'emploi: Transformations du travail et devenir du droit du travail en Europe. Rapport pour la Commission des Communautés Européennes* (Paris, Flammarion, 1999); V. Schultz, 'Life's Work' (2000) 100 *Columbia Law Review* 1881; K. Rittich, 'Feminization and Contingency: Regulating the Stakes of Work for Women' in Conaghan *et al.*, above n 24, at 117.

[26] S. Deakin, 'The Contract of Employment: A Study in Legal Evolution' (2001) 11 *Historical Studies in Industrial Relations* 1.

it became a logical site to administer educational programmes, savings for retirement, access to health, and the other aspects of the welfare apparatus of modern states.[27]

Our problem today is that none of these four foundational assumptions of labour law is still true. The employment relationship is no longer the site of the greatest oppression, or the greatest inequality of bargaining power, or the most revolting excesses of power, or the greatest social conflict. In every country, the employed have it quite a bit better than the unemployed, or those excluded from the labour market by age or gender or immigration status or lack of skills. In every country, serious oppression, inequality and conflict are found among these individuals outside the labour market, per- haps recipients of public assistance, perhaps working in relationships that are difficult to characterise as employment: for example, genuinely self- employed marginal labourers who work for many different people, or self- employed tenant farmers. The chapters in this volume offer many pictures of workers in informal sectors who may or may not be employed in a legal sense, but surely lie outside effective legal regulation.[28]

It matters not how we redraw the boundaries. The problem is the con- cept of employment itself. As a foundation for legal regulation, it is simul- taneously under-inclusive and over-inclusive. It leaves out many who might benefit from legal attention. Indeed, it leaves out precisely the neediest. Since the employment relationship (or even the work relationship) excludes many; it is thus neither the only nor the best way of creating social equali- ty or security or education or training.[29] At the same time, the concept of employment includes many whose needs are far less urgent. The public image of labour law suffers when working people who do not need its pro- tections find themselves frustrated by its restrictions.[30]

Worse yet, the very boundaries of employment, as Hugh Collins shows in his discussion of the different employment status of nurses at the same hos- pital,[31] enforce distinctions that frustrate substantive equality. Pinning legal treatment to employment status is not, in other words, a recipe for basic fairness that will, however, require minor adjustments. Rather, tying legal

---

[27] J.S. Hacker, *The Divided Welfare State: The Battle over Public and Private Social Benefits in the United States* (Cambridge, Cambridge University Press, 2002).

[28] Benjamin, this volume; Sankaran, this volume.

[29] Supiot, above n 25, Gunter Schmid as discussed in Benjamin, Sciarra.

[30] I have argued that this is true of self-employed individuals in the US who, as a group, are better compensated than employed individuals and do not wish to change their status: A. Hyde, *Working in Silicon Valley: Economic and Legal Analysis of a High-Velocity Labor Market* (Armonk, NY, ME Sharpe, 2003), 112–9; see also S.R. Barley and G. Kunda, *Gurus, Hired Guns, and Warm Bodies: Itinerant Experts in a Knowledge Economy* (Princeton, NJ, Princeton University Press, 2004).

[31] This volume.

status to employment status is constituted by, and thus builds in, the very unfairness and arbitrary treatment. To try to deliver equality through work law is constantly to be arguing that two relationships distinguished in law should, after all, be treated alike. But it is the law that creates the distinctions. And since the concepts that law uses to draw those distinctions, such as 'subordination', turn to paper in our hands, the distinctions resulting from these unsatisfactory tests will inevitably seem arbitrary.[32]

The result is inevitable. If law pins different status to the boundaries of employment—wherever, and however broadly, it draws those boundaries—it invites employers, workers, and their organisations (e.g. Restaurant Opportunities Center) to treat that boundary strategically. Which they do. When labour market regulation is followed by increased informalisation or self-employment, this is not a regrettable and unforeseeable by-product of regulation. Rather, it demonstrates the rationality of employers and employees.

It is long past time to stop tweaking the boundaries of employment and instead to try to remember why we were concerned with employment in the first place.

3. TWO JUSTIFYING NARRATIVES FOR LABOUR LAW: NON-MARKET VALUES; CONFLICT RESOLUTION

A. Labour Law as Upholding Values against the Market

Brian Langille has risen to this challenge.[33] Joining others, such as Clyde Summers,[34] Langille suggests that the distinct role of labour law is to uphold important values against the market:

> [L]abour lawyers see the development of labour law, certainly within recent memory, as one of the elaboration and remedying of a series of disenchantments with this contractual reality. Labour law is thus primarily conceived as a set of interventions in the labour market, that is, in the negotiation process for contracts of employment. The point of all this is, of course, 'justice' in this part of our lives, that is, in employment relationships. The idea of justice does

---

[32] Goldin, this volume.

[33] This volume.

[34] C.W. Summers, 'What We Should Teach in Labor Law: The Need for a Change and a Suggested Direction' in *The Park City Papers: Papers Presented At The Labour Law Group Conference on Labour and Employment Law in Park City, Utah, 29 June–1 July, 1984,* (Nashville, Tenn, The Labour Law Group, 1985) 195-96 (employment law organised around the theme of 'the role of the law in aiding the weaker party').

not need, for most Labour lawyers, a complete theoretical account. The more sophisticated will likely be able to draw upon ideas elaborated by John Rawls or Ronald Dworkin about a liberal theory of justice containing two elements, sometimes expressed as, 'concern' and 'respect'. Others may now draw upon the human development approach elaborated by Sen. But the core normative claim which the received wisdom makes is that justice for employees will never be completely secured as long as the relationship is analyzed in purely [common law] contractual terms.[35]

I daresay that every participant in this volume would agree that labour law intervenes in markets to achieve justice that will not emerge from unregulated contracting. I agree with it, as far as it goes. The problem is that it does not go far enough in specifying *which* non-market values will or should count as labour law values. Langille's eclecticism in finding values is certainly attractive (and accurate descriptively). That is, as Langille says, few labour lawyers could articulate a comprehensive theory of justice, and most would derive their views from various sources. However, this eclecticism undermines any attempt to find a unified core in the field. And, again, while we can (and do) continue our daily tasks without such a core, we find ourselves speechless when confronted increasingly with new ways of working, or engaging in economic activity, and a request to include or exclude these from labour and employment law as we know it.

Upholding values that do not emerge from an unregulated labour market will be a necessary condition of any coherent account of what labour law is all about—tautologically, one might say, since values that emerge from the market, such as efficiency, do not (by definition) require legal specification. However, the problem with formulations of this kind is that they do not provide *sufficient* conditions to identify labour law. They tend to break down except at very high levels of generality. They are useless in solving boundary problems, such as the six problems of borders with which we began. The cry for justice is as strong outside the boundary as within it.

We could adopt a purely descriptive theory of labour law. It would consist of the complete set of all non-market values imposed by law on labour markets. This would be a way of conceding that the field lacks coherence. The problem with this way of thinking is that one can easily convince oneself that, if one's labour law proposal has never emerged from voluntary negotiations between an employer and an employee, and has never been adopted by a democratically elected legislature, then it must be a good value and one must be doing the right thing.

---

[35] Langille, this volume.

If not the complete set of non-market values, then which? In the discussion of this paper at the conference 'The Scope of Labour Law: Re-drawing the Boundaries of Protection', Silvana Sciarra argued that the universe of labour rights now found in transnational and national law formed a coherent, if evolving, body of law, often constitutional. I think this is true only at a very high level of generality, for example if one said that labour law stood for values of 'solidarity' and 'collectivity' as against 'individualism'. For purposes of this chapter, I will consider only one example: the four core values of the International Labour Organisation's Declaration on Fundamental Principles and Rights at Work (1998), that is, freedom of association and the effective recognition of the right to collective bargaining; the elimination of all forms of forced or compulsory labour; the effective abolition of child labour; and the elimination of discrimination in respect of employment and occupation.[36] I am in total agreement with the concept that the ILO needed to set some priorities and focus on the most crucial and widely-accepted labour rights. I regard the Declaration as an enormous step forward for manageable and usable transnational labour rights, now placed in a form in which they can and will be incorporated increasingly into domestic legislation and negotiated trade agreements. I do not regard the Declaration as in any way a 'shrinking' or 'retreat' of transnational labour law; rather it is a vehicle for that field's expansion in scope and effectiveness.[37]

Nevertheless, one cannot regard the Declaration as a coherent *definition* of labour rights. The Declaration is a compromise.[38] It is designed to function at a high level of generality, to be included in legislation and trade agreements, and this it does. But rights such as the right to bargain collectively, or to be free of discrimination, are implemented in very different ways in different countries, sometimes in different regions or sectors within countries. Rights excluded from the Declaration do not for that reason cease to be part of labour law. I am thinking particularly of the right to be free of threats to health and safety, omitted from the Declaration. I have argued on theoretical grounds that, in order to build transnational labour law, the ILO would be well-advised to return to its traditional posture and

---

[36] See www.ilo.org/public/english/standards/decl/declaration/index.htm.

[37] For the contrary argument, see P. Alston, '"Core Labour Standards" and the Transformation of the International Labour Rights Regime' (2004) 15 *European Journal of International Law* 457; P. Alston and J. Heenan, 'Shrinking the International Labor Code: An Unintended Consequence of the 1998 ILO Declaration on Fundamental Principles and Rights at Work' (2004) 36 *New York University Journal of International Law & Policy* 221.

[38] In particular, a compromise designed to win US approval. See Alston, above n 37, at 466–9; G. Mundlak, 'The Transformative Weakness of Core Labour Rights in Changing Welfare Regimes' in E. Benvenisti and G. Nolte (eds.), *The Welfare State, Globalization, and International Law* (Berlin, Springer, 2004) 231.

devote more attention to technical matters such as workplace toxins and hazards.[39]

The point here however is that the boundaries of the field cannot emerge in a principled way from the inevitably political process of defining specific rights, such as the right to work or bargain or be free of discrimination or threats to safety. If this is the process that will answer our six problem cases at the beginning of this chapter, we have nothing principled to say about those cases. If industrial relations tribunals take jurisdiction of claims by tenants or farm workers, then those must be within the definition of labour law, but if not, not. If a legal system protects some group's right to organise, or be free of discrimination, it is necessarily enforcing a core principle of the ILO, but this would equally be true if that group did not consist of employees, traditionally defined.

Once again, we need either a defence of the centrality of employment or a workable way of moving 'beyond employment'. We cannot get either by summing up the legal norms relating to employment even within a single jurisdiction. The task is more, not less, hopeless if we focus on transnational norms. While labour law will indeed turn out to defend a coherent set of value as against the norms of the market, we will need a more precise definitional tool than simply to observe that our daily work has strayed quite far from market norms.

B. Labour Law as Conflict Resolution

So, while a good starting point in defining labour law is this concept of norms that must be defended but will not emerge from market transactions, we need to refine and supplement this idea.

As an American, I was intrigued by Brian Langille's claim that his vision of norms-against-the-market was not merely theoretically attractive, but would be the natural and received response of lawyers practising in the

---

[39] This claim is part of a larger argument, to be elaborated later in this chapter, that labour law should focus primarily on the set of values that is rational for societies but will not emerge from unconstrained markets because of coordination problems, of which low trust is the most important. Focusing on technical issues, such as annual identification of the world's 20 most hazardous work processes, publicising safer alternatives, and technical assistance to developing countries in adopting safer processes, has more potential to build the long-term trust necessary for an effective system of transnational labour law, than focusing on such necessarily more contentious issues as discrimination, child labour, or the design of collective bargaining, around which no international consensus exists below a very general level: A. Hyde, 'A Game-Theory Account and Defense of Transnational Labour Standards: A Preliminary Look at the Problem' in J. Craig and S.M. Lynk (eds.), *Globalization and the Future of Labour Law* (Cambridge, Cambridge University Press, forthcoming, 2006), 143, available at: http://law.bepress.com/rutgersnewarklwps/fp/art11.

field. This thought-experiment is another way to advance the project of defining the field. While I defer to Langille's sense of the Canadian legal community, and while I have not conducted any actual survey of US labour and employment lawyers, I strongly suspect that few, if any, non-academic lawyers south of the parallel would define their field as a set of non-market values. The received tradition in the US views collective labour law, at least, as primarily advancing a social interest in the reduction of conflict.[40] The very identification of the employment relationship as a subject of particular legal attention no doubt reflects, in large part, the perception of the nineteenth century that the 'labour question' was the primary source of social conflict.

The narrative identifying labour law with the management and reduction of conflict has doubtless passed from fashion outside the US. It is amazingly absent from the chapters in this volume, entirely so as nearly as I can see. Yet this project has been the site of some of labour law's finest achievements: works councils, participation in enterprise, social dialogue, collective bargaining, arbitration, labour courts. I have argued that labour law is typically a vehicle for public concessions to a disruptive worker movement, because of its value in reducing and channelling conflict.[41]

I argued that the narrative of values-against-the-market provides no limitations and no reason either to extend, or refuse to extend, the boundaries of the field. By contrast, the narrative of conflict resolution provides a simple, if crude, test for the boundaries of the subject. If disputes between hoteliers and their landlords, or agricultural workers and fast-food chains, or

---

[40] The opening sentence of the *National Labour Relations (Wagner) Act*, s 1, 29 USC s 151:

'Findings and declaration of policy: The denial by some employers of the right of employees to organise and the refusal by some employers to accept the procedure of collective bargaining lead to strikes and other forms of industrial strife or unrest, which have the intent or the necessary effect of burdening or obstructing commerce . . .'

The Supreme Court picked up just this message in upholding the constitutionality of the Act. 'Experience has abundantly demonstrated that the recognition of the right of employees to self-organisation and to have representatives of their own choosing for purpose of collective bargaining is often an essential condition of industrial peace. Refusal to confer and negotiate has been one of the most prolific causes of strife. This is such an outstanding fact in the history of labour disturbances that it is a proper subject of judicial notice and requires no citation of instances . . .': *National Labour Relations Board v Jones & Laughlin Steel Corp.* (1937) 301 US 1, 42. It continues to be conventional in the US to justify labour policy by its supposed tendency to reduce conflict. The rights of employees to organise 'are protected not for their own sake but as an instrument of the national labour policy of minimizing industrial strife "by encouraging the practice and procedure of collective bargaining"': *Emporium Capwell Co. v Western Addition Community Organization*, 420 US 50. Labour 'arbitration is the substitute for industrial strife': *United Steelworkers v Warrior & Gulf Navigation Co.* (1975) 363 US 574, (1960).

[41] A. Hyde, 'A Theory of Labor Legislation' (1990) 38 *Buffalo Law Review* 383.

doctors and insurance companies are a 'prolific cause of strife' that has led to public demands for concessions to workers or mechanisms of conflict control, then by all means hoteliers and agricultural workers ought to be included before industrial tribunals. If not, not.

Although this account of labour law has some descriptive power, it is normatively unappealing as a complete account of the field. However, I do not think the role of labour law in managing social conflict should be entirely absent from the substitute narrative we might construct, to which I now turn.

4. WHAT IS LABOUR LAW, AND WHAT ARE ITS BOUNDARIES?

Labour and employment law is the collection of regulatory techniques and values that are properly applied to any market that, if left unregulated, will reach socially sub-optimum outcomes because economic actors are individuated and cannot overcome collective action problems. Labour and employment law can reach socially beneficial outcomes in such markets through some combination of the following techniques. Individual actors can be permitted to form organisations and protected against retaliation for doing so. These organisations may be monitored or regulated in the interest of the public or of their principals. These organisations may conclude binding agreements. The agreements may be enforced through special institutions outside the general run of contract. Minimum contractual terms may be socially specified. Institutions of dispute resolution may be socially provided or encouraged, such as labour courts, arbitration, or mediation. Ground rules for economic conflict may be enacted.

For historic reasons, these techniques originated and achieved maturity, though surely not perfection, in the market for employment. Within the memory of senior practitioners in the field, this market represented simultaneously the site of the greatest exploitation, inequality, market failure, and social conflict. The labour market had already been shaped by legal doctrines that made worker organisation difficult or impossible, and thus needed legal reforms to define any legitimate role for worker organisation.

However, these techniques of a mature system of labour law are not restricted to the market for employment. They may be invoked whenever social efficiency is impeded by bars to organisation, collective action problems that prevent the adoption of efficient cooperative solutions, wasteful conflict, low trust, high information costs, or similar problems. The case for inclusion or exclusion of a particular category of disputes or contracts from the world of labour law is a combined empirical and economic inquiry that asks—always in the particular case, in the particular legal system: what, if any, barriers to socially optimum solutions exist in this particular market? Would any of these barriers be usefully addressed through techniques such as collectivised actors, socially-provided contractual minima, or institutions of dispute resolution? What social costs would be imposed by application of these traditional techniques of labour law, and would these costs be outweighed by the likely benefit? Treatment of a particular matter as one of labour law should normally depend on an affirmative answer to these three questions, rather than the similarity or not to a traditional relationship of subordinate employment.

On this view, labour law is not the set, in theory infinite, of human values that might rationally be imposed by societies on markets. Rather, labour law is the much narrower set of values that correct market failures through particular legal techniques.

A. What Kinds of Market Failure does Labour Law Address?

Only in the magical world of those ignorant of professional labour economics do labour markets function like the idealised neoclassical markets in economics textbooks that swiftly adjust price and quantity until no more efficient transactions can occur and the market has cleared. Labour law grows up to meet a clear and defined list of market failures common to labour markets, though in no case restricted to those markets. The most important economic aspects of labour markets for understanding labour law include: (1) inelasticity of supply; (2) collective action problems; (3) low trust and opportunism that prevent the formation of efficient long-term contracts; (4) inadequate incentives for investment in human capital; and (5) information asymmetries.[42] When labour law addresses these (and similar) market failures, it does not stand against the market. It enables it.

1. Inelasticity of Supply

The most important difference between labour markets and neoclassical markets is perhaps the most obvious but least-discussed. In most societies, people who reach adulthood are compelled, in order to survive, to enter the labour market and sell their labour, no matter how many others do the same and no matter how poor a price their labour fetches. In neoclassical markets, when the price of a commodity drops, sellers produce less of it, or none at all, or put their stocks into silos and farm something else. Sellers of

---

[42] A fuller treatment might also include: (6) monopsonistic buyers with ability to set the price of labour: D. Card and A.B. Krueger, *Myth and Measurement: the New Economics of the Minimum Wage* (Princeton, NJ, Princeton University Press, 1995); A. Manning, *Monopsony in Motion: Imperfect Competition in Labour Markets* (Princeton, NJ, Princeton University Press, 2003); (7) bilateral monopolies between employers and long-term employees; (8) cognitive disabilities resulting from individuals' use of decisional heuristics or other rational refusals to invest in information.

labour power have these options only in highly restricted forms, if at all. (The government may provide higher education that delays their entry into the labour market, what economists call 'disguised unemployment'. Or they may have the good fortune to be supported by another family member.) Most people must sell their labour power to survive. The inability of sellers to restrict supply necessarily drives prices down and prevents labour markets from clearing; there will always be unemployed people.

2. Collective Action Problems

Sellers of labour power, and sometimes buyers, may therefore sometimes benefit from agreements to limit competition, set floors, restrict entry, and the like. Today we think of this as a branch of game theory. However, this may be the oldest idea in labour law, part of its justificatory narrative since the beginning, long before scholars employed the formal language of game theory. Child labour, noted John Stuart Mill in 1832, is a case 'in which it would be highly for the advantage of every body, if every body were to act in a certain manner, but in which it is not the interest of any *individual* to adopt the rule for the guidance of his own conduct, unless he has some security that others will do so too'.[43]

Today, however, we may employ the tools of game theory to identify more of the situations that Mill intuited, in which agreements that are in the advantage of everybody will not emerge from the market because of low trust, misperceptions, information asymmetries, or other factors that will prevent individuals from reaching efficient cooperative solutions, forcing them instead to bargain against each other, driving standards down and wasting resources in duplicative and unnecessary bargaining.

To pick just one example, in a working paper I model the adoption of transnational labour standards as cooperative solutions to Stag Hunt games, in which all players will benefit from the adoption of a cooperative solution but will not adopt it if they anticipate even one defection from the cooperative process (such anticipation of defection thus becoming the defection itself). To present intuitively what can take more space to present formally: It is clearly in the long-term interest of India, Bangladesh and Pakistan that all their children go to school and not work in factories. Going to school builds human capital, attracts more and better foreign investment, and generally results in a richer society for all. However, if (contrary to fact) India and Pakistan actually were to succeed in getting all their children out of

---

[43] J.S. Mill, 'Employment of Children in Manufactories' in *Newspaper Writings August 1831–October 1834*, 23 *Collected Works of John Stuart Mill* (Ann P. Robson and John M. Robson (eds.), Toronto, University of Toronto Press, 1986) [1832] 398, at 399.

workshops and into schools, there are certain specific foreign investments and gains from trade that would flow to Bangladesh to take advantage of its child labour, and this would be true even if (as we suppose) Bangladesh knows that it is in its long-term interest that children learn instead of work. This is a classic Stag Hunt. If all countries cooperate in ending child labour, all will be better off. Jobs will be taken by unemployed adults, and children will go to school. But if even one country defects by letting children work, it will capture a certain stream of foreign direct investment that others will not. So, if you think one of your rivals will be selfish, it is rational for you to be selfish, too. On this view, labour standards in trade agreements and even ILO Conventions can be seen as coordination devices among countries with poor labour standards to ensure that they move forward together.[44] We can generalise this approach to most aspects of labour law.

3. Overcoming Low Trust, Opportunism, and Sub-optimum Investment in Human Capital

Stag Hunts epitomise a kind of contract in which a cooperative solution exists and is rationally in the interest of all but will not be adopted because players do not trust others to stick to the deal. There are, however, many others. One that has received a great deal of attention from economic and legal scholars of employment in recent decades is the contract between an employee and an employer that, for whatever reason, anticipates its highest gains if it can effectively hire an employee for a very long term. In one version, this permits the employer to train and share other information with the employee, secure in the knowledge that the employee and the information will not immediately migrate to a competitor. However, there are other versions of the 'implicit lifetime employment contract' that do not depend on investments in human capital.[45]

The economists who first modelled the implicit contract assumed it was self-enforcing.[46] Legal scholars, by contrast, quickly saw the possibilities

---

[44] Hyde, above n 39.

[45] The airline US Airways successfully went to the US Supreme Court to defend its practice of reserving desk jobs for senior baggage handlers, thus defeating the claim that the Americans with Disabilities Act 1990, 42 U.S.C. s 12101–12212, required it to open these jobs to disabled workers: *U.S. Airways, Inc. v Barnett* 535 US 391 (2002). It is not easy to say precisely why it is in US Airways' interest to create lifetime careers for baggage handlers, though plainly the airline thinks that it is. Healthy young people who can load suitcases onto aeroplanes may be found on street corners all across America and might be hired for minimum wage. Nor were the positions in question covered by a collective bargaining agreement. We might speculate that the airline's policies permit it to hire better quality (more reliable) workers, reduce turnover, and save constant hiring and search costs. However, it is unlikely that the airline makes substantial investment in the human capital of baggage handlers or is concerned about losing it to competitors.

[46] E. Lazear, 'Why Is There Mandatory Retirement?' (1979) 87 *Journal of Political Economy* 1261; S. Rosen, 'Implicit Contracts: A Survey' (1985) 23 *Journal of Economic Literature* 1144.

that the employer might behave opportunistically by renouncing its implicit promise of a lifetime job, a promise often unenforceable at common law.[47] Labour unions sometimes appeal to employers who want to establish such contracts. Unions reduce employee turnover, reinforce returns to experience, and provide enforcement mechanisms for what the law might regard as vague or unenforceable promises.[48] It is fairly clear that such implicit lifetime contracts have been less popular among US employers in recent decades.[49] Employers that see little value in stable employment relations have more reason to oppose unionisation, as of course has occurred.

4. Information Asymmetries

Information is expensive, and individual bargainers may rationally not invest in it. Their bargains may be poorly priced; they may over-invest in unnecessary protections because they misestimate risk, the employer's or employee's needs, and the like. Permitting collective bargainers, who can afford to invest in information, may result in more efficient bargains. Facilitating works councils, worker directors, collective bargaining, and other consultative structures may increase trust, lower information costs, and permit parties to reach more efficient bargains with lower transaction costs.

B. How does Labour Law Address these Market Failures?

This is far from an exhaustive list of market failures addressed by labour law, but it is more than enough to illustrate the basic point. When labour law permits workers to form organisations and bargain as a group, it may—depending on circumstances—counteract the natural tendency toward over-supply of labour, permit controls on entry (some of which may of course harm the public and be worse than the disease), permit efficient sharing of risks of loss or gain, or lower information costs for workers and employers. When labour law creates consultative institutions, it may further lower transaction and information costs, build trust, and facilitate efficient cooperative solutions that will not be adopted because of low trust. When minimum terms of employment are specified, this may prevent a ruinous race to the bottom or reinforce the implicit efficient agreement among private parties (for example, to abolish child labour, if Mill is correct). Of

---

[47] S.J. Schwab, 'Life-Cycle Justice: Accommodating Just Cause and Employment at Will' (1993) 92 *Michigan Law Review* 8.

[48] R.B. Freeman and J.B. Medoff, *What Do Unions Do?* (New York, Basic Books, 1984).

[49] Hyde, above n 30; K.V.W. Stone, *From Widgets to Digits: Employment Regulation for the Changing Workplace* (Cambridge, Cambridge University Press, 2004).

course, such terms might, in other circumstances, tax job creation and reduce employment.[50]

The point is that there is nothing about these efficiency-promoting features of labour law that is restricted to traditional contracts of subordinate employment. If there are other markets in which efficiency may be promoted by collectivised bargaining agents, minimum terms, consultative structures, or ground rules for economic conflict, then labour law ought to apply.

C. Is there no Room for Human Values in Labour Law that Cannot be Recast into Economic Language?

Of course there is, but one would expect employers to resist such humane, non-economic values strenuously, and for law to have major problems in efficacy.

As mentioned, I first began thinking about Stag Hunts in the context of transnational labour standards such as ILO Conventions, treaties and corporate codes, all of which may lack effective enforcement mechanisms and which therefore may not even seem like law, to sceptical observers. The point of the Stag Hunt model, in that context, is to show that even law that lacks effective sanctions may still be worth having, when it provides coordination points for agreements that would be Pareto-optimal for private parties or governments, but will not be voluntarily adopted. We may certainly generalise this model to other systems of labour law that lack sanctions. These, too, are not necessarily useless. They may provide coordination points and spread to larger groups solutions that are both just and efficient.[51]

Most real-world systems of labour law include sanctions that can change actors' incentives, and make rational courses of conduct that were not rational before. If a society wants to encourage behaviour that it regards as humane, such as restricting the grounds for dismissal from employment, labour law provides the tools for doing so (taxes or fines on dismissal, mandatory severance pay, labour courts or tribunals to adjudicate the grounds of dismissal). So there is no theoretical reason for labour law to restrict itself to facilitating efficiency.

There are, however, practical reasons for focusing on efficient solutions to market failure. For labour law to achieve other values, it must have sanctions, and as a practical matter that usually means that a democratic legislature

---

[50] The best economic introduction is Card and Krueger, above n 42.

[51] B. Skyrms, *The Stag Hunt and the Evolution of Social Structure* (Cambridge, Cambridge University Press, 2004) shows that in large groups cooperative solutions may be reached only when neighbours can negotiate with each other and copy their successes.

has invested an agency or tribunal with such power. Sanctions are rarely part of harmonisation projects. Democratic legislatures, in turn, have limited scope for imposing on private actors results that are inefficient from the private actors' point of view—not zero scope, but limited. Persistent attempts to impose inefficient solutions engender non-compliance, off-the-books employment, informalisation, and similar responses that put all of labour law into poor repute. Since the set of such humane values is in any case thin and contested, and since the scope for efficient solutions (properly understood) is large and still poorly-mapped, it is rational for theorists and administrators of labour law to focus their energies on the kinds of reforms mentioned here, that facilitate Pareto-optimal solutions but do not emerge from atomised markets.

D. Redrawing the Boundaries

If labour law is understood as the collection of techniques and practices that overcome specific market failures (inelasticity of supply, collective action problems, low trust and opportunism, information asymmetry) with specific techniques (collectivised actors, minimum terms, institutions that build trust), what are its boundaries? Viewed in this way, the answer to this question calls for diagnosis of potential market failure and the likely prognosis for application of labour law techniques. The similarity or difference between the case at hand and traditional nineteenth-century subordinate employment is rarely, if ever, of any importance.

Some norms of labour law are, or should be understood as, basic human rights that pertain to every human being, without any reference to the details of that individual's work supervision or compensation. This is particularly true of norms of health and safety. The right of a banana picker not to be exposed to a toxic nematocide is a human right, in the sense that it should have nothing to do with whether the banana picker is on the payroll of the plantation, or is a self-employed migrant who works for many farms over a season, or works off-the-books, out of sight of the tax authorities, or, for that matter, grows bananas on his own plot. In fact, courts in the US have had a difficult time classifying migrant farm workers, who are typically very poor people with nothing to sell but their labour power, but who equally typically work for many different farms, depending on the season, and are not in fact economically dependent on any single farmer.[52] This dispute may have ramifications for the most efficient way to collect taxes,

---

[52] Compare *Donovan v Brandel*, 736 F 2d 1114 (6th Cir, 1984) (migrant farm workers are independent contractors) with *Secretary of Labor v Lauritzen*, 835 F 2d 1529 (7th Cir, 1987) (migrant farm workers are employees, applying multi-factor approach).

but should be completely irrelevant in guaranteeing the workers' freedom from exposure to toxins. Similarly, just because the student intern is unpaid is no reason to assume that Congress intended that she could be sexually harassed.[53]

Collective labour rights call for a different, more economic inquiry, looking at the public interest. If the public would be served by collective negotiations between physicians' or dentists' organisations and insurance companies, or service station or other franchisees and franchisors, or hoteliers and landlords, then labour law stands ready to mediate. We know in advance that relationships of this kind will bear *some* resemblance, but not *total* resemblance, to subordinate employment. The question is not how many factors on an eight- or 20-factor list flip to favour the weaker party, but what kinds of market failures disserve the public, and whether the practices of labour law would, on balance, better serve the public.[54]

Our current narratives of labour law (as the extension of subordinate employment) share the same fault with narratives of taming the market. Both narratives struggle, as all the papers of the conference show, with their inability to apply concepts like subordinate, dependent, unequal. By contrast, the approach of this chapter has no such limits or concepts, so it has no *a priori* issues of exclusion and inclusion. Rather, the application of labour law rests on affirmatively finding a useful task for it to perform. This means a problem amenable to legal solution, such as a Stag Hunt, amenable precisely to collective solutions. Labour law as a set of techniques rests on no *a priori* definition. Its application is subject always to demands of efficiency and social value.

5. CONCLUSION: THE FUTURE OF LABOUR LAW

Labour law has a bright future, once it understands itself as a collection of regulatory techniques, not a sidecar on the motorcycle of subordinate employment.

The most exciting current development in the economics of work and employment, still in its infancy, is the emerging field of network economics.

---

[53] *Contra, O'Connor v Davis*, 126 F 3d 112 (2d Cir, 1997) (student intern may not sue under Civil Rights Act). Compare, *US v City of New York (Colon v City of New York)*, 359 F 3d 83 (2d Cir, 2004) (recipient of public assistance, required to perform uncompensated work for city as condition of welfare grant, is employee of city for purposes of Civil Rights Act).

[54] In discussion following these remarks at the conference 'The Scope of Labour Law: Redrawing the Boundaries of Protection', Simon Deakin observed that terms like subordination and dependence are just code by which lawyers work out the details of overcoming collective action problems. This is the process I favour. However, too often, in the real world, those words are the code for *not* working out these problems. The limits of the contract of employment are too often the boundaries of any legal intervention at all.

In network economics, economic actors are typically networks of actors rather than individual firms; careers, and communities of employees and their organisations, occur within networks but transcend firm boundaries; information can be more valuable when held by many than by few; discrimination can be rational and require legal, rather than self-, correction. Legal issues concern exclusion from networks, new forms of employer and worker organisation, new forms of holding intellectual property, new ways of administering training and benefits.[55] The sooner that labour law expands its vision 'beyond employment', the sooner it will participate in the more important economic relations of the new century.

---

[55] See, eg, C. Shapiro and H. Varian, *Information Rules: A Strategic Guide to the Network Economy* (Boston, Mass, Harvard Business School Press, 1999); Hyde, above n 30; K. Arrow, 'What Has Economics to Say About Racial Discrimination' (1998) 12 *Journal of Economic Perspectives* 91, at 98; P.M. Romer, 'Endogenous Technological Change' (1990) 98 *Journal of Political Economy* S71.

4

Using Development Approaches to Address the Challenge of the Informal Economy for Labour Law

ANNE TREBILCOCK*

1. INTRODUCTION

A S THE VARIETY of forms of work expands, the growth in what is termed the 'informal economy' and 'informal employment' poses major challenges to traditional labour law. In most of the developing countries of the world, development frameworks largely set the tone for law reform processes. These are driven largely by economists, with some reliance on statistics. An inter-disciplinary dialogue with legal experts around fundamental labour market issues is rare. One way to stimulate a productive interchange may be found in development frameworks.

This chapter reviews different approaches to 'informality' from the perspectives of the International Labour Conference, statistics, poverty reduction, selected labour market analysis and three schools of thought with their origins in the development community: sustainable livelihoods, human capabilities, and empowerment. It explores which of these approaches seems to be most promising for labour law in light of the challenges posed by 'informality'. Looking at labour law through a development lens may give rise to new perspectives as the basis for fresh solutions.

A. What is Meant by 'Informality'?

A wide-ranging vocabulary has been used to describe a wide range of phenomena that have both shared and unshared characteristics: informal, irregular, unofficial, unregulated, non-standard, hidden, shadow, underground,

* Legal Adviser and Director, Office of Legal Services, International Labour Office. The views expressed are those of the author alone.

parallel, non-structured, unorganised, illegal, unmeasured, unrecorded, undeclared or 'non-observed'.[1] Some of these terms are in fact rather misleading, since many activities in the 'informal economy' are well structured and highly stratified according to complex social rules.[2] 'Illegal' is a particularly unhelpful designation, since it confuses activity that is inherently immoral and criminal—such as narcotics trafficking—with otherwise socially legitimate economic activity that has been branded unlawful in civil and/or criminal law for often diverse reasons.

While not containing a definition per se of the informal economy, the conclusions adopted by the government, employer and worker delegates to the International Labour Conference in June 2002, used the term to describe:

> All activities by workers and economic units that are—in law or in practice—not covered or insufficiently covered by formal arrangements. Their activities are not included in the law, which means that they are operating outside the formal reach of the law; or they are not covered in practice, which means that—although they are operating within the formal reach of the law, the law is not applied or not enforced; or the law discourages compliance because it is inappropriate, burdensome or imposes excessive costs.[3]

The ILC conclusions further distinguished these informal activities from 'criminal and illegal activities, such as smuggling of illegal drugs, ... [which] are not appropriate for regulation or protection under labour or commercial law' (paragraph 5). We will return to the second part of this phrase as a potential avenue to pursue. The way countries address informality depends on how the underlying problem is framed and what legal provisions are already in place.

The shift from talking about the informal 'sector'[4] to the informal 'economy' was more than semantic. Although admittedly still speaking of two economies, the ILC conclusions rejected a dualism in which the formal and

---

[1] OECD, ILO, IMF, CIS Stat, *Measuring the Non-observed Economy: A Handbook* (Paris, OECD, 2002).

[2] A. Sindzingre, 'The Relevance of the Concepts of Formality and Informality: A Theoretical Approach' in EGDI and UNU-WIDER Conference, *Unlocking Human Potential: Linking the Informal and Formal Sectors* (Helsinki, Finland, 17–18 Sept. 2004), 9.

[3] *Conclusions concerning Decent Work and the Informal Economy* (Provisional Record No 25, International Labour Conference, 90th Session, Geneva, International Labour Office, 2002), para 3. The distinction between non-application and non-enforcement is explored further by J.L. Daza Pérez, 'Informal Economy, Undeclared Work and Labour Administration', *Dialogue Paper No 9* (Geneva, International Labour Office, 2005), 9.

[4] Keith Hart, an anthropologist, coined the term 'informal sector' in describing income opportunities in 'Informal Income Opportunities and Urban Employment in Ghana' (1973) 11 *Journal of Modern African Studies* 61. Before its publication, an ILO report on Kenya kicked off its use in development and labour market academic circles: *Employment, Incomes and Inequality: A Strategy for Increasing productive Employment in Kenya* (Geneva, International Labour Office, 1972).

informal 'sectors' were seen as distinct entities, in favour of the idea of 'a continuum of production and employment relations'.[5] Three factors explained this. The first is that the workers and enterprises considered to be 'informal' cut across many sectors of economic activity, rather than constituting a sector of their own. The second is the interdependencies and linkages that exist between formal and informal activities (referred to in paragraph 3 of the conclusions), in part reflecting changes in global production systems. The third is the long-standing criticism of the dualistic formal/informal analytical framework for being 'both over-simplified and blurred'.[6]

While this new approach to the 'informal economy' captures the heterogeneity of informality, it is precisely this heterogeneity that presents difficulties for policy makers, including labour lawyers and legislators. Recent investigation into segmentation of the labour market within the informal economy has led to proposals for a more precise categorisation as a basis for meaningful policy formulation.[7]

At the same time, the analytical power of the notion of 'informality' is weakened by the fact that workers and economic units can operate as 'formal' for some purposes and as 'informal' for others. What really matters is whether informality is having negative consequences for workers and entrepreneurs that need to be addressed. In developing countries, many workers engage in multiple activities, whether formal ones supplemented by informal ones, or several informal activities pursued simultaneously. Similarly, entrepreneurs may operate both formally and informally. This dimension of 'multiple activity' has important implications for how law, including labour law, can operate effectively.

The notion of 'informality' sits uneasily in law, and at first blush the term 'informal employment' sounds like an oxymoron. This leads some to make the often unwarranted assumption that international labour standards 'do not apply' to the informal economy.[8]

For a lawyer, the term 'employment' conjures up legal notions of contracts of employment, whether written, oral or implied, which are enforceable

---

[5] L. Lim, 'Highlights of the ILC Conclusions', presentation to the Turin Workshop on the Follow-up to the ILC Conclusions on Decent Work and the Informal Economy (ILO, International Training Centre, 10–12 Feb. 2003). The 'continuum' approach has been picked up by K.F. Becker, *The Informal Economy: Fact Finding Study* (Stockholm, Sida, 2004) and Sindzingre, above n 2.

[6] *Ibid.*, at 3. For a history of how the concept was used in the ILO until the 15th International Conference of Labour Statisticians, see P.E. Bangasser, *The ILO and the Informal Sector: An Institutional History* (Geneva, International Labour Office, Employment Paper 2000/9, 2000).

[7] M. Chen, J. Vanek, F. Lund, J. Heintz, R. Jhabvala and C. Bonner, *Women, Work and Poverty, Progress of the World's Women 2005* (New York, UNIFEM/UNDP/ILO, 2005).

[8] A. Trebilcock, 'International Labour Standards and the Informal Economy' in J.-C. Javillier, B. Gernigon and G. Politakis, *Les Normes Internationales du Travail: Un Patrimoine pour l'Avenir* (Geneva, International Labour Office, 2004), 585.

between the parties, through a judicial and/or an administrative system. Nonetheless, the term 'informal employment' has gained considerable currency in development circles and, increasingly, in statistical parlance. That is why this chapter seeks to explore whether development paradigms might hold some promise for the fulfilment of the core purpose of labour law: to tip an inherently unequal balance of power in favour of those who provide their labour as their means to live.

B. Extent of the Informal Economy and its Gender Dimension

However the informal sector or informal economy is defined, it is widely recognised that the phenomenon is huge in many developing countries, mushrooming in Eastern and Central Europe, and growing in importance in some developed nations. The estimated shares of non-agricultural employment that are in the informal economy are: 48 per cent in North Africa, 51 per cent in Latin America, 65 per cent in Asia and 72 per cent in Subsaharan Africa.[9] In countries that include informal employment in agriculture, these percentages go even higher: a composite figure for India, to take an extreme but frequently cited example, counts 93 per cent of total employment as working informally. While much less significant than in developing countries, informality is growing in some developed countries as well.[10]

The United Nations Commission for Latin America and the Caribbean reported that of the fully 51.9 per cent of non-agricultural employment in the informal sector in 2000,[11] 15.6 per cent were as employers or workers in firms of with up to five employees, 24.3 per cent were classified as independent or own-account workers and 5.3 per cent engaged in domestic work. Data from *Panorama Laboral/Labour Overview* for 2004 have confirmed a continued expansion of employment in the informal sector, as well as its strong feminisation (one of every two employed women is found in this sector).[12] These data pose difficulties for lawyers, since a firm employing fewer than five people may or may not be beyond the formal reach of labour law. A similar question arises for domestic work.

---

[9] *Women and Men in the Informal Economy: A Statistical Picture* (Geneva, International Labour Office, 2002).

[10] P. Renooy, S. Ivarsson, O. van der Wusten-Gritsai and R. Meijer, *Undeclared Work in an Enlarged Union: Final Report* (Brussels, European Commission, Directorate-General for Employment and Social Affairs, 2004).

[11] V.E. Tokman, *Las dimensiones laborales de la transformación productiva con equidad* (Santiago de Chile, Unidad de Estudiso Especiales, CEPAL, Oct 2004), 56, citing ECLAC, based on household surveys.

[12] *Panorama Laboral/Labour Overview* (Lima, International Labour Office, 2004).

Overall, women predominate in informal work throughout the world. Chen, Vanek and Carr have come up with a pyramid that illustrates its gender-related segmentation. In terms of earnings, employers and own-account operators—who are predominantly men—come out on top. Then, in descending order are unpaid family members (both men and women), followed by employees of informal enterprises and other informal wage workers. At the bottom of the heap are industrial outworkers/homeworkers—categories where women are in the vast majority.[13] Echoing the ILO report, *Working out of Poverty* (2003), these authors recall that the vast majority of the poor work and that the vast majority of the working poor, especially women, are engaged in the informal economy.

2. PERSPECTIVES ON INFORMALITY

In this section, informality is seen from the perspectives of development for poverty reduction, ILO constituents represented at the International Labour Conference, labour markets, and statistical measurement.

A. Informality as a Development Issue

There is substantial but not total overlap between the incidence of informal economic activity—especially the type that features an irregular and precarious income—and of poverty. Thus informality is at heart a development issue. A recent report by one leading European agency, the Swedish International Development Agency, shows how it perceives informality:

'The informal economy, which presently harbours many of the workers in the developing countries, has grown substantially during the last decades. The main reason for this growth appears to be that the formal labour markets have not been able to generate sufficient amounts of jobs and absorb a continuously growing and many times unskilled workforce. The informal economy thus provides opportunities for income earning for those that have no other means to survive. However, it is also believed that people voluntarily engage in informal economic activities because of excessive taxation and regulation from the part of governments.'[14]

Informal enterprises are much more vulnerable in relation to obstacles faced by formal enterprises (including too restrictive or cumbersome taxation systems and certain labour laws).[15]

---

[13] M. Chen, J. Vanek and M. Carr, *Mainstreaming Informal Employment and Gender in Poverty Reduction* (London, Commonwealth Secretariat, 2004), 40.
[14] Becker, above n 5, at 5.
[15] *Ibid.*, at 22.

In its conclusions on policy and strategy development, SIDA identifies its areas of intervention in relation to the informal economy: streamlining the regulatory framework for business in order to reduce the costs for small enterprises to become formal, address property rights in the informal sector, assist government to eliminate gender discrimination in business, support efforts to spread micro-credit programmes, and support training and capacity building of entrepreneurs. At the same time, SIDA acknowledges that the lack of incomes and assets, and of voice and power, has an important impact on the lives of those in the informal economy.[16]

These views reflect the tension between the concern for the worker and the concern for the firm, a tension that can be seen throughout various approaches to development. They also suggest a lack of appreciation of the *positive* function of labour law, seeing it principally as a constraint. This has also been the perspective of much of the reform of laws governing micro and small businesses[17]—which has in effect been 'undercover' labour law reform. What has received much less attention is the lack of a job creation dividend for the countries that have followed the economic presecriptions by eliminating labour market regulations that were seen as responsible for job loss.

B. The 2002 International Labour Conference Conclusions

The discussion of the informal economy at the International Labour Conference inevitably brought together the concerns of the individual worker (through a representative organisation) and of the enterprise (through an employers' organisation), along with the role of government. It is not surprising, then, that the ILC conclusions identified the informal economy above all as a governance issue.

While both the employers' and the workers' groups at the International Labour Conference identified governance issues as critical, their emphasis differed. The employers stressed the need for appropriate regulatory frameworks, noting that it was important not to drive informal operators out of existence. While acknowledging the contribution that the informal economy makes to providing low cost goods and services, the employers highlighted the unfair competition aspects (the 'free rider' phenomenon). For the workers, governance and representation were seen as critical. They called for 'good law and its proper application'. Both groups saw a need to

---

[16] *Ibid.*, at 36.

[17] Vega Ruiz analyses how such reform has dominated the labour law agenda in Latin America over the past decade: M.-L. Vega Ruiz, *Libertad de asociación, libertad sindical y el reconocimiento efectivo del derecho de negociación colectiva en América Latina* (Geneva, International Labour Office, 2004), 74 ff.

reach out to people in the informal economy, with the workers in particular emphasising the importance of respect for the right to self-organisation and collective action. The conclusions stress in paragraph 24 that '[n]ational legislation must guarantee and defend the freedom of all workers and employers, irrespective of where and how they work, to form and join organizations of their own choosing without fear of reprisal or intimidation'.[18]

The conclusions note in paragraph 22 that labour law 'often does not take into account the realities of the modern organisation of work. Inappropriate definitions of employees and workers may have the adverse effect of treating a worker as self-employed and outside the protection of labour law'.[19] Thus, 'to ensure that labour law affords appropriate protection for all workers, Governments should be encouraged to review how employment relationships have been evolving and to identify and adequately protect all workers'.[20] This may involve measures that fall outside the scope of traditional labour law. The phrase in paragraph 5—'appropriate for regulation or protection under labour or commercial law' would suggest this. (Other branches of law could be added.) The phrase also casts the net wide enough to catch both situations in which there is genuinely no employer and those where one can be identified.

C. Labour Market Views of Informality

While this chapter does not intend to provide an exhaustive review of labour market theory in relation to informality, it highlights some relevant recent work. Labour market analysts concur in seeing informality as a reflection of a structural imbalance between too many job seekers and too few jobs. Those who don't find a 'formal' job swell the informally economy.

In relation to this, Robert Fragale Filho sets out four types of tensions that could explain the changes that labour is experiencing today: capital v. labour, qualified (skilled) labour v. non-qualified labour, social inclusion v. social exclusion and labour v. post-labour. In the last scenario, labour law 'could no longer be based on subordination but would have to create new forms of integration, social solidarity and maintenance of the social body's integration, taking into consideration the world of "non-labour" and the importance acquired by "free time"'.[21] (The latter is a questionable notion in the case of women, particularly in developing countries.) The precise

---

[18] *Conclusions*, above n 3, at para 24.
[19] *Ibid.*, para 22.
[20] *Ibid.*
[21] R. Fragale Filho, 'Celebrating Twenty-Five Years and Speculating over the Future from a Brazilian Perspective' (2003) 25 *Comparative Labor Law and Policy Journal* 21, at 23, 25.

ways in which this could be done in various legal systems continues to stymie experts.

In addition, interaction between the formal and the informal is now embedded in certain industries as the way business operates, reflected in many supply chains.[22] Lund and Nicholson have taken value chain analysis and expanded it for the informal economy. Along with Sindzingre,[23] they have observed that production, transformation, export and sale of products—from commodities to manufactured goods—involve segments and channels that resort to both the informal and formal aspects of the economy.[24] They suggest that a more nuanced approach is introduced by focusing on the workers at different positions in the value chain, and on their needs for security for themselves and their households. The value added to a commodity may end up with less security for the worker and his/her family. 'The focus on short-term competitiveness detracts attention from the need for human capital formation of the present generation of workers, and for the access to education of their children—the next generation of working people.' The value chain approach, they note, 'offers the opportunity to understand better how workers at different points in the chain of production may have different access to a "ladder of protection"'.[25]

Tokman, whose work has influenced thinking about informality over several decades, still uses the term 'informal sector' as 'the last link in the chain of heterogeneity that characterizes the structure of production in Latin America'.[26] Recently, he reviewed economic reforms that have taken place in Latin America and concluded that the informal sector had been overlooked. He sees informality from three perspectives: as a survivalist strategy, as a mechanism of decentralisation and flexibility, and as an instrument of reducing costs and evading inadequate regulations. The first stresses social policies to combat poverty. The second two, in his view, reflect the current situation in light of more open and integrated economies, and focus on promoting the productive development of the informal economy.

Another policy direction, promoting the incorporation of informal activities into the formal economy by facilitating such a transition and creating incentives, would in Tokman's view call for transformation on a larger scale. In any event, he correctly observes that the end result is a multiplicity of institutions addressing what is essentially the same problem, but from

---

[22] See, eg, S. Hayter, 'The Social Dimension of Global Production Systems: A Review of the Issues', *Working Paper No 25* (Policy Integration Department, World Commission on the Social Dimension of Globalization, Geneva, International Labour Office, 2004).

[23] F. Lund and J. Nicholson (eds), *Chains of Production, Ladders of Protection: Social Protection for Workers in the Informal Economy* (Durban, School of Development Studies, University of Natal, 2003), 102.

[24] Sindzingre, above n 2, at 18.

[25] Lund and Nicholson, above n 23.

[26] Tokman, above n 11, at 55.

different orientations. Beyond a duplication of effort, contradictory policies can result.[27]

As Tardanico and Menjívar Larín argue, the deterioration of conditions and erosion of job stability in the formal sector/economy have blurred the boundary between the two.[28] This observation is shared by Maloney, who argues that 'the urban informal sector should be viewed as a part of a voluntary small firm sector similar to those in advanced countries that, due to the laxity of enforcement of labor and other codes, is able to choose the optimal degree of participation in formal institutions'.[29] (Is this an invitation for them to ignore the rule of law?) He further suggests that 'a worker with few skills that would be rewarded in salaried work may prefer to be independent ...; the informal option may actually offer a measure of dignity and autonomy that the formal job does not'.[30]

While this is probably true at the high end of the informality continuum, it is a far cry from the reality of most people in the informal economy. Over the 1990–2000 decade, for instance, the largest wage gap emerged between own-account workers in formal and informal settings, followed by that of employees of formal and informal micro-enterprises.[31] Like many other economists addressing labour regulation, Maloney's preoccupation is not with workers, but rather with firms and how to improve their economic outcomes. It is also based on a theoretical notion of independence that does not square with contemporary organisation of production chains. More fundamentally, however, it reflects a concept of choice that presupposes freedoms—freedoms that the poor often do not enjoy in practice.

For, as Jacoby observes, '[t]he reallocation of risk, from business to individuals, and with government playing a smaller role, has been the central dynamic of Anglo-American labour markets during the past thirty years'.[32] In contrast to Western Europe, he notes, policy changes in the United Kingdom and the United States have accentuated rather than counteracted market effects. The same is true of many developing countries. 'One serious effect of unrectified inequality is to weaken the political influence of those in the bottom half of the income distribution. A feedback is created, whereby individuals already falling behind are unable to prevent regulatory

---

[27] *Ibid.*, at 64–5.

[28] R. Tardanico and R. Menjivar Larin, 'Restructuring Employment and Social Inequality: Comparative Urban Latin American Patterns' in R. Tardanico and R. Menjivar Larin (eds.), *Global Restructuring, Employment and Social Inequality in Urban Latin America* (Miami, North-South Center Press, 1997), at 231.

[29] W. Maloney, 'Informality Revisited' (2004) 32 *World Development* 1173. His conclusions are based on panel data on male microentrepreneurs in three Latin America countries.

[30] *Ibid.*

[31] Tokman, above n 11, at 57.

[32] S. Jacoby, 'Economic Ideas and the Labor Market: Origins of the Anglo-American Model and Prospects for Global Diffusion' (2005) 25 *Comparative Labor Law and Policy Journal* 43 at 60.

changes that cause them to slip even further.'[33] The Anglo-American perspective on labour markets is precisely the one adopted in law reform efforts pursued by most development economists.

A rather different approach is suggested by Chen, Vanek and Carr. They stress promotion of opportunities (microfinance, skills training, improved technologies, business development services), securing of rights by extending the scope of existing legislation, promoting collective bargaining and/or enforcing labour standards, protection of informal workers through existing and/or alternative insurance coverage, and the organisation of informal workers and their representation in policy making institutions.[34] They call for better integration of the ILO's Decent Work Agenda in poverty reduction initiatives, along with renewed attention to employment in economic planning.

D. Statistical Measurement of 'Informal Employment' and 'Informal Sector'

What is measured matters. The adoption, at the 17th International Conference of Labour Statisticians in 2003, of guidelines on a statistical definition of informal employment has a history that goes back to 1982, when the 13th ICLS adopted a resolution endorsing the development of appropriate methodologies and data collection programmes on the urban informal sector and rural non-agricultural activities.[35] The 14th ICLS, held in 1987, concluded that the 'economic unit' was the most appropriate measurement unit to define the informal sector. This was, and still is, a tendentious issue, as Bangasser has observed: '[s]hould the unit of analysis be the individuals working in these conditions; or should it be the "enterprises" where they work even though these are typically very small, owned by the workers themselves and hard to catch and delineate statistically? ... Which unit of analysis is chosen influences what kinds of remedies are envisaged.'[36]

The 15th ICLS adopted an international statistical definition of the informal sector, which was picked up in a major revision of the international System of National Accounts in 1993. As Hussmanns has explained, to arrive at an internationally agreed definition of the informal sector acceptable both to labour statisticians and national accountants,

---

[33] *Ibid.*
[34] Chen *et al.*, above n 13, at ix and xx.
[35] Bangasser, above n 6, at 20.
[36] *Ibid.*
[37] R. Hussmanns, *ILO Guidelines on the Measurement of Employment in the Informal Sector and the Informal Economy*, Presentation to the Goskomstat of Russia/GUS Seminar on the Non-Observed Economy: Issues of Measurement (St Petersburg, 23–25 June 2004).

the informal sector had to be defined in terms of characteristics of the production units (enterprises) in which the activities take place (enterprise approach), rather than in terms of the characteristics of the persons involved or of their jobs (labour approach).[37] The 15th ICLS also adopted a resolution on a related topic, but with less resonance: the new International Classification of Status in Employment (ISCE 1993). It corresponds only very loosely to definitions that appear in labour laws.

With a variety of 'informal' phenomena being measured, comparisons, estimates and above all policy prescriptions based on such data make for risky business indeed. Part of the difficulty lies in the attempt to match the measurement of informality at the macro-economic level (where national accounts seek to capture all economic production for purposes of calculating Gross Domestic Product) and at the micro-economic level of firms and households.[38]

To respond to criticisms of the 15th ICLS resolution, including the failure to capture the increasing informalisation of employment, the Expert Group on Informal Sector Statistics (known as the Delhi Group) concluded that 'the definition and measurement of employment in the informal sector needed to be complemented with a definition and measurement of informal employment'.[39] In Hussmanns' view, '[t]hey are both useful for analytical purposes and hence, complement each other. However, the two concepts need to be defined and measured in a coherent and consistent manner....'[40] The Delhi Group tested what became the guidelines on a statistical definition of informal employment. It rests on a conceptual framework set out in a matrix that combines production units by type (formal sector enterprises, informal sector enterprises, and households) and jobs by status in employment (own-account workers, employers, contributing family members, employees, members of producers' cooperatives).

Some, but not all, of the categories identified have identifiable counterparts in laws and regulations.[41] This mismatch could spell trouble for policy makers. However, it should not be forgotten that the statistical community came up with these constructs precisely to fill a gap identified by the policy makers who were anxious to measure what they saw springing up around them.

Two other initiatives in the ILO have been developing measurement of elements relevant to work in the informal economy: Decent Work Indicators,[42] which basically involve expansion of labour statistics, and

---

[38] Sindzingre, above n 2, at 12.

[39] *Ibid.*

[40] *Ibid.*

[41] A. Trebilcock, 'Decent Work and the Informal Economy' in EGDI and UNU-WIDER Conference, *Unlocking Human Potential: Linking the Informal and Formal Sectors* (Helsinki, 17–18 Sept. 2004), 17.

[42] See R. Anker, J. Chernyshev, P. Egger, F. Mehran and J. Ritter, 'Measuring Decent Work with Statistical Indicators' (2003) 142 *International Labour Review* (Geneva) 147.

Socio-economic Security Indices, which are part of a separate research tool. Both offer some prospects for capturing certain aspects of the dimensions of informality that affect peoples' lives. For instance, the economic security approach identifies five criteria: regularity status (in regular wage labour, full-time or part-time, or in registered self-employment), contract status (having a written contract of employment), workplace status (working in or around a fixed workplace), employment protection status (being protected against arbitrary dismissal or entitled to severance pay), and social protection status (being entitled to medical care). The results of the surveys that have used these measures show a much greater degree of informality than suggested by methods that use an enterprise-based concept.[43]

The work on labour statistics in relation to decent work picks up on the ICLS recommendations by including measurement of informal employment in labour force, household and special surveys.[44] It holds promise for moving beyond long-criticised measures of 'employment' and 'unemployment' that capture only formal phenomena and presume a single economic activity for each person.

Chen, Vanek and Carr have recommended that '[l]abour statisticians, labour lawyers and researchers working on labour issues need to collaborate on the development of an overarching framework that allows the classification, comparison and analysis of the full set of employment statuses/work arrangements that exist in both developed and developing countries. This will contribute to improved understanding of the changing nature of work as well as the links between employment and poverty.'[45]

E. Perceptions of Labour Law

While the Washington Consensus has been declared officially dead, it shows signs of life in the literature and on the ground when it comes to labour law reform. Although a quite recent report on employment, both formal and informal, by the Asian Development Bank suggests a more nuanced approach,[46] the report of the UN-established Commission on the Private

---

[43] *Economic Security for a Better World* (Geneva, International Labour Office, 2004), 141–5.

[44] See R. Hussmans, 'Measuring the Informal Economy: from Employment in the Informal Sector to Informal Employment', *Policy Integration Working Paper No 53* (Geneva, International Labour Office, 2005) and ILO Bureau of Statistics/Department of Statistics and Sociology of the Republic of Moldova, 'Employment in the Informal Economy in Moldova', *Policy Integration Working Paper No 41* (Geneva, International Labour Office, 2005).

[45] Chen *et al.*, above n 13, at 196.

[46] Asian Development Bank, *Labor Markets in Asia: Promoting Full, Productive and Decent Employment* (Manila, ADB, 2005), which acknowledges that, 'overall, labour market rigidities are not to be blamed for poor labour market outcomes (based on country studies of India, Indonesia, Philippines and Viet Nam).'

Sector and Development, *Unleashing Entrepreneurship: Making Business Work for the Poor,*[47] takes the more common economic view. It focuses attention on the positive role that firms can undoubtedly play in enhancing welfare. The measures by which this is judged, however, reflect certain assumptions about the operation of labour legislation.

The Commission's report relies on the World Bank's regular review of doing business. This review involves 145 countries that are scored in relation to simplifying some aspect of business regulations, strengthening property rights or making it easier for businesses to raise financing. The most recent report gives high marks to Slovakia for, inter alia, introducing flexible working hours and easing the hiring of first-time workers.[48] The report notes that when registering property is accompanied by 'improvements [note: no further definition] in ... employment regulation' and other aspects, the benefits are much greater.[49] The report continues: '[with] rigid employment regulation, few people will be hired, with women, young and low-skilled workers hurt the most. .... Their only choice is to seek jobs in the informal sector.'

With this familiar approach, there is no questioning of the possible relationship between *specific* measures (various types of employment protection, social protection, limits on working hours etc.) and the incidence of poverty for the individuals affected, or the consequences of reduced social protection coverage after reform. Perhaps the most disingenuous assertion in this report lies in an attempt to explode a 'myth' that social protection requires more business regulation by citing Nordic countries. True, they tend to have light legal regulation, but they also have active labour market policies, broad collective bargaining coverage and extensive social protection. These aspects are not mentioned.

The category in the table entitled 'Enforcing contracts' highlights summary proceedings for debt collection, case management in courts, limitation of appeals and enforcement moved out of court. What about the enforcement of contracts of employment or the payment of contributions to social protection funds? In short, the survey itself reveals a number of value judgements about what is important and what is an improvement.

Finally, while high unemployment rates and the growth of the informal economy have been attributed to labour market inflexibility, Mkwandawire and Rodríguez note that available evidence suggests that the situation is much more complex:

In most countries, labour has indeed become more "flexible," and the labour supply more elastic. Yet increased growth has been accompanied by decreasing real

---

[47] Report to the Secretary-General of the United Nations (New York, UNDP, 2004).
[48] World Bank, *Doing Business in 2005* (Washington, DC, World Bank, 2005), 1.
[49] *Ibid.*, at 3.

wages, suggesting that the low employment intensity of growth cannot be attributed to rigid labour markets. ... In the absence of fundamental questioning of the premises of the dominant economic policy package, measures intended to mitigate the now widely admitted negative social consequences of the orthodox policy package will fail. ... What is clearly necessary is social policy that no longer serves as a handmaiden to socially flawed economic policies, but is an integral part of the development model itself. It is now widely accepted that many objectives of social policy constitute the key instruments of development, because they enhance the productive capacity of society, improve the efficiency of institutions (including markets) and ensure social stability.[50]

The new ADB report reflects such points to an encouraging degree.

3. A LOOK AT THREE DEVELOPMENT PARADIGMS

This section explores the potential of three development paradigms for labour law: the sustainable livelihoods approach, the human capabilities approach and the empowerment approach.

A. Sustainable Livelihoods Approach

The sustainable livelihoods approach was articulated in the early 1990s and became current within the United Kingdom's Department for International Development (DFID) by the end of that decade.[51] It can be summed up in these terms:

A livelihood comprises the capabilities, assets and activities required for a means of living. A livelihood is sustainable when it can cope with and recover from stresses and shocks and maintain or enhance its capabilities and assets both now and in the future, while not undermining the natural resource base.[52]

While still in use within DFID, this approach is facing competition from increasing emphasis from the 'pro-poor growth' school of thought. Pro-poor growth is defined as the average growth rate of the incomes of poor people. DFID has identified four conditions for accelerating pro-poor growth: creating strong incentives for investment, fostering international economic links, providing broad access to assets and markets, and reducing risk and vulnerability. Research indicates that pro-poor growth is faster in

---

[50] T. Mkandawire and V. Rodríguez, 'Globalization and Social Development after Copenhagen', *UNRISD, Occasional Paper No 10* (Geneva, UNRISD, 2000), 29.

[51] R. Chambers and G. Conway, 'Sustainable Rural Livelihoods: Practical Concepts for the 21st Century', *IDS Discussion Paper 296* (Brighton, IDA, 1992).

[52] D. Carney, M. Drinkwater, T. Rusinow, K. Neefjes, S. Wanmali and N. Singh, *Livelihoods Approaches Compared* (DFID, Nov. 1999), mimeo, 8.

countries where the informal economy is smaller, a result equated with less burdensome regulation of business (not further specified), which leads to greater willingness of firms to participate in the formal economy.[53]

The sustainable livelihoods approach is described by its proponents as being a people-centred, holistic and dynamic means of reaching development goals.[54] The approach uses a framework for diagnosis and planning that radiates from the livelihood assets that people possess: human assets/human capital (skills, knowledge, ability to work, good health), physical assets (e.g. basic infrastructure and production equipment/technology), natural assets (e.g. land, water, biodiversity), financial assets (savings, credit, remittances etc.) and social assets/social capital (networks, membership of groups, trust relationships, access to wider institutions in society). From these perspectives, it looks at the vulnerability context (eg, shocks, trends and seasonality) and the policies, institutions and processes involved, including laws.

The approach identifies the livelihood strategies that people pursue with various livelihood outcomes. It is supposed to build on people's strengths, promote links between policies and institutions that operate at the macro and the micro levels, encourages broad partnering from the public and private sectors and aims at long-term sustainability. Among the development agencies in addition to DFID that are using the sustainable livelihoods approach are the United Nations Development Programme, the Food and Agriculture Organisation and several NGOs.

Among the factors that are significant for the sustainable livelihoods approach are:

- Raising human capital through health and education;
- Enhancing social capital through raising people's awareness of their rights and obligations;
- Expansion of options and opportunities through responding to evolving global markets;
- Improvement in the policy and institutional context of livelihoods, due to the whole array of factors tackled by efforts to improve governance.[55]

While this framework certainly contains elements relevant to labour law—from training to good governance to rights at work and organisation—these emerge more clearly from the two other development frameworks

---

[53] *Pro-Poor Growth Briefing Note 2: How to Accelerate Pro-Poor Growth: A Basic Framework for Policy Analysis* (London, DFID, 2004).

[54] *Sustainable Livelihoods—Current Thinking and Practice* (London and Rome, DFID and FAO, 2000); *Background Briefing: Sustainable Livelihoods and Poverty Elimination* (London, DFID, 1999), mimeo.

[55] F. Ellis and J. Seeley, *Background Briefing: Globalisation and Sustainable Livelihoods: An Initial Note* (London, DFID/ODG/UEA, 2001), mimeo, 2.

under examination. This is probably because the sustainable livelihoods approach, while attractive because of its emphasis on people's strengths as well as their vulnerabilities, does not directly address power relationships. As du Toit has observed, 'It is important to understand not only household-level livelihood components, but the local, regional and global institutions, power relationships and processes that perpetuate and create marginality. Ultimately, tackling chronic poverty requires tacking those power relations.'[56]

B. A Human Capability Perspective

While many find the term 'human capital' deeply troubling (the ILO Constitution does, after all, declare that 'labour is not a commodity'), it has been one of the main sources of thinking in relation to human capability. The dominant paradigm as reflected in OECD publications of the 1990s focused on the employability of human capital. The UNDP, however, has a broader notion, derived from work of Amartya Sen:

> The concept of human capital or human resource development is mostly about individual agency for production. ... [T]he idea of agency in human development is also about collective agency for influencing political processes. People aiming to influence public decisions, whether for access to schooling, the right to vote, or decent working conditions can rarely be effective on their own. This requires a process of forming associations, making alliances, generating public debates.[57]

Human rights and the legal frameworks that guarantee them are important in the human development approach both for their intrinsic value and as instruments in promoting individual and collective agency.[58]

However, as Bartley *et al.* have stated, '[o]ne concern about the human capital approach is its assumptions of individuals as rational maximisers of individual utility: that is, that people make decisions about maximizing their own opportunities and develop their potential to maximize future opportunities based upon rational considerations of self-interest and unlimited choice'.[59] This basically ignores family life and social being. The

---

[56] A. du Toit, 'Forgotten by the Highway: Globalisation, Adverse Incorporation and Chronic Poverty in a Commercial Farming District of South Africa', *Eldis Poverty Reporter* (25 Feb. 2005), 3, available at: www.eldis.org/cf/rdr/rdr.cofm?doc=DOC17762.

[57] S. Fukuda-Parr, 'Operationalizing Amartya Sen's Ideas on Capabilities, Development, Freedom and Human Rights—the Shifting Policy Focus of the Human Development Approach', 9, available at: www.ids-ps.org/doc/Oxford/w5.PDF.

[58] *Human Rights and Development* (New York, Human Development Report, UNDP, 2000).

[59] A. Bartley, R. Cremer, A. de Bruin, A. Dupuis and P. Spoonley, '"We Might Call them Once": Mediating Supply and Demand in Regional Labour Markets?', *Working Paper No 2* (Labour Market Dynamics Research Programme, Massey University, Auckland, 2001), 150,

Human Capability Framework, on the other hand, sees individuals as embedded in a variety of social relations that affect their choices and aspirations. The economist Amartya Sen points out that a capability perspective encompasses the direct relevance of human capabilities to the well-being and freedom of people, as well as their indirect role through influencing social change and economic production.[60] Labour law can easily identify with Sen's notions of freedom (of association/from forced labour, discrimination and child labour), well-being (at the work place and through social protection), social change (the political and technical role of trade unions, employers' associations, social dialogue institutions). And yet the development discourse and the labour law discourse seldom cross paths.

An exception is Hepple, who argues for expanding the scope of national labour law to bring about 'an equality of capabilities. This embraces the substantive freedoms that individuals need in order to survive and prosper, including freedom to pursue education and training and a career of their choosing, freedom of association and freedom to participate in economic and political decision-making that affects their lives as well as the capacity to obtain decent work.'[61]

Bartley *et al.* argue that the Human Capability Framework provides an 'integrated view of key economic and social objectives, and an understanding of the role of the labour market in achieving them'.[62] The labour market dimension involves matching capacity and opportunities. In this constellation, '"[c]apacity" refers to the skills, knowledge and attitudes people possess and how in using these skills, they can take advantage of the labour market and other opportunities available to them. . . . "Opportunities" are the alternatives available to people to use their capacity (i.e., skills, knowledge and attitudes) as a way in which they gain financial or personal reward.'[63]

Examination of the matching process permits identification of factors that influence capacity formation and opportunity creation. While reminiscent of the supply and demand sides of the labour market in economic terms, the human capability framework goes beyond the simplistic idea that the matching is determined purely by the price of wages.[64]

Since its appearance in the late 1990s, the Human Capability Framework has been picked up by researchers as a means of investigating

---

quoted in R. Tipples, 'The Human Capability Framework—An Important and Useful Framework for Understanding the Labour Market?' (2004) 29 *New Zealand Journal of Employment Relations* 3, at 5.

[60] A. Sen, *Development as Freedom* (New York, Anchor Books, 1999), 296–7.

[61] B. Hepple, *Labour Law, Inequality and Global Trade* (Amsterdam, Hugo Sinzheimer Instituut, 2002), 31.

[62] Bartley *et al.*, above n 59, at 149, cited in Tipples, above n 59, at 4.

[63] *Ibid.*, at 5.

[64] *Ibid.*, at 6.

the complexities of labour markets. In the case of New Zealand, the government has used it to integrate policies on employment, labour markets and welfare. The New Zealand Department of Labour provides a working definition of human capability as 'the ability of people to do things—both the capacity and the opportunities to do things'.[65]

While beyond the scope of this chapter, the experience of New Zealand in developing this framework over two ideologically distinct governments and applying it in day-to-day practice offers considerable food for further study and reflection. Specifically, the HFC serves as a key organising and analytical framework for the government's employment strategy. This strategy involves alignment of government interventions with those of training providers, regions, community, organisations and employers as well as matching employers and employees. It stresses fostering good connections and networks to develop community capability as a source of employment opportunities.[66] The matching function is to provide for: '[e]stablishment of an employment relationship framework that provides flexibility to accommodate a range of relationships and outcomes, underpinned by statutory minima to ensure clarity, stability and fairness; [and] clarity/stability of rules to manage conflicts and disputes through: information provision and specific institutional mechanisms to mediate and settle employment relationship problems'.[67]

In addition, the Framework helps to address particular situation of disadvantaged groups, including indigenous people, various age groups, and women in the labour market. Analysis of pay equity within the Human Capability Framework, for instance, encompasses: capability skills, responsibility, effort, working conditions; work and family balance; employment opportunities; pay equity and equal employment opportunity policies.

Each is seen as interrelated and impacted upon by capability influences and labour market opportunity influences.[68] One of the benefits identified of the HFC is the 'relative ease with which it can be used by key authorities and stakeholders to convert ideas and concepts about employment into real actions fostering jobs'.[69] The 'good relationship' formed depends on a high level of agreement between the wants, needs and expectations of the parties, at both legal and psychological levels.[70]

The claim that the HCF provides a 'pictorial framework capable of expressing key linkages in employment from the individual employment relationship to the global economy'[71] is doubtful, however, in the face of

---

[65] Bartley, above n 59, at 4, citing Department of Labour, *Human Capability: A Framework for Analysis* (Wellington, Department of Labour, 1999), 4.
[66] Tipples, above n 59, at 8.
[67] *Ibid.*, at 9.
[68] *Ibid.*, at 10.
[69] *Ibid.*, at 12.
[70] *Ibid.*
[71] *Ibid.*

growing informality in the labour market. In an increasing number of industrial and service industries, the labour market has moved beyond the national level, working through supply chains across a number of countries and communities.

The capabilities approach measures the presence of basic opportunities by looking at what individual women and men are actually able to do and to be. 'If human development focuses on the enhancement of the capabilities and freedoms that the members of a community enjoy, human rights represent the claims that individuals have on the conduct of individual and collective agents and the design of social arrangement to facilitate or secure these capabilities and freedoms.'[72]

The human capabilities approach contains several elements that are highly relevant to labour law, especially in light of its application in practice. More thought needs to be given to its application above the national level and in the context of different legal cultures.

C. An Empowerment Approach

In its background publication to the *World Development Report* 2000/01, *Voices of the Poor*, the World Bank identified three pillars of poverty reduction—vulnerability and assets (which can be seen as a sustainable livelihoods approach), opportunity (which could be analogous to the human capabilities approach) and empowerment.

While the sustainable livelihoods approach and the human capability perspective take the individual as their point of departure, an empowerment perspective adds a stronger dimension of the power of collective action.

The World Bank has identified four elements of empowerment—information, inclusion/participation, accountability, and local organisational capacity.[73] The Bank asserts that these elements can be combined to create more effective, responsive, inclusive and accountable institutions which in turn enable people to develop their own capacities, increase their assets and move out of poverty. The focus on local rather than national organisational capacity is curious when power relationships are at stake, since they operate at both levels. Noteworthy as well is the reference to participation rather than representation.

Nonetheless, among the lessons learned by the Bank across various contexts are several of relevance to the labour field:

---

[72] *Human Rights and Development*, above n 58, at 20.
[73] D. Narayan, 'Chapter 3: Applying Empowerment Principles' in *Empowerment and Poverty Reduction: A Sourcebook* (Washington, DC, World Bank, 2002), 31.

- Poor people's realities are the starting point;
- Respect, trust and social relations matter;
- Participatory processes and conflict management go together;
- Poor people's membership-based organisations are overlooked (note: trade unions and producers associations are among those mentioned);
- Changes in rules and institutional processes enable large-scale change[74]

It would be interesting to apply these criteria in the context of labour law reform processes in which the Bank itself has been involved. A measure of success identified by DFID could be used in relation to workers in the informal economy: '[p]oor people need to be empowered in their capacity to interact with other private sectors agents (local landlords, sellers of inputs, providers of financial services, owners of factories) as well as with public service. ... Successful interventions for empowerment include strengthening the participation of people in decision-making processes by promoting their political rights, securing their rights to information, providing accessible skills training, and increasing the accountability of governments to citizens both directly and through democratic institutions'.[75]

A human rights perspective must be embedded in the empowerment paradigm, as implied by Häusermann: '[a] human rights approach to development is one that moves the debate from handouts to empowerment, from charity to securing the rights of people to the requirements, freedoms and choices necessary for life and development in dignity'.[76]

While the rights and principles in the 1998 ILO Declaration on Fundamental Principles and Rights at Work have been termed 'enabling rights', they could just as well be seen as 'avenues to empowerment'. As the preamble to the Declaration notes, they are the basis for people to 'claim freely and on the basis of equality of opportunity, their fair share of the wealth which they have helped to generate, and to achieve fully their human potential'. 'The human rights approach to development requires a focus on overcoming the inequities and discrimination that are at the root cause of poverty and social exclusion. It focuses on overcoming systemic obstacles to the enjoyment of human rights ...'[77]

---

[74] These and other lessons are summarised in R. Rinehart, *Designing Programmes to Improve Working and Employment Conditions in the Informal Economy: A Literature Review* (Geneva, International Labour Office, Conditions of Work and Employment Series No 10, 2004), 49–50.

[75] *Halving World Poverty by 2015—Economic Growth, Equity and Security* (London, DFID, 2000), 38.

[76] J. Häusermann, *Rights and Humanity: A Human Rights Approach to Development* (London, Rights and Humanity, 1998), 60.

[77] *Ibid.*, at 205.

A meeting between staff of the World Bank and the Department for International Development of the United Kingdom in March 2004 produced a collection of essays that explore the concept of empowerment, its measurement and its close affinity with a human rights approach to development.[78] This is not surprising since; as Moser notes, human rights are *a priori* about power relationships. She cites a definition of a rights-based approach to development which describes its aim as promoting justice, equity and freedom. The approach addresses power issues that lie at the heart of poverty and exploitation.[79] Underlying it are these ideas: people are citizens with rights rather than beneficiaries with needs; government has a central role to play; grass roots participation is critical for the poor to be heard. Relying on Amartya Sen and Deepak Narayan, Moser points out that human freedom is the common purpose and motivation of human rights and human development.

However, as Moser notes, the final Social Development Strategy of the Bank issued in 2004 makes no reference to human rights. Her own work acknowledges the role of labour standards at the international level, but not in regard to statutory law within countries. Labour rights appear again in a matrix on 'channels of contestation', where they are seen as a type of claim and referred to in relation to implementation of entitlements. Another participant in the DFID–Bank discussions, Mosse, observes that '[p]ower sharing involves conflict; successful power sharing involves conflict resolution mechanisms that can be made more successful through deliberate power sharing institutions'.[80] The considerable body of work on dispute resolution in the labour field could be brought to bear on this analysis, and may be one way of bridging the labour law and development divide.

In addition to the concept of empowerment, its measurement is of interest to labour law in the context of the informal economy. One analytical framework for use in measuring and monitoring empowerment processes and outcomes has been developed by Alsop and Heinsohn.[81] The framework assesses empowerment in different domains of a person's life (the state, the market—of which labour is an aspect along with credit and goods) and at different levels (macro, intermediary and local). Degrees of empowerment are measured by the existence of choice, the use of choice and the achievement of choice. While not yet applied in the domain of labour, it would be interesting to see what the results would be, particularly in relation to the operation of various aspects of labour law and the informal economy.

[78] R. Alsop (ed.), *Power, Rights and Poverty: Concepts and Connections* (Washington, DC, World Bank, 2004).

[79] C. Moser, 'Rights, Power and Poverty Reduction' in *ibid.*, 34.

[80] D. Mosse, 'Power Relations and Poverty Reduction' in *ibid.*, at 86.

[81] R. Alsop and N. Heinsohn, 'Measuring Empowerment in Practice: Structuring Analysis and Framing Indicators', *World Bank Policy Research Working Paper No 3510* (Washington, DC, World Bank, Feb. 2005).

Indicators proposed by other researchers as they relate to labour are also interesting.[82] These include membership of an organisation as an organisational asset and an index of civil liberties that encompasses freedom of association.[83] And in the market domain, they refer to the number of core labour standards ratified as well as the number of laws 'supporting pro poor labour shifts in labour market segmentation'. Other elements cited are diversity of national labour organisations, number of industrial disputes resolved, number of collective bargaining mechanisms over wage rights and employment conditions.

The implicit assumption here, that more labour organisations and more collective bargaining mechanisms equate to greater empowerment, is certainly questionable, since this may simply reflect fragmentation. Nevertheless, the fact that such indicators go beyond 'participation' to encompass representation and negotiation is already a step in the right direction. A serious empowerment approach to development must necessarily place freedom of association and organisation for collective action at its core. As recognised in the 2002 ILC conclusions, these are critical elements for people in the informal as well as in the formal economy.

Interestingly, Hernando De Soto's message about the importance of property titling for the poor has extended recently to include association building as a necessary complement to such measures.[84] Indeed, if states paid as much attention to ensuring freedom of association as securing property rights, true empowerment of the poor could ensue. Moreover, it would be administratively much cheaper for states to do this, since at one level they need only to refrain from interfering with this freedom, rather than surveying land, maintaining registries, issuing titles and resolving disputes claims. Of course, where an employer could be found, the state would also need to ensure that he or she was respecting freedom of association—a much more active role that entails some resource outlay. Tokman has gone one step further, by suggesting that the notion popularised by De Soto for recognition of property rights be extended to the 'contractual recognition of the labour relationship'.[85]

---

[82] J. Holland and S. Brook, 'Measuring Empowerment: Country Indicators' in Alsop, above n 78.

[83] The work of Galli and Kucera has already explored this. See, for instance, R. Galli and D. Kucera, 'Informal Employment in Latin America: Movements over Business Cycles and the Effects of Worker Rights', *Discussion Paper No 145* (Geneva, International Institute for Labour Studies, 2003).

[84] Compare H. De Soto, *The Mystery of Capital: Why Capitalism Triumphs in the West and Fails Everywhere Else* (New York, Basic Books, 2000) with his keynote address to the UNU/WIDER Conference on Unlocking Human Potential: Linking the Formal and Informal Sectors (Helsinki, 17 Sept. 2004).

[85] Tokman, above n 11, at 69.

4. CONCLUSION

Why is there economic activity that escapes the law, with negative consequences for those affected? One factor identified in the literature is the law itself, either because of its lack of application/enforcement and/or because it is 'inappropriate, burdensome or imposes excessive costs' (ILC conclusions, paragraph 3). The debate over what constitute 'good', 'appropriate' or 'non-burdensome' labour regulations will continue. Those who attack labour legislation are specific: they target any collective bargaining above the enterprise level, provisions that protect against dismissal, severance pay, minimum wages, and some aspects of social protection (such as paid maternity leave) as harmful labour market rigidities that stifle formal employment creation.

But in the development community recommendations on legislation that should be retained or enacted remain somewhat vague. They place emphasis on two things: social protection mechanisms (all very well, but without details about how they would be articulated or financed) and legislation targeting particular categories of workers, such as street vendors and home workers.[86] The latter of these in particular fails to get at the essence of the problem. Where the circumstances in which work is carried out are unique—as in street vending, home work and domestic work—it may make sense to have at least some specific legal provisions to address these particular situations. But for most issues, and for most workers, their concerns will be the same regardless of the circumstances in which they work.

Essentially, the ILC conclusions struggled to address the question '[h]ow can people, no matter how their work is designated, be both empowered and protected using law?'.[87] They contain many useful pointers for reorienting labour law as an effective development tool, and have engendered thinking around a 'model of change' that calls for simultaneous action to prevent a slide into the negative situations associated with informality, to support formalisation where feasible and to improve conditions of those who are stuck in the informal economy.[88] It is critical to see this interconnected picture.

In relation to formalisation, Tokman has observed that '"[f]ormalization" of the labour relationship constitutes the first necessary step from informality to regulated and protected labour relationships. . . . Something

---

[86] For recommendations on, respectively, street vending and social protection, see eg Chen *et al.*, above n 13, at 187–9 and 192–4.

[87] This is an extension of Arturo Bronstein's question, 'how to protect the unprotected?': A. Bronstein, 'Labour Law and the Informal Sector' (Workshop on Regulatory Frameworks and their Economic and Social Impact, Unpublished Paper, Geneva, 4–5 Feb. 1999), 1.

[88] For more on the model of change, see R. Diez de Medina, 'A Model of Change for the Informal Economy' in the Informal Economy Resource Database (Geneva, International Labour Office, 2005), available at: http://www.ilo.org/public/english/knowledgefair/download/model/presentation.pdf.

seminal occurs with the recognition of labour contracts, since the objective should not be to sanction illegality, but rather to constitute subjects or citizens who have the credentials to become covered by labour protection in the case of workers and by the logic of market rules in the case of microentrepreneurs who have to live up to a formal labour relationship'.[89] This suggestion actually begs the question and returns labour law to square one. Labour law's solution to the lack of protection has been the contract of employment—a legal institution that—precisely because it affords certain protections—is avoided by those operating in circumstances of informality. A fundamental rethinking of legal techniques is needed.

To stimulate a dialogue linking labour law and development, this chapter has suggested that using notions of sustainable livelihoods, human capabilities and empowerment in the labour context may be a means of moving the debate forward. The role of law, especially labour law, in producing better outcomes for the poor, remains largely unexplored. The challenge is crafting 'good' legislation that is enforceable and enforced for everyone, while promoting economic growth with equity.

As Kalula has argued in relation to Southern Africa, '... the future of labour law ... lies in seeking to recognise that labour law is rather a sharper instrument of social policy. Labour market regulation must strive to influence work beyond the formal sector narrowly defined. It must strive to treat social protection as a central objective. ... Labour law must be part of the alleviation of poverty agenda'.[90] Labour lawyers surely have a lot of work to do!

---

[89] Tokman, above n 11, at 68.
[90] E. Kalula, 'Present at the Creation or Another False Start in Africa: Labour Market Regulation, Social Protection and the Future of Labour Law in Southern Africa' (Inaugural Lecture, Faculty of Law, University of Cape Town, New Series No 229, July 2003), 14.

II

The Employment Relationship as a Vehicle for the Delivery of Rights and Entitlements

5

The Comparative Evolution of the Employment Relationship

SIMON DEAKIN*

1. INTRODUCTION

It is widely believed that labour law is currently undergoing a 'crisis' of core concepts.[1] This is exemplified, above all, by the growing number of labour relationships which fall outside the scope of protection provided by the concept of the contract of employment or employment relationship. This chapter aims to contribute to the debate over the present and future scope of labour law by examining the evolution of the contract of employment from an historical and comparative perspective. A principal reason for doing so is that the conditions under which the contract of employment began to take shape as a core institution of labour law, around the turn of the twentieth century, were in certain significant respects similar to those of today.[2] Then, as now,

* Acting Director, Centre for Business Research, University of Cambridge, UK. I am grateful to the editors of this collection and to Joern Janssen for comments on an earlier draft.

[1] This has been a consistent theme of labour law writings since the early 1980s. See J. Clark and Lord Wedderburn, 'A Crisis in Fundamental Concepts', in Lord Wedderburn, R. Lewis and J. Clark (eds.), *Labour Law and Industrial Relations: Building on Kahn-Freund* (Oxford, Clarendon Press, 1983), 110, in particular at 153. More recently a key point of reference is A. Supiot (ed.), *Au delà de l'emploi. Transformations du travail et devenir du droit du travail en Europe* (Paris, Flammarion, 1999).

[2] A number of historical studies have explored the conditions which accompanied the emergence of the modern employment relationship and the core institutions of the welfare state, including collective bargaining and social insurance, at the turn of the twentieth century. For the US, see S.M. Jacoby, *Employing Bureaucracy: Managers, Unions and the Transformation of Work in the 20th Century*, revised edn, (Mahwah, NJ, Lawrence Erlbaum Associates, 2004), in particular ch 1; for the UK, S. Deakin and F. Wilkinson, *The Law of the Labour Market: Industrialization, Employment and Legal Evolution* (Oxford, Oxford University Press, 2005); for France, M. Mansfield, R. Salais and N. Whiteside (eds.), *Aux sources du chômage 1880–1914* (Paris, Belin, 1994), R. Castels, *Les métamorphoses de la question sociale: une chronique du salariat* (Paris, Fayard, 1995), and C. Didry, *Naissance de la convention collective: Débats juridiques et luttes socials en France au début du XXᵉ siècle* (Paris, Editions de l'EHESS, 2002); on Germany (with a comparison to the British case), R. Biernacki, *The Fabrication of Labour: Britain and Germany, 1640–1914* (Berkeley, Cal, University of California Press, 1995); and on general European developments in this and earlier periods, B. Hepple (ed.), *The Making of Labour Law in Europe* (London, Mansell, 1986).

there was widespread concern in many countries about the negative implications for the social fabric of a system of industrial enterprise which appeared to be entrenching inequality.[3] The persistence of poverty meant that the supposed benefits of the market economy could not, as its proponents had claimed, be made universally available.[4] At the same time, the few, fragile social compromises which had been established through early forms of collective bargaining and labour legislation were being undermined by technological innovation and changes in the structure of the firm.[5] The internationalization of trade and the interlinking of economies—then called 'imperialism'—undermined appeals for social protection in much the same way as 'globalisation' does now.[6] The intellectual orthodoxy of the day was provided by 'iron laws' of economics, which proclaimed, just as they do again, the futility of regulation in the face of market forces.[7]

The emergence of the modern 'welfare' or 'social' state from these highly unpromising circumstances was, of course, not simply or even principally the consequence of an intellectual revolution.[8] The beliefs which projected the free market credo of the nineteenth century well into the twentieth became impossible to maintain as a result of the unprecedented global crisis of the 1920s and 1930s.[9] It would, however, be wrong to assume that a cataclysm on that scale is needed if new ideas and solutions are now to come forward. Whether a crisis of some kind is unavoidable, given the protean nature of modern capitalism, remains to be seen, and perhaps this broader question should be seen as outwith the present debate within

[3] For the UK, this is most clearly evident in the Minority Report of the Poor Law Commission of 1909: S. and B. Webb, *The Public Organisation of the Labour Market: Being Part Two of the Minority Report of the Poor Law Commission* (London, Longmans, Green & Co., 1909) and in the contemporaneous study of William Beveridge, appropriately entitled *Unemployment: A Problem of Industry* (London, Longmans, Green & Co., 1909).

[4] On the evolution of concepts of 'poverty' in this period in Britain, assessing the work of Charles Booth and of Seebohm Rowntree, see K. Williams, *From Pauperism to Poverty* (London, Routledge and Kegan Paul, 1981).

[5] On the significance of the comparison, in this regard, between today's trend towards vertical disintegration and the experience of the early twentieth century, see P. Cappelli, 'Market-Mediated Employment: The Historical Context' in M. M. Blair and T. A. Kochan (eds), *The New Relationship. Human Capital in the American Corporation* (Washington, DC, Brookings Institution, 2000), 66.

[6] There is a growing literature considering the parallels between the 'first' globalisation of the late nineteenth century and more recent developments. See, in particular, S. Berger, *Notre première mondialisation: leçons d'un echec oublié* (Paris, Seuil, 2003).

[7] See Deakin and Wilkinson, above n 2, at 242–3.

[8] On the respective roles of social forces and intellectual movements in the development of modern labour law, see A. Supiot, 'Introduction' in Supiot, above n 1, at 7.

[9] See K. Polanyi, *The Great Transformation: The Political and Economic Origins of Our Time* (Boston, Mass, Beacon Press, 1957) (originally published 1944). Polanyi wrote: 'the origins of the cataclysm'—referring here to the crisis of the 1930s—'lay in the utopian endeavour of economic liberalism to set up a self-regulating market system' (*ibid.*, at 29).

labour law. Rather, the task—which is no doubt difficult enough—is to challenge neoliberal and neoconservative dogmas which might otherwise become so deeply entrenched that only another upheaval of catastrophic dimensions could shift them.

Part of that task is an engagement with historical evidence.[10] Reform does not start with a blank slate—for better or worse, we have to deal with the conceptual legacy of twentieth century labour law, to reshape it where necessary, but also to appreciate its malleability, and its capacity for adaptation. We can understand better the limitations of existing models if we improve our knowledge of the conditions under which they emerged and then developed. The study of their origins will help to reveal whether their weaknesses are structural and deep-rooted, or merely contingent and temporary.

The analysis must also be comparative. The current fashion is for 'end of history' type analyses which predict the convergence of systems around a supposedly functional core of rules and precepts which support economic growth.[11] Labour law is, in principle, no more immune from this all-embracing neo-functionalism than those areas, such as company and commercial law, to which it has already been extensively applied.[12] Under these circumstances it is essential to see comparative law as the study of systemic diversity,[13] and to revisit the lessons of an earlier generation of scholars which identified the risks associated with the transplantation of legal rules and techniques across systems.[14] The task is to understand the variety of solutions and the specificity of the local and national conditions which gave rise to them, rather than trying at every point to fit divergent experiences into a single, universal model.

The centrepiece of this project is an analysis of the contract of employment as a juridical concept, which explores its complex links to the wider economic and social environment of industrial capitalism. Disentangling the multiple strands of meaning in the legal concept of the contract of employment (and its civil law equivalents) is part of this process, but wider questions must also be addressed. What was the relationship between the

---

[10] For defences of this methodology, see Berger, above n 6, and Castels, above n 2.

[11] H. Hansmann and R. H Kraakman, 'The End of History for Corporate Law' (2001) 89 *Georgetown Law Journal* 439.

[12] R. Kraakman, P. Davies, H. Hansmann, G. Hertig, K. Hopt, H. Kanda, and E. Rock (eds), *The Anatomy of Corporate Law: A Comparative and Functional Approach* (Oxford: Oxford University Press, 2004).

[13] B. Aherling and S. Deakin, 'Labour Regulation, Corporate Governance and Legal Origin: A Case of Institutional Complementarity?', *CBR Working Paper No 312* (Cambridge, Centre for Business Research, 2005), available at: http://www.cbr.cam.ac.uk/pdf/WP312.pdf.

[14] Most importantly, the work of Otto Kahn-Freund: see his 'On Uses and Misuses of Comparative Law' (1974) 37 *Modern Law Review* 1.

emergence of the employment model and phases in the evolution of capitalist labour relations? How far was the employment model a by-product of
the welfare state? In what ways did the different national trajectories of economic growth under capitalism influence the evolution of the rules and
principles of labour law, and what, in turn, was the influence of that body
of law upon economic growth?

Some answers to these questions have already been suggested for the
British case.[15] The experience of Britain is significant because it was the first
nation to industrialise, but, precisely for that reason, it may be difficult to
draw generalisations from that case. A comparative perspective is required,
but the potential scale of the project is vast. This chapter is a first attempt
to map out some of the issues and suggest solutions.[16] Section 2 summarises
the argument recently presented in the work just referred to in relation to
the evolution of the contract of employment in British labour law. Section
3 draws on comparative material on the experience of continental
European systems in order to put the British case in context. Section 4 offers
some first conclusions on the significance of the analysis for the contemporary debate over the scope of labour law and the future of the contract of
employment.

2. THE EVOLUTION OF THE CONTRACT OF EMPLOYMENT IN BRITAIN: AN OVERVIEW

However British 'industrialisation' is defined—as the rise of the factory, the
shift from a rural to an industrial and urban economy, the transition from
agricultural subsistence to dependence on wage labour, or, more abstractly,
as the movement from status to contract—it is apparent that, by comparison with the experience of most other countries, it was a lengthy process,
lasting several centuries. The institutional roots of a market economy can
be found in the later Middle Ages and in the early modern period; the stim-
ulus provided to innovations in governance by such events as the Black
Death and the dissolution of the monasteries have been extensively documented.[17] England already had a mature *national* legal system at this stage,

---

[15] See generally Deakin and Wilkinson, above n 2.

[16] Because of shortage of space, an analysis of the US case is beyond the scope of the present chapter. The reasons for the appearance of a distinctive US version of 'employment at will'
in the late nineteenth and early twentieth century, the point at which American and English
law diverged, are discussed by Deakin and Wilkinson, above n 2, at 82–6.

[17] See, respectively, R. C. Palmer, *English Law in the Age of the Black Death, 1348–1381: A
Transformation of Governance and Law* (Chapel Hill, University of North Carolina Press,
1993), and D. Woodward, 'The Background to the Statute of Artificers: The Genesis of Labour
Policy, 1558–63' (1980) 33 *Economic History Review (NS)* 32.

the significance of which for its economic development is only now beginning to be understood. The first labour statutes, passed by way of response to the labour shortage which followed the Black Death of 1346, indicate the growing importance of legislation as a mechanism of state control of the economy, and are testimony to the existence at that point of an early system of contracting over the performance of work, already displacing compulsory labour in the form of villeinage or serfdom.[18] The Statute of Labourers of 1351 did not just formalise the system of wage regulation; it also helped to seed legal innovations which led to the promissory action of assumpsit, the forerunner of modern contract law.[19] The sixteenth century saw, alongside the diminution in the role of the Church as an institution of social protection, the extension of state control over labour, through the passage of numerous poor law statutes and of the pivotal Statute of Artificers of 1562, which was to provide the legislative foundation for wage setting, service in agriculture and the activities of the urban guilds up to the early nineteenth century.[20]

Formally, labour was not yet completely 'free': under the Statute of Artificers, service in agriculture was compulsory for those without property or other independent means of subsistence. Within the guilds, relations between masters, journeymen and apprentices were more akin to those of producers who were equally subject to the rules of the trade than to those between capitalists and subordinate workers. Putting-out systems resembled extended networks of independent contractors linked by merchant capitalists, rather than integrated industrial enterprises. Thus it is not possible to point to the existence of wage labour in the modern sense of that term. For this reason, the terms used by the Statute of Artificers and the poor law legislation of this period, including 'servant' and 'labourer', have to be treated with care; it would be a mistake to see them as simply the functional equivalents of the much later concept of the contract of employment.[21]

At the same time, the corporative system of the seventeenth and eighteenth centuries can be understood as responding in a number of ways to the growing dependence on wages of the large part of the English population. The poor law provides the clearest indication of this. A sophisticated framework of taxation and mutual insurance was put in place, based on the

---

[18] 'As villeinage ceases, the poor law begins' was Tawney's assessment (R. H Tawney, *The Agrarian Problem in the Sixteenth Century*, edited with an introduction by L. Stone (New York, Harper and Row, 1967), 47), and the point can be extended to wage regulation more generally.

[19] See Palmer, above n 17, for details of this process.

[20] See Deakin and Wilkinson, above n 2, at 44–51.

[21] For a more complete account of the points made in this paragraph, see Deakin and Wilkinson, above n 2, ch 2.

concept of the poor law 'settlement', through which annual service provided an entitlement to cash doles in the event of a loss of income through sickness or old age. The system was administered locally, at parish level, but it was national legislation which required each of the 15,000 parish units to raise local taxes for the purpose of supporting poor relief, and to suppress indiscriminate charitable giving. Anticipating the modern welfare state, the English poor relief system was both publicly instituted and legally mandated.[22]

The 'old' or pre-1834 poor law undoubtedly had disciplinary objectives. One of these was the control of labour mobility. Migrants were characterised as the 'vagrant' or 'wandering' poor; 'masterless men' who refused to work at customary wage levels or absconded from service were liable to severe punishments including branding and imprisonment.[23] Poor law officers enforced the 'removal' of paupers to their parishes of settlement. At best, the old poor law constituted a paternalist code, in which cash doles were combined with payments in kind and what remained of access to common land to ensure little more than the bare minimum of subsistence. But the confinement of the recipients of relief in workhouses, a regular feature of the system after 1834, was rare at this stage. The reality of economic insecurity was not lost on some of those who administered the system: according to a mid-eighteenth century edition of a leading treatise for justices of the peace, the 'poor' were 'here to be understood not vagabond beggars and rogues, but those who labour to live, and such as are old and decrepit, unable to work, poor widows, and fatherless children, and tenants driven to poverty; not by riot, expense and carelessness, but by mischance'.[24]

The poor law also provided the occasion for the first significant attempt to systematise the law governing the service relationship.[25] Disputes between parishes over the allocation of responsibility for poor relief led to an enormous body of litigation for that time. From the mid-seventeenth century the Court of King's Bench used the recently developed prerogative writs to impose a degree of administrative uniformity on settlement practice. Hundreds of settlement cases were reported, specialised law reports on the subject were compiled, and textbooks were written to guide justices of the peace and poor law officers. In the process, the juridical concept of service began to take shape as a reciprocal relationship, founded on contract while also incorporating status-based obligations on both sides, including

---

[22] See generally P. Slack, *The English Poor Law 1531–1782* (London, Macmillan, 1990).

[23] A.L. Beier, *Masterless Men: The Vagrancy Problem in England 1560–1640* (London, Methuen, 1985).

[24] M. Dalton, *The Country Justice: Containing the Practice, Duty and Power of the Justices of the Peace, as Well in as Out of their Sessions* (London, Lintot, 1746), 164.

[25] See generally K. Snell, *Annals of the Labouring Poor: Social Change and Agrarian England 1660–1900* (Cambridge, Cambridge University Press, 1985).

the servant's open-ended duty to obey orders and the master's obligation, as Blackstone put it, to maintain the servant 'throughout the revolution of the respective seasons, as well when there is work to be done as when there is not'.[26] It is also possible to see, in the eighteenth century case law, numerous decisions on what would now be called task contracts and casual labour relationships, as well as attempts by masters to avoid the application of the settlement laws by dismissing servants just before they completed a year's service. There is some evidence to suggest that the attitude of the courts to the definition of annual service shifted over the economic cycle, with the concept becoming more rigid and narrow at times of hardship when claims increased and parishes sought to restrict payments of relief.[27] It would seem that difficulties in the application of abstract juridical concepts to the 'reality' of labour relationships are nothing new.

The century after 1750 which is conventionally associated with the period of the 'industrial revolution' in Britain was, in addition to being a time of rapid technological and social change, also a period of legal innovation; hence Arnold Toynbee's suggestion, made in the 1870s, that the essence of the industrial revolution was not to be found in the adoption of steam power or the advent of factory labour, but in 'the substitution of competition for the medieval regulations which had previously controlled the production and distribution of wealth'.[28] Unmediated competition in the labour market was promoted through the repeal of the wage-fixing laws and apprenticeship regulations which had formed the main body of the Statute of Artificers (in 1813 and 1814 respectively). It is not clear how far the 1562 Statute had ceased to be enforced by this point, but it does not seem that it was a complete dead letter. The removal of legal support for apprenticeship controls was resisted by a series of strikes in the 1810s, and there was considerable litigation around the same time, in the course of which the courts watered down the Statute's restrictions on entry into the regulated trades.[29] Where a seventeenth century court had concluded that 'he who cannot use a mystery himself, is prohibited to employ any other men in that trade; for if this should be allowed, then the care which has been taken to keep up mysteries, by erecting guilds or fraternities would signify little',[30] by 1811 Lord

---

[26] W. Blackstone, *Commentaries on the Laws of England: A Fascimile of the First Edition of 1765–69*, edited with an introduction by S. N. Katz (Chicago, University of Chicago Press, 1979), 413.

[27] The case law is discussed by Deakin and Wilkinson, above n 2, at 118–24.

[28] A. Toynbee, *Lectures on the Industrial Revolution in England*, edited with an introduction by T. S. Ashton (Newton Abbott, A.M. Kelley, 1969) (originally published 1884), 92.

[29] I. Prothero, *Artisans and Politics in Early Nineteenth Century London: John Gast and His Times* (Folkestone, Dawson, 1979).

[30] *Hobbs v Young* (1689) 1 Show KB 267.

Ellenborough CJ could refuse to convict an unqualified mill owner of a breach of the Statute on the ground that 'persons of the first families of this kingdom' could not be expected 'to serve regular apprenticeships as millers'.[31] In this way a potential legal constraint on the form of the capitalist enterprise, which would in future be based on the clear separation of labour from ownership of the means of production, was removed.

A parallel change which occurred in the sphere of the poor law was the dismantling of the institution of annual service upon which access to poor relief as of right (or, at least, on the basis of a customary expectation) had depended. The courts were the first to restrict the notion, by introducing the concept of the 'exceptive' hiring to explain why industrial workers, who did not live in the household of the master and so were deemed not to be continuously under his authority, could not acquire a settlement.[32] In 1834 Parliament abolished the category of settlement by hiring altogether. This was part of the wider reform, embodied in the Poor Law Amendment Act of that year, which saw the legal instantiation of the principle of 'less eligibility'. This was a reaction to what had been seen as the excesses of the old poor law, and in particular the variant of the Speenhamland system, which from the late eighteenth century had encouraged the payment of poor relief to subsidise low wages. The problem with the old poor law, and in particular with Speenhamland, according to the political economists of the time, was that it distorted the working of the market. As Bentham put it, 'if the conditions of individuals, maintained without property of their own, by the labour of others, were rendered more eligible than that of persons maintained by their own labour, then, in proportion as this state of things were ascertained, individuals destitute of property would be continually withdrawing themselves from the class of persons maintained by their own labour, to the class of persons maintained by the labour of others'. This would have the all too troubling consequence, if it continued, that 'at last there would be nobody left to labour at all, for anybody'.[33] The solution, adopted in the Act of 1834, was known as the principle of less eligibility: no pauper should be better off than the least well-off 'independent' workers and their families. This meant confinement in the workhouse for the able-bodied poor. But because even this might give rise, on occasion, to an improvement in the condition of the pauper, since 'humanity demands that all the bodily wants of the inmates of a public establishment should

---

[31] *Kent v Dormay* (1811) Kingston Assizes, 14 August, reported in J. Chitty, *A Practical Treatise on the Law Relating to Apprentices and Journeymen, and to Exercising Trades* (London, W. Clarke & Sons, 1812), 122.

[32] Deakin and Wilkinson, above n 2, at 122.

[33] J. Bentham, 'Essay II: Fundamental Positions in regard to the Making of Provision for the Indigent Poor' in *Essays on the Subject of the Poor Laws* (1796), reproduced in M. Quinn (ed.), *The Collected Works of Jeremy Bentham: Writings on the Poor Laws* (Oxford, Clarendon Press, 2001) 39.

be provided for', a level of subsistence which the market itself was not able to guarantee, it was essential 'to submit the pauper inmate of a public establishment to such a system of labour discipline and restraint as shall be sufficient to outweigh, in his estimation, the advantages which he derives from the bodily comforts which he enjoys'.[34]

In these ways, what were seen as 'distortions' or 'interferences' with the working of the market for labour were removed. It might be thought that this would have led to the contractualisation of labour relations, and hence to the recognition in the courts of the concept of the contract of employment as the paradigm legal form of the work relationship. However, this is not what happened. For some occupational groups, a type of employment contract did indeed emerge, to which the courts attached status obligations in the form of implied contractual terms. The common law action for wages due as earned under the contract and the action for damages for wrongful dismissal can be identified in cases from the early decades of the nineteenth century.[35] However, these decisions were almost without exception based on the employment of managerial, clerical or professional workers. Manual workers fell under the distinctive legal regime of the Master and Servant Acts, under which breach of the service contract was a criminal offence, for which thousands of workers were fined or imprisoned each year up to the 1870s.[36]

The master–servant model was not a hold-over from the corporative regime of the Statute of Artificers and old poor law. On the contrary, most of the disciplinary powers used by employers and courts were additions from the mid-eighteenth century and early nineteenth century, the result of parliamentary action to bolster the prerogatives of the new employer class. The nature of the paradigm legal form of the labour relationship under early industrial capitalism in England was statutory and hierarchical, rather than common law and contractual. The legal influence of the master–servant regime was just as far reaching as its considerable social and economic impact. The model of a command relation, with an open-ended duty of obedience imposed on the worker, and reserving far-reaching disciplinary powers to the employer, spilled over into the common law, so that long after the repeal of the last of the Master and Servant Acts in 1875, not just the terminology of master and servant but also many of the old assumptions of unmediated control were still being applied by the courts as they developed the common law of employment.[37]

---

[34] *Report on the Continuance of the Poor Law Commission* (1839), reproduced in H.R. Jenner-Fust, *Poor Law Orders* (London, P.S. King, 1907), 4.

[35] A watershed decision, synthesising these developments, was *Emmens v Elderton* (1853) 13 CB 495.

[36] See generally Deakin and Wilkinson, above n 2, at 61–74.

[37] *Ibid.*; see also the comprehensive survey of master–servant laws in the British Empire: D. Hay and P. Craven (eds), *Masters, Servants and Magistrates in Britain and the Empire* (Chapel Hill, NC, University of North Carolina Press, 2004).

It took the advent of the welfare state and the extension of collective bargaining, with state encouragement, to achieve a more complete 'contractualisation' of employment relations.[38] The persistence of the master–servant model in employment law, and the enduring influence of the principle of less eligibility in the long transition from the poor law to social security, which was completed only in the 1940s, delayed the advent of the contract of employment. If the contract of employment is identified, above all, with a classification of labour relations which incorporates the 'binary divide' between employees and the self-employed, we have to look to the middle of the twentieth century to find it in British labour law. The first statutes to adopt the binary divide in a clear form were concerned with income taxation and social insurance. Even then, it cannot be found in the first income tax and national insurance measures of the 1910s, which adopted slightly different classification schemes from those used later, retaining the distinction between manual and non-manual workers. The National Insurance Act 1946, which incorporated Beveridge's plan for social security, marked the turning point; its clear division between those employed under a 'contract of service', a term which gradually became interchangeable with the term 'contract of employment', and those who were 'self-employed' or independent contractors was then carried over into early employment protection statutes in the 1960s. The term 'employee' is truly a very recent innovation in British labour law.

3. THE ORIGINS OF THE EMPLOYMENT RELATIONSHIP IN THE CIVIL LAW SYSTEMS OF CONTINENTAL EUROPE

There is also evidence from the civil law systems to support the claim that the modern contract of employment is an invention of the late nineteenth and early twentieth centuries, associated with the rise of the integrated enterprise and the beginnings of the welfare or social state. However, it is also clear that the experience of the civil law systems was far from uniform. Distinct conceptions of the employment relationship took shape in different systems, reflecting variations in economic conditions and in legal cultures, and further reinforcing divergence through their influence on the development of labour law.

The starting point for the analysis is the process by which the emerging forms of wage labour were grafted on to the traditional Roman law concept of the *locatio conductio* in the post-revolutionary codes. In relying on the model of the *locatio*, the drafters of the codes were grouping labour

---

[38] See Deakin and Wilkinson, above n 2, at 86–100, for a fuller account of the development described in this paragraph.

relationships with other types of contracts, the effect being to stress that, in common with them, they were based on exchange. Thus labour, or in some versions labour power—as, for example, in the German term *Arbeitskraft*—thereby became a commodity which was linked to price (not necessarily the 'wage'), through the contract. The further consequence was to align the labour relationship with the law of things rather than the law of persons: the notion of the personal 'subordination' of the worker was absent from the formulae used by the codes.[39] The reality was rather different, since more or less all systems acknowledged the power of the employer to give orders, to issue rules which had binding force (in the form, for example, of the French *livret* or work book), and to retain the worker in employment, without a testimonial, until it considered the work to be complete. However, this body of legislation and practice was formally separated from the general private law of the codes, and administered by police authorities and specialised labour tribunals; as a result, it remained under-developed from a conceptual point of view.

Two versions of the *locatio conductio* were contained in the French *Code civil* of 1804: one, the *louage d'ouvrage*, was loosely based on the Roman law idea of the *locatio conductio operarum*, or hire of work (in the sense of a piece of work or completed task); the other, the *louage de services*, had some affinity to the *locatio conductio operis*, or hire of services. In each case, the link to Roman law concepts was more tenuous than it might seem at first sight. The concepts used in the *Code civil* were adaptations—they were 'the same as the old *locatio conductio* in name only'.[40] This was because they aimed to replace the Roman law notion of the *locatio conductio* as a form involving the subjection of the individual worker with the liberal idea of formal equality between contracting parties. Even in the case of the *louage de services*, the form which most closely resembled an agreement to serve, the *Code civil* insisted (in Article 1780) that services could be provided only for a certain purpose or limited period of time. A commitment to lifelong service, for example, would be void.

It is possible to see, in the distinction between the *louage d'ouvrage* and the *louage de services*, the essence of the division between independent contractors and servants in English law, and perhaps, the origins of the binary divide itself. However, to take this view would be to run the risk of viewing what was in practice a highly complex and differentiated set of categories

---

[39] S. Simitis, 'The Case of the Employment Relationship: Elements of a Comparison' in W. Steinmetz (ed.), *Private Law and Social Inequality in the Industrial Age: Comparing Legal Cultures in Britain, France, Germany and the United States* (Oxford, Oxford University Press, 2000), 181.

[40] B. Veneziani, 'The Evolution of the Employment Relationship' in B. Hepple, above n 2, 31 at 32.

through the lenses of alternative systems of classification. Under the system of the *Code civil*, those falling under the concept of the *louage de services* were domestic servants (*domestiques*) and day labourers (*journaliers*), leaving the *louage d'ouvrage* to cover all others. Although the *Code civil* placed the risks of non-completion of the task on the worker in the case of the *louage d'ouvrage*, upon completion the property in the relevant goods, and any surplus, vested immediately in the employer (Article 1790). Under the *louage de services*, the employer was to be the sole judge of whether the work had been completed (Article 1781), so in practice the allocation of risks differed little between the two forms. Neither relation could give rise to an indeterminate or open-ended contract. Cutting across the classifications contained in the *Code civil*, the regulatory jurisdiction associated with the *livret* or workbook was strengthened by legislation just before the *Code* was adopted (law of 12 April 1803). It is arguable that both of the categories set out in the *Code* were, in practice, closer to wage labour than to relations between commercial parties.[41]

Nor should it be assumed that there is a direct line of descent between the *louage de services* and the notion of the contract of employment or *contrat de travail*. Although the existence of such a link was posited at the end of the nineteenth century by a number of labour law jurists, this was, it has been more recently claimed, a 'mystification' of the process involved: 'republican writers on labour law pretended to themselves and persuaded others that "service hiring" was a category of the Civil Code that had applied to the employment of workers from the outset'.[42] This was done to lend the appearance of continuity to the law at a time when the concept of the *contrat de travail* was still relatively new. The term itself appears not to have been in use before the mid-1880s.[43] The main impetus for its adoption was an argument by employers in larger enterprises that the general duty of obedience should be read into all industrial hirings. However, once the term became established, it was used in turn of the century legislation on industrial accidents,[44] and its adoption was promoted and systematised by commissions of jurists charged with developing a conceptual framework for collective bargaining and worker protection.[45] At the core of the concept

---

[41] H. Petit and D. Sauze, 'Une lecture historique de la relation salariale comme structure de repartition des aléas. En partant du travail de Salais', in F. Eymard-Duvemay (ed) L' économie des conventions: méthodes et résultats. Tome II Développements (Paris, La Découverte) 309–11; A. Cottereau, 'Droit et bon droit: Un droit des ouvriers instauré, puis évincé par le droit du travail (France XIXe siècle)', [200] *Annales HSS*, Nov.–Dec., no. 6, 1521.

[42] A. Cottereau, 'Industrial Tribunals and the Establishment of a Kind of Common Law of Labour in Nineteenth Century France' in Steinmetz, above n 39, 203 at 220.

[43] *Ibid.*

[44] Veneziani, above n 40, at 64.

[45] *Ibid.*, at 68.

was a notion of 'subordination' in which the open-ended duty of obedience was traded off in return for the acceptance and absorption by the enterprise of a range of social risks.

The terminology used in the German Civil Code, the *BGB*, adopted in 1896, is superficially similar to that used in the French *Code civil* at the beginning of the nineteenth century, with the *Dienstvertrag*, literally the 'contract for service', distinguished from the *Werkvertrag*, the contract for work or sub-contract. The *BGB* nevertheless marked a significant break with the Romanist model of the *locatio*. This was not just because the two categories were placed in separate volumes of the code, signifying the fragmentation of the *locatio* concept; more substantively, the *Dienstvertrag* came to embody the idea of the employer's duty of care (*Fürsorgepflicht*), the counterpoint to the duty of loyalty (*Treuepflicht*) owed by the worker. This reflected the influence of Gierke, who argued for the integration into the Code of the principles of social solidarity which, he argued, were to be found in the historical antecedents of the *Dienstvertrag*. In this way, the emerging employment law was realigned with the law of persons and with the notion of the enterprise as an employing community.[46] At the same time, there is no clear reference in the *BGB* to the binary divide between employees and the self-employed: 'at the time the *BGB* was drafted the distinction between employment and services had not been established, so the term *Dienstvertrag* covered both types of agreement. This means that in the context of Art. 611 [*BGB*], *Dienstvertrag* refers both to the contract for service and the contract of employment'.[47] The modern notion of the employment relationship or *Arbeitsverhältnis* came later, as in France, with the adoption of protective legislation and the legal accommodation of collective bargaining.

Both France and Germany saw the late development of the contract of employment. What emerged, however, were forms which reflected the distinctive legal cultures of the two systems.[48] In the French-origin systems, the power of the state to regulate conditions of work was instantiated within the legal system through the concept of *ordre public social*, that is, a set of minimum, binding conditions which applied as a matter of general law to the employment relationship. The implicit logic of this idea was that, in recognising the formal contractual equality of the parties to the employment relationship, the state also assumed, by way of symmetry, a responsibility for

---

[46] *Ibid.*, at 59; V. Sims, *Good Faith in Contract Law: A Comparative Analysis of English and German Law* (Ph.D. Thesis, University of Cambridge, 2002), 85–86.

[47] *Ibid.*, at 83.

[48] U. Mückenberger and A. Supiot, 'Ordre public social et communauté: deux cultures du droit du travail' in B. Zimmermann, C. Didry and P. Wagner (eds), *Le travail et la nation* (Paris, Éditions de la Maison des Sciences de l'Homme, 2000), 81.

establishing a form of protection for the individual worker who was thereby placed in a position of 'juridical subordination'. In German-influenced systems, by contrast, a 'communitarian' conception of the enterprise qualified the role of the individual contract. This approach was summed up at the end of the nineteenth century by Gierke's argument that the supposedly 'eternal juridical truths' of the modernised Romanist tradition simply served to conceal 'formulas expressing individualistic and capitalistic assumptions'.[49] Under Gierke's influence, the employment relationship was orientated away from the law of obligations and towards the law of persons; thus in contrast to the French approach, German law came to recognise the 'personal subordination' of the worker in the form of 'factual adhesion to the enterprise' or *Tatbestand*, a process which conferred 'a status equivalent to membership of a community'.[50]

Alain Supiot has suggested that 'there is no European country in which the conception of the employment relationship has not been influenced to some degree by each of these two legal cultures, the Romanist and the Germanic'.[51] The influence of communitarian thinking was particularly strong in all continental systems, French-origin included, in the first part of the twentieth century, when it overlapped to some degree with fascist ideologies. At the same time, it would be excessively reductive to identify this line of thought with fascist notions of the corporative state. The idea of the 'interests of the enterprise' as a reference point for the mutual obligations of employer and employee has had a wider resonance, since it predated the rise of authoritarian regimes and retained an influence after their fall. It owed much to the concentration of industry and the emergence of vertically integrated and bureaucratically-organised enterprises during the same period, a process which, as we have noted, began earlier and was more complete on the continent than in Britain. The result was a 'synthesis' of contractual and communitarian elements that has been ever since a source of 'structural ambivalence'[52] in the conceptual framework of European labour law.

4. INITIAL REFLECTIONS ON THE SIGNIFICANCE OF COMPARATIVE AND HISTORICAL ANALYSIS

What is the significance of the analysis set out above for our understanding of the contemporary debate over the scope of labour law and in particular over the future of the contract of employment? The following conclusions may, tentatively, be advanced.

---

[49] O. von Gierke, *Das Deutsches Privatrecht: Systematisches Handbuch der deutschen Rechtswissenschaft* (Leipzig, Duncker & Humblot, 1895), 32.

[50] A. Supiot, *Critique du droit du travail* (Paris, Presses Universitaires de France, 1994), 18.

[51] *Ibid.*, at 19.

[52] *Ibid.*

1. The concept of the contract of employment or employment relationship has roots in the process of industrialisation but it owes its full development to the further intervention of the welfare state.

Were it not for the social legislation of the welfare or social state, and for the related development of collective bargaining, there would not be a 'contract of employment' or 'employment relationship' as we have come to understand it. The earliest antecedent for the modern employment contract in Britain is the eighteenth century institution of annual service, which emerged from what was essentially a prototype of the welfare state, the poor law system of settlement by hiring. In all systems, it was twentieth century social insurance and employment protection legislation which stabilised the employment relationship and, together with the macro-economic policy of that period, actively sought, for a period, to suppress casualisation. In Britain, collective bargaining assisted the process further as unions encouraged employers to replace the internal contracting system with direct employment relations.

On the continent, there is evidence of a longer continuous tradition of an 'integrative' conception of the enterprise. As industrialisation occurred later, vertical integration of the enterprise occurred more quickly. There is also evidence that labour shortages in regions of France and Germany where workers retained a tie to the land for longer than was the case in Britain, providing them with an alternative to wage labour, made employers more ready to assume responsibility for social risks arising from employment, as the quid pro quo for the acceptance by workers of managerial direction and control.[53]

However, in all systems it is arguable that without certain institutional interventions, the employment model would be confined again to particular occupational groups, in particular professional and managerial workers occupying a relatively secure and protected market segment. That is essentially what is happening now, thanks to the diminishing influence of collective bargaining, the encouragement by government policy of outsourcing, and attempts by employers to exploit possibilities for the fragmentation of the legal form of the enterprise. This is a process which, rather than being the inevitable consequence of technological shifts or structural changes in the economy, has in many cases has been set in motion by legislative changes and by reversals of policy, particularly in macroeconomic policy.[54]

---

[53] P.K. O'Brien, 'Path Dependency, or why Britain became an Industrialized and Urbanized Economy Long before France' (1996) 52 *Economic History Review* 213.
[54] Deakin and Wilkinson, above n 2, ch 4.

2. There is nothing new about the claim that the contract of employment is an 'artificial' model imposed on a more complex 'reality' of labour relations.

The debate about 'scope' is essentially an argument about how to apply protective labour statutes. Work relations which fall on the 'margins' of the employment category, because they involve casual or part-time work, or work at a distance from the workplace, have always posed a problem of classification. As we saw above, this was the case as early as the poor law legislation of the eighteenth century. Again, in the early twentieth century, arguments about the meaning of the terms 'servant' and 'workman' were concerned with the same issues of workplace fragmentation and the disintegration of the employing enterprise that today are regarded as imposing new constraints on the ability of labour law to protect workers. To point to the recurring nature of the problem is in no way to underestimate the problems involved in solving it today, since the techniques of avoidance used now inevitably differ from those of a century or more ago. However, it may serve as a reminder that what appears to be the consequence of technology or ineluctable economic changes is instead often the result of political decisions (such as the decision in the 1980s to reverse the trend in macroeconomic policy towards the stabilisation of the employment relationship) and managerial strategies (such as the current vogue for outsourcing) which history shows are by no means irreversible.

3. The concept of the contract of employment serves important functions in a market-based economy even in an era of deregulation and liberalisation, and is unlikely to be replaced by a radically new model in the near future, even if there is some 'rebranding' of concepts.

The trajectory of the contract of employment suggests that as a legal concept it embodies at least two significant functions: one is to assist in the managerial task of the coordination of work within the enterprise, a task signified by the 'control' and 'integration' tests of employee status; the other is to serve as a device for shifting and controlling for the social risks of a loss of income through sickness, unemployment and old age which are inevitable and unavoidable in an economy in which the vast majority of the population is dependent, directly or indirectly, on wages for subsistence, a function signified by the 'economic reality' test. The risk-shifting function, and hence some form of social security for at least some workers, is just as much an integral feature of a market system as the capitalist enterprise is. This is not to say that the emergence of a mature welfare state is inevitable in a given system, any more than one can say that we inevitably and always find democracy and human rights in capitalist economies. It is simply to say that the presence of an advanced social security and employment protection system is by no means incompatible with a market economy, or necessarily hostile to it. It is possible that an advanced social model of this kind is best represented in the western Europe experience; however, to argue, on 'cultural' grounds, that it can *only* flourish there, or possibly in parts of north America, is to make very strong and arguably untenable assumptions about the evolutionary path which capitalism is taking, or may take, in other systems.

The enduring presence of the contract of employment in most developed economies, even in those which have undergone considerable liberalisation and deregulation over the past two decades, is striking. Thus in Britain, notwithstanding some decline in job tenure rates for male workers and some growth in flexible forms of work, the vast majority of workers have employment status. This figure reaches 90 per cent if self-employed 'workers' are included;[55] and the 'worker' concept is arguably nothing more than a rebranding exercise, designed to overcome the difficulties created by the highly artificial 'mutuality of obligation' test. Self-employment has not grown much, if at all, over the past decade, suggesting that its incidence is cyclical (in the sense of being associated with falls in overall employment) rather than structural. The same pattern is broadly observable in other EU Member States.

4. However, the contract of employment is the product of those historically contingent features which accompanied its mature development in the mid-twentieth century; as those particular features of the economy and social policy fade away, there are growing problems in using the existing form of the contract of employment as a device of classification.

The employment model is useful, even indispensable, to labour lawyers, but it bears the marks of its origin. It reflects, in particular, the context in which the mid-twentieth century compromise between labour and capital was struck. It assumes not simply that the employing entity is a large, vertically integrated enterprise, characterised by unified management and by an internal labour market based on bureaucratic control, for which the regulation of workplace relations through collective bargaining is well suited; it also makes assumptions about the household division of labour. In Britain, the instantiation of the male breadwinner model in the legislation of the welfare state was a reaction to the extreme forms of competition between men and women which the nineteenth century poor law embodied.[56] The poor

---

[55] B. Burchell, S. Deakin and S. Honey, *The Employment Status of Individuals in Non-standard Employment*, EMAR Research Series no 6 (London, Department of Trade and Industry, 1999).

[56] Deakin and Wilkinson, above n 2, ch 3. It does not of course follow that the employment contract is *inevitably* tied to the male breadwinner model; indeed, it is arguable that the model of the employment contract can be renewed or modified in the context of a less gendered division of labour. See J. Browne, S. Deakin and F. Wilkinson, 'Capabilities, Social Rights and European Market Integration' in R. Salais and R. Villeneuve (eds.), *Towards a European Politics of Capabilities?* (Cambridge, Cambridge University Press, 2004).

law was more gender neutral than might be supposed;[57] but this was a world in which the workhouse was used to break up family relations as a warning to the improvident, and where the male and female able-bodied were equally subject to the harsh impositions of the duty to work. In the twentieth century, in sharp contrast, the preservation of the male bread-winner wage became the goal of collective bargaining, and the social insurance rights of married women were almost entirely derivative of those of their male partners. Restricting the scale of female employment and confining it to the margins of the economy was to some degree the goal, and in any case certainly the effect, of Beveridge's supply side reforms and macroeconomic policy.[58]

The erosion of the male breadwinner model has accelerated rapidly since the 1970s.[59] This has been the result of changes in the economy, associated with growing female participation in paid employment, rising divorce rates, the fragmentation of family structures. At the same time, the male bread-winner model has ceased to serve as a normative point of reference, as it has been judged to be incompatible with the principle of equal treatment between men and women in both employment law and social security law.[60] However, as yet, no clear alternative to that model has emerged. Full-time employment for men is no longer guaranteed, and since, for women, it never was, some kind of parity has been restored; but one effect is growing poverty and social exclusion in 'workless households' where neither partner is in employment.[61] No matter how imperfectly, the male breadwinner model protected individuals and households from the effects of unmediat-ed competition in the labour market. Its eclipse has led to new forms of insecurity and social exclusion.[62]

---

[57] See A. Clark, 'The New Poor Law and the Breadwinner Wage: Contrasting Assumptions' (2000) 34 *Journal of Social History* 262; M. Levine-Clark, 'Engendering Relief: Women, Able-Bodiedness and the New Poor Law in Early Victorian England' (2000) 11 *Journal of Women's History* 107.

[58] See Deakin and Wilkinson, above n 2, at 171–5.

[59] *Ibid.*, at 319–26.

[60] This is particularly clear in the case law on Art 141 (ex Art 119) of the EC Treaty, which has had major implications for pay systems and for systems of social security in Member States of the EU. Thus just as differences in pay between men and women for work of equal value cannot be justified by the supposed need to pay a male breadwinner wage (Case 170/84 *Bilka-Kaufhaus GmbH v Weber von Hartz* [1986] IRLR 317), so the principle of equal treat-ment has led to an equalisation of pensionable ages in occupational social security (Case C-262/88 *Barber v Guardian Royal Exchange Assurance Group* [1990] IRLR 240), which can imply a 'levelling down' of provision (Case C-408/92 *Smith v Avdel Systems Ltd.* [1994] IRLR 602).

[61] See Deakin and Wilkinson, above n 2, at 319–26.

[62] C. Creighton, 'The Rise and Decline of the "Male Breadwinner Family" in Britain' (1999) 23 *Cambridge Journal of Economics* 519.

5. The timing of industrialisation and the form taken by the welfare state shape the evolution of labour law in a given system and influence the form taken by its core concepts including the contract of employment.

The most distinctive feature of the British case is *early industrialisation,* that is to say, industrialisation which occurred *before* the putting in place of many of the social and legal institutions which support and sustain a market economy. This had profound implications for the nature of industrial enterprise in Britain and for the form of the welfare state, which are reflected in labour law. Thus the development of legal forms which could support the vertically integrated enterprise and unified management had to wait until the mid to late nineteenth century. Industrial enterprise developed before there was limited liability and a straightforward incorporation process; thus to a greater extent than in continental Europe, British firms in the formative early phases of industrialisation were small scale, relied heavily on internal contracting in lieu of unified management, and made little use of the capital market. This explains, in part, the predominant role of master–servant legislation in the British experience: this offered a form of legal support for managerial prerogative at a time when the typical enterprise lacked managerial capacity of its own.

This might be of just antiquarian interest, were it not for the path-dependent nature of legal change. The master–servant model long outlived its usefulness to employers in early industrial England, and, thanks to the global influence of the English common law, was exported worldwide, with far-reaching and arguably negative results in terms of the entrenchment of an adversarial conception of the employment relationship.[63] That conception arguably still influences British labour law, and the labour law of many other systems, today. The principal tests used to classify labour relationships—control, integration, economic reality and mutuality of obligation—all too clearly bear the signs of their origins as responses to particular phases in the evolution of the employing enterprise and the growth of the welfare state, a legacy which continues to cause confusion in the application of labour law. But path dependence can have much more negative effects than even that. The peculiar mix of Speenhamland-type wage subsidisation and Benthamite less eligibility which characterises the social security policy of today's New Labour government suggests that history can cast a very long shadow indeed.

This is not just to argue that 'history matters' to our understanding of contemporary labour law. From a wider perspective, the most important question is the following: which features of the British case offer insights

---

[63] See generally Hay and Craven, above n 37.

into the general, structural features of the relationship between labour law and industrialisation, and which are unique to the British experience? If the concept of the contract of employment was a relatively late arrival in Britain, what was the experience elsewhere? In this regard, Mark Freedland[64] has posed the critical question of whether the distinction between employees and the self-employed, rather than being 'contingent and circumstantial a product of a particular set of social policies, imposed by legislation upon a specific labour market in a certain jurisdiction at a given moment of time', could instead very well be regarded as 'a much more universal and deeply embedded one which permeates the jurisprudence, as well as the legislation, of many legal systems over very long historical periods of time'.

While a certain amount of progress in understanding the nature of the employment model can arguably be made on the basis of a single-country study or a two-or three-country comparison,[65] resolution of the wider question posed by Freedland can be achieved only through a broader comparative analysis. This chapter has made an attempt to point the way to some of the answers. The evidence reviewed here supports the view that the contract of employment or employment relationship, understood as a juridical concept, has a highly complex lineage. It has roots in the adaptation of Roman law concepts to liberal economic philosophies in the post-revolutionary period, and in the commingling of contractual ideas with legislative regulation of the service relationship. However, just as in the British case, the conceptual classifications used in the nineteenth century codes do not map precisely on to the binary divide between employees and the self-employed which is at the core of modern labour law. What emerges again is the importance of specific national and local conditions in shaping the development of the employment model, and the role, above all, of a particular historical conjunction, associated with the coevolution, at the end of the nineteenth century, of the welfare state and the modern industrial enterprise. The next step in this research is to fill in the gaps in our knowledge, in particular concerning the relationship between the evolution of the law and wider changes in the economy during and after the industrial revolution.

---

[64] M. Freedland, *The Personal Employment Contract* (Oxford, Oxford University Press, 2003), 19–20.

[65] As in the works by Biernacki, above n 2, and Mückenberger and Supiot, above n 48. More broadly comparative works, such as those, cited above, Veneziani, above n 40, and Simitis, above n 39, are rare.

6

Labour Subordination and the Subjective Weakening of Labour Law

ADRIÁN GOLDIN*

1. A DEFIANT AND COMPLEX CONTEXT; THE SUBJECTIVE WEAKENING OF LABOUR LAW

A. About a Trend

To place in the right context the subject this work is about, it is necessary, in my opinion, to see it within a process that, with different nuances and intensities, seems to have an almost universal extension. We are talking about the weakening tendencies that appear to affect the social law and which are seen in, at least, three dimensions that will be schematically stated below:

i. The social law suffers a *normative weakening* as a result of labour flexibility demands, deregulation, reduction in the intensity of protection. In short, *a loss of resources of protection*.

ii. It also experiences a *subjective weakening* as a result of a number of phenomena such as unemployment, increasing informality, the vertical disintegration of companies and the productive decentralisation trends, fraud by evading obligations and several signs of the so–called 'escape from labour law',[1] public policies that allow the treatment of dependant workers as if they were not (eg, home workers, lorry drivers, apprentices etc.), ambiguous relations in which it is highly difficult to establish the nature (dependent or autonomous) of the links.[2] In short, a *loss of personal scope of the social law*.

iii. Finally, it suffers an *applicative weakening* which is the indirect consequence of the phenomena already mentioned above and of others

---

* Professor Plenario, Unversidad de San Andrés, Argentina.
[1] M. Rodriguez Piñero, 'La huida del derecho del Trabajo' [1992] *Relaciones Laborales (Madrid)* 85.
[2] The latter will be, precisely, the subject we are aiming at in these lines.

such as the decrease of political significance or the limitation of the competences of the political actors who are in charge of the application of labour law and social protection (Labour Ministry, labour inspection, labour courts[3] etc.) or its plain and simple suppression, together with the scattering of its powers,[4] as well as the social actors' (weakening and loss of unions' influence), all of which usually goes together with the ideological devaluation of the labour law and other forms of social protection, despised as signs of anachronistic paternalism, etc. In other words, a *loss of effectiveness* 'stricto sensu' *of the social law.*

Certainly, this is not the occasion to deal with the causes of and reasons for such critical processes, which, in any case, have been thoroughly explored by specialised literature.[5]

Nevertheless, it must be said that those generic biases of *normative, subjective and applicative weakening of social law* do not necessarily lead us to a pessimistic vision of its future, since together with those tendencies and those critical causation factors other important counterbalances—institutional, political, ideological, economic, productive and technical—that seem to sustain the logic of protection coexist.

B. The Subjective Weakening of Labour Law

The modern debate around labour subordination undoubtedly fits in the subjective facet of that process of weakening of labour law. However, this facet includes other convergent factors of reduction of the personal scope of labour law. Among them—as stated before—are the high levels of unemployment, the growing incidence of informality, the processes of vertical disintegration of companies and decentralisation of the ways of organising production, fraud and other ways of escaping from labour law,[6] the legislative policies that consider certain dependant labour relations as if they were not, the ambiguous relations, ie those which even showing a strong economic worker's subjection do not seem to include the feature of labour dependence.

---

[3] This is the case in Argentina, where competences previously given to labour courts have been transferred to other jurisdictions (the commercial one, specifically in the case of bankruptcy) as well as granting labour courts competences that did not belong to them (dealing with statutory protections provoked by the restriction on the availability of bank deposits).

[4] A process described by Harry Arthurs (of York University, Toronto, Canada) in his contribution to this volume.

[5] See, for the whole and for its great power of synthesis, the very recent Arturo Bronstein study, 'Los retos actuales del derecho del trabajo' [2006] *Derecho del Trabajo* (forthcoming).

[6] See above n 1.

This subjective weakening of labour law appears both in industrialised economies and in those still in process of developing. But while in the former factors prevail that are consequences of technological and organisational innovation (though other less sophisticated ones, such as informality and fraud, are also present in a lesser extent), in developing countries the subjective weakening process finds its most deeply rooted expressions in informality and other analogously primitive factors. Notwithstanding, in the latter, though to a lesser degree, other more modern and newer factors can also be recognised, especially in the more advanced technological areas.

2. LABOUR DEPENDENCE; A CATEGORY PUT TO THE TEST

A. What's it All About?

In such a context, and among those factors which determine that process of the subjective weakening of labour law, it is my belief that the institution of labour *dependence or subordination*, given its virtual condition of 'master key' that enables the effective application of the rules of labour law to the specific relations containing them, is one of those (the institutions) which require a most careful follow-up. It remains to be seen whether, both at present and in the not so distant future, the idea of labour subordination itself keeps correspondence with the prevailing ways in which human labour is hired and carried out, whether all of them fit into that traditional mould and, as a consequence, whether they provide an answer to their specific needs of regulation and protection; whether, in any case, the universal categorisation of the traditional concept of subordination leaves enough room for the regulatory diversity which is required by the growing productive heterogeneity.

Nevertheless, one cannot help wondering what the importance of these theoretical reflections is in countries such as those in Latin America, where the systems for the protection of work and workers are impaired by some other prevailing factors of subjective weakening, like those which were mentioned above. We should ask ourselves then, given the existence of such circumstances, if it would not be enough to make use of the traditional concept of subordination to encompass in a satisfactory manner 'the remains' of protected work? Isn't wondering in this way 'about the margins' of the system of protection to be under a kind of intellectual delusion, when such a great number of the most intimate components of its condition are within a danger zone, or even directly in a catastrophic situation? From my point of view, this latter thought—even under the circumstances we are going through—does not deserve those objections if we refer to the subject in its plain terms: 'raising the issue' of the category of subordination is worthwhile and sensible only if it is unreservedly admitted that such *issue still has not achieved a quantitative centrality.* However, the crisis in the capacity of labour subordination to cover a wide number of cases is undoubtedly *a far from negligible part, in qualitative terms,* of what is currently taking place. To ignore this involves the risk of leading the system of protection to its own lethargy and death, after its centre of subjective imputation has been gradually wasted away.

B. An Early Hypothesis about the Relative Validity of the Category

By the way, it is convenient to remember that the recognition of the theoretical consistency of the category—even at the height of its success—has been far from peaceful. Not long ago, Paul Davies, quoting Wedderburn, suggested its possible falsehood.[7] Gérard Lyon-Caen would moderate the accusation: he said it was not necessarily false but that it prevailed in the absence of a better one.[8] According to Deveali, this would be, just as happens in other branches of the law and even in other sciences, a concept that is formulated initially to serve as grounds for a specific solution and from then onwards it steadily acquires a general scope and is accepted without further argument, *as if such concept were true and definite, and without taking into account the special circumstances which gave rise to its appearance.*[9]

At the same time, I would like to add a hypothesis to which I will return when I ponder about the necessity to re-formulate the category: the concept of labour subordination was effective until the present because the large majority of the relations it attempted to cover was either clearly within its frontiers or clearly outside them, and neither of these two variations demanded an effort to be qualified. The concept had been conceived from a *dominant social type i*n whose presence the process of qualification of the relation—*simple, evident and almost intuitive*—did not require the formulation of the logical, volitive and complex operation inherent in the practice of using the *indicia* procedure.[10] And here is where its hypothetical weakness

---

[7] P.L. Davies, 'El empleo y el autoempleo. El punto de vista del common law' in *Actas del VII Congreso Europeo de Derecho del Trabajo* (Varsovia, Wydawnictwo Naukowe, 'Scholar', 1999), 175.

[8] G. Lyon-Caen, *Le droit du travail non salarié* (Paris, Sirey, 1990).

[9] M.L. Deveali, *El derecho del trabajo: en su aplicación y sus tendencias,* (Buenos Aires, Astrea, 1983) 179.

[10] A. Montoya Melgar, 'El futuro de la subordinación en la evolución del Derecho del Trabajo' in *Le transformazioni del lavoro. La crisi della subordinazione e l'avvento de nuove forme di lavoro* (Milan, Fondazione Giulio Pastori, Diritto e politiche del lavoro—Franco Angeli, 1999). The indicia procedure is a legal technique used to determine a particular relationship between a worker and someone who pays his wages constitutes—whether or not—an employment contract. This procedure considers a set of factical indicia illustrating the presence of a dependent (in both economic and legal aspects) relationship to establish whether all these indicia, considered as a whole, are more significant that others, detected in the same relationship, suggesting the independent character of the worker.

lies. This technique, which is apt for providing marginal answers in the so-called 'grey cases' (those with a significant low impact in proportion[11]) would have brought to light its evident unfeasibility in terms of *effectiveness and efficiency* if reality had claimed for its systematic 'try out'. What I am suggesting is that the indicia test is a good one only if it is used in a marginal way (to solve situations which exceptionally drift away from the strict model) or that, in other words, the fewer times it is applied, the much more effective it is. The hypothesis would be complete by putting forward the fact that what is happening these days, as regards the deep transformations under way, is that the 'simple, evident and almost intuitive' application is losing its historic prevalence; the exploration of the frontiers of the employment relationship becomes more and more habitual and the technique of the set of indicia unveils—on account of its increasing use—its congenital weakness.

3. THE TRANSFORMATIONS UNDER WAY

This is not the opportunity to enumerate all the determining factors in raising the issue of the category of subordination;[12] it seems more proper to achieve that by referring to the literature which has unveiled more rigorously its judicial, technological and organisational features.[13] Nevertheless, it is convenient to give some information with a view to preventing further thoughts from sinking in the sheer abstraction of theoretical categories.

A. The Changing Work Conditions

Among other phenomena, talk about the changing work conditions is about the dismemberment of the old factory practices which are increasingly diluting due to the increasing circulation of capital,[14] the transformations in

---

[11] And which as a consequence labour law, being busy with social effects of a higher impact, can deal with. On this, I refer to M.L. Deveali, 'El elemento cuantitativo en las normas del derecho del trabajo' in Deveali, above n 9, 84.

[12] In an accurate expression, a basic technical document prepared under the direction of Enrique Marín Quijada for the 'Reunión de expertos sobre los trabajadores en situaciones en las cuales necesitan protección' meeting, convened by the ILO in Geneva from May 15th May 19th 2000, p 25 N0.134 suggested that there was an 'out of focus' approach betweento the (labour) rule and the person whom it must protect, as if such person is displaced or dissociated of the rule's sphere.

[13] Among many others, see J.-E. Rey in several studies, such as 'Le droit du travail . . . une nécessaire adaptation' [1996] *Droit Social* 351; 'Nouvelles technologies et nouvelles formes de subordination' [1992] *Droit Social* 52; 'Le Droit de Travail à l'épreuve du télétravail; le statut de télétravailler' [1996] *Droit Social* 121; 'De Germinal a Internet; Une nécessaire évolution du critère du contrat de travail' [1995] *Droit Social* 634. Also, see J.-L. Beffa, R. Boyer and J.P. Touffut, 'Le droit du travail face à l'héterogénéité des relations salariales' [1999] *Droit Social* 1039, as well as 'Le travail dans vingt ans' rapport de la commission présidée par Jean Boissonat, 'Le travail dans vingt ans' La documentation française (Paris, Editions Odile Jacob, 1995).

[14] J. de Maillard, 'Scolie sur le rapport de subordination' [1982] *Droit Social* 20.

qualifications and the trend towards the prevalence of executives and middle management, intellectual professions, the trades in education and information.[15] It is also about the trends towards less physical and more intellectual work and its consequence, about working hours, which are no longer those of Taylorism, when time was delimited and perfectly measurable in time units. Now time has become diffuse and fragmented, and therefore reluctant to be captured by a labour law that regulates employment in the traditional dimension of time. Such a devaluation of material time, a consequence of the de-materialisation of work, causes the substitution of the subject-matter of the obligations undertaken, which, in turn, becomes more difficult to be expressed as an *obligation of means* (action to be taken), but instead is more easily seen as an *obligation of result*. The institutions and categories of the labour law of arms and bodies and of the labour law of the factory should give way to a labour law of minds;[16] something which implies, without a shadow of a doubt, a noticeable change as regards the level of technical and functional autonomy of the worker but, even greater still, a change in the ways of exercising power by the employer.

B. The Productive Decentralisation

At the same time, the phenomena of productive decentralisation and the strong trend towards the outsourcing of functions, together with the appearance or the widespread use of practices which, in different ways, imply directly or indirectly the recruitment of human labour (subcontracting, casual work, and other means of intermediation, franchising, engineering, supply of goods, concession, distribution, and so on), pose an additional threat to the traditional concept of dependence. Such types of contract actually imply a growing segmentation of attributes and responsibilities inherent in the condition of employer, by virtue of which the power of direction, the appropriation of the fruits of labour, the determination of the place of work, the ownership of the economic interest under whose name the service is rendered, the authority to organise the work to be done, the responsibility for the fulfilment of the services derived from the obligations undertaken, among other attributes and responsibilities, are fragmented or distributed among various contracting parties.

In many of these assumptions, the figure of the 'immediate' employer seems diminished by what we once called the *inconsistency of the employer* derived from the fact that the latter is not, in many of these assumptions,

---

[15] Boissonnat Commission, above n 13.
[16] J.-E. Ray, 'De Germinal', above n 13, and also in 'Nouvelles Technologies', above n 13.

the owner of the main productive asset for which the services are actually rendered.[17] In such cases, the type of relation or the rate that normally exists between the number of workers that the employer hires to work under his charge and the fixed capital destined for its exploitation is broken.[18] Such outsourcing is directed both at auxiliary companies—here is where the possibility for the monetary 'inconsistency' of the employer lies—and at external collaborators under the ever growing form of self-employment, to the detriment of dependent work and not always in violation of the law.[19] Often, those collaborators set up relations that are exclusive, stable and lasting, and which have technical and functional autonomy but which lack a material equality of positions.

D'Antona states that some of the productive transformations of outsourcing make it possible for certain professional services to be hired either under a regime of subordinate employment or under a self-employment one.[20] Pedrazzoli warns that the wide range of labour regulatory schemes blurs the limit between both systems of providing services (subordinate and self employment) 'resulting in a *continuum*; a greater propensity to the blending of the previous forms comprised in either of the two systems'.[21] This blending would be confirmed by 'a wider liberalization . . . of the regulations governing subordinate employment',[22] 'making labour cheaper'[23] and which would replicate such *continuum* in the legislation.

C. Public Policies and Actions by Employers

In many of the phenomena described so far, the will of those who create public policies and that of the parties to the contract would come together, if it actually did, under the utilisation of the contractual options permitted by new technological or organisational advances which would carry the greatest innovative potentialities. Furthermore, we should consider those cases in which resorts to will prevail more directly (the will of the legislating bodies

---

[17] See my 'Trabajo precario y negociación colectiva' in *El empleo precario en Argentina* (Buenos Aires, CIAT/OIT, 1988), 107.

[18] Our communication to the 'Seminario sobre *Libertad de empresa y Relaciones Laborales*' La Toja-Santiago de Compostela, 12–16 Apr., 1993 on the topic 'Las empresas de trabajo temporal en la Argentina', reproduced at Derecho del Trabajo L III B 1031.

[19] W. Sanquinetti Raymond, 'La dependencia y las nuevas realidades económicas y sociales; ¿un criterio en crisis?' [2000] *Doctrina Judicial Laboral* No 2, 5.

[20] M. D'Antona, 'La subordinazione e oltre. Una teoria giuridica per el lavoro che cambia' in M. Pedrazzoli (ed.), *Lavoro subordinato e dintorni. Comparazione e prospettive* (Trento, Il Mulino, 1989), 43.

[21] M. Pedrazzoli, 'Las nuevas formas de empleo y el concepto de subordinación o dependencia' [1989] *Derecho del Trabajo* 1481.

[22] *Ibid.*

[23] Such is the expresion used by A Ojeda Avilés, 'Encuadramiento profesional y ámbito del Derecho del Trabajo' [1988] *Relaciones Laborales (Madrid)* 148.

or, in the proper case, that of the contracting parties). The phenomena of treating salary as if it is another kind of payment (using a spanish neologism, *'desalarización'*, in English, perhaps de-salarisation) or treating a dependent worker as if he is an independent one (also in Spanish, *'deslaboralizacion'*, perhaps de-laborisation) are settled by law itself.[24] A certain reversion in the expansive trend of labour law—here legislation and judicial precedents go hand in hand—should also be considered.[25] Contrary to that expansive trend, 'de-laborisation' is now growing, and the presumptions of labour relationships lose effectiveness and prestige. A certain revaluation of the qualifying capacity of the free will of the parties to a contract[26] can be noticed, which revaluation is sometimes introduced in the legislation itself.[27]

Finally, the growing trend towards what we named 'de-laborisation' at the instance of the employers themselves in a situation which Rodríguez Piñero not long ago called 'avoidance of Labour Law', should be mentioned.[28] This trend also expresses itself by simulation of other types of contracts, the generalisation of the 'atypical' contractual modalities, the 'individualisation' of the labour relationships (avoidance of collective law and of collective activities per se). It also expresses itself by certain expressions of productive decentralisation and, off with modalities previously attributed to the process of organisational transformation, the deliberate and increasing recourse (whether actual or faked) to independent or self-employment.

---

[24] In Argentina, Law 24.700 'de-salarised' several additional benefits, while transporters or freighters were 'de-laborised' by Presidential Decree 1494/92 as well as the contract of apprenticeship by Law 24.465 ('re-laborised' later by Law 25.013). The same logic was applied to mechanisms such as scholarships and traineeships, vouchers and food baskets, etc. As from 1994, the Spanish Employment Legislation (s 1.3 g) excluded 'from the labour area the activity of the people who, holding duly authorised administrative permits, render transport services charging the corresponding price with commercial vehicles fit for public transport whose ownership or direct power of disposition they hold, even when those services are rendered in a continuous way for the same carrier or marketer'.

[25] This trend was based on a complete denial of the capacity of the free will of the parties to qualify the nature (dependent or self-employed) of the employment contract and the validity of a virtual 'in dubio pro laborale': Melgar, above n 10.

[26] M. Rodriguez Piñero, 'La voluntad de las partes en la calificación del contrato de trabajo' (1996) 18 *Relaciones Laborales (Madrid)* 1, states—in my opinion—the matter in its precise terms when he affirms that the will of all of the parties is relevant at the time of choosing and carrying out the true nature of the relationship—the actual character of the services rendered by the worker—but it is not relevant at the time of qualifying the relationship, whenever such qualification intends to depart of the relationship's true nature.

[27] It is the case of the so-called Madelin law passed in France on 11 February, 1994, establishing that the worker's registration as self-employed expressed an act of will that make possible the presumption of his independent insertion into his job. It was a simple presumption, according to public order character of the contract of employment, and could be enervated by means of the accreditation of one performance in a permanent juridically subordinated relationship. Strongly criticised by one part of the doctrine, and without visible effects on the employment situation, this presumption was abrogated by the second law on the 35 hour week (law of 19 Jan., 2000): J. Pelissier, A. Supiot and A. Jeammaud, *Droit du Travail*, (20th edn, Paris, Précis Dalloz, 2000).

[28] Piñero, above n 1.

4. MORE HYPOTHESES FOR A RE-DEFINITION OF THE CENTRE OF IMPUTATION OF LABOUR LAW

A. A Defensive Reaction

It is true and also noticeable that, in a context where such deep transformations are taking place, the traditional concept of labour dependence is aligned with a tendency—which seems to be increasing and irreversible—towards narrowing its scope.[29] This implies that constantly growing cohorts of workers do not respond, as they clearly did in the past—in a way that I have already referred to as 'simple, evident and almost intuitive'—to the paradigmatic figure of the salary-earner. This is why their belonging to the area of protected labour has become doubtful, to say the least.

This time it is not about demands for the softening of the intensity (in scope and contents) of the protection regime, which has always been demanded (but in a much stronger way and by more people during recent decades) by economists and businessmen in an attempt for flexibility or even de-regulation. It is more than that. It is the plain and simple suppression of the condition of protected worker. *It is the most direct path to a situation of 'zero protection'*; a path which, in addition, shows a notorious resistance to ideological challenge since, as it is derived from a whole net of transformations that cannot always be attributed to the will of the interested parties, it does not allow charging responsibilities, requiring compensations or moderating effects by way of settlement in all cases.

Nevertheless, we, should not be surprised by the fact that, even in times of involution of protection, labour law scholars unanimously concur in recognising the importance of this problem.[30] I do not believe this is the time in which the prospective generalisation of labour law will materialise finally to encompass all forms of labour activities.[31] On the contrary, I

---

[29] The process is especially slow in less technically advanced countries, such as those in Latin America. However, in any case, this matter is also present and is part of the current context in these countries.

[30] It was analysed in the European Regional Congress which was held in Warsaw (1999), the World Congress on Labour Law and Social Security (Jerusalem, 2000) and the American Regional Congress (Lima 2001). Also, in the so-called 'Supiot Report' (*Au delà de l'emploi. Transformations du travail et devenir du droit du travail en Europe* (Paris, Flammarion, 1999). It is also being considered and analysed in the ILO (see above n 14). In Argentina, the topic had been discussed in the Jornadas de la Asociación Argentina de Derecho del Trabajo y de la Seguridad Social held in Córdoba in 1995.

[31] I am not referring here to the modern form of the contract proposed by the Boissonnat Report—discussed in the last paragraphs of this chapter—but to the one proposed by Gérard Lyon-Caen (above n 8) which includes salaried and non-salaried workers, who together are the *active workers*. I am also refering to the contracts of activity which Mario Deveali discussed (above n 9, at 163), who held that at one time it would be necessary to abandon the concept of labour contract to group in a large family—that of the contracts of activity—all the contractual forms regulating human activities, such as contracts for services, professional services, agency, industrial companies, cooperatives of production, etc.

believe we face a strictly *defensive* exercise of a regulated system that runs the risk of losing the very cause of its existence[32] if it tolerates losing its subjects.

How is that *defensive* reaction to materialise? Jurists tend to think that if the application of labour law rested on a generic category—that of the *dependent worker* or, more theoretically, that of *dependence or subordination*—and if hypothetically this category stopped interpreting the reality that it intended to refer to, it would be necessary to re-design or create an alternative category, one that has a better correspondence with that reality. As evidenced by the theoretical efforts made in recent years, this task is far from being simple and, moreover, one that I am not able to carry out. But I will try to identify some of the factors that explain the difficulties that hinder the fulfilment of such task. It does not matter how complex it may be, it always seems more proper than the attempt to accommodate by force the facts and relations that currently prevail within the categories formerly used to contain them.

B. 'De-construct' in order to Understand

In an attempt to understand, I have chosen to analyse the way in which the category of subordination was constructed. To do this, one has to retrace the logical path along which it was created to see to what extent it is possible to use a similar methodology and a similar starting point to reach another destiny (another reality, another category).

Even acknowledging that it is possible to decline into simplification, I consider it useful to characterise the process of construction of the concept of labour dependence as a product of the inductive examination of the features characterising the manner in which a typical industrial worker and the owner of a productive organisation related in the setting of the capitalist society. In other words, first came the relationship (what an evocation of Aristotle!) and only after that the theoretical construction of the concept, using the factual contents perceived in every typical individual relationship, reproduced as constants in those relationships of the same type, and transferred inductively to higher levels of abstraction. In this way, a reference 'matrix' is created and this matrix is the conceptual and abstract projection of the actual and material figure of the typical subordinate worker.

From then onwards, the determination of the existence of a dependence relation in each of the specific relationships is the result of its comparison with and adjustment to that 'matrix'. Or, as D'Antona proposes, in a closer

---

[32] Of course, the fact that from such a big crisis a broadening of the centre of imputation of labour law may result cannot be disregarded, nor predicted. As I said earlier in the text, I do not believe this is the perspective that explains the urgent need to think about this topic.

manner (and anticipating the conceptual 'expansion' which I will describe shortly): 'closer to a similarity judgment, in a case by case basis, to the figure of a subordinate worker which has been empirically re-constructed than to an inclusion judgment of a legal type'.[33]

The truth is that labour dependence, whether as a conceptual matrix of reference or as a simple figure, satisfactorily fulfilled the qualifying 'inclusive/excluding' role that the regulatory system assigned to it. It expressed a dominant way of working that enabled the vast majority of relationships to identify themselves without any difficulty at all—I repeat once again, *simple, evident and almost intuitive*. But that matrix also meant a *stylisation of the determinant social type* that would allow the inclusion of other subjects demanding protection,[34] normally in a trial, only now not by means of a strict adjustment operation but by means of a resemblance, similarity,[35] or likeness judgment, whose judicial instance—if it has the appearance of a dependant relationship, then it will be treated as one; if the relationship is too different from a dependant one, then it will be treated as an autonomous one—has always been a political option which the judges have set aside to exercise in each case.[36]

From my point of view, in that process—and in its sustainability—what had a significant impact was the presence of that dominant figure that, in most cases allowed, one to do without that logical and voluntary operation as is the application of the *indicia* method, a method which would only be put to the test marginally, to those cases which are not clear enough and are tried before the courts of law.[37]

Even though the true original rationale of labour legislation lies in the *economic hypo-sufficiency*, as Deveali reminds us, the dominant type mentioned is better noticed in the personal subordination which derived almost invariably from such economic relationship.[38] Hence, the correlative preponderance of the indicators of the *juridical aspect of*

---

[33] Above n 20.

[34] According to M. Rodríguez Piñero ('Contrato de trabajo y autonomía del trabajador' in *Trabajo subordinado y trabajo autónomo en la delimitación de las fronteras del derecho del trabajo* (Estudios en homenaje al Profesor José Cabrera Bazán) (Madrid, Tecnos y Junta de Andalucía, 1999) 23, such separation of the social model of origin—that which, in my opinion, is the product of the 'stylisation' exercise—permitted the construction of a general and universal category of worker, an extremely broad category that surpasses and exceeds the initial range of the industrial labourer, 'even though this will continue being the ideal model of reference for a long time'.

[35] When M. D'Antona refers to 'a similarity judgment on a case by case basis to the figure of a subordinate worker reconstructed empirically' (above n 20), he summarises the whole process: the formulation of a similarity judgment involves both the total adjustment to the conceptual 'matrix' and the use of what we call 'approximation parameters'.

[36] T. Sala Franco, *Lecciones de Derecho del Trabajo* (Valencia, Tirant lo Blanch, 1987), 243.

[37] In absolute terms, a lot; but very few if considered as a percentage of the aggregate number of situations in which services are rendered in an employer–employee relationship.

[38] Deveali, above n 9, at 179.

dependence (instead of its economic one) in the theoretical construction of the concept.[39]

The importance awarded to the juridical-personal aspects of dependence is improper but it has not been problematic so far.

It is improper because, as evidenced by the very protective system,[40] there is no protection regarding the power of direction within the contract—a functional or organizational instrument that does not necessarily result in consequences which are likely to get social reproach—while there is protection regarding the unilateral areas enjoyed by the employer (given his patent bargaining power superiority, of a clear economic nature) at the time of fixing (and later keeping or changing) the working and employment conditions. A careful observation of the rules of protection proves that their purpose is to restrict the otherwise unlimited and unilateral power over fixing such conditions initially and, subsequently, over limiting the employer's hierarchical authority with a view that such conditions cannot be amended unilaterally. Thus, the limits to *ius variandi* (in order to avoid an improper amendment of the contents of the contract), to the *power of direction* in general (to prevent abuse of the employer's authority to specify the contents that were not defined in the contract), to the *disciplinary power* (when exercised, the fulfilment of the contractual conditions is questioned). Contrary to what Deveali stated,[41] it is not the duty to obey but the contractual unilateralism at the time of fixing (and, if applicable, keeping or changing) the working and employment conditions that justifies the protection.

But it has not been problematic so far because in the dominant social type—the one perception of which we have already characterised as simple, evident and almost intuitive—the *power of direction, expressed in the juridical aspect of subordination, coincides in a correlative and general manner with the unilateral predominance of the employer in his power to fix and keep/amend the terms and conditions set out in the contract.* In other words, upon the existence of the legal-personal aspect of dependence what was also implied—being *quod plerumque accidit*—was the contractual predominance of the employer and the resulting social ineffectiveness of the exercise of individual self-regulation, something which justified the collective action and the protective regime.

---

[39] Its economic aspect has been considered a prejudicial fact, 'a fact prior to the contract and alien to it . . . and therefore not useful to qualify it', whereas 'the distinction between contracts should take into account, not the economic standing of the parties, but the legal relations arising from them' (several citations of A. Plá Rodríguez, Cursode Derecho Laboral (Montevideo, ACALI, 1978), ii, at 129 and of A. Rouast, 'Contrat de Travail' in M. Planiol and G. Ripeat, Traité Pratique de Droit Civil Français (Paris, LGDJ, 1932), XI at 13.

[40] I believe, as I will try to propose later, that not only is the protection regime a prescriptive correlation of categories but that such protective regime has a strong influence in the configuration of the category.

[41] Above n 9, at 181.

C. New Ways of Exercising Power

There are changes, such as the ones I have summarised under the previous heading, that involve, as regards matters concerning this analysis, a noticeable alteration in the exercise of power and a tendency towards the vanishing of the dominant type. Both factors tend to undermine that implied idea. In many cases the legal-functional dependence does not last long (*however, not necessarily) regarding the contractual unilateralism to fix the working and employment conditions nor with the resulting need for protection)* and, in any case, the dominant type bursts into a spectrum of growing heterogeneity whose inclusion in the category of legal dependence, for this reason and for the ones mentioned before, ceases to be simple, evident and almost intuitive.[42]

Regarding the first of those factors—noticeable alteration in the exercise of power—it is enough to go over the incomplete inventory of technological, legal and social transformations that I have already mentioned to notice—as obvious as it is—how such alteration shows. One can appreciate the manner in which the discretionary power gives way to the functional power that shows in more complex and diffuse forms.[43] It shows the greater the functional autonomy, the fewer obligations of means, the removal of controls—from the regulation of operations, as is proper of the scientific organisation of work, to the regulation of the criteria for people's performance, according to company principles, rules and standards whose internalisation is required.[44] Outsourcing introduces mediations in the exercise of power which, as a consequence, becomes less consistent; the enjoyment of unspecific and fundamental rights at work is claimed, which rights involve further limitations on such exercise. The de-materialisation of labour and the preponderance of intelligence over the effort of arms and bodies render senseless strict hierarchies, legal subordination, fixed and collective timetables, and disciplinary power.[45]

These and other reasons—namely, the urgent phenomenon of de-standardisation of labour,[46] reclassification and the growing productive heterogeneity—wear down the *dominant type*, which by its gravitation alone legitimated the use of a category, that of legal subordination, which that type invariably displayed.

---

[42] M. Rodríguez Piñero, citing Luca Tamajo, states that the social type and the regulatory prototype—related to a protection system—lose coherence and interdependence when the social changes fragment the unity of the typical social model, allowing the emergence of a plurality of figures that require a differentiation and modulation of the *quantum* and of the modality of rights (above n 34).

[43] See, eg, 'Supiot Report', above n 30.

[44] *Ibid.*

[45] Ray, above n 16, at 647.

[46] A.G. Baylos, 'Igualdad, uniformidad y diferencia en el derecho del trabajo' in [1998] *Revista de Derecho Social* 11.

D. Another Equation to Determine the Needs for Protection

The formula which served as grounds for the application of the protection system [labour + legal-personal subordination] implied, in fact, the bargaining power hypo-sufficiency at the time of fixing and keeping the employment conditions because that was the way the dominant type showed. In an elliptical and pragmatic exercise the focus was placed on the legal aspect of dependence, the easiest to apprehend, actually to reach the ever implied phenomenon of unequal bargaining power, a conspicuous manifestation of economic hypo-sufficiency. Today, legal subordination is losing consistency and the type that contains it, in turn, tends to lose its dominant character. In a constantly increasing number of cases, it has ceased to appear, or, if it appears at all, such presence has a tendency towards not being 'simple, evident and almost intuitive' and requires legal proceedings to be acknowledged.[47] In the best of cases, it seems it is bound to be just one of the varieties in which the formula which really requires a protection system shows, such formula being [labour + contractual inequality], one that lacks novel components. The need for protection has always had its deepest grounds in the terms of that binomial; what is novel is the fact that contractual inequality no longer finds in the legal aspect of dependence its most visible material 'alter ego', its effective intermediary criterion.[48]

[47] J.L. Ugarte Cataldo, *La subordinación jurídica; crónica de una supervivencia anunciada* (document presented in the V American Regional Congress on Labour Law and Social Security, Lima, 16–19 Sept., 2001) affirms that the legal aspect of dependence can more satisfactorily meet the requirements of *effectiveness and efficiency*, since it is perceived more easily by courts. However, if effectiveness involves achieving the goal of protecting all those persons who need such protection and efficiency involves doing that at the lowest possible cost, those requirements are only truly met when the need to resort to the courts is only marginal (as it was until not long ago, on account of the immediate capacity of the legal aspect of dependence of being perceived—in a simple, evident and almost intuitive manner).

[48] Almost 50 years ago (!), Deveali said, with an ability for anticipation which will never cease to surprise, (in *Derecho del Trabajo* [1953]53) that 'it is our opinion that the *concept of legal subordination . . . is doomed to disappear*'. That prediction was not grounded on the relative positions of the planets, but on the idea that 'the concept of legal subordination adopted to characterize the employment contract does not always coincide with that of hypo-sufficiency, which constitutes the real rationale behind labour legislation'. This should be understood as follows: whenever it becomes impossible to sustain the dominant coincidence between economic hypo-sufficiency and legal subordination, the latter criterion will lose its qualifying effectiveness at that moment (at this moment?) and we will have 'to start again from scratch'.

E. The 'Third Category'

The efforts made in recent years by theory, by the legislation of some countries[49] and even by the system of international rules on labour[50] seem to confirm that the matter goes along those paths: the greater the contractual subjection—the contractual inequality—the less perceivable the legal—personal subordination as a generic indicator of imputation of the protection system.[51]

By the way, the response to the challenge of facts—of those facts—is far from being unanimous. In some countries, such as Italy and Germany,[52] the strategy has consisted in tracing the contours of some collectives of autonomous workers in unequal contractual conditions and assigning them protective legislation[53] (I am referring to the *para-subordinate worker* of the Italian experience and the *quasi-employee* of German legislation). However, it should be pointed out that such movement, which was started some decades ago, still did not acknowledge the most recent 'inclusion crisis' of the legal-personal aspect of dependence, but, instead, it did acknowledge dissatisfaction with the dichotomy criterion—dependence/autonomy[54]—which had been taking place over time, and which left (leaves) certain situations that had always included contractual inequality without protection. As Paul Davies has perspicaciously pointed out, this way of constructing the 'third category'—one which many view as an alternative solution to the more modern conceptual problem generated with regard to the centre of imputation of labour law[55]—involves 'penetrating' the interior territory of autonomous workers in order to draw there inner borders (businessman, individual entrepreneur, simple autonomous worker), an exercise we are not used to undertaking.[56] The

---

[49] As pointed out, the Italian legislation, as from Law 533/1973, which introduces the idea of 'para-subordination' and the German legislation, with the figure of the 'quasi-employee', defined in s 12 of the 1974 Law on Collective Agreements. In a less 'intense' way, we should mention the Canadian Code on Labour Matters, which grants the right to collective negotiation to every person, whether or not such person has been hired under a contract of employment or renders services for another person under a contract for services, and the relationship with this person is one of economic dependence (see Davies, above n 7, at 197). Also the first of the final provisions of the Spanish Employment Law which allows progress towards a figure analogous to that of the 'para-subordinate' (the autonomous worker in a situation of economic dependence who needs protection), while it provides that 'work done in condition of self-employment shall not be subject to the labour legislation, except for those aspects specifically and expressly prescribed by law' (Raymond, above n 19).

[50] In the process tending to promote the approval of an international agreement on employment that takes responsibility for the needs of protection of workers whose relationships cannot be clearly included within the category of labour dependence (see, specially, n 12 above).

[51] A. Supiot, 'Trabajo Asalariado y trabajo independiente' in *Actas*, above n 7, at 137.

[52] The German experience has been described by M. Weiss, in 'The Evolution of the Concept of Subordination: The German Experience' in *Le transformazioni*, above n 10, at 57.

[53] Raymond, above n 19.

[54] M. Grandi, 'El problema della subordinazione tra attualita e storia' in *Le transformazioni*, above n 10, at 11.

[55] Among others, J. Barthélémy, 'Le professionnel libéral et les 35 heures' [2000] *Droit Social* 490.

[56] Davies, above n 7.

concept of the autonomous worker has been built in most countries by means of a residual technique (all those workers who are not salaried) which means that the conceptual effort has been invariably oriented towards the salary-earner.[57]

F. Economic Dependence, another 'Set of Indicia'?

There is a second path in sight, which is that of attempting the recovery of the inclusive capacity of the concept of labour dependence by letting it lie mostly on its economic aspect. Of course, it is not enough to state that criterion; in order to make it 'earthly' it would be necessary to rebuild the set of indicia—the indicia system—so that it is fit to fill the set of assumptions to which we intend to submit the protection regime.

Legal scholars, case law and several national pieces of legislation have undertaken this venture, after the purpose of identifying the traces of economic subjection.[58] It is not my aim, at this point, to devote to those traces the analytical efforts they truly deserve; therefore, I shall now proceed, by way of illustration only, to enumerate some of them and continue to sustain hypotheses and interrogations.

As is evident, and before any other consideration, this is about the personal performance of the labour; that condition is present in the Italian concept of *para-subordination,* in the German *quasi-employee,* in some legislation in the Netherlands and even in the United Kingdom, where the distinction lies between the contract for personal services and that contract which can be performed by means of the provision of workers.[59] Another relevant matter is related to the intensity of the performance and, particularly, to the priority the payment of salary has in the worker's income. Also connected to this matter, but in different ways, are the exclusiveness, the ownership (or not) of a client portfolio by the person who considers himself a worker,[60] the continuity of performance.

An interesting experience, described by Manfred Weiss, reports on the efforts of a group of German scholars in search of a new criterion to replace

---

[57] Lyon-Caen, above n 8.

[58] A venture whose viability, anyway, Paul Davies questions in the light of the energetic resistance that nowadays opposes any form of growth of the system of protection (above n 7).

[59] P. Davies and M. Freedland, 'Labour Markets, Welfare and the Personal Scope of Employment Law' (2000) 16 *Oxford Review of Economic Policy* 84.

[60] V. Renaux-Personnic, *L'avocat salarié: entre independence et subordination* (Marseilles, Presses Universitaires d'Aix, 1998), 106, wonders what employer would allow a full-time dependent to develop a personal client portfolio in the same area of business as he acts for such employer? The non-salaried worker owns his tools, bears the risks of his economic activity and enjoys the benefits. Specifically, he chooses his clientele. On the possibilities of an autonomous worker of building his own personal clientele, see also M. Fabre-Magnan, 'Le contrat de travail défini par son objet' in *Le travail en perspectives dirigé par Alain Supiot* (Paris, LGDJ, 1998), 101.

the declining category of subordination.[61] Based on the notion of 'company risks', their research is about a proper balance between the risks and the chances of the company. From this perspective, when an individual is undergoing a situation which poses a business risk to him, but does not allow him to enjoy the correlating advantages, such individual is an employee. On the contrary, he is not an employee if he can act as a businessman in his sole interest and can also enjoy the advantages derived from his activity. Logically, each criterion has its own characterising set of *indicia*: the individual does not own a business organisation, has no collaborators (except for the members of his own family), carries out his activities personally, does not have offices or capital, does not perform activities in the market by himself, is not free to choose the work place or the timetable, does not have his own clients and is not free to set the price of the goods or services. Tested on 938,000 people, the system evidenced superior capacity to acknowledge economic subjection.[62] However, even Manfred Weiss warns about the doubtful usefulness of the proposed criterion. It is a very complex approximation, a new set of indicia whose confirmation would require the formulation, case by case, of a complex, descriptive and logical operation, incompatible with the criteria of *effectiveness and efficiency* that demands the application of legislation such as that of employment protection, characterised by the quantitative data.[63]

It would seem, and this is the hypothesis I consider relevant to formulate at this stage, that in the absence of a perceivable dominant type with the simplicity and evidence which denoted the historical dependent worker, an indicia system built with components such as those proposed—whose reasonableness does not seem debatable to us—may be theoretically rigorous and valid, but, even so, not apt to ensure the efficient allocation—universal, fast, of limited costs—of the protection resources which were created to shelter it.[64]

---

[61] Weiss, above n 52.

[62] While with the traditional criterion of subordination 48% of self-employed workers (19% were clearly employees and the remaining 33% could not be characterised) were registered, with the concept experimented the percentage of self-employed workers decreased to 30% (44% included in the protected category of employees, and 26% who could not be qualified).

[63] Deveali, above n 11.

[64] We mean the criterion of effectiveness described by *ibid.* where he states that while civil law, in seeking perfect justice, usually limits itself to abstract statements which are difficult—sometimes impossible—to apply to the multifarious reality, thus creating conflicts between justice and equity. Labour law, whose rules often have a circumstantial character as they are passed to solve some problems which require an urgent solution (without concern about the principles that could be affected or about the influence the extension of the new rule could have), sacrifices the view of perfect justice for the need of less perfect justice, but one of easy and certain application to all cases. An *indicia test* of such a complex application would not meet such sense of effectiveness, in my opinion. This sense of effectiveness is also implied—although in support of the preservation of the traditional categories—in Grandi's call for attention regarding the risk of substituting the regime of dichotomy of types and subtypes for another regime that introduces the seed of uncertainty and precariousness by compelling attendance to judges in order to confirm their adscription (above n 54).

G. The Hypothesis of Protection Segmentation and the Qualifying Capacity of the Protection Techniques

Another possible response could recognise anticipatory signs in the cases of certain professional groups that were assigned specific protective legislation on account that, in spite of not showing clearly the functional-legal subordination, they did evidence, from an economic perspective, a clear situation of subjection and a resulting need for protection.[65] We might sustain the hypothesis that if a generalisation process of this trend were unleashed, the construction of new conceptual categories would demand a subsequent inductive process, after which they would be the result of the regulations on protected groups, more on account of the assigned protection techniques than on defining features nor necessarily homogeneous.

The starting point of that assumption is the idea that, just as nobody programmed the theoretical construction of the concept of labour dependence, in my opinion, nobody will be able to programme the construction of the categories that will replace this concept. Even so, it is worth formulating some hypotheses which may allow us to interpret some of the directions this process may take. One of them refers to the qualifying capacity of the techniques and contents of protection. This idea, broken into concepts, proposes that the categories in whose search theory displaces, do not refer to an ontological condition that calls for discovery, but they are or will be—at least in a significant dimension—the product of the way (needs, techniques, contents) in which they are assigned a regime or system of protection. Because this is about protection, and the categories that are to have specific protection treatment shall be recognisable '*ex post*', on account of the common legislation they have been assigned.

I think that Rodriguez Piñero, in the negative, evokes a hypothesis such as that when, citing Luca Tramajo, he points out that the social type and the regulatory prototype (our 'reference matrix', or the 'figure' of the remembered D'Antona) that relates to a whole compact protection system loses coherence and interdependence when social changes fragment the unity of the social model, allowing the emergence of a plurality of figures that call for a differentiation and modulation of the *quantum* and of the modality of guarantees.[66]

In that same orientation—acknowledging protection as determinant to the conceptual qualification—we could include the phenomenon of broadening the category of dependence, which took place in France when it was

[65] In Argentina, it is the case of fruit and vineyard contractors, diary middlemen and 'talleristas' (the owner of a small textile factory who works on demand, according to the orders of an entrepreneur). In France, in the words of the Book VII of the Labour Code, it would be the case of certain home-workers, travelling salesmen, and sales persons dedicated to specific territorial areas, reporters, artists and models, maternal assistants, branch managers, etc: Lyon-Caen, above n 8, at 42.

[66] Above n 42.

necessary to provide more people—legally non-dependent—with access to social security protection.[67] I believe we could also add (although this time not as from the construction of the category but as from its effects[68]) when, as Thérèse Aubert-Monpeyssen wittily points out, they choose a particular worker, or they choose the contract that will govern his performance, not due to circumstances conceptually linked to his category, but by the protection legislation that he has with him.[69]

According to this hypothesis, if the fragmentation already mentioned of the dominant type, the growing heterogeneity of the working processes, their de-standardisation and correlative fragmentation of the traditional categories[70] generated a massive assignation of differentiated protection legislation—also breaking the logic of a sole legislation as historically corresponded to that dominant type[71]—it is probable that the construction of broader centres of imputation of the labour legislation will materialise 'ex post', by means of regrouping the categories resulting from such fragmentation on account of common needs—and availabilities—of resources and protection.

If this were the case, these new centres of regulatory imputation, beneficiaries of some common protective content but different in each case in the rest of their legal regimes, would be the result of a specific re-qualifying process. This process would be determined, to a lesser extent, by the subjective nature of the beneficiaries, and to a greater extent, by the common techniques conceived for their protection.

The process could have one more component. On one hand, such correspondence between the sole and exclusive feature of its centre of regulatory imputation (based on the notion of dependence) and the subsequent unity and universality of its protection legislation could 'burst' into a plurality of legislation which would, in turn, determine a correlative variety of specific groups.[72] On the other hand it is probable that another convergent movement, which makes no difference between the more independent (from a juridical perspective) wage-earner and the self-employed, tied by a growing economic subjection impinges on this situation.[73] The definition of some

---

[67] Supiot, above n 51.

[68] Effects that may rebound on the category originating them, requiring their re-definition or that of its legislation.

[69] T. Aubert-Monpeyssen, 'Les frontières du salariat à l'epreuve des stratégies d'utilisation de la force de travail' [1997] *Droit Social* 616.

[70] Baylos, above n 46.

[71] The fragmentation of the protection legislation, which used to be considered a pathological phenomenon, should now be admitted as a natural phenomenon and even as a condition to enable the integration of situations which were previously difficult to incorporate: J. Cruz Villalón, 'El proceso evolutivo de delimitación del trabajo subordinado' in *Trabajo subordinado y trabajo autónomo en la delimitación de las fronteras del derecho del trabajo, Estudios en Homenaje al Profesor José Cabrera Bazán* (Madrid, Ed. Tecnos y Junta de Andalucía, 1999), 170.

[72] Renaux-Personnic, above n 60.

[73] Supiot, above n 51.

new categories—new centres of imputation of labour law—would be in that case the complex expression of those simultaneous trends of diversification and convergence.

5. INCLUSIVE CAPACITY OF DEPENDENCE AND CONTINUITY OF PROTECTION

Together with the conceptual 'out of focus'[74] put forward by what we have denominated 'inclusion crisis' of the idea of dependence, there is one additional 'out of focus' stemming out from the other term of the protection equation.[75] We will deal now with the loss of effectiveness of the protection system owing to the temporal asymmetry paradox between the needs for protection and performance at work: the continuity of the need for protection is impaired by increasing discontinuities of performances and careers.

To pose both problems in a way that relates them, we could say that, in the first case, the problem is how, from a synchronous perspective, we can make the system of labour protection protect, at the same time, all of the persons entitled to protection; in the other case, the question raised, from a sequential perspective, is how to protect each one of them all the time.

Indeed, this is an issue different from that of the *frontiers of labour dependence* and that is why, I will not deal with this in depth (it deserves reflections much lengthier than the whole of this document); I just want to point out in what way they are different, but also to what extent the answers to one of those issues could prove functional to solve the following.

Speaking more generally, the problem consists in securing the continuity of the protection during the transition between one paid job and another, of 'filling the gaps'. Apart from the working times paid (dependent, autonomous, assimilated to one or the other), this is about the times of unemployment, but also of professional training, of paying attention to family commitments, of solidarity work, of performing civic duties, of resting.[76]

---

[74] An image the origin of which we identified in n 12 above.

[75] An equation that relates the protected subject (centre of imputation of the labour legislation) to the legislation that defines techniques and contents included in such protection.

[76] Alain Supiot states that the rights of workers should concern all forms of personal activity at somebody else's service, which forms may mix and take place in the life of any of them. This includes voluntary work which, in the author's opinion, is fundamental for survival in a certain society (he gives as an example work within the family in order to enhance working power). As long as the job is useful for society, it would be convenient to assign it a set of social rights and a protection system (his introduction in *Le Travail en perspective* (Paris, LGDJ, 1998), 1.

The Boissonat Report[77] states that situations such as those can be dealt with through traditional insurance techniques which 'rest on the ground of quotation—service', a solution which would not introduce significant fragmentation with the current management forms. However, the Boissonat Report itself also states that such a solution would only provide a response to those situations under the classical labour contract and, therefore, would exclude those who are outside it (for example, independent work and its own 'gaps').

A. Some Proposals

And that is why, in the context of a proposal for a radical transformation of the legal and institutional frame, the Boissonat Report proposes the creation of a new legal category consisting in a framework agreement with a moral person (association, group of public interest, local states, local companies, institutions of public or private education), which coordinates employment policies together with their needs and guarantee the employee, during his dependent performance, but also at different stages in his career (such as those of autonomous work, the time of training, resting time, time for paying attention to family commitments, of solidarity work, of performing civic or family duties, etc.) the continuity of minimum compensation and certain social protection.[78]

In this way, the limitation of an individual relationship to a contract between a salaried worker and a legally defined employer responsible for only one company would be avoided, allowing the diffusion of social and economic liability beyond the company, particularly in the area of sub-contracting and co-contracting. From that perspective, the contract of activity would favour mobility, which would not amount to precariousness, insecurity or exclusion; in turn, the system would itself benefit from the adaptation skills required and those companies with flexibility and ability to react will contribute to improving their competitiveness starting from a cooperative organisation and a mutual flexibility. To that end, the contract of activity would enjoy productive flexibility, work evolution and continuity of personal careers.

A further consideration, that of the Supiot Report, adds that the construction of the contract of activity brings to life the idea of defining

---

[77] This is what the research work *Le travail dans vingt ans*, rapport de la Commission présidée par Jean Boissonnat, La documentation francaise (Paris, Editions Odile Jacob, 1995) is called.

[78] I choose a grossly schematic characterisation, for the purposes of this mention, even at the risk of incurring disloyal simplification. See F. Gaudu, 'Travail et activité' [1997] *Droit Social* 119. By same author and about the same topic, also see 'Du statut de l'emploi au statut de l'actif' [1995] *Droit Social* 535.

professional legislation to form part of the demands for individualisation and mobility of the professional careers required by employers and that labour law should take into account so as not severely to hinder the display of the modern methods of work organisation. In such context, he concludes, there is an attempt to guarantee, by all means, the continuity of protection, not necessarily on the grounds of holding a job, but about the continuity of protection legislation that transcends the various situations a worker experiences along his professional career.

B. A Latin American Appreciation

It is evident that they are highly sophisticated institutional constructions, whose financial mechanics seem far out of reach at present in the countries of Latin America, given the scarcity of economic and organisational resources.[79] However, it is interesting to include in this chapter this reference by the strength with which both documents—the Boissonat and Supiot Reports—have caused figures of this type to be present in the European debates. It is also interesting because institutional creations of this type, even far from their integral materialisation, may serve to lead the way and explain the direction of the intermediary stages in a sequence of conceiving a new design which labour law will hardly be able to prevent.[80]

Finally, it is interesting (and mainly this is why we have given it this schematic mention) because it enables us to perceive in what way a figure like the one proposed, when the protection system is assigned exterior frontiers significantly more inclusive—and included within such frontiers we can find dependent or autonomous employment, and all the intermediary variations, time for professional training, for resting, for paying attention to family commitments, etc.)—it certainly reduces the negative balances that, in terms of protection resources, can be noticed in its limits or interior frontiers (in such context, the frontiers of dependence are circumscribed).

---

[79] It can be financed by the State, by the social security institutions, by mutual joint committees, by companies, by the worker himself in the form of credit for time worked but not paid, waiver of part of a previous income, etc. (from the Supiot Report; in the same sense see Gaudu, above n 78). Its utilisation is proposed in the Supiot Report; it should be subject to a financial logic proper of the social drawing rights which the worker holder of a contract of activity could use to apply them to a specific social imputation (that of its support). This would be a function—right, which means it could not be freely endorsed for the benefit of a third party. I considered this proposal (specially the version included in the Supiot report) from a Latin-American point of view in a paper published in (1999) 20 *Comparative Labour Law and Policy Journal* 681, under the title 'Labour Law beyond Employment: A Latin-American Perspective'.

[80] T. Priestley, 'A propos du "contrat d'activité" proposé par le rapport Boissonnat' [1995] *Droit Social* 955.

6. BY WAY OF CONCLUSION

Not long ago, Robert Castel wondered whether the labour protection system would undergo either a process of mere re-deployment (to recover or include those categories of workers which currently seem to have been left out of its rules and institutions) or a deeper transformation, a true *institutional re-foundation*.[81]

Castel was inclined, very cautiously, to believe the first of these two alternatives.

I am not quite sure. If it is true that labour law is trying to lay new foundations on an equilibrium which still has to be achieved, if the policies on labour law cannot recognise and adapt to contexts that have changed considerably and keep doing so, if the prevailing techniques will no longer be necessarily the same, if the legislation will have to re-define its very centre of imputation of labour rules and regulations, then we should not discard the possibility that labour law has a *re-foundational*[82] destiny ahead.

A re-foundation without founders, as was the origin of the labour law we are engaged in, but which should also express that fight, probably never-ending, that mankind has always taken part in for equity and justice.

---

[81] R. Castel, 'Droit du travail: redéploiement ou refondation?' [1999] *Droit Social* 438.

[82] It is probable that this reference to the idea of *re-foundation* has, in the French experience and in Castel's evocation, a specific meaning linked to episodes and proposals that were generated in their own context. My use of the term was not intended to convey such specific national background.

7

The Reports of My Death are Greatly Exaggerated: 'Employee' as a Viable (Though Over-used) Legal Concept

GUY DAVIDOV*

1. INTRODUCTION

'WHO IS AN employee' has always been a tough question, and in recent years an increasing number of commentators is tempted to answer 'don't ask'. Calls for dissolving the employee/independent contractor distinction are increasing.[1] Indeed, when one is repeatedly confronted with a difficult question, it is worth pondering every once in a while whether there is still point in asking it. And so with the age-old employee/independent contractor distinction, it is pertinent to examine whether the continued use of the distinction in law is justified—whether the concept of 'employee' is still viable and can play a useful role.

While the concept of 'employee' is used in various areas of law, this chapter is limited to the context of protective labour and employment laws. In this particular setting, the distinction between employees and independent contractors purports to separate those who require protection, and there is

* Faculty of Law, University of Haifa, Israel. Thanks go to Ruth Ben-Israel, Judy Fudge, Oren Gazal and Sharon Rabin-Margalioth for insightful comments on an earlier draft; remaining shortcomings are of course solely my own.
[1] See A. Brooks, 'Myth and Muddle—An Examination of Contracts for the Performance of Work' (1988) 11 *University New South Wales Law Journal* 48; M. Linder, 'Dependent and Independent Contractors in Recent U.S. Labor Law: An Ambiguous Dichotomy Rooted in Simulated Statutory Purposelessness' (1999) 21 *Comparative Labor Law & Policy Journal* 187; R. R. Carlson, 'Why the Law Still Can't Tell an Employee When It Sees One And How It Ought to Stop Trying' (2001) 22 *Berkeley Journal of Employment and Labor Law* 295; J. Fudge, E. Tucker and L. Vosko, 'Employee or Independent Contractor? Charting the Legal Significance of the Distinction in Canada' (2002) 10 *Canadian Labour and Employment Law Journal* 193.

a specific employer that can and should take responsibility for their well-being, from those who can (presumably) take care of themselves in the market environment.[2] The discussion is not merely conceptual, then. It is rather an examination of the viability and usefulness of an important instrument for the delivery of workers' rights.

Scholars have raised a number of arguments in opposition to the continued use of the employee/independent contractor distinction (and the concept of 'employee') in law. Four arguments merit attention: that the concept of 'employee' serves to exclude some people who are not employees nor independent contractors; that basic assumptions at the heart of the distinction concerning inequality of bargaining power are no longer valid, if they ever have been; that the concept of employee is vague and 'indefinable'; and that the classification into groups of workers is too rigid and should give way to context-specific determinations of the scope of each regulation. The purpose of this chapter is to examine the merits of these four arguments. It will be shown that none of them can justify abandoning the concept. At the same time, they all provide important and useful insights into the way this concept should be practically used.

2. 'EMPLOYEE'—EXCLUSIONARY?

The first argument against the employee/independent contractor distinction does not concern the different treatment of those employed and those who are self-employed, but rather focuses on those excluded from the inquiry altogether. If we assume, at this stage, that independent contractors are those who can (broadly speaking) take care of themselves, and that it is somehow possible to differentiate independent contractors from employees, then there is nothing unjustified in excluding independent contractors from some regulatory protections. But the distinction can be attacked for excluding unpaid work, particularly the work of many women at home.[3] More generally, it has also been argued that excluding the unemployed in this framework is unjustified.[4]

---

[2] See G. Davidov, 'The Three Axes of Employment Relationships: A Characterization of Workers in Need of Protection' (2002) 52 *University of Toronto Law Journal* 357.

[3] See J. Conaghan, 'Work, Family, and the Discipline of Labour Law' in J. Conaghan and K. Rittich (eds.), *Labour Law, Work and Family: Critical and Comparative Perspectives* (Oxford, Oxford University Press, 2005), 19. For critiques of the paid/unpaid work distinction, although not specifically in the context of the definition of 'employee,' see also, eg, M.M. Ertman, 'Love and Work: A Response to Vicki Schultz's Life's Work' (2002) 102 *Columbia Law Review* 848; K. Rittich, 'Transformed Pursuits: The Quest for Equality in Globalized Markets' (2000) 13 *Harvard Human Rights Journal* 231, at 244.

[4] See M. Linder, *The Employment Relationship in Anglo-American Law: A Historical Perspective* (Westport, Conn, Greenwood, 1989) 239–41. Linder seems to argue against the employee/independent contractor distinction in general, although he refers almost entirely to the context of social security in his reasoning. His argument is tied with criticism on the uncertainty of the distinction, which is discussed here separately at sect. 4 below.

However, the most basic characteristic of 'employees' is that they require protection in their relationship vis-à-vis a specific employer, and at least to some extent the employer is seen as responsible for such protection. This is both at the administrative level—the employer is the one often required to make sure that some work rules (e.g. maximum hours) are observed; and at the distributive level—the employer is often required to bear the costs of workers' protection, to internalise the indirect costs of employing people rather than externalising them. Unpaid workers, on the other hand, do not have an 'employer' who benefits from their labour and can be asked to pay the costs of their protection. This is not to suggest that their work is less beneficial or important, or that it is not productive. But there are significant differences that justify differential treatment as far as protective labour and employment laws are concerned. There is no 'employer' who can bargain individually or collectively with them. Nor is there an 'employer' who can be required to ensure that certain rules are obeyed concerning their work. The separation of the employed from the unemployed is even more fundamental—not only that there is no employer to deal with, there is not even 'work' that requires certain kinds of protection.

So when it comes to hours of work, or minimum wages, or collective bargaining for example, there is clearly a difference between 'employees' and unpaid workers, or the unemployed, that justifies differential treatment. At least in some contexts, the concept of 'employee' relates to legally significant factual differences among individuals, even if it appears to exclude certain people from its ambit. But while the under-inclusiveness critique is not compelling as far as the existence and viability of 'employee' as a legal concept is concerned, it is certainly relevant in determining where exactly this concept should be put to use. This critique is best understood as directed against the instances in which the employee/independent contractor distinction is used, not against the distinction itself.

Numerous rights are tied to the existence of an employment relationship, in some cases without valid justification. The employment relationship has been used for many years as a vehicle to deliver a set of entitlements, based on two presumptions: that almost all people who work for remuneration do so as employees, and that the vast majority of employees fit the traditional mould, ie they are men who support families, in long-term, full-time, stable jobs. As these traditional assumptions increasingly lose their validity,[5] the ties between the employment relationship and different entitlements must be revisited to ensure that some people (whether they are unemployed, unpaid workers or independent contractors) are not unjustly excluded.

---

[5] See recently K.V.W. Stone, *From Widgets to Digits: Employment Regulation for the Changing Workplace* (Cambridge, Cambridge University Press, 2004), ch 4.

Indeed, in recent years there is a growing consensus among scholars that the concept of 'employee' has been over-used, in the sense that some of the rights that currently apply only to employees should be enjoyed by broader groups.[6] Human rights are an obvious example; there seems to be no reason why protection against racial discrimination, for example, should not apply to independent contractors just like employees.[7] Health care, basic social security and health and safety protection should similarly be available to independent contractors as well. But the critique goes further than that; the linkage between employment and other rights must also be questioned. The British legislature appears to have been attuned, more than many others, to these concerns. Over the past few years a number of rights (concerning working time, minimum wage, deductions from wages, grievance hearings and part-time work) have been broadened to apply to all 'workers', rather than merely employees.[8] Then again, these developments have been more of a (limited) response to the narrow interpretation given by British courts to the concept of 'employee', rather than the result of an overall rethinking of the appropriate uses of the concept.[9]

---

[6] See *Meeting of Experts on Workers in Situations Needing Protection (The Employment Relationship: Scope)—Basic Technical Document* (Geneva, International Labour Office, 2000), available at: http://www.ilo.org/public/english/dialogue/ifpdial/publ/mewnp/; A. Supiot, *Beyond Employment: Changes in Work and the Future of Labour Law in Europe* (Oxford, Oxford University Press, 2001) (previously published as European Commission, *Transformation of Labour and Future of Labour Law in Europe: Final Report* (Brussels, European Commission, 1999)); Linder, above n 1; B. Langille and G. Davidov, 'Beyond Employees and Independent Contractors: A View From Canada' (1999) 21 *Comparative Labor Law & Policy Journal* 7.

[7] See A. Hyde, *Classification of U.S. Working People and its Impact on Workers Protection: A Report Submitted to the International Labour Office* (January 2000), s 7.1.4, available at: http://www.ilo.org/public/english/dialogue/ifpdial/downloads/wpnr/usa.pdf; L.L. Maltby and D.C. Yamada, 'Beyond "Economic Realities": The Case for Amending Federal Employment Discrimination Laws to Include Independent Contractors' (1997) 38 *Boston College Law Review* 239; P. Davies and M. Freedland, 'Employees, Workers, and the Autonomy of Labour Law' in H. Collins, P. Davies and R. Rideout (eds), *Legal Regulation of the Employment Relation* (London, Kluwer, 2000) 267; S. Engblom, 'Equal Treatment of Employees and Self-Employed Workers' (2001) *International Journal of Comparative Labour Law and Industrial Relations* 211.

[8] Employment Rights Act 1996, s 230(3); National Minimum Wage Act 1998, s 54(3); Working Time Regulations 1998, reg 2; Employment Relations Act 1999, ss 12(6), 13(1); Part-Time Workers (Prevention of Less Favourable Treatment) Regulations 2000, reg 1.

[9] See G. Davidov, 'Who is a Worker?' (2005) 34 *Industrial Law Journal* 57. And see B. Burchell, S. Deakin and S. Honey, 'The Employment Status of Individuals in Non-Standard Employment' (March 1999), available at: http://www.dti.gov.uk/er/emar/emar6.pdf; P. Davies and M. Freedland, 'Labor Markets, Welfare and the Personal Scope of Employment Law' (1999) 21 *Comparative Labor Law & Policy Journal* 231, at 241; S. Anderman, 'The Interpretation of Protective Employment Statutes and Contracts of Employment' (2000) 29 *Industrial Law Journal* 223, at 240.

An impressive attempt at such rethinking was included in the influential 'Supiot Report', a report prepared by a group of experts led by Alain Supiot for the European Commission, which challenges the dominance of employment status as a basic requirement for various entitlements.[10] Given the lack of security in today's jobs, the rise in self-employment, the need for constant training, and particularly the frequent shifts from one status to the other (employee, self-employed, unemployed, unpaid worker, training)— the Report recommends that emphasis be shifted from employment status to 'labour force membership status'. The idea is to provide security by allowing people to preserve their rights throughout their working lives and especially through changes in status.

More generally, the Report points out that labour and social security laws are currently divided, in terms of the scope of their application in different European countries, between four concentric circles.[11] The outer circle is universal, ie covers 'everyone irrespective of any kind of work'. Rights for health care, for example, are guaranteed, at least in most countries and to some extent universally.[12] The second circle covers unpaid work, such as care for other people, training on one's own initiative or voluntary work. People within this circle enjoy, in some countries, retirement benefits linked to child rearing, accident coverage for certain kinds of volunteer work, etc. The third circle covers any kind of paid work. Health and safety regulations, for example, usually cover independent contractors as well as employees. Lastly, the fourth (inner) circle covers only 'employees', who enjoy all the previously mentioned rights and numerous others. The Report offers this typology as a framework for defining 'labour force membership status'. There is no intention to supersede the employment status. 'Labour force membership status' is intended to point out the different circles involved, to trigger a rethinking of the appropriate circle of application for each right, and especially to address the shifts between the circles and point towards the need for some continuity and security in this regard.

These goals are laudable and the Supiot Report does an admirable job in addressing them. It is important to make clear, however, that nothing in the Report argues against the employee/independent contractor distinction or the concept of 'employee' per se. It is rather an argument regarding the proper use of this concept and the need to address changes in status that people go through throughout their adult lives. Indeed, where the Report

---

[10] Supiot, above n 6, ch 2.

[11] *Ibid.*, at 54.

[12] To be more precise, such rights can be limited to citizens or residents. But for our purposes here the important point is their availability irrespective of one's labour market status.

deals directly with the employee/independent contractor distinction,[13] some possible improvements to the application of the distinction are put forward, but it is not suggested that the distinction should be abandoned.

3. INEQUALITY OF BARGAINING POWER

While the first argument was directed against the exclusion of people who are neither employees nor independent contractors, the second argument challenges the distinction between these two familiar groups, arguing that the basic assumptions behind the distinction are mistaken or at least anachronistic.

It is often said that the basic characteristic of an employment relationship—which is also the background reason for all protective labour and employment regulations—is the inequality of bargaining power between the individual employer and the individual employee.[14] The existence of unequal bargaining power is usually taken for granted by labour lawyers, but for many economists the whole idea is conceptually flawed. They believe that labour markets—like all other markets—work according to principles of supply and demand, and 'power' is not a factor in these calculations.[15] This challenge requires some exploration into the meaning of 'inequality of bargaining power'.[16]

For current purposes, the concept of unequal bargaining power can be understood at two levels, one within and the other outside the confines of neo-classical economic theory.[17] Understood from within economic theory,

---

[13] *Ibid.*, ch 1.

[14] See P. Davies and M. Freedland, *Kahn-Freund's Labour and the Law* (3rd edn, London, Stevens, 1983), 18.

[15] See, eg, A.A. Alchian and W.R. Allen, *University Economics: Elements of Inquiry* (3rd edn, Belmont, Cal, Wadsworth, 1972), 427–8; M.O. Reynolds, 'The Myth of Labor's Inequality of Bargaining Power' (1991) 12 *Journal of Labor Research* 167; S.J. Schwab, 'The Law and Economics Approach to Workplace Regulation' in B.E. Kaufman (ed.), *Government Regulation of the Employment Relationship* (Madison, Wis, IRRA, 1997) 91, at 111.

[16] It should be noted that the concept of 'inequality of bargaining power' has a different meaning when invoked in the context of contract law. In the latter context, it refers to a doctrine which assumes that power is usually equal; only in the exceptional cases where power is unequal is there justification for not enforcing a contract (see D. Kennedy, 'Distributive and Paternalistic Motives in Contract and Tort Law, With Special Reference to Compulsory Terms and Unequal Bargaining Power' (1982) 41 *Maryland Law Review* 563, at 621). Note, however, that 'inequality of bargaining power' in employment relationships is assumed to be the *norm* rather than an exception. Moreover, in the context of labour and employment laws the concept is used to justify protection ex ante rather than ex post.

[17] See B.A. Langille, 'General Reflections on the Relationship of Trade and Labor (Or: Fair Trade is Free Trade's Destiny)' in J. Bhagwati and R.E. Hudec (eds), *Fair Trade and Harmonization (Vol 2): Legal Analysis* (Cambridge, Mass, MIT Press, 1996) 231, at 243. At both levels, my reference—in accordance with the common usage of the concept—is not specifically to bargaining, in the sense of negotiating or haggling, but more generally to power inequalities in setting the terms of the relationship. See C.E. Lindblom, '"Bargaining Power" in Price and Wage Determination' (1948) 62 *Quarterly Journal of Economics* 396, at 400 and 411.

the phrase 'unequal bargaining power' is simply a shorthand for a number of market failures,[18] resulting in the relative inability of the employee (compared with the employer) to influence the wage rate and other contract terms. In theory, in a perfectly competitive full-employment market the wage is determined by supply and demand, and neither party has any ability to influence it. But this is hardly a prevalent scenario in real life. Whenever employers' competition for labour is limited—ie there are impediments to the ability of workers to take other, comparable jobs—employers have the power to lower wages and working conditions below those that employees would have accepted in a perfectly competitive full-employment market.[19] Thus, for example, monopsony conditions (few buyers of labour) in local labour markets and collusive agreements among employers leave workers with little choice but to accept the terms dictated to them.[20] Information asymmetries mean that employees are often unaware of the terms that they can achieve and thus are willing to work for less.[21] Bounded rationality, together with information deficiencies, also means that many employees do not fully understand the terms of their engagement, particularly with regard to pensions or other complex benefits. The costs of searching for and moving between jobs are often significant, similarly impairing workers' ability to enter and exit employment freely.[22] Firm-specific training, pension rights and benefits based on tenure all tie workers to the specific firm and limit their ability to find a suitable substitute elsewhere, thus also allowing the employer to pay less than the fully competitive wage rate. Finally, the existence of unemployment (due to the other failures) gives employers—who no longer face unlimited competition for labour—further powers to lower wages and working conditions.[23] All of these discrepancies between the perfectly competitive full-employment market and real life

---

[18] See F. Machlup, *The Political Economy of Monopoly: Business, Labor and Government Policies* (Baltimore, Mid, Johns Hopkins, 1952), 369–70.

[19] B.E. Kaufman, 'Labor's Inequality of Bargaining Power: Changes over Time and Implications for Public Policy' (1989) 10 *Journal of Labor Research* 285; B.E. Kaufman, 'Labor's Inequality of Bargaining Power: Myth or Reality?' (1991) 12 *Journal of Labor Research* 151; A. Manning, *Monopsony in Motion: Imperfect Competition in Labor Markets* (Princeton, NJ, Princeton University Press, 2003).

[20] Monopsony has traditionally been considered by economists to be extremely rare, if not merely theoretical. But recently many economists are willing to relax the definition and consider it more common. See D. Card and A.B. Krueger, *Myth and Measurement: The New Economics of the Minimum Wage* (Princeton, NJ, Princeton University Press, 1995), ch 11; W.M. Boal and M.R. Ransom, 'Monopsony in the Labor Market' (1997) 35 *Journal of Economic Literature* 86; Manning, above n 19, at 3.

[21] See S.L. Willborn, 'Individual Employment Rights and the Standard Economic Objection: Theory and Empiricism' (1988) 67 *Nebraska Law Review* 101.

[22] See Manning, above n 19; J. Stiglitz, 'Democratic Development as the Fruits of Labor' (Keynote Address, IRRA Conference, Boston, Jan. 2000), available at: http://www.lera.uiuc.edu/meetings/Annual/2000/StiglitzSpeech.PDF.

[23] See Kaufman, above n 19.

explain why employers often enjoy a superior market position over employees, and these situations can usefully be considered 'inequality of bargaining power'. The existence of such inequality thus becomes an empirical question. Economically speaking, inequality of bargaining power exists in a given employment relationship when there are market failures resulting in the employer having more ability than the employee to influence the terms of the contract.

A market analysis can be useful, as it holds the theoretical promise of not only efficiency but the promotion of liberty and autonomy as well.[24] But this is hardly the whole picture, as is bluntly revealed when reading the following argument by two market enthusiasts:

> Suppose the proposition is true that employers as a class are wealthier than employees. What follows is an 'inequality of bargaining power' only in the sense that employers systematically could outbid employees for resources in the open market . . . Conceive of a 'job' as an amount of time held by employees, which they can spend on themselves or in the service of employers . . . Because employees need money more than employers do, employees will surrender their 'leisure' time, the time that employees 'purchase' from themselves, in order to work for the richer class of employers. By the same token, rich employers will be in a position to outbid employees for terms of employment . . . If this is the sense in which inequality of bargaining power is thought to exist between employers and employees, it demonstrates not market failure but market success. A market is successful when it moves resources from lower-value to higher-value uses.[25]

This is undoubtedly true from a pure market perspective, but the 'success' of the market can be devastating for the individual employee. Indeed, even when the market works perfectly, and the worker is able to secure her competitive wage, it is still possible that some aspects of the contract will not be considered acceptable by society. For example, it may sometimes be efficient, and an employee may agree, that the employer act with discrimination, or ignore safety requirements, or pay below the minimum wage, or for the employee to work 18 hours each day—but society does not accept these arrangements. Broadly speaking, the reason is that in some circumstances

---

[24] See generally M.J. Trebilcock, *The Limits of Freedom of Contract* (Cambridge, Mass, Harvard University Press, 1993).

[25] M.G. Freed and D.D. Polsby, 'Just Cause For Termination Rules and Economic Efficiency' (1989) 38 *Emory Law Journal* 1097, at 1100. See also H. Collins, 'Justifications and Techniques of Legal Regulation of the Employment Relation' in H. Collins, P. Davies and R. Rideout (eds), *Legal Regulation of the Employment Relation* (London, Kluwer, 2000), 3, at 11 (noting that according to regulation theory, 'poor pay for arduous jobs is the product of a competitive market, not a sign of market failure that might justify intervention').

market ordering does not promote—but rather infringes upon—liberty and autonomy, or simply that society insists on the primacy of other values.[26] And at least in some cases, it means that we do not allow a certain arrangement—even if it is efficient—because the existing distribution of resources made the acceptance by the employee a hollow one.[27] The acceptance of an unreasonable offer due to lack of freedom to chose otherwise can also be seen as inequality of bargaining power.[28]

The concept of unequal bargaining power can thus be understood as referring to any situation in which the employer has more power than the employee to affect the terms of the engagement, whether due to market failures or the background allocation of resources. At the end of the day, the existence of such inequality is therefore an empirical question, and one that is extremely difficult to measure. Although there is certainly specific evidence that labour markets are not competitive,[29] and although historically this was

---

[26] Langille, above n 17, at 244–5.

[27] As Adam Smith famously noted, 'it is not . . . difficult to foresee which of the two parties must, upon all ordinary occasions, have the advantage in the dispute, and force the other into a compliance with their terms. . . . The masters can hold out much longer. . . . Many workmen could not subsist a week, few could subsist a month, and scarce any a year without employment': Adam Smith, *The Wealth of Nations* (Harmondsworth, Penguin, 1970), 169. The length of time and the severity of the situation may be somewhat different in a modern welfare state (particularly thanks to unemployment insurance), but the basic inequality of power is still obvious. Another way to put this, which is perhaps more 'internal' to economic theory, is to say that since employees are normally less wealthy than their employers, they are more risk averse to the possibility of unemployment, and will thus accept terms which they would not have accepted as risk-neutral: see M.W. Reder, 'On Labor's Bargaining Disadvantage' in C. Kerr and P.D. Staudohar (eds.), *Labor Economics and Industrial Relations: Markets and Institutions* (Cambridge, Mass, Harvard University Press, 1994), 237.

[28] See D.M. Beatty, 'Labour is Not a Commodity' in B.J. Reiter and J. Swan (eds.), *Studies in Contract Law* (Toronto, Butterworths, 1980), 313, at 334–5. As it is often put, workers often face a 'take it or leave it' choice, and they have to accept the terms stipulated by their employers in order to subsist. See M. Weber, *Economy and Society* (G. Roth and C. Wittich eds., Berkeley, Cal, University of California Press, 1978), 730. It has been argued that a shopper faces the same 'take it or leave it' choice, without ability to influence the price of commodities: W.H. Hutt, *The Strike-Threat System: The Economic Consequences of Collective Bargaining* (New Rochelle, NY, Arlington House, 1973), 67; and see A.A. Alchian and H. Demsetz, 'Production, Information Costs, and Economic Organization' (1972) 62 *American Economic Review* 777. But a shopper regularly has a wide range of such choices in competing shops, while workers often face only a single offer. Furthermore, shopping for a product is not like looking for a job that one must have in order to subsist. Indeed, the sale of basic subsistence products and situations of lack of competing shops are both heavily regulated just like the labour market.

[29] See, eg, D. Watson, 'U.K. Wage Underpayment: Implications for the Minimum Wage' (2000) 32 *Applied Economics* 429 (showing that workers commonly accept wages below their marginal productivity); Card and Krueger, above n 20 (showing that markets do not behave according to the expectations of the competitive model); Manning, above n 19 (showing that labour markets are usually characterised by monopsony); S. Machin and A. Manning, 'A Test of Competitive Labor Market Theory: The Wage Structure Among Care Assistants in the South of England' (2004) 57 *Industrial and Labor Relations Review* 371 (finding that the wage structure deviates in important respects from what would be expected in a competitive labour market).

obvious to most prominent economists from Adam Smith onwards,[30] the reining Chicago School insists that imperfections are relatively unimportant and labour markets can be treated as if they were fully competitive. While this is contested by many others,[31] it does reveal the difficulty of relying on the concept of inequality of bargaining power as the basis for labour and employment laws. And proving that someone accepted a job because the allocation of resources left her with no other choice is not less difficult. It is practically impossible to show, empirically, that this is the regular scenario for defined groups of workers; especially given that some degree of inequality of resources always exists in the market. Indeed, inequality of bargaining power, as defined above, exists in various degrees not only in employment relationships but in many commercial relations as well.

Hence, while not meaningless, as some economists argue, the concept of unequal bargaining power certainly appears to be problematic. It suffers from inherent vagueness, and in itself, it cannot provide much help in determining who should be considered an 'employee'. But this does not mean that employment is a relationship between equals, or that there is no difference between employees and independent contractors. To be sure, there have always been exceptionally powerful employees, and their numbers are rising as knowledge becomes so crucial for businesses. But the paradigm continues to be a relationship of asymmetric vulnerability, unlike the situation in business relations between independent contractors.

As far as the concept of 'employee' is concerned, the solution is simple. Rather than focus on the background (but problematic) fact of inequality in order to give it meaning and draw its borders, we should shift our attention to more discernible characteristics of the relationship that justify regulatory interventions. Elsewhere I have suggested that democratic deficits and dependency (economic or otherwise) are the main characteristics that justify labour and employment laws and the concept of 'employee' should be interpreted accordingly.[32] Other solutions are of course also possible. We could, for example, focus directly on specific results that we find unacceptable, whether because they create distributive injustice, or because they are detrimental to autonomy, democracy or other values. The point is that difficulties with the concept of inequality of bargaining power say nothing about the existence of a difference between employees and independent contractors that justifies this division. It simply means that the differences should be articulated at a different level of generalisation.

---

[30] See B.E. Kaufman, 'The Evolution of Thought on the Competitive Nature of Labor Markets' in Kerr and Staudohar, above n 27, at 145.
[31] *Ibid.*
[32] Davidov, above n 2.

To be sure, we may wish to define or interpret the group of 'employees' differently from current judicial practices. Doctrine can be improved; its failures do not say anything about the existence of a difference between different groups of workers in real life. There are data in some countries to shows that, among those currently considered independent contractors, many have similar characteristics to employees.[33] But these people, if they share the characteristics that justify the protection of labour and employment laws, should simply be included within the group of employees. The question is not whether there is a difference between employees and independent contractors as these groups are currently defined by the courts, but more generally whether a difference between different workers can be observed, no matter how they are currently classified. It would be difficult to deny that, at least in some cases, such a difference exists, whether we separate the groups by looking for democratic deficits and dependency, or by using some other yardstick.[34]

4. 'EMPLOYEE'—INDEFINABLE?

A third line of argument maintains that it is simply impossible to define employment. 'As with the unicorn', argues Adrian Brooks, 'there is no such beast as "employment contract"'.[35] She explains that:

A 'definition' of something, to be worthy of the name, must be both inclusive and exclusive, must state elements which will be present in all instances of that something, and which will not be present in other things. This can be done by putting together a group of criteria which will always be found together in a thing of that nature, and never found together in any other type of thing. Thus, we have not properly defined a cat if we say that a cat is an animal with four legs, fur and a tail. We have described a substantial

---

[33] For an analysis of data from Canada and Germany see, respectively, J. Fudge, 'Labour Protection for Self-employed Workers' (2003) 3 *Just Labour* 36; W. Däubler, 'Working People in Germany' (1999) 21 *Comparative Labor Law & Policy Journal* 77, at 85.

[34] A lot has been written in recent years about the change in the basic exchange of subordination for security. More and more firms now attempt to achieve more flexibility by freeing themselves of the rigidities associated with employment security. But it would be very difficult to argue that subordination is no longer the norm. The loss of security for many employees does not mean a relaxation of subordination. It usually just means that employees are forced to assume more risks than before. See R. Breen, 'Risk, Recommodification and Stratification' (1997) 31 *Sociology* 473 at 477; P. Cappelli, L. Bassi and H. Katz, *Change at Work* (New York, Oxford University Press, 1997); S. M. Jacoby, 'Are Career Jobs Headed for Distinction?' (1999) 42 *California Management Review* 123; D. Gallie, M. White, Y. Cheng and M. Tomlinson, *Restructuring the Employment Relationship* (Oxford, Clarendon, 1998), 300; U. Beck, *Risk Society: Towards a New Modernity* (London, Sage, 1992), ch 6.

[35] Brooks, above n 1, at 49.

number of cats by doing that, but we have not defined the concept 'cat'. First, the purported definition is not inclusive—it is not true of all cats. Manx cats have no tail; some breeds of cat have no fur. Second, the purported definition in not exclusive—lots of animals have four legs, fur and a tail, yet are not cats. The alleged definitions of employment contracts fail in the same way. They neither include all contracts which have been judicially accepted as employment contracts, nor do they exclude all contracts judicially proclaimed independent.[36]

Brooks then goes on to show why the tests currently used by the courts (particularly the 'control' and 'integration' tests) do not deliver the desired conclusive results. Hence, she concludes that there is no definition which enables us to say that one contract for the performance of work is employment while another is not. However, as already noted, the inadequacy of current tests and definitions says nothing about the ability to develop better ones. Moreover, it is mistaken to view our task as providing a definition for 'employee' in the same sense that a cat can be defined. A cat is a fact of life. With better efforts, and some basic knowledge of biology, its unique characteristics can probably be defined conclusively. The concept of 'employee', on the other hand, is not a fact of life but a legal construct. We do not 'find out' who or what an employee (legally speaking) is. It is open for us as a society to decide.

Still, one could argue, once we define in principle the category of workers who should be considered employees, we are left with the challenge of identifying the people who fall into this category, and the borders tend to be indeterminate and vague. This is certainly true as a matter of positive law; courts all over the world have been struggling throughout the past century with putting the employee/independent contractor distinction into practice. It is also understandable as a matter of theory and hence can be expected to continue.[37] The variety of work arrangements is endless and changing all the time, and it would be impossible to define in detail the characteristics of workers that should put them in the protected group of employees. Indeed, we are not likely to find detailed characteristics that will make the definition of employee inclusive or exclusive. Any attempt to do so will leave us protecting a certain *form* of relationship, rather than those workers who are in *substance* in need of protection. The examination of

---

[36] *Ibid.*, at 50. See also J. Fudge, 'New Wine Into Old Bottles?: Updating Legal Forms to Reflect Changing Employment Norms' (1999) 33 *University of British Columbia Law Review* 129, at 144–46 (citing Brooks and concluding that 'employment contracts are impossible to define').

[37] 'It is . . . unlikely that a single criterion will one day suffice to characterize wage-earning status. This is not a given, something which exists in itself, but rather a legal construct continually in the making': Supiot, above n 6, at 17.

every different set of facts must be left to the rather wide discretion of the courts. Some degree of uncertainty is thus unavoidable.[38]

Does this render the concept of employee 'indefinable' or useless? Not at all. Concepts like employee simply have a different kind of definition from what Adrian Brooks had in mind.[39] The different particulars of the group of employees do not have any specific (detailed) characteristics that are necessarily shared by all of them, but rather a relationship which can be likened, following Wittgenstein, to 'family resemblance'.[40] To be sure, we can always 'draw a boundary' for a special purpose, as Wittgenstein explained.[41] Indeed, we sometimes draw boundaries that define the group of 'employees' for particular purposes. But we do not, and should not, draw a boundary based on detailed characteristics, because this will subvert the very purpose for which we use the legal concept of employee: the identification of workers in need of protection in their relationship *vis-à-vis* their employers, whatever detailed characteristics they may or may not have.[42]

Nothing said so far is meant to dismiss or underestimate the need for more certainty and clarity in the application of the employee/independent contractor distinction. Achieving more certainty, with clearer tests, is certainly an important goal and not an impossible one, as long as it is understood that some degree of uncertainty is necessary for the meaningful use of the employee/independent contractor distinction. It would make sense to put the line between employees and independent contractors in a way that ensures that those who really need protection will not fall outside the protected group; in other words, it would be appropriate to define the group of employees somewhat over-inclusively regarding aspects that tend to be

---

[38] Indeed, the concept of 'employee' is more a 'standard' than a 'rule'. On this basic distinction and the inevitable degree of uncertainty which 'standards' create see R. Pound, 'Hierarchy of Sources and Forms in Different Systems of Law' (1933) 7 *Tulane Law Review* 475, at 482–6; H.H. Hart and A.M. Sacks, *The Legal Process: Basic Problems in the Making and Application of Law* (Westbury, Foundation Press, 1994), 139–41.

[39] See Langille and Davidov, above n 6.

[40] L. Wittgenstein, *Philosophical Investigations* (Oxford, Blackwell, 1957), para 67.

[41] *Ibid.*, para 69.

[42] And see H.L.A. Hart, *The Concept of Law* (Oxford, Oxford University Press, 1961), 125:

'Uncertainty at the borderline is the price to be paid for the use of general classifying terms in any form of communication concerning matters of fact. Natural languages like English are when so used irreducibly open textured. It is, however, important to appreciate why, apart from this dependence on language . . . we should not cherish, even as an ideal, the conception of a rule so detailed that the question whether it applied or not to a particular case was always settled in advance, and never involved, at the point of actual application, a fresh choice between open alternatives. Put shortly, the reason is that the necessity for such choice is thrust upon us because we are men [sic], not gods. It is a feature of the human predicament (and so of the legislative one) that we labour under two connected handicaps whenever we seek to regulate, unambiguously and in advance, some sphere of conduct by means of general standards to be used without further official direction on particular occasions. The first handicap is our relative ignorance of fact: the second is our relative indeterminacy of aim.'

difficult to apply, in order to make sure that uncertainty does not mean exclusion of workers in need of protection. But attempts to achieve too much certainty run the risk of losing sight of the purpose of the distinction.

Such attempts have recently come from two main directions. In a number of different countries legislatures introduced detailed lists of indicators to assist in identifying 'employees'. These lists have not been defined as exclusive, but rather as creating a presumption of an employment relationship.[43] Theoretically, then, one can still be considered an 'employee', even when the legislated indicators do not apply. In practice, however, this is unlikely to happen the more the requirements for the presumption are defined in detail. Thus, for example, in Germany there is now a list of five specific indicia, and a worker is presumed to be an employee when at least three of them apply.[44] Similarly, in Portugal, a list of five detailed indicia must all apply in order for a presumption of employment to take effect.[45] While I generally support the use of presumptions of employment, such lists of detailed indicia are likely to turn from merely creating presumptions into defacto definitions. Indeed, elsewhere legislatures have managed to avoid detailed definitions, even when introducing presumptions.[46] It may be tempting to use a definition that is relatively rigid and easy to apply, but such a definition is likely to exclude workers in new and non-traditional work arrangements or otherwise unexpected circumstances, even when such workers are in need of protection just like any other employee. Perhaps in the context of administering tax contributions it is necessary to create a clear-cut and determinate line.[47] But in the context of labour and employment

---

[43] For an up-to-date and very useful review see *Report V(1): The Employment Relationship* (International Labour Conference, 95th Session, Geneva, International Labour Office, 2005), 29–38, available at: http://www.ilo.org/public/english/standards/relm/ilc/ilc90/pdf/rep-vi.pdf.

[44] Social Security Code (SGB IV), s 7 para 4. This definition is expected to apply in the context of labour law (and not only social security) as well: see R. Wank, 'National Study for Germany' (prepared for the ILO Meeting of Experts on Workers in Situations Needing Protection, held May 2000), available at: http://www.ilo.org/public/english/dialogue/govlab/pdf/wpnr/germany.pdf. The 5 indicia are: (1) the person does not employ employees working 15 hours a week or more and earning more than 630 DM; (2) the person works permanently and primarily for one contractual partner; (3) corresponding work for the contractual partner is usually performed by employees of the contractual partner; (4) the work does not show the typical characteristics of entrepreneurial activity; and (5) the outward appearance of the work corresponds with that of an activity the person has previously performed as an employee of the contractual partner. See M. Weiss, 'Federal Republic of Germany' in R. Blanpain (ed.), *International Encyclopedia for Labour Law and Industrial Relations* (Deventer, Kluwer, 2000), para 82.

[45] See *Report V(1)*, above n 43, at 30.

[46] See, eg, Argentina (presumption of employment in case of personal service) and South Africa (presumption of employment when *either one* of seven broadly framed indicators exist)—both reviewed in *Report V(1)*, above n 43.

[47] For an example of a detailed definition, used in the context of workers' compensation and unemployment insurance laws, see Oregon's Independent Contractors Statute, ORS. § 670.600 (1999) (detailing 7 necessary conditions plus 4 out of 6 conditions that must be met to be considered an independent contractor). A relatively detailed definition for tax purposes has also been introduced in Australia; see A. Stewart, 'Redefining Employment? Meeting the Challenge of Contract and Agency Labour' (2002) 15 *Australian Journal of Labour Law* 235.

protections, the benefits from determinacy are outweighed by the risk that those most in need of protection will find themselves excluded.

From an opposite direction, but also in an effort to tackle the uncertainty that comes with the existing tests, scholars have called for replacing the category of 'employee' with a unified category of 'contracts for the performance of work'.[48] But this means one of two things: either that general contract law will be applied to employment contracts, or that independent contractors who sell labour power to numerous clients (eg plumbers) will be treated like the employees of each of their clients. Both options are clearly unacceptable. As long as there is some difference, in real life, between employees and independent contractors—a difference with significance for the purpose of providing workers' protection—this difference must be recognised in legal regulation or employees will end up losing their basic rights. And it would be difficult to deny that at least in the context of some kinds of protection such a difference exists, if only because of two basic reasons that were already mentioned above. First, the fact that there are some workers ('employees'), typically with one specific employer, that are in need of protection, while at the same time there are others who are capable of protecting themselves in a market environment. And secondly, in the case of employees there is a corresponding employer who can and should take responsibility for their well-being. The lack of such an employer in the case of the independent plumber (or consultant) with numerous occasional clients dictates a very different regulatory regime.

In short, we must be careful not to devise our legal constructs in a way that will subvert their own purposes. While certainty and determinacy are undoubtedly highly important in law, the purpose of the laws themselves— in our own context, the protection of workers—must remain our primary concern.

5. 'EMPLOYEE'—TOO RIGID?

A fourth line of argument starts from this last premise: that the concept of 'employee' must be interpreted purposively. This is an important point, which unfortunately has often been neglected by courts in the context of the employee/independent contractor distinction. Over the years, judges

---

[48] Brooks, above n 1, at 90–2; Fudge, above n 36, at 147–8. For another formulation see Fudge *et al.*, above n 1, at 230 (arguing that 'all workers dependent on the sale of their capacity to work' should be covered by protective regulations). Marc Linder has similarly argued that 'entitlements should be decoupled from the existence of an employment relationship', since the process of identifying indicia of dependency appears to him 'so fraught with uncertainty and costs that the game is no longer worth the candle': Linder, above n 4, at 240–1. See also Linder, above n 1.

around the world have repeatedly given the concept of employee a formalistic interpretation, which ignored the purpose for which the concept has been invoked by legislatures in a given context. Thus, for example, the judicially developed 'control test', which is still dominant in many countries, has its origins in the vicarious liability context,[49] which has little to do with the goals of protective regulations.[50] Perhaps most dramatically, the current US Supreme Court insists that the term 'employee' must retain its 'common law' meaning, no matter what the purpose of the regulation is.[51] Another example is the insistence of the UK courts that, in order for one to be considered an employee, she must be contractually obligated to work (repeatedly) for the employer and the employer must be contractually obligated to offer her the work.[52] This 'mutuality of obligations' requirement means that a worker who works regularly for the same employer, subject to his control and fully dependent on him economically, may be considered an 'independent contractor' because there is no formal obligation to offer or accept work.[53] Yet, if one is concerned with the worker's need of protection, this formal obligation should hardly be relevant when the worker in fact works regularly for the same employer.

Another British example of formalism concerns the preliminary requirement that the work must be performed personally, although 'a limited or occasional power of delegation' is acceptable.[54] Thus, for example, the English Court of Appeal decided that Mr Tanton, a driver picking up newspapers and delivering them on a fixed route with the employer's vehicle,

---

[49] See P.S. Atiyah, *Vicarious Liability in the Law of Torts* (London, Butterworths, 1967), ch 5.

[50] According to another view, which refers to Britain but may apply to other countries as well, the control test was developed in the context of protective regulations, at the beginning of the 20th century, especially to limit the scope of these regulations, which were at odds with the conservative views of judges: see S. Deakin, 'The Evolution of the Contract of Employment, 1900–1950' in N. Whiteside and R. Salais (eds.), *Governance, Industry and Labour Markets in Britain and France* (London, Routledge, 1998), 212. Marc Linder has also argued that the judiciary's choice to apply the control test in the context of protective legislation resulted from social class bias: Linder, above n 4, at 135, 174. In any case, whether judges simply ignored the purpose of the legislation or specifically tried to subvert it, it is obvious that their actions were not justified.

[51] *Nationwide Mutual Insurance Co v Darden*, 503 US 318 (1992). And see Linder, above n 1.

[52] See *Wickens v Champion Employment* [1984] ICR 365 (EAT); *Carmichael v National Power Plc* [1999] 4 All ER 897 (HL).

[53] See, eg, *Stevedoring and Haulage Services Ltd v Fuller* [2001] EWCA Civ 651 (CA). According to the Court of Appeal, dockers who worked as permanent employees of a firm for a number of years, then dismissed but accepted back immediately as 'casual workers', continuing to work on most days and working only for that firm, do not have an overarching contract of employment with the firm because of the express terms of the contract set by the employer. The lack of a *formal* obligation to offer or accept work was crucial for the judges; they did not bother themselves with the *reality* of the relationship.

[54] *Ready-Mixed Concrete (South East) Ltd v Minister of Pensions and National Insurance* [1968] 2 QB 497 at 515 (CA).

was an independent contractor, based on the factual conclusion that Mr Tanton was not contractually obligated to perform his work personally, but was rather allowed (indeed required) to arrange for a substitute driver when he was unable or unwilling to drive himself.[55] The Court went on to rebuke the Employment Appeal Tribunal for being 'more concerned with what actually occurred than with the obligations of the parties as contained in the documents'. But any employer can easily insert such a clause into the written agreement (which, incidentally, Mr Tanton refused to sign). Indeed, the Court itself admitted that a tribunal should consider whether the clause is not merely a sham, and it is difficult to see how this can be examined if not by reference to what actually occurred. In the case of Mr Tanton, apparently he had arranged for a substitute driver for a period of six months while he was ill, which on the face of it indeed shows that he was not obliged to work personally. On a second look, however, this fact only reveals how ironic and unjust the Court's decision is. Since the company considered Mr Tanton an independent contractor, he received no sick pay. To keep his job he had to arrange a substitute for the time of his sickness. In other words, although he had no opportunity for profit, he had to bear all the risks himself, while the company avoided both the sick pay and the need to look for a substitute. To add insult to injury, these aspects of the contract, which were imposed on him and were only to his disadvantage, were used by the Court to revoke his employee status.[56]

Other examples of courts losing sight of the purpose behind the employee/independent contractor distinction (or, more broadly, the purpose of labour and employment regulations) exist all over the world.[57] At the same time, some courts have explicitly chosen the purposive approach in recent years.[58] Elsewhere, legislatures now attempt to correct this failing, in specific

---

[55] *Express and Echo Publications Ltd v Tanton* [1999] ICR 693, [1999] IRLR 367 (CA).

[56] An example of one (American) case that got this right is *Donovan v Sureway Cleaners* 656 F 2d 1368 (9th Cir, 1981), in which operators of retail outlets were ruled to be employees for the purpose of the Fair Labour Standards Act. Discussing the issue of control, the Court explicitly maintained that 'the test is not what the "agent" could do but what in fact the agent does do'. Therefore, 'the fact that Sureway's "agents" possess, in theory, the power to set prices, determine their own hours, and advertise to a limited extent on their own is overshadowed by the fact that in reality the "agents" work the same hours, charge the same prices, and rely in the main on Sureway for advertising': *ibid.*, at 1371. More specifically, in some countries the case law explicitly maintains that the contractual ability to hire assistants is not enough to negate 'employee' status; the worker has to make actual use of those rights (eg, Belgium, as reported in C. Engels, 'Subordinate Employees or Self-Employed Workers? An Analysis of the Employment Situation of Managers of Management Companies as an Illustration' (1999) 21 *Comparative Labor Law and Policy Journal* 47, at 75).

[57] See Langille and Davidov, above n 6; Linder, above n 1.

[58] See, eg, in the particular context under discussion, *Pointe-Claire (City) v Quebec (Labour Court)* [1997] 1 SCR 1015 (Supreme Court of Canada); *Sarusi v National Labour Court et al.*, adopted 14 Oct. 1998 (Supreme Court of Israel); *Konrad v Victoria Police* (1999) 165 ALR 23 (Federal Court of Australia).

instances, by broadening the ambit of regulations to include some independent contractors.[59]

But this can be taken a step further. A purposive approach, one could argue, means that the concept of employee has a different meaning for every piece of legislation, sometimes even every section in any given legislation, according to its particular purpose. And since the concept has numerous different meanings, there is not really any point to it. Indeed, so this argument goes, a classification into categories only leads to a rigid application of the law. It is better simply to state in each specific regulation the scope of its application.[60] Thus, for example, when a legislature is drafting a law dealing with maximum hours of work, it must decide which group of people should enjoy the protection of such a law, and define this group accordingly for purposes of this specific legislation. Alternatively, this task can be left to the courts, to interpret the law according to its purpose and taking into consideration the particular circumstances, the time and place and current societal values. Every piece of regulation should thus state (whether explicitly or by interpretation) the scope of its application according to its particular purpose.

This critique seems appealing at first. It attempts to avoid rigid and sometimes outdated and irrelevant classifications. And it strives to ensure that protection is given only to those who need it, and to all the people who need it, in any given context. But there are strong arguments in favour of a unified concept as well. First, legal concepts are important tools we use to preserve stability, determinacy and certainty in the application of the law.[61] They offer a useful starting point that captures the experience and insight of generations. They also make it possible for people to know their status and rights. Secondly, a relatively stable and unified meaning of the concept of employee is probably necessary for the existence of group consciousness and solidarity. If the legal rights of every worker are examined separately in every context, workers will have very little in common as far as their legal status is concerned, and they can be expected to feel much less connection to their peers. Finally, and most important, the approach suggested above would lead to never-ending contentions by employers regarding the status of employee for each and every section in each and every item of legislation, which would seriously undermine workers' protection.

The case for a general understanding of 'employee'—a relatively unified concept—is even stronger when taking into account the current state of the law. Given the fact that legislatures have already chosen to use the same

---

[59] See, eg, the use of the term 'worker' by the British legislature, discussed above.

[60] See Carlson, above n 1.

[61] 'If the law is not to degenerate into an unwieldy mass of isolated rules the proper use of legal concepts must retain an important place in legal technique': Atiyah, above n 49, at 33.

concept ('employee') for different regulations, giving it numerous meanings would result in a serious frustration of legislative intent.

The various considerations for and against a unified concept of employee must be balanced if we are to achieve a sensible solution. While I whole-heartedly share the view that the concept of employee should be interpreted purposively,[62] and that the concept can have different meanings in different contexts, dismantling the concept altogether takes this approach too far. For the reasons set out above, the purposive approach must have its limits. A purposive analysis should be performed at a certain level of generality or abstraction and not with regard to every detail separately. An appropriate balance is to separate protective labour and employment regulations from other areas of law in which the concept of employee is used, such as tort law and taxation; and maintain a unified definition of 'employee' for pro-tective labour and employment regulations, based on their common goals, while allowing room for extensions or exceptions in particular instances. This approach balances between sensitivity to particular purposes and the need to create a stable and relatively determinate group of people who are considered employees, at least for protective regulations.[63]

6. CONCLUSION

There are four arguments against the continued use of the legal concept of 'employee' and the employee/independent contractor distinction. We have seen that none can justify abandoning the concept of 'employee'; indeed, the discussion reasserts the importance and viability of this concept. But all four arguments raise valid concerns regarding the proper use of the concept.

First, the concept of employee is not exclusionary in itself. But we must be mindful not to over-use this concept when there is no real difference in a given context between employees and other groups of people. Secondly, the basic premise on which the concept of employee is based—that some workers (but not others) are in a position of unequal bargaining power—is probably true, but too vague to be used as a yardstick. The scope of the concept should be defined based on more specific (and less controversial)

---

[62] See Davidov, above n 2; Langille and Davidov, above n 6; Davidov, above n 9; G. Davidov, 'Joint Employer Status in Triangular Employment Relationship' (2004) 42 *British Journal of Industrial Relations* 727.

[63] Support for this approach can be found in B. Hepple, 'Restructuring Employment Rights' (1986) 15 *Industrial Law Journal* 69, at 74 ('The starting-point should be a unified definition, while allowing for specified exceptions and extensions as to the scope of application of partic-ular rights and obligations'). Support for a unified test was also voiced in the American 'Dunlop Report': see US Department of Labor, *Commission on the Future of Worker-Management Relations* (June 1994), s 5, available at: http://www.dol.gov/asp/programs/history/reich/reports/ dunlop/dunlop.htm.

characteristics, such as democratic deficits and dependency. Thirdly, a concept like 'employee' can be neither exclusive nor inclusive, which means that some degree of uncertainty with regard to the exact group of employees is unavoidable. But this does not make the concept 'indefinable' or useless. Attempts to achieve more certainty in this area, while understandable, must be mindful of the risk of subverting the goal of protective regulations themselves. Finally, the concept of employee should be interpreted purposively, although this should not be taken to the point of having a different group of employees for each specific section in any given regulation. There is merit in maintaining a relatively unified understanding of 'employee' for purposes of protective labour and employment laws, while leaving some room for exceptions and extensions where necessary.

Change is certainly needed. It should involve re-thinking of the proper role for the concept of 'employee', along the lines suggested above. It may also be useful to add new, intermediate categories, in between 'employees' and 'independent contractors'.[64] But the old distinction can still play a useful role.

---

[64] See Davidov, above n 2; Davidov, above n 9.

III

Bringing Atypical Work Arrangements into the Scope of Labour Law

8

*Rethinking Labour Law: Employment Protection for Boundaryless Workers**

KATHERINE V.W. STONE**

T HE AMERICAN WORKPLACE has changed dramatically in recent years, forcing us to rethink the framework of the labour and employment laws that were established during the New Deal period. For much of the twentieth century, the prevailing employment paradigm was that employees had a long-term relationship to a firm and enjoyed a large amount of de facto long-term job security. Their firm provided job security, training, social insurance, and orderly advancement opportunities and obtained a loyal and knowledgeable work force in return. The longer employees stayed on the job, the more their wages rose and their benefits vested, giving them a greater stake in the firm over time. While not all employees had the secure and comfortable work life that the model envisaged, many did, particularly blue collar men in basic industry after the great union drives of the 1930s. The labour laws of that era were based upon the long-term attachment model of employment.

The twentieth century ideal of work has come and gone. Job security in the private sector, in the form of long-term attachment between a worker and a single firm for the duration of the worker's career, is a vestige of the past. New ideas about how to organise work have generated new work practices that are proliferating throughout American enterprises. Today workers expect to change jobs frequently and employers engage in regular churning of their workplace, combining layoffs with new hiring as production demands and skill requirements shift. There has been an explosion in the use of atypical workers such as temporary workers, on-call workers,

* Presented at the Workshop on the Scope of Labor Law: Re-Drawing the Boundaries of Protection, Bellagio Study and Conference Centre, Italy, May, 2005. Portions of this chapter are derived from the author's book, K.V.W. Stone, *From Widgets to Digits: Employment Regulation for the Changing Workplace* (Cambridge, Cambridge University Press, 2004).
** Professor of Law, UCLA School of Law, California, USA.

leased workers, and independent contractors. Furthermore, 'regular' full-time employment no longer carries the presumption of a long-term attachment between an employee and a single firm with orderly promotion patterns and upwardly rising wage patterns. No longer is employment centered on a single, primary employer. Instead, employees now expect to change jobs frequently. At the same time, firms now expect a regular amount of churning in their workforces. They encourage employees to manage their own careers and not to expect long-term career-long job security. Indeed, the very concept of the workplace as a *place,* and the concept of employment as involving an *employer,* are becoming out-dated.[1]

The transformation of work requires a transformation in labour law. Historically, labour laws have been enacted to address the social problems created by production arrangements of the current era. Each era has unique forms of work arrangements that generate their own forms of worker vulnerability. For example, workers compensation laws were passed by state legislatures in response to public concern about mounting workplace injuries in the early twentieth century. The National Labour Relations Act and the Fair Labour Standards Act were enacted in the 1930s in the midst of the Great Depression, when unprecedented numbers of workers lost their jobs, their homes and their livelihoods. In the twentieth century industrial era, employers did not always live up to their promises of long-term jobs with rising wages and secure retirements, but the labour and employment laws were designed to protect employees against the vulnerabilities and possibilities of exploitation present in the then-prevailing work relationship. The employment laws provided a floor of minimum wages and maximum hours, old age and disability insurance, minimal safety and health standards, and the right to organise into unions to bargain collectively for higher standards on a firm by firm basis.

As a result of the transformation of work, the current regulatory regime is seriously out of alignment with the reality of today's workplace. In the United States, the labour and employment laws give 'regular' workers—those with long term, steady jobs with stable employers—a right to unionise and bargain collectively, social insurance against unemployment and workplace injuries, a minimum wage guarantee, and health and safety protection. Atypical workers—those lacking a long-term relationship with a particular employer—are usually not eligible for those employment rights. But today we are witnessing an inversion of the Lake Wobegon syndrome in the labour market. Lake Wobegon is the imaginary town in Minnesota where all of the children are above average. In the labour market today, all of the workers

---

[1] For a detailed description of the changing workplace, see K.V.W. Stone, *From Widgets to Digits: Employment Regulation for the Changing Workplace* (Cambridge, Cambridge University Press, 2004).

are becoming atypical.[2] Soon the atypical workers will be typical and the only really atypical ones will be those we today consider 'typical'.

The labour law regime we have inherited was compatible with and tailored to the job structures of the industrial era, and does not fit the reality of the workplace today. In light of the transformation of work, it is necessary to rethink the nature of employment regulation at a fundamental level. This article describes the changes in the nature of work, explains how the labour laws in the United States have been built upon a long-term attachment template, and suggests ways in which labour law protection should be expanded to include new types of workers.

1. THE CHANGING NATURE OF EMPLOYMENT

During the twentieth century, most large firms organised work in ways that have come to be called 'internal labour markets'. In internal labour markets, jobs are broken down into minute tasks and then are arranged into hierarchical ladders in which each job provides the training for the job on the next rung up. Employers who utilised internal labour markets hired only at the entry level, then utilised internal promotion to fill all of the higher rungs.[3] These practices were based upon the teachings of the scientific management theories of Frederick Winslow Taylor and those in the personnel management movement. Thus in the early and mid twentieth century, management reduced the skill level of jobs, while at the same time encouraging employee–firm attachment through promotion and retention policies, explicit or de facto seniority arrangements, elaborate welfare schemes and longevity-linked benefit packages. Because employers wanted employees to stay a long time, they gave them implicit promises of long-term employment and of orderly and predictable patterns of promotion.[4] While these systems had their origins in the blue collar workplace of the smokestack industrial heartland, by the 1960s they were adapted to large white collar workplaces such as insurance companies and banks.

Sometime in the 1970s, employment practices began to change. Since then, there have been widespread reports that large corporations explicitly

---

[2] For references on the Lake Wobegon Syndrome in cognitive psychology, see http://en.wikipedia.org/wiki/Lake_Wobegon_effect.

[3] For a discussion of the operation of internal labour markets, see P. Doeringer and M. Piore, *Internal Labour Markets and Manpower Analysis* (Lexington, Mass, DC Heath, 1971). On the origin of internal labour markets, see K.V.W. Stone, 'The Origin of Job Structures in the Steel Industry' in R.C. Edwards, D.M. Gordon and M. Reich (eds.), *Labor Market Segmentation* (Lexington, Mass, DC Heath, 1975). See also P. Osterman, 'Introduction' in P. Osterman, *Internal Labor Markets* (Cambridge, Mass, MIT Press, 1984); S. Jacoby, 'The Development of Internal Labor Markets in American Manufacturing Firms' in *ibid.*, 23, at 38–9.

[4] S.M. Jacoby, *Employing Bureaucracy: Managers, Unions and the Transformation of Work in American Industry, 1900–1945* (New York, Columbia University Press, 1985).

reject the notion that their employees should expect long-term, no less life-time, employment. Hence the attachment between employees and their firms has been weakened. At the same time, firms have increasingly turned to temporary, provisional, and contingent employees rather than utilise a 'regular' workforce.[5] This casualisation of work has reportedly become a fact of life both for blue collar and for high-end professionals and managers. This was expressed eloquently by Jack Welch, the notorious former CEO of General Electric Company, in an interview with the Harvard Business Review in 1989 when he said:

> Like many other large companies in the United States, Europe, and Japan, GE has had an implicit psychological contract [with its employees] based on perceived lifetime employment. People were rarely dismissed except for cause or severe business downturns. . . . This produced a paternal, feudal, fuzzy kind of loyalty. You put in your time, worked hard, and the company took care of you for life. . . . But given today's environment, people's emotional energy must be focused outward on a competitive world where no business is a safe haven for employment unless it is winning in the marketplace.[6]

Labour economists have documented the trend away from long-term firm–worker attachment and toward short-term employment relationships. The Department of Labour's Current Population Survey (CPS), found dramatic declines in job tenure between 1983 and 2002 for all men over the age of 20, with the most significant declines amongst men in the age groups over age 45.[7] This is precisely the group who were the beneficiaries of the old model of long-term employment relationships. In addition to the job tenure data, the CPS found a significant decline in the number of men who had been with their current employer for 10 years or more. Similar large declines occurred for men in every age group over 45.[8] These are dramatic changes. For women, there was not such a marked decline, and in some

---

[5] See F.J. Carré, 'Temporary Employment in the Eighties' in V.L duRivage (ed.), *New Policies for the Part-Time and Contingent Workforce* (Armonk, NY, Economic Policy Institute Series, ME Sharpe, 1992), 48 (on growth of temporary employment); P.F. Drucker, *Managing in a Time of Great Change* (New York Truman Talley Dutton, 1995), 66–7 (describing change in the composition of temporary workers); C. Tilly, 'Short Hours, Short Shrift: The Causes and Consequences of Part-Time Employment' in Carré, above 15, at 17, fig 1.

[6] N. Tichy and R. Charan, 'Speed Simplicity, Self-Confidence: An Interview with Jack Welch' (Sept.–Oct. [1989]) *Harvard Business Review* 1, at 9.

[7] BLS News Releases, 'Employee Tenure in 2002' (25 Sept. 2002), available at: http//146.142.4.23/pub/news.release/tenure.txt.

[8] For men between 55 and 65, the average time with a given employer declined from 15.3 to 10.2 years over the 20-year period; for men between 45 and 54, it declined from 12.8 to 9.1; for men between 35 and 44, it declined from 7.3 to 5.1 (*ibid.*). Several economists who have analysed this and other data sources have concluded that since 1980 there has been a significant decline in job tenure. See D. Jaeger and A. Huff Stevens, 'Is Job Security in the United States Falling?' (1999) 17 *Journal of Labor Economics* S1; R.G. Valletta, 'Declining Job Security' (1999) 17 *Journal of Labor Economics* S170 (citing numerous studies).

cases even a modest rise. However, because women were not generally part of the long-term employment system, the overall percentages of women working for 10 years or more is significantly lower than men at every stage.[9]

Sociologists have also noted the change in job patterns for workers today. For example, Richard Sennett, interviewed a number of younger employees about their experiences in the labour market, and reports:

> The most tangible sign of that change might be the motto 'No long term'. In work, the traditional career progressing step by step through the corridors of one or two institutions is withering. . . . Today, a young American with at least two years of college can expect to change jobs at least eleven times in the course of working, and change his or her skill base at least three times during those forty years of labour.[10]

In the late twentieth century, employers began to dismantle their internal labour market job structures. Facing rapidly expanding and increasingly competitive global product markets, they began to create new types of employment relationships that provided them the flexibility to make quick adjustments in production methods, product design, marketing strategies and product mixes. To respond to intense global competition, firms needed the ability to decrease or redeploy their work forces quickly as market opportunities shifted. Hence management theorists and industrial relations specialists developed what they call the 'new psychological contract',[11] or the 'new deal at work'.[12] In the new deal, the long-standing assumption of long-term attachment between an employee and a single firm has broken down. It has been replaced by other implicit and explicit understandings of the mutual obligations of employees and the firms that employ them.

While the new employment relationship does not depend upon long-term employment, attachment or mutual loyalty between the employee and the firm, it also does not dispense with the need for motivated and committed employees. Indeed, firms today believe that they need not merely predictable and excellent role performance; they need what has been described as 'spontaneous and innovative activity that goes beyond role requirements'. They

[9] *See* F.D. Blau, M.A. Ferber and A. Winkler, *The Economics of Women, Men and Work*, (3rd edn, Upper Saddle River, NJ, Prentice Hall, 1998), 113–5.

[10] R. Sennett, *The Corrosion of Character: The Personal Consequences of Work in the New Capitalism* (New York, WW Norton, 1998), 22.

[11] See eg, S.L. Robinson and D.M. Rousseau, 'Violating the Psychological Contract: Not the Exception But the Norm' (1994) 15 *Journal Organizational Behavior* 245, at 246; N. Anderson and R. Schalk, 'The Psychological Contract in Retrospect and Prospect' (1998) 19 *Journal Organizational Behavior* 637, at 637; M.A. Cavanaugh and R.A. Noe, 'Antecedents and Consequences of Relational Components of the New Psychological Contract' (1999) 20 *Journal Organizational Behavior* 323, at 323.

[12] P. Cappelli, *The New Deal at Work: Managing the Market-Driven Work Force* (Boston, Mass, Harvard Business Scholl Press, 1999), 217.

want employees to commit their imagination, energies and intelligence on behalf of their firms. They want employees to innovate, to pitch in, to have an entrepreneurial attitude toward their jobs. Thus current best management practices dictate that they give employees discretion, but they want to ensure that the discretion is exercised on behalf of the firm. Thus they want to elicit behaviour that goes beyond specific roles and job demands, and gives the firm something extra. Organisational theorists characterise this something extra as organisational citizenship behaviour, or 'OCB'.[13]

Much of current human resource policy is designed to resolve the following paradox: Firms need to motivate employees to provide the OCB and the commitment to quality, productivity and efficiency while at the same time they are dismantling the job security and job ladders that have given employees a stake in the well-being of their firms for the past 100 years. Hence managers have been devising new organisational structures that embody flexibility while also promoting skill development and fostering organisational citizenship behaviour.

A new employment relationship is emerging through such theoretical and experimental programmes as total quality management (TQM), competency-based organisations, and high performance work practice programmes. The advocates of the competency-based organisation emphasise skill development by insisting that employees be paid for the skills they have, rather than according to lock-step job evaluation formulas.[14] Skill-based pay, they claim, will give employees an incentive to acquire new skills and also make it incumbent upon employers to provide training and career development opportunities.[15] Advocates of TQM, meanwhile, counsel firms to involve every employee, at every level, in continuous product and service improvement. Some of the specific recommendations of TQM are to provide continuous training and opportunities for individual improvement, and to give workers direct contact with customers, external suppliers and others who do business with the firm.[16]

Despite differences in emphasis, the various approaches that comprise the new employment relationship share several common features.[17] A defining

---

[13] See D.W. Organ, *Organizational Citizenship Behavior: The Good Soldier Syndrome* (Lexington, Mass, Lexington Books, 1988), 4–5.

[14] See E.E. Lawler, III, *The Ultimate Advantage: Creating the High-Involvement Organization* (San Francisco, Cal, Jossey-Bass, 1992), 156.

[15] See *ibid.* at 144–56. See generally, K.V.W. Stone, 'The New Psychological Contract: Implications of the Changing Workplace for Labor and Employment Law' (2001) 48 *UCLA Law Review* 519, at 560–5.

[16] See J.G. Rosett and R.N. Rosett, 'Characteristics of TQM', NBER Working Paper No. 7241 (1999); E.E. Anschutz, *TQM America* (Bradeuton, Flo, McGuinn & McGuire Pub, 1995). See generally, Stone, above n 15, at 565–8.

[17] M.V. Roehling, M.A. Cavanaugh, L.M. Moynihan and W.R. Boswell, 'The Nature of the New Employment Relationship(s): A Content Analysis of the Practitioner and Academic Literatures', Centre for Advanced Human Res. Studies, Working Paper No. 98–18 (1998), 2.

characteristic of the new employment relationship is that employees do not have long-term job security with a particular employer. Employees have episodic jobs, sometimes as regular employees, sometimes as temporary workers, and sometimes as independent contractors. Employment relationships are complex, without any one-size-fits-all model of what it means to be a worker.

When employees are with a firm in an employment relationship today, they are given implicit understandings that provide a substitute for the job security of the past. Many employers explicitly or implicitly promise to give employees not job security, but 'employability security'—i.e. opportunities to develop their human capital so they can prosper in the external labour market.[18]

Another feature of the new employment relationship is that it places emphasis on the worker's intellectual and cognitive contribution to the firm. Unlike scientific management, that attempted to diminish or eliminate the role of workers' knowledge in the production process, today's management theories attempt to increase employee knowledge and harness their knowledge on behalf of the firm.[19]

The new employment relationship also involves compensation systems that peg salaries and wages to market rates rather than internal institutional factors. The emphasis is on offering employees differential pay to reflect differential talents and contributions.[20]

Another feature of the new employment relationship is that firms provide employees with opportunities to interact with a firm's customers, suppliers and even competitors.[21] Regular employee contact with the firm's constituents is touted as a way to get employees to be familiar with and focused on the firm's competitive needs, and at the same to raise the employees' social capital so that they can find jobs elsewhere. The new relationship also involves a flattening of hierarchy, the elimination of status-linked perks,[22] and the use of company-specific grievance mechanisms.[23] We can thus summarise the major differences between the new employment relationship and the old as follows:

---

[18] R.M. Kanter, *E-Volve!* (Boston, Mass, Harvard Business School Press, 2001), 192.

[19] T.A. Stewart, *Intellectual Capital: The New Wealth of Organizations* (New York, Currency/Doubleday, 1997), ix; T.O. Davenport, *Human Capital: What it Is and Why People Invest in it* (San Francisco, Cal, Jossey Bass, 1999), 152–6.

[20] Kanter, above n 18, at 175 (reporting that the tide is moving 'toward more varied individual compensation based on people's own efforts').

[21] Anschutz, above n 16, at 53.

[22] See J. Klein, 'The Paradox of Quality Management: Commitment, Ownership, and Control' in C. Heckscher and A. Donnellon (eds.), *The Post-Bureaucratic Organization* (London, Sage, 1994), 178, at 178–82.

[23] See J. Greenberg, *The Quest for Justice on the Job* (Thousand Oaks, Cal, Sage, 1996), 32–9. See generally, J.A. Colquitt, D.E. Conlon, M.J. Wesson, C. Porter and K Yee Ng, 'Justice at the Millennium: A Meta-Analytic Review of 25 years of Organizational Justice Research' (2001) 86 *Journal of Applied Psychology* 425, at 435–6.

old employment relationship	new employment relationship
job security	employability security
firm-specific training	general training
deskilling	upskilling
promotion opportunities	networking opportunities
command supervision	micro-level job control
longevity-linked pay and benefits	market-based pay

2. THE LABOUR LAWS AND THE OLD WORKPLACE

The labour and employment laws are neither compatible with, nor responsive to the problems generated by the new employment relationship. The basic framework of the labour and employment laws in the United States originated in the New Deal period, when President Franklin D. Roosevelt and a Democratic Congress took affirmative steps to assist American workers who had been devastated by the Great Depression. In that decade, four significant labour statutes and two major Supreme Court opinions established a framework for governing labour relations that persists to this day.[24] This framework consists of two types of regulation—statutory protections establishing minimal standards for individual employees, and regulation to facilitate collective bargaining to enable unionised workers to establish employment terms by contract. Both were structured in ways that assume long-term, stable employment relationships.

A. The Collective Bargaining Law

The collective bargaining law—the National Labour Relations Act—was designed to promote the self-organisation of workers to enable them to constitute a countervailing power so they could bargain with employers about the operation of internal labour markets. In the bargaining process, labour and management were encouraged jointly to determine the rules by which the workplace would be governed.

In many respects, collective bargaining under the NLRA assumes the existence of stable employment of long-term employees. For example, under the Act, the unionised workplace is divided into discrete bargaining

[24] *Norris La Guardia Act*, 29 USC. ss 101–115; *National Labor Relations Act*, 29 USC ss 151–169; *Social Security Act* of 1935, 14 Aug. 1935, Ch 531, 49 Stat 620, codified as amended in scattered sections of 42 USC; *Fair Labor Standards Act* of 1938, 29 USC ss 201–219. The two Supreme Court decisions are *N.L.R.B. v Jones and Laughlin Steel Corp.* 310 US 1 (1937) (holding that it is not a violation of the Commerce Power for Congress to legislate about private employment) and *West Coast Hotel Co. v Parrish* 300 US 379 (1937) (holding that it is not a violation of substantive due process for a state law to set the maximum hours of work for women workers).

units, each unit a well defined, circumscribed and economically stable group. While the individuals in the unit could and did change, the bargaining rights and bargaining agreements applied to the unit. Unions negotiated agreements that contained wages, work rules, and dispute resolution systems for those individuals working in the unit. The terms and benefits applied to the job—they did not follow the worker to other jobs when they left the unit. Job-centred benefits were not problematic in a workplace in which jobs themselves were stable and long-term, but as individuals move between departments and jobs, bargaining unit based unionism means that union contractual gains are ephemeral from the workers' point of view.

The assumption of long-term employment has also permeated union bargaining goals. Many of the benefits and work rules unions negotiated rewarded long-term employment and were thus consistent with the implicit lifetime employment commitment. Wages, vacations and sick leave policies in collective bargaining agreements are usually based upon length of service. Employers insisted on long vesting periods for pensions, thereby reinforcing the norm of long-term employment. Unions have been quite effective in policing employers' implicit promises of long-term employment and preventing employer breaches. They almost invariably insist on seniority and just-cause-for-discharge clauses to protect against opportunistic employer behaviour. At the same time, unions establish grievance and arbitration systems to give workers an expeditious and inexpensive mechanism to enforce the psychological contracts of the industrial era workplace.

B. Social Insurance Laws

In addition to the laws to promote collective bargaining, Congress in the New Deal period enacted minimal employment standards for individual employees not covered by collective bargaining. Federal and state employment laws provided a safety net and set a floor of benefits for those workers who remain outside the bilateral collective bargaining system. In 1935 Congress enacted the Social Security Act which provided old-age assistance and disability insurance.[25] It also had provisions for unemployment compensation for workers who lost their jobs through no fault of their own. In 1938, Congress enacted the Fair Labour Standards Act (FLSA) which established a federal minimum wage and set maximum hours for employment.[26]

An important feature of the New Deal social security and unemployment insurance programme was that they were not universal in their coverage. Rather, they tied crucial social insurance protections to employment, thereby reinforcing the bond between the employee and the firm. Furthermore, they

---

[25] *Social Security Act* of 1935, above n 24.
[26] *Fair Labor Standards Act* of 1938, 29 USC ss 201–19.

did not provide mandatory and universal health insurance. Thus workers were left to obtain health insurance from individual employers, usually as a product of labour–management negotiations.

Over the past 30 years, the employment laws have expanded in number and scope as the extent of the collective bargaining system has contracted. In the 1970s, individual employment protections were expanded by national legislation to provide occupational safety and health protection,[27] pension insurance,[28] expanded protection against discrimination for government employees[29] and pregnant women,[30] and protection for federal employee whistleblowers who report employer wrong-doing.[31] In the 1980s, the federal government enacted the Worker Adjustment and Retraining Notification Act (WARN) to require that employers give their employees advance notice of plant closings and mass layoffs,[32] and the Employee Polygraph Act to provide protection for worker privacy interests.[33] In the same period, numerous states enacted legislation to protect the job security, privacy, dignity, and other concerns of employees. Thus as union density has declined in the private sector, statutory protections have become the main source of worker rights. Yet most of those statutory protections are available only to workers who have an on-going relationship with a specific employer.

C. Job Security and At-will Employment

In addition to the legislative developments of the 1970s and 1980s, many states in the United States revised their at-will doctrines and restricted employers' right to fire employees, thereby giving workers in those states judicial protection against unfair dismissal. Some states adopted a common law tort of unjust dismissal, imposing tort liability when an employer discharged an employee for a reason that violates public policy. For example, a court found an employer liable in tort for dismissing an employee who missed work to serve on a jury.[34] Another imposed liability for dismissing an employee who refused to commit perjury.[35] In addition, a small number

---

[27] *Occupational Safety and Health Act* of 1970 (OSHA) (Pub.L. 91–596, 29 Dec. 1970, 84 Stat 1590), codified and amended in scattered sections of 5, 15, 18, 29, 42, & 49 USC

[28] *Employee Retirement Income Security Act* of 1974 (ERISA) (Pub.L. 93–406, 2 Sept. 1974, 88 Stat 829), codified at 29 USC 1001 ff.

[29] *Rehabilitation Act* of 1973, Pub. L. No 93–112, 87 Stat 355 (codified and amended in scattered sections of 29 USC).

[30] *Pregnancy Discrimination Act* of 1978, Pub. L. No 95–555, 42 USC 2000e.

[31] *Civil Service Reform Act* of 1978 (Pub.L. 95–454, 13 Oct. 1978, 92 Stat 1111), codified as amended in scattered sections of 5 USC.

[32] *Worker Adjustment and Retraining Notification Act* 1988(WARN) (Pub.L. 100–379, 4 Aug. 1988, 102 Stat 890), codified at 29 USC ss 2101–2109.

[33] *Employee Polygraph Act*, 29 USC ss 2001–2009.

[34] *Needs v Hocks* 536 P 2d 512 (Oregon, 1975).

[35] *Petermann v International Bhd. of Teamsters*, 174 Cal App 2d 184 (1974).

of states implied a covenant of good faith and fair dealing into employment contracts, thus finding that an employer breached an employment contract by discharging an employee in a situation that demonstrated egregious bad faith. The prototype situation in which a court found an employer liable for breaching an implied covenant was when an employer discharged a salesman just before a large commission on a sale he had completed became due and payable.[36]

A third type of exception to the at-will doctrine, adopted by 43 U.S. states, was an implied-in-fact contract exception. In these cases, employers who made express or implicit promises of job security were held liable for breach of contract if they did not honour them. For example, in 1984, the Supreme Court of Washington held that when an employer puts promises of fair treatment and limitations on its powers of arbitrary dismissal in an employee handbook, the employer is obligated to act in accordance with those promises.[37] In addition, some US courts imposed contractual liability on employers who engaged in arbitrary dismissals after giving verbal promises of lifetime employment and fostering a corporate culture that assured its employees that they would not be fired unfairly.[38]

The exceptions to the at-will rule were not uniform—some US states recognised a tort of unjust dismissal, some imposed implied terms of good faith and fair dealing into employment contracts, and some expanded the situations in which they would enforce implied contracts for job security. In the same period, some US courts became more receptive to the application of conventional torts to workplace harms. Thus, for example, some U.S. courts permitted workers to sue for intentional infliction of emotional distress when they were the victims of extremely abusive employer treatment.[39] Despite these exceptions, however, the vast majority of non-union workers remained subject to the at-will doctrine, lacking job security or regulatory protection for their job-related grievances.

3. THE PROBLEM OF BOUNDARYLESS WORKERS WITH BOUNDED PROTECTIONS

The changes in workplace practices described above have rendered many features of the existing regulatory framework obsolete. The former regulatory

---

[36] *Foley v National Cash Register Co.* 364 N E 2d 1251 (Mass, 1977).

[37] *Thompson v St. Regis Paper Co.* 685 P 2d 1081 (Wash, 1984).

[38] See, eg, *Pugh v See's Candies* 171 Ca Rptr 917 (Ca, Ct App, 1981), overruled in part on other grounds by *Guz v Bechtel Nat'l, Inc.* 24 Cal 4th 317 (2000).

[39] See, eg, *Bodewig v K-Mart, Inc.* 54 Or App 480, 635 P 2d 657 (App Ct 1981); *Tandy Corp. et al. v Bone* 283 Ark 399, 678 S W 2d 312 (Ark 1984); *Moniodis v Cook* 64 Md App 1, 494 A2d 212 (1985); *Smithson v Nordstrom, Inc.* 63 Or App 423, 664 P 2d 1119 (App Ct 1983); *Shipkowski v United States Steel Corp.* 484 F Supp 66 (E D Penn, 1983).

structure was based on the template of long-term employment relationships and is not well suited to the newly emerging employment system in which firms engage people in non-traditional relationships and employees have several short-term relationships with a variety of employers over their working lives. As more and more workers are de-linked from a particular employer, workers' legal rights change dramatically. They lose many of their protections and benefits, be they contractual, common law, or statutory. Atypical employees and independent contractors fall outside the coverage of many labour laws. At the same time, the new employment relationship collapses the distinctions between regular employees and temporary workers, and between employees and independent contractors. The result is that workers increasingly fall outside the scope of labour law protections. Further, the existing laws do not respond to the needs of either regular or atypical employees because they do not address the important sources of vulnerability.

Two features of the new employment relationship require us to rethink labour law and devise some new types of employment protections. First, the changing nature of work involves a redistribution of risk from the firm to the employee so that any labour regulation needs to respond to the new risks that are currently generated. Secondly, the new work practices are collapsing the distinction between regular and atypical employees, so that many who are in most need of social protection fall outside the ambit of the regulatory regime. As a result, we need to rethink the labour and employment laws, and ensure that regulations be devised that address the risks and vulnerabilities of both regular and atypical employees.

A. New Risks for 'Regular' Employees

1. *The Decline in Job Security*

Regular employees face new risks under the new employment relationship. First and foremost, they face a risk of losing their jobs. To be sure, regular employees in the United States have always been hired under an at-will employment contract. An at-will contract is one that can be terminated by either party at any time for any reason. Given the at-will rule, one might say that all employees in the United States are temporary employees because they have no legally enforceable right to an on-going employment relationship. However, until recently, many employees had some job security through a combination of customary, contractual and common law protections. This is no longer the case.

As explained above, until recently many employees had the protection of internal labour markets and their implicit promises of job security. In internal labour markets, the implicit promise was part of a workplace culture in which employees were not fired unless there was good cause. With the rise of the new employment relationship, this form of customary job security is waning. Employers no longer promise to, nor are they are expected to, keep employees on the payroll when demand for the product fluctuates downward. Rather, in the new employment relationship, the risk of the firm's short-term and long-term success is placed squarely on the employee.

Contractual job security was a second source of job security for many employees in the past, and it too is waning. For the past half century, many private-sector employees had unions that negotiated collective bargaining agreements containing job security provisions. Most labour–management contracts have a provision that specifies that an employer can dismiss an employee only for 'just cause'. 'Just cause' is an amorphous concept, but it has been given meaning over the past 50 years by labour arbitrators on a case-by-case basis. Most union contracts also establish grievance and arbitration procedures to provide an informal tribunal to enforce the contractual job security protection. In the 1960s and 1970s, when unions were prevalent in the private sector, many non-union firms emulated their union counterparts by promising job security and some even instituted non-union grievance procedures to adjudicate allegations of wrongful discharge.[40] However, union density has declined drastically since 1980, so that today less than 9 per cent of private-sector workers have unions at all.[41] As unions decline, the number of employees who have contractual protection for job security also declines. Further, as unions decline, non-union employers no longer feel the need to emulate the union workplace, so non-union job security provisions also wane.

A third source of job security came from the US courts. As discussed above, in the mid-1980s, some state courts began to provide common law job security protection to fill the vacuum created by the steep union decline. However, the legal changes in the at-will rule of the 1980s and 1990s have been undermined in recent years. In many states, courts have limited the tort of unjust dismissal and the covenant of good faith and fair dealing to cases of extremely abusive employer conduct, so that there have been relatively few cases in which employers were found liable either for unjust dismissal or breach of an implied covenant of good faith and fair dealing. In addition, some courts have eliminated the possibility of punitive damages in wrongful dismissal cases, making the remedy less meaningful. In addition, employers in implied contract jurisdictions can avoid liability by placing an explicit disclaimer of just cause liability and a clear statement that the employment relationship is at-will in their employment manuals. There is evidence that employers are increasingly doing just that.[42] Furthermore,

---

[40] T.A. Kochan, H.C. Katz and R.B. McKersie, *The Transformation of American Industrial Relations* (New York, Basic Books, 1986).

[41] Stone, above n 1, at 123.

[42] M. Berger, 'Unjust Dismissal and the Contingent Worker: Restructuring Doctrine for the Restructured Employee' (1997) 16 *Yale Law & Policy Review* 1, at 5–6.

an employer can avoid liability for unjust dismissals by establishing a mandatory arbitration system for disputes concerning terminations and designing the systems to make it difficult for employees to prevail. The use of employer-promulgated arbitration systems has been growing at a rapid rate as employers seek to limit their liability both for employment discrimination and for wrongful dismissal.[43]

As the customary, contractual and common law protections for the job security of regular employees are disappearing, those employees revert to their default status as at-will employees. Under the new employment relationship, regular employment has been transformed into a relationship of de facto as well as de jure free agency. Lacking customary, contractual or common law job security, today's regular employees are difficult to distinguish from temporary ones.

2. Other Risks for Regular Employees

In addition to the risk of job loss, the new employment relationship shifts onto regular employees many other risks that were previously borne by the firm. For example, the new employment relationship generates a level of wage inequality and wage uncertainty that was not feasible under the old internal labour market arrangements. In internal labour markets, wages were set by institutional factors such as seniority and longevity. Wages today are increasingly pegged to individualised factors such as pay for performance, and to the external labour market through techniques such as bench-marking. One result is wage uncertainty for employees. Gone are the days of reliable and steadily progressing pay levels along some pre-arranged or pre-agreed-upon scale. Instead, an individual's pay can fluctuate greatly from month to month, or even week to week.

In addition to job insecurity and wage uncertainty, the new employment practices place on employees the risk of losing the value of their labour market skills. When jobs are redesigned to provide greater flexibility, their skill requirements often increase.[44] Newly trained employees thus have an advantage over older ones, and ongoing training becomes not an opportunity for advancement but a necessity for survival. The new employment practices thus impose not only risks of job loss on employees, but also risks of depreciation of their skill base. Rather than being able to count

---

[43] In 2001, the Supreme Court gave its approval to the use of these systems in *Circuit City Stores v Adams* 532 US 105 (2001). See also *Gilmer v Interstate/Johnson Lane* 500 US 1 (1991). *See* K.V.W. Stone, 'Employment Arbitration Under the Federal Arbitration Act' in A.E. Eaton and J.H. Keefe (eds.), *Employment Dispute Resolution and Worker Rights in the Changing Workplace* (Champaign, Ill, Industrial Relations Research Association, 2000), 27.

[44] For a series of case studies that illustrate how job redesign lead to changing skill requirements, see H.C. Katz, 'Industry Studies of Wage Inequality: Symposium Introduction' (2001) 54 *Industrial & Labor Relations Review* 399.

on a rising wage level and a comfortable retirement, many workers are anticipating a lifetime of retooling just to stay in place.

Another type of risk that is generated by the new employment relationship involves the dissolution of stable and reliable employee old age and social welfare benefits. In the United States, social insurance is linked to employment. Workers obtain health insurance, pensions, disability, long-term care, and most other forms of social insurance from their employers, when they can get it, rather than from the state. Even most forms of state-mandated insurance benefits, such as unemployment compensation and workplace accident insurance, require a worker to have a relationship with a specific employer to be eligible for benefits. Because social insurance is tied to employment, as job security wanes and workers move from job to job, they usually lose whatever employer-sponsored benefits they once had. Therefore, even if a new employer offers a health benefit plan that is comparable to that of the former employer, most plans impose waiting periods for health coverage and exclusions for pre-existing conditions that leave many effectively uninsured. Further, most pension plans do not vest for several years, so that mobile workers are often not covered.

The impact of the new employment relationship on social insurance goes beyond simply the change in job longevity. Employers are also restructuring their plans so as to shift more risk of uncertainty onto employees. In the area of pensions, there has been a historic shift in the past two decades. In the past, almost all private pensions were 'defined benefit' plans. In a defined benefit plan, employers contribute to a fund on behalf of their covered employees, and each employee is guaranteed a specified benefit level at the time of retirement, a benefit determined by the individual's length of service and final out-going salary level. Since the 1980s, many employers have terminated their defined benefit plans altogether or have converted them to defined contribution plans. The result is that today, defined contribution plans have overtaken defined benefit plans as the dominant form of employer-provided pension in the United States.[45] In defined contribution plans, the employer contributes a fixed amount into an account for each worker based on the number of person-hours worked. Often the worker is given some choices about how the funds in his/her account shall be invested. Upon retirement, the amount of the worker's pension is determined by the value of that account at that time. If the funds were invested well, or if the market did well overall, the worker's pension could be high. But if they were invested poorly or if retirement occurred amidst a market downturn, the pension could be paltry. The risk, both of the market and of bad decisions, falls on the individual employee.

In all, the new free agency model of employment has put regular employees at risks in many respects. Indeed, as free agents, regular employees have

---

[45] E.A. Zelinsky, 'The Defined Contribution Paradigm' (2004) 114 *Yale Law Review* 451.

come to resemble atypical workers in many respect. They can be dismissed at any time, they have no reliably rising wage scales, their benefits are non-existent or ephemeral, and they do not have an orderly path of progression to define their working careers. Thus regular workers are coming to share with their less privileged counterparts the problems of risk and uncertainty that the atypical have long endured.

B. Problems of Atypical Workers

Atypical workers—temporary workers, leased workers, part-time workers, trainees and apprentices, and 'dependent' independent contractors—are a growing portion of the American labour force. In 2005, the Department of Labour classified 16.2 million people—12.1 per cent of the workforce—as contingent workers. Of these, there were an estimated 10.3 million independent contractors, 2.5 million on-call workers, 1.2 million temporary help agency workers, and 813,000 workers for contract work companies out of a total full-time workforce of 139 million.[46] In addition, in 2003 the Department of Labour found that there were over 5,000,000 involuntary part-time workers—those who want but do not have regular employment.[47] A survey of firms in all industries and of all sizes conducted by the Upjohn Institute found that 78 per cent of all private firms used some sorts of flexible staffing arrangements.[48]

Atypical workers have long experienced risks of joblessness, pay variability, skill obsolescence and benefit gaps. Indeed, unlike regular employment, atypical employment does not convey even the illusion of job security. Temporary workers can spend years working alongside a regular permanent employee without any expectation of continued employment nor right to participate in the employer's benefit plans.[49] Temporary workers move from firm to firm, often dispatched for short-term assignments by a temporary help agency. On-call workers are either retained by a specific

[46] US Dept of Labor, Bureau of Labor Statistics, 'Contingent and Alternative Work Arrangements–February 2005' (USDL 05-1433, Gov't Printing Office, 27 July, 2005). See also S.R. Coheny, 'Workers in Alternative Working Arrangements' (Nov. 1998) 121 *Monthly Labor Review* 3, at 4–6.

[47] US Dept. of Labor, Bureau of Labor Statistics, 'A Profile of the Working Poor, 2003 Table 1' (Gov't Printing Office, Report 983, Mar. 2005), 6. See also C. Tilly, *Half a Job: Bad and Good Part-Time Jobs in a Changing Labor Market* (Philadelphia, Penn, Temple University Press, 1996). Writing in 1996, Rebecca Blank estimated that between 4.6 and 8.5% of the workforce is in contingent or part-time work involuntarily and would prefer regular, full-time employment instead. See R.M, Blank, 'Contingent Work in a Changing Labor Market' in R. Freeman and P. Gottschalk (eds.), *Generating Jobs* (New York, Russell Sage Foundation, 1998), 258.

[48] S. Houseman, 'Why Employers Use Flexible Staffing Arrangements' (2001) 55 *Industrial & Labor Relations Review* 149.

[49] See *Vizcaino v Microsoft* 103 F 3d 1006 (1997).

employer to work on an as-needed basis or placed on-call by a temporary help agency. They are required to be available for work without knowing their next place or hours of work. 'Independent contractors' are often unskilled workers who face shape-ups in ad hoc hiring halls on street corners every morning.[50] None of these types of workers have a reasonable expectation of long-term employment with a particular employer even though they can spend years in the labour force doing the same kind of work in the same geographic area. Atypical workers receive significantly less pay than their regular employee counterparts and are less likely to receive health insurance or pensions from their employers.[51]

1. Atypical Workers under the Labour Law

The labour laws in the United States make sharp distinctions between regular workers and atypical workers, and between employees and independent contractors. Atypical workers—contingent, temporary and part-time workers—enjoy some protections of the employment laws. They are covered by the minimum wage legislation, workers' compensation, and occupational health and safety legislation. If they earn more than $500 in a quarter, their employer is required to make social security payments on their behalf. However, there are many statutory employment protections from which atypical workers are explicitly or as a practical matter excluded. For example, unemployment insurance, family and medical leave and social security disability insurance have minimum hours eligibility requirements that temporary workers and part-time workers often cannot satisfy.[52]

Temporary workers also lack meaningful rights to engage in collective bargaining because, under a recent National Labour Relations Board (NLRB) ruling, temporary workers are not able to organise in the same bargaining units with the permanent workers they work alongside unless both the agency and the user employer consent.[53] In overturning a prior decision, the NLRB held that, absent employer consent, temporary workers can only organise into a unit with other temporary workers who work at their temporary agency. Given that agency temporary workers spend their days at widely disparate and varying workplaces, without opportunities to meet each other or know of each other's existence, organising a temp agency is difficult if not impossible to achieve.

---

[50] See, eg, J. Gordon, *Suburban Sweatshops* (Cambridge, Mass, Harvard University Press, 2005).

[51] See, S.F. Befort, 'Revisiting the Black Hole of Workplace Regulation: A Historical and Comparative Perspective on Contingent Work' (2003) 24 *Berkeley Journal of Employment & Labor Law* 153, at 164; P. Ball, 'The New Traditional Employment Relationship' (2003) 43 *Santa Clara Law Review* 901, at 909–13; C. Summers, 'Contingent Employment in the United States' (1997) 18 *Comparative Law Journal* 503, at 510.

[52] Befort, above n 51, at 162–4; Ball, above n 51, at 917.

[53] *Oakwood Care Center and SEIU*, 343 NLRB No. 76, 176 LRRM 1033 (2004), overruling *In Re M.B. Sturgis, Inc.*, 331 NLRB 1298 (2000).

Atypical workers often lack coverage under the employment discrimination laws that prohibit employment on the basis of race, gender, ethnicity, age, religion or disability status. The discrimination laws apply only to employers who have a set minimum number of employees. Employers can avoid coverage by keeping the number of employees below the statutory minimum by designating the majority of their workforce as independent contractors.[54]

The Employment Retirement Income Security Act (ERISA) permits employers to exclude temporary workers and part-time workers who work less than half a year from their pension plans. Hence many temporary workers are let go after five and a half months in order to preclude coverage from pension plans. And those who work for more than half a year may still never receive a pension because many pension plans provide that benefits do not vest for five years.

In addition, most common law courts that grant dismissal protection to employees deny protection for temporary workers on the ground that they had no reasonable expectation of long-term employment in the first place.[55]

2. Independent Contractors under the Labour Law

In contrast to atypical employees, independent contractors are not eligible for any of the protections provided by the employment law statutes because they are not considered 'employees'. Unlike in Europe and Canada, in the United States there have not been legislative efforts to create an intermediate category between 'employee' and 'independent contractor' that would give atypical workers some of the employment protections available for standard workers.[56] Rather, in the United States there are only two categories— employee and independent contractor—where the former gets some employment law protections and the latter does not. Increasingly employers attempt to reclassify employees and to vary their employment practices so as to transform their former 'employees' into 'independent contractors'.[57] Many

---

[54] For example, in *Arbauch v Y & H Corp.*, the plaintiff experienced severe sexual harassment on the job but was not able to sue because her employer had classified its truck drivers as independent contractors, leaving it with less than the requisite 15 'employees' necessary to trigger the protection of Title VII: *Arbaugh v Y & H Corp.* Civ. 03–30365 (5th Cir, 18 Aug. 2004).

[55] Berger, above n 42.

[56] For an analysis of the use of the intermediate category in the U.K, see G. Davidov, 'Who is a Worker?' (2005) 34 *Industrial Law Journal* 57. See also S.F. Befort, 'Labor Law at the Millennium' (2002) 43 *Boston Col. Law Review* 351 (discussing the development of an intermediate category of dependent independent contractors in Canada, Sweden, and Germany).

[57] See, A.H. Brustein, 'Casual Workers and Employee Benefits: Staying Ahead of the Curve' (2005) 7 *Univ. Pa. J. of Labor & Empl. L.* 695; P. Ball, 'The New Traditional Employment Relationship' (2003) 43 *Santa Clara Law Review* 901. See also L. Lawlor Graditor, 'Back to Basics: A Call to Re-evaluate the Unemployment Insurance Disqualification for Misconduct' (2003) 37 *John Marshall Law Review* 27, at 60–1 (employers regularly misclassify employees as independent contractors to avoid paying unemployment insurance).

low-paid employees such as janitors, truck loaders, typists, and building cleaners have been redefined as independent contractors even when they are retained by large companies to work on a regular basis. Independent contractors are not covered by minimum wage, workers' compensation, unemployment compensation, occupational safety and health laws, collective bargaining laws, social security disability, anti-discrimination laws, or any of the other employment protections discussed above.[58]

There has been a great deal of litigation in recent years about whether particular individuals or jobs should be classified as employees or independent contractors.[59] Two different tests have been used for distinguishing an employee from an independent contractor. Under the National Labour Relations Act, courts use a restrictive common law agency test that focuses primarily on the employer's right to control the work tasks of the putative contractor.[60] Under the Fair Labour Standards Act, the courts use a broader 'economic realities' test that looks at numerous factors to determine whether the individual is in fact dependent upon the employer.[61] For other purposes, some courts developed a hybrid of the two tests that uses a multi-factored economic realities test but gives particular weight to the employer's right to control the employee's work.[62] However, in 1992, the Supreme Court in *National Mutual Insurance v. Darden* rejected the hybrid test and insisted that for ERISA, and by implication for all the employment statutes other than the Fair Labour Standards Act, the common law agency test should be applied.[63] The Court explained that the employer's right to control the work was paramount. It enumerated thirteen factors to use to determine the application of test in any given case. The factors are:

> (1) the hiring party's right to control the manner and means by which the product is accomplished; (2) the skill required; (3) the source of the instrumentalities and tools; (4) the location of the work; (5) the duration of the relationship between the parties; (6) whether the hiring party has the right to assign additional projects to the hired party; (7) the extent of the hiring party's discretion over when and how long to work; (8) the method of payment; (9) the worker's role in hiring and paying assistants; (10) whether the work is part of the regular business of the hiring party; (11) whether the hiring party is in business;

[58] See generally, L. Horwedel Barton, 'Reconciling the Independent Contractor Versus Employee Dilemma: A Discussion of Current Developments as they Relate to Employee Benefit Plans' (2002) 29 *Capital University Law Review* 1079.

[59] *Mendoza v Bishop* 2005 WL 123982 (*Ohio App*, 2005); *Burditt v Kerr-McGee Chem. Corp.* 982 F Supp 404 (ND Miss, 1997) For discussions of misclassification disputes, see S.J. Arensault, M.E. Hass, J.H. Philbrick and B. Bart, 'An Employee By Any Other Name Does Not Smell As Sweet: A Continuing Drama' (2000) 16 *The Labor Lawyer* 285; Barton, above n 58.

[60] *Roadway Package System* 326 NLRB 842 (1998).

[61] *Real v Driscoll Strawberry Associates, Inc.* 603 F 2d 748 (9th Cir, 1979).

[62] *Spirides v Reinhardt* 613 F 2d 826, 831 (DC Cir, 1979); *Equal Employment Opportunity Comm'n v Zippo Mfg. Co.* 713 F 2d 32, 38 (3d Cir, 1983).

[63] *National Mutual Insurance v Darden* 503 US 318 (1992). See Befort, above n 56.

(12) the provisions of employee benefits; and (13) the tax treatment of the hired party.[64]

None of these factors looks to the individual's economic dependency on the employing firm. The Ninth Circuit recently applied these factors in *Vizcaino v Microsoft* to find that Microsoft had deprived numerous individuals of benefits because it had misclassified them as independent contractors when they were, in fact, employees.[65]

C. Collapsing the Distinctions

In today's workplace, it is often difficult to distinguish between employees and independent contractors. Both are expected to use discretion, to manage their own careers, to move from job to job and project to project. Under the right to control test, 'employees' are defined as those whose work tasks are controlled by the employer and 'independent contractors' are those whose work tasks are not controlled by the employer. Yet in the new employment relationship, employers grant more and more discretion to lower level employees and attempt to give even the lowest level of employee considerable control over her day-to-day work tasks. Indeed, the wisdom of total quality management, competency-based organisation theory, and other contemporary high performance work programmes is that when employees are given discretion to use their judgment, creativity and knowledge, they develop organisational citizenship behaviour and bring valuable ideas to the firm. These approaches attempt to encourage employees to innovate and to have an ownership attitude toward the work process. Therefore the trend toward granting of discretion to employees collapses the distinction between employees and independent contractors under the right to control test. So not only are employers restructuring tasks to turn employees into independent contractors, they are also making the distinction between the two groups almost meaningless. Just as the atrophy of internal labour markets makes all workers 'temporary' in a real sense, so too does the employer's quest for OCB render all workers 'independent contractors'.

As employment tasks are revised and employment relationships are redefined in order to transform more and more employees into independent contractors, more and more individuals are left without the protections of the labour and employment laws. Yet many of these individuals share the vulnerabilities of regular and atypical employees. Some have termed these types of workers 'dependent independent contractors'. Their jobs are insecure, their incomes fluctuate, they lack reliable and affordable benefits, and

---

[64] *Ibid.*, at 323–4.
[65] *National Mutual Insurance v Darden*, above n 64, at 323–4.

they need constantly to upgrade their skills. Hence any reform in labour law has to include these dependent independent contractors if it is to address the problems of the new workplace.

4. RECOMMENDATIONS FOR REFORM

The employment laws need to be revised in many ways if we are going to address the vulnerabilities of both regular and atypical employees. As I have tried to show, the two groups are quickly becoming indistinguishable, and hence it is necessary to think about legal reforms that do not distinguish between regular and atypical workers, be they temporary workers, part-time workers, independent contractors or others in dependent employment relationships. Some of the reforms that will be required are described below.

A. Expanding Collective Bargaining Rights

The labour laws need to be reformed so that workers can organise across employer units without limitation by narrow notions of bargaining units, and so that they can assert economic pressure beyond the boundaries of the firm without constraint by secondary boycott laws. Labour laws also need to permit or even promote a form of organisation that includes atypical together with regular, employed together with unemployed, part-time as well as full-time, and independent contractors as well as employees. Such an organisation might play a representational function in a particular workplace, but its primary role will be as a political and economic force that can protect workers' interests and rights on a region or local basis.[66]

B. Employment Rights for All Employees

Individual employment rights, such as unemployment insurance, workers compensation, minimum wage, social security disability, rights to organise, and so forth must be broadened so they apply to all workers, be they regular, temporary or dependent independent contractors.

C. Protection for Independent Contractors

It is necessary to revise the test for independent contractor status so that they come under the labour law protections. One way to accomplish this

---

[66] I describe this type of unionism in detail in Stone, above n 1, at 219–39.

would be to return to the economic realities test that looks to the degree of dependency of the worker. However, simply instituting the economic realities test is not enough because it runs the risk of depriving workers who have several employers of protection. A better approach is to base employee status on the individual's vulnerability and relative power *vis-à-vis* the party who pays for her services. The relevant question to ask is whether the individual is so situated that she requires the protections the law provides.

D. Making Training a Priority

In the new workplace, all workers need continual training to upgrade their skills and develop new ones. Employers promise employability, but they do not always provide it. Hence there is a role for local government, working with local companies and representatives of local unions and civil organisations, to identify the training needs of the community and insure that workers have access to training and re-tooling throughout their lives. These training needs should be offered for free to all in a community, through the community college system or other state-sponsored training programme.

E. Shoring up the Social Safety Net

In order for individuals to survive and thrive in the new boundaryless labour market, they need child care for young children, after-school care programmes for school age children, school vacation and snow day coverage, educational activities and homework assistance.

Individuals also need affordable and reliable health insurance, disability insurance, and old age assistance. These should be provided by the state and available to everyone. However, if national insurance is not politically feasible, then employers should be encouraged or required to form multi-employer plans that enable workers to keep their benefits as they move amongst employers in a given locality. The state should also require employers to expand eligibility to all who work for them, in any capacity.

F. Transition Assistance

In the current era, it is inevitable that many will have periods in which they are not in the labour force. Sometimes these will be involuntary periods of unemployment between jobs. Sometimes individuals will take time out of the workplace to care for a young child or an elderly dependent. At other times, workers will need to retool, learn new skills, or reposition themselves in relation to the changing requirements of work. Thus one of the most pressing needs of workers today is to have income support for these times of transition. To design meaningful employment protections we need to design ways to support workers as they move in and out of the changing, boundaryless workplace. That is, we need to find a way to provide everyone with transition assistance.

There are various approaches we could take to the problem of transition assistance. One would be to expand the welfare system by eliminating the work requirement and time limits. However, given the intense opposition to welfare in any form in the United States, this approach is politically inconceivable. Alternatively, we might consider a proposal that has been much discussed in Europe—a proposal for social drawing rights.

The concept of social drawing rights grew out of a study in 1999, sponsored by the European Commission and conducted by a group of labour relations experts. The group, of which Alain Supiot was the chair, was charged with considering the impact of changes in the workplace on labour regulation in Europe. In 2000 it issued a report, known as the Supiot Report. The Report describes a changing employment landscape in Europe that mirrors changes that have occurred in the United States—a movement away from internal labour markets toward more flexible industrial relations practices. It found that the new work practices have entailed a loss of job and income security for European workers. The Report called for new mechanisms to provide workers with 'active security' by which they meant mechanisms that equip individuals to move from one job to another.[67]

The Supiot Report contained a number of suggestions for changes in the institutions regulating work to provide active security. Its most visionary proposal was for the creation of 'social drawing rights' to facilitate worker mobility and to enable workers to weather transitions. Under the proposal, an individual would accumulate social drawing rights on the basis of time spent at work. The drawing rights could be used for paid leave for purposes of obtaining training, working in the family sphere, or performing charitable or public service work. It would be a right that the individual could invoke on an optional basis to navigate career transitions, thereby giving flexibility and security in an era of uncertainty. As Supiot writes, 'They are *drawing* rights as they can be brought into effect on two conditions: establishment of sufficient reserve and the decision of the holder to make use of that reserve. They are *social* drawing rights as they are social both in the way they are established . . . and in their aims (social usefulness)'.[68]

---

[67] See A. Supiot, *Beyond Employment: Changes in Work and the Future of Labour Law in Europe* (Oxford, Oxford University Press, 2001), 56; A. Supiot *et al.*, 'A European Perspective on the Transformation of Work and the Future of Labor Law' (1999) 20 *Comparative Labor Law & Policy Journal* 621. See also, D. Marsden and H. Stephenson, 'Discussion Paper, Labor Law and Social Insurance in the New Economy: A Debate on the Supiot Report' (London School of Economics, Centre for Economic Performance, July 2001).

[68] Supiot, *Beyond Employment*, above n 67, at 56.

The concept of social drawing rights is derived from existing arrangements in which workers have rights to time off from work for specified purposes, such as union representation, maternity leave, and so forth. The Report makes an analogy to sabbatical leaves, maternity leaves, time off for union representatives and training vouchers to observe that 'we are surely witnessing here the emergence of a new type of social right, related to work in general'.[69] Social drawing rights, it is said, would smooth these transitions and give individuals the resources to retool and to weather the unpredictable cycles of today's workplace.

In the United States, we have precedents for the concept of paid time off with re-employment rights to facilitate career transitions or life emergencies. There are well established precedents for paid leaves for military service, jury duty, union business, and other socially valuable activities. Some occupations also offer periodic sabbatical leaves. The concept is also built into the idea of temporary disability in state workers' compensation and other insurance programmes, which provide compensation and guarantee re-employment after temporary absences. The recent Parental Leave Act extends the concept of leave time to parenting obligations, although it does not mandate that such leave time be compensated. These programmes all reflect and acknowledge the importance of subsidised time away from the workplace to facilitate a greater contribution to the workplace. They could serve as the basis for developing a more generalised concept of career transition leave.

5 CONCLUSION

The workplace is changing and the labour laws must change as well. Workers today are forced to bear many new risks in the labour market—risks of job loss, of wage variability, of benefit gaps, of skill obsolescence, and of intermittent prolonged periods of unemployment. Our labour laws do not address these problems, either for regular or for atypical workers.

The changing nature of work creates new opportunities for workers, but also new types of vulnerabilities. As employer–employee attachment is episodic rather than long-term, the problem of transitions has risen to the fore. Thus the challenge for regulation today is not to recreate the era of worker–employer attachment, but to find a means to provide workers with support structures to enable them to weather career transitions.

This chapter has made some proposals for reform that are designed primarily to provide livelihood security and ease transitions as workers move

---

[69] *Ibid.*

around in the boundaryless labour market. The proposals only scratch the surface of the profound changes in our labour laws that are necessitated by the changing workplace. Simply enumerating these proposals demonstrates both how far-reaching change has to be and how difficult it will be to attain. Yet if we are going to formulate policy that is relevant to the present era, it is necessary to think broadly, no matter how quixotic it may seem.

9

Beyond The Boundaries: Prospects for Expanding Labour Market Regulation in South Africa

PAUL BENJAMIN*

1. INTRODUCTION

L ABOUR LAW IS playing a perpetual game of catch-up. New forms of work are continually emerging and the law is called on to respond. But the rules of the game are unequal. Legal change works through slow processes of commissions of inquiry, draft proposals and public and parliamentary debates. Sometimes, courts may devise creative responses to extend labour law's boundaries but more often than not it falls to elected legislatures to reshape legislation. And by the time new regulations or standards are in place the world of work has revolved another few degrees and the process starts all over. Or the same old issues of a lack of enforcement raise their head.

It is now an article of faith that the traditional model of labour regulation is in crisis. The point of departure of this chapter is an attempt to understand the specific form of the challenges facing labour market regulation in South Africa. The efficacy of the extensive body of labour law enacted during the first democratic parliament is under threat. While there have been calls to shift the boundaries of labour law during the last decade, reform has been hampered by a lack of information on the precise nature of labour market change. A recent government report has drawn a clearer picture of these changes and will provide the basis for the next phase of policy debate. At the same time, calls for extensive de-regulation of the labour market initially proposed by employer groupings, are being debated within the ruling African National Congress.

* Director, Cheadle, Thompson & Haysom Inc. Attorneys, Cape Town, South Africa; Adjunct Professor, Institute of Development and Labour Law, School of Law, University of Cape Town.

This chapter examines a range of possible regulatory responses to South Africa's new and increasingly informalised labour market. It seeks to place this discussion within an international context by exploring the relevance for developing countries such as South Africa of theoretical models developed to understand the contemporary European labour market in Europe as well as looking at developments elsewhere in the developing world.

This chapter proceeds from the assumption that the labour markets of the twenty-first century are not homogenous, or even, relatively homogenous. They consist in varying proportions of a combination of employees in standard employment (however defined); those in old and new forms of non-standard employment and the self-employed. The forms and proportions of employment vary from country to country, but the diversity of employment relationships is generally present. A generalised conception of the employment relationship will at best apply to a portion of the workforce.[1]

Much of the focus of recent debates has been on the protection of the 'employee-like'[2]—those whose employment conditions defy the conceptual tools of traditional labour law. While some of these workers are the knowledge workers of the new economy, the majority (even in developed economies) are in marginal employment with inadequate (and often decreasing) protection. Developing appropriate protection for this group of workers should be the focus of debates to extend the boundaries of labour law.

After the advent of democracy in 1994, South Africa's new government moved swiftly to enact a quartet of labour laws: the Labour Relations Act of 1995 the Basic Conditions of Employment Act of 1997 the Employment Equity Act of 1998 and the Skills Development Act of 1999. In broad terms, these laws sought to establish core worker rights, facilitate South Africa's reintegration into the world economy and overcome the apartheid inheritance of a labour market marked by high levels of inequality and unemployment and low levels of skill and productivity. However, the new Acts were constructed primarily on a foundation of the conventional employment relationship. Trends towards informalisation which were already present by 1994 have accelerated and a very significant proportion of the workforce earns its livelihood through insecure and unprotected work in which employer power is unrestrained. Figures for 2002 show that in South Africa out of a total economically active population of 20.3 million people, 6.6 million were in full-time employment; 3.1 million were in atypical employment;[3] 2.2 million in informal work and 8.4 million were unemployed.[4]

---

[1] See for instance J. Conaghan, 'Labour Law and New Economy Discourse' (2003) 16 *Australian Journal of Labour Law* 9.

[2] Sometimes referred to as 'employee-lite'.

[3] This includes temporary, part-time and outsourced work as well as approximately 1 million domestic workers.

[4] E. Webster and K. von Holdt, 'Work Restructuring and the Crisis of Social Reproduction: A Southern Perspective' in E. Webster and K. von Holdt (eds.), *Beyond the Apartheid Workplace: Studies in Transition* (Durban, University of KwaZulu-Natal Press, 2005), 3 at 28.

The South Africa government has characterised the country in terms of a 'two economies' paradigm. The first economy consists of that part of the population included in the world economy. The second economy consists of those who through lack of education, skills or exploitable assets are excluded. Government policy seeks to design and manage interventions to build a staircase between the two economies and meld them together.[5] In this context, there is a tendency to characterise labour law as a system that protects the relatively privileged 'insiders' of the formal economy at the expense of the unemployed and those within the informal sector and hampers the development of indigenous small businesses.[6]

2. UNDERSTANDINGS OF THE NEW LABOUR MARKET

The new labour markets of the developed world have been the subject of intense scrutiny. What significance do these debates have for the more informalised and less protected labour markets of the South? These societies have been described as constituting a 'missing middle'[7]—lacking the skills base to reap the benefits of the globalised knowledge economy but also unable to compete (either as exporters or often in their domestic markets) with the economies of scale found in India and China.[8]

The starting point of the European Commission's much-cited Supiot Report (an interdisciplinary assessment of the future of work and labour law) is that the classic socio-economic model that underpinned labour law during the twentieth century is in crisis.[9] To prevent the working world being split in two, the Commission suggests a 'redesigned notion of security'. The elements of this notion are that:

(a) employment status should be redefined to guarantee the continuity of employment status in order to protect workers during transitions between jobs;

[5] A. Hirsch, 'South Africa's Development Path and the Government's Programme of Action' (2004), available at: http://www.sarpn.org.za/documents/d0001084/index.php (accessed 21 Nov. 2005). For a fuller account, see A. Hirsch, *Season of Hope: Economic Reform under Mandela and Mbeki* (Durban, University of KwaZulu-Natal Press, 2005).

[6] See African National Congress, 'National General Council Discussion Document: Development And Underdevelopment Learning From Experience to Overcome the Two-economy Divide' (2005), available at: http://www.anc.org.za/ancdocs/ngcouncils/2005/ 2economy-divide.html (accessed 21 Nov. 2005).

[7] See G. Garret, 'Globalisation's Missing Middle' (2004) *Foreign Affairs* 84.

[8] For instance, between 2002 and 2004 imports of clothing from China increased fourfold, while in the same period 36,000 workers (approximately 20% of the total workforce) in the clothing and textile sectors lost their jobs due to the closure of businesses (*Business Report* (Johannesburg), 8 Apr. 2005).

[9] A. Supiot, *Beyond Employment: Changes in Work and the Future of Labour Law in Europe* (Oxford, Oxford University Press, 2001).

(b) new legal instruments should be designed to ensure continuity of employment above and beyond cycles of employment and non-employment;

(c) labour force membership should be determined on the basis of the broader notion of work.

The Commission proposes a number of reforms to labour law to deal with the growth of atypical, disguised and triangular employment. These are that:

(a) labour law should be expanded to apply to all forms of work performed for others, and not merely to subordinate work;

(b) the status of temporary employment businesses should be clarified;

(c) certain aspects of labour law should be extended to those workers who are neither employers nor employees.

An influential approach to explaining evolving modes of employment is the 'transitional labour market' proposed by Gunter Schmid as a basis for combating unemployment in European economies.[10] This work has also been influential in Australian debates.[11] This approach suggests that there are five types of major life course transitions. These are between:

(a) education and employment;

(b) (unpaid) caring and employment;

(c) unemployment and employment;

(d) retirement and employment;

(e) precarious and permanent employment.

In adapting this model for presentation to a South African audience, Clive Thompson, mindful of the HIV-AIDS epidemic, suggests the addition of a further transitional factor: absence from the workplace to deal with health impairment.[12]

Transitional labour markets, it is argued, should provide institutional arrangements which support flexibility and security and are stepping-stones from precarious to stable jobs. New institutional arrangements should increasingly take account of the need for ongoing training, that the diversity of individual needs requires greater flexibility in the organisation of work

---

[10] G. Schmid, 'Is Full Employment Still Possible? Transitional Labour Markets as a New Strategy of Labour Market Policy' (1995) 16 *Economic and Industrial Democracy* 429.

[11] See I. Watson, J. Buchanan, I. Campbell and C. Briggs, *Fragmented Futures* (Sydney, Federation Press, 2003).

[12] C.R. Thompson, 'The Changing Nature of Employment' (2003) 24 *Industrial Law Journal (SA)* 1793, at 1813.

and that atypical work calls for reconsideration of the relationship between paid work and other socially useful activities. In term of this approach, social policy should move from passive social protection to the social management of risk. Social policy should promote social inclusion through jobs based on proper social standards, rather than merely alleviating poverty. For example, it has been suggested that unemployment insurance should be transformed to an employment insurance to provide income security during transitions between education, training and employment.

It has been suggested that these approaches (while developed to explain transitions in the European labour market) may offer a useful framework for understanding work within the informal sector in developing countries.[13] The emphasis on the need to identify the specific forms of insecurity encountered by workers in marginal work is of great value. Any re-evaluation and expansion of labour law must be preceded by an identification of the insecurities and risks associated with marginal work, including those that occur at points of transition between different forms of employment. Where traditional labour law protects employees against these risks, a case can be made for extending protection to additional workers at risk. Where labour law does not protect employees against a particular risk, consideration will have to be given to developing new forms of protection. This may result in expanding the boundaries of labour law in a second sense, in developing new forms of protection to provide appropriate protection for previously unprotected workers. Without this, the expansion of labour law may do no more than provide protection on paper.

An influential analysis has classified South Africa as well as India and many countries in Latin America and Eastern Europe, as 'lean' social democracies that have cultivated a system of rights but abrogated the responsibility of the state to provide a universal system of social security support.[14] The security that conventional labour law protection can provide is much reduced by the de facto flexibility that employers enjoy due to the high rate of unemployment. An ILO country study of South Africa points out that unemployment has been the 'handmaiden' of flexibility.[15] Protection against dismissal becomes a key area of focus because of the dire consequences for an individual of losing a job. Once employees have exhausted their unemployment insurance benefits, they fall through (what

---

[13] J.-M. Servais, 'Globalization and Decent Work Policy: Reflections upon a New Legal Approach' (2004) 143 *International Labour Review* 185, at 199.

[14] See H. Bhorat and P. Lundall, 'Employment and Labour Market Effects of Globalization: Selected Issues for Policy Management' (Employment Strategy Paper 2004/3, Geneva, International Labour Office, 2004), available at: http://www.ilo.org/public/english/employment/strat/download/esp3.pdf.

[15] G. Standing, J. Sender and J. Weeks, *Restructuring the Labour Market: The South African Challenge. An ILO Country Review* (Geneva, International Labour Office, 1996).

a government-appointed commission of inquiry has described as) a 'vast hole in the social safety net'.[16]

'Lean' social democracy can be contrasted with labour market policies that seek to achieve labour market security by promoting 'protected mobility'. These policies of 'protected flexibility' or 'flexicurity' offer adaptability for firms and security for workers. Proponents of this approach argue that institutions and policies for protected mobility are necessary for efficiency and equity in labour markets in open economies as globalisation increases the need for insurance against labour market risks and transitions. Flexibility, stability and security are required for a productive economy and a well-functioning labour market for decent work.[17] The model of protected flexibility emphasises that social protection can be used both to stabilise employment and for employment promotion.

A significant feature of policies in these countries is Social Pacts developed in representative institutions which set levels of flexibility and protection broadly across the economy. Policies of protected flexibility represent an attempt to move away from a situation in which flexibility creates insecurity to one in which security promotes flexibility.

While these polices are associated with successful small European economies such as Ireland, the Netherlands and Denmark, the use of social protection to promote employment creation is not confined to the most developed countries. The ILO suggests that exceptionally good social security is one of the explanations for successful job growth in some countries in Central Europe, the Republic of Korea and Malaysia. For example, the Korean system of social security which combines unemployment insurance with an employment stabilisation programme and a skills development programme to prevent unemployment and stimulate re-employment is seen as a successful linking of active labour market policies to unemployment assistance and unemployment benefits.[18]

The immense costs of expanding social protection in economies with low levels of formal employment raises significant issues as to the feasibility of these possibilities. However, they raise an important question whether employment protection and employer flexibility can be enhanced by policies not dealing directly with the content and duration of the employment

---

[16] *Transforming the Present—Protecting the Future: Report of the Committee of Inquiry into a Comprehensive System of Social Security for South Africa* (Consolidated Report, Mar. 2002), ch 2, available at: http://www.sarpn.org.za/CountryPovertyPapers/SouthAfrica/march2002/report/index.php.

[17] See, for instance, P. Auer, 'Protected Mobility for Employment and Decent Work: Labour Market Security in a Globalised World' (Employment Strategy Paper 2005/1, Geneva, International Labour Office, 2005), available at: http://www.ilo.org/public/english/employment/strat/download/esp2005-1.pdf.

[18] C. Harasty, 'Successful Employment and Labour Market Policies in Europe and Asia and the Pacific' (Employment Strategy Papers 2004/4, Geneva, International Labour Office, 2004), available at: http://www.ilo.org/public/english/employment/strat/download/esp4.pdf.

relationship. If this can be done, it will expand the options for extending the boundaries of labour law.

Any use of these theoretical models must also take a measured view of the capacity of labour law to provide security. Sandra Fredman, in examining the underlying reality of precarious work by women in the UK, argues that despite the rhetoric of 'flexicurity' in European labour law, 'flexibility proceeds apace but security remains a rhetorical gesture'.[19] Increased legal security may not always be translated into real security, particularly in societies with high levels of unemployment.

3. LESSONS FROM THE DEVELOPING WORLD

Before proceeding to examine the contemporary reality of the South African labour market, it is useful to alter perspective and look at .developments in the rather more studied (when compared to Africa) labour markets of Latin America and East Asia. Studies of Latin America suggest that labour regulations do contribute to shaping employer practices but that they do not seem to have influenced employment generation. It is possible to reject the simplistic argument that relaxing constraints on contracts and dismissals will suffice to improve economic performance. Labour regulation is only one of the multiple causes relevant to job creation. A study of Argentina, Brazil and Mexico suggests that, irrespective of the level of labour regulation, precarious wage employment (employment forms not complying with labour and social security law) has increased in all three countries in the 1990s. This involves an advance of flexibilisation via actual employer practice adopted mainly by smaller firms trying to survive in difficult economic contexts. This has been facilitated by a lack of control and enforcement. The same study suggests that labour market programmes contribute more concretely to alleviating the problems of the unemployed than 'indirect incentives' such as dismantling labour protection. Programmes developed for the mid-1990s onwards in these countries include cash transfers, direct state employment creation, subsidies to the private sector in exchange for hiring additional workers, assistance to sectors with potential for employment creation, public employment services and supply-side measures such as training for the unemployed.[20]

A recent study of labour law in East Asia suggests that labour laws have very little to do with the construction and functioning of labour markets.

---

[19] S. Fredman, 'Women at Work: the Broken Promise of Flexicurity' (2004) *Industrial Law Journal* 299.

[20] A. Marshall, 'Labour Market Policies and Regulations in Argentina, Brazil and Mexico: Programmes and Impacts' (Employment Strategy Paper 2004/13, Geneva, International Labour Office, 2004), available at: http://www.ilo.org/public/english/employment/strat/download/esp13.pdf.

Labour law has often been subordinated to political considerations to bolster political power in authoritarian regimes and has often been subordinated to the need of industrialisation strategies. In general, there is a significant gap between law and practice. This has manifested itself in a number of ways, including the fact that labour movements have not been sufficiently developed to oppose the state, low levels of collective bargaining and low levels of industrial action under legal procedures.[21]

In his discussion of labour law in the Southern African Development Community (SADC) countries, Kalula argues that labour laws in the region are concerned with the regulation of formal labour markets to the exclusion of 'irregular' workers, particularly those in the informal sector. In spite of the increasing size of the informal sector and the rise of atypical workers, the focus of emerging new systems of labour market regulation remains the formal employment sector. To the extent that vulnerable workers are targeted at all, this applies to limited categories, with the vast majority of workers being left out. The future of labour law in Southern Africa depends upon its capacity to 'embrace the realities of deprivation and social needs'.[22]

4. HOW HAS WORK CHANGED IN SOUTH AFRICA?

Getting a grip on changing work patterns in South Africa has been difficult, particularly as official statistics throw little light on the problem. The picture has been somewhat clarified by a recent report summarising the conclusions of a research project commissioned by the Department of Labour on the changing nature of work and atypical forms of employment.[23]

The project conceptualises the changes in work in terms of two interrelated processes—casualisation and externalisation. Both represent shifts from the norm of the standard employment relationship which is understood as being indefinite (permanent) and full-time employment, usually at a workplace controlled by the employer. Casualisation is used to refer to displacement of standard employment by temporary or part-time employment (or both). Externalisation is used to refer to a process of economic restructuring in terms of which employment is regulated by a commercial contract rather than by a contract of employment. Informalisation refers to the process by which employment is increasingly unregulated and workers

---

[21] S. Cooney, T. Lindsey, R. Mitchell and Ying Zhu (eds), *Law and Labour Market Regulation in East Asia* (London, Routledge, 2002).

[22] E. Kalula, 'Beyond Borrowing and Bending: Labour Market Regulation and Labour Law in Southern Africa' in C. Barnard, S. Deakin and G.S. Morris, *The Future of Labour Law: Liber Amicorum Sir Bob Hepple QC* (Hart, Oxford, 2004), 275 at 287.

[23] Department of Labour (South Africa), *Synthesis Report: Changing Nature of Work and Atypical Forms Of Employment In South Africa* (2004, Unpublished). A summary of the Report is available in (2005) 30 *SA Labour Bulletin* 30.

are not protected by labour law. 'Informalisaton' covers both employees who are nominally covered by labour law but are not able to enforce their rights and those who are not employees because they have the legal status of independent contractors. In the case of externalised work, this includes situations where the nominal employer does not in fact control the employment relationship.

Despite the limited data, we now know that there has been a rise in self-employment in both the formal and the informal sector in the last 10 years. It has also been shown that changes in the labour market have taken the form of externalisation rather than casualisation. The motor for the development of externalisation has been an exponential increase in the incidence of labour broking (temporary employment services (TESs). The wages of workers in externalised employment are significantly lower than those employed in the firms whom they supply with goods or services.

Legislation may have provided an impetus for this development in two ways. First, the avoidance of legislation has provided the motive to externalise and the legislative provisions concerning TESs which are discussed below have provided the opportunity. Certainly, nothing in labour legislation has impeded the growth of labour broking.

Firms have restructured to reduce standard employment to a minimum. The primary benefit for employers has been to reduce labour costs and minimize risks associated with employment. Two forms of labour market segmentation have been produced—between those employed in an enterprise in full-time employment and those who have been casualised (part-time or temporary workers) and between those employed by an enterprise and those employed by labour brokers or contractors.

Those employed in these outsourced and informalised employment relations constitute the first of three concentric circles that surround full-time employment in the formal economy. Outside this are the informal sector proper and beyond that the unemployed. During a working life, many workers will spend time outside formal employment; some may never enter formal employment.

5. DEFINITIONS AND PRESUMPTIONS

Employment involves a 'basic exchange' between security and dependence. Those who are classified as being in a position of dependence receive a range of protections: those who are not must live their working lives in terms of commercial contracts. Put differently, the employer's social responsibility arises only as a quid pro quo for the worker's full commitment to the employment relationship.[24]

---

[24] See, for instance, Fredman, above n 19, at 300.

A number of scholars have argued for employment rights to be divorced from the employment relationship and to be afforded to all who participate in the paid workforce, however marginally. However, this describes the challenge facing labour law in only the most general of terms. A remade labour law must address the question which rights should be expanded to (or created for) which categories of workers. This will require a multiplicity of definitions. If we accept, for instance, that rights to freedom of association or collective bargaining should be guaranteed to a wider category of workers than should be protected against unfair dismissal, we need to define those different categories. This can be achieved by developing a global definition of a 'worker' and then indicating which workers do not receive particular protections. Alternatively, the boundary can be shifted by creating ancillary definitions such as that of the dependent contractor to whom some aspects of labour law will be extended.

Developing a wider definition as a cornerstone of a revised body of labour law would appear to offer a better prospect of expanding the boundary while at the same time maintaining a relatively cohesive body of labour law. However, it is also likely to attract a more hostile response from the opponents of expanded protection. Political realities may dictate that an incremental approach is more effective as protection is expanded on a relatively piecemeal basis to deal with the worst abuses of informalisation. However great the conceptual appeal of the 'big bang' approach may be, there are few, if any, governments which are likely to be able to pull off this approach.

In 2002 the South African government introduced a rebuttable presumption of employment into the principal labour statutes.[25] This approach has already influenced other African countries, and an equivalent provision is included, for instance, in Tanzania's 2004 Employment and Labour Relations Act. The presence of any one of seven factors in an employment relationship brings the presumption into operation. The factors included those traditionally used by the courts to determine the existence of a contract of employment (control, supervision) as well as one ('economic dependence') which has never formed part of South African law and one (being part of the employer's organisation) which has previously been rejected by the courts. These amendments were justified in government policy documents on the basis that they would assist vulnerable workers to assert their rights as employees. Significantly, the presumption applies irrespective of the form of the employment relationship, emphasising that the court must inquire into the realities of an employment relationship rather than being content to scrutinise the wording of the contract. Once the employee satisfies the presumption's relatively low hurdle of establishing that one of the factors is present,

---

[25] The presumption is found in s 200A of the Labour Relations Act 66 of 1995 and s 83A of the Basic Conditions of Employment Act 75 of 1997.

the employer must lead evidence about the nature of the employment relationship to show that the claimant is not an employee.

The presumption was a response to a widespread practice of disguised employment in terms of which employees were 'converted' into independent contractors by contractual stipulations to avoid labour legislation. The multi-factoral 'dominant impression' test used by South African courts to distinguish employment from self-employment caused uncertainty in which this practice could flourish. By the time, the presumptions became law, the courts had seen through this crude form of avoidance, describing it as a 'bizarre subterfuge' and a 'cruel hoax and sham' to deprive employees of the protection of labour law.[26]

It has been suggested that the presumption offers an opportunity to initiate a process of challenging the assumptions that underlie the traditional distinction between employees and independent contractors.[27] While the courts have not yet had an opportunity to apply the presumption to the position of marginal workers, the Labour Appeal Court has felt sufficient confidence to make expansive interpretations of who is an employee. In the first of these, the court held that the definition of an 'employee' includes a person who has concluded a contract of employment to commence work at a future date but who has not yet started work. The court acknowledged that while this construction did not accord with a literal construction of the definition of an employee, an expansive interpretation was justified to avoid hardship and absurdity and was consistent with the progressive legislative development of labour protection.[28]

The Labour Appeal Court has held also that even in cases in which the presumption is not applicable because the employee earns above the applicable earnings threshold, the factors listed in the presumption may be used as a guide in determining whether a person is in reality in an employment relationship or is self-employed.[29] The less formalistic approach to considering who is an employee is shown in the finding that an arrangement in terms of which a person renders personal services through the vehicle of a legal entity such as a company or a closed corporation does not prevent the relationship being covered by labour legislation. Previously, the court had expressed its displeasure at well-paid employees who used these stratagems to obtain tax benefits but then sought the protection of the unfair dismissal jurisdiction when the relationship soured. Such was the anger directed

[26] *Motor Industry Bargaining Council v Mac-Rites Panel Beaters and Spray Painters (Pty) Ltd* (2001) 22 Industrial Law Journal (SA) 1077 (N); *Building Bargaining Council (Southern & Eastern Cape) v Melmon's Cabinets CC & another* (2001) 22 Industrial Law Journal (SA) 120 (LC).

[27] J. Theron, 'The Erosion of Workers Rights and the Presumption as to who is an Employee' (2002) 6 *Law, Democracy and Development* 27.

[28] *Wyeth SA (Pty) Ltd & others v Manqelea* (2005) 26 Industrial Law Journal (SA) 749 (LAC).

[29] *Denel (Pty) Ltd v Gerber* (2005) 26 Industrial Law Journal (SA) 1256 (LAC).

against these employees that the courts forgot that in the process they were letting the employer scot-free off a range of other obligations. This state of affairs was allowed to continue for a number of years because it was only well-paid consultants who were being deprived of labour protection. However, the court has now accepted that even those employees may not require the protection of labour law, there are social policy reasons why they should not be entitled to contract out freely. In particular, they should remain entitled to the protection of minimum standards and should be required to make their contribution to social insurance funds and pay the skills development levy. However, where employees have represented to the tax authorities that they are not employed by their employer but rather by a 'front' personal services company that they control, the court will now use the doctrine of 'clean hands' to deprive the employees of unfair dismissal protection.

At the same time, the point has been made that problems that the presumption sought to address in respect of disguised employment were largely problems of enforcement, and that the state had not simultaneously committed greater resources to enforcing existing laws.[30] This raises a very significant issue of the relationship between the 'boundaries' debate and the issue of enforcement. Many of the most marginal workers (homeworkers, for instance) are covered by existing definitions. The pursuit of the new in legislation will do no more than distract attention from the same old failures if enforcement remains inadequate and under resourced.

6. WHOSE DECISIONS?

Conventional definitions of an employee have allowed wide scope for the courts to determine who is covered by labour law. In some countries, judicial activism has led to expansion of the boundary of protection; in others courts have continued to place formalistic or restrictive interpretations on open-ended definition. However, the remarkable fact is that the key question in labour market regulation (who should receive the protection of labour laws) is left for the courts to determine, with legislation often giving very little guidance.

Should the courts continue to perform this function? The argument for courts to adopt a purposive approach to the interpretation of the scope of legislation has been made on several occasions. While a purposive approach to interpretation is better than one that is not, too much reliance on this places a huge responsibility on the courts to determine questions of labour market policy which may be beyond their competence or expertise. This

---

[30] S. Godfrey and M. Clarke, 'The Basic Conditions of Employment Act Amendments: More Questions than Answers' (2002) 6 *Law, Democracy and Development* 1.

battle has also been played out in the terminology of definitions and the tendency for courts in some countries to assert common law principles, even where these conflict with the purpose of legislation.[31] Likewise, this approach places a huge emphasis on the efficacy of litigation processes and favours those groups which are more able to mount challenges through the courts.

One response has been to develop definitions which give greater guidance to the courts, employers and employees. There has been a tendency to move from more abstract definitions to ones which specify whether or not the legislation applies to specific categories of employees. However, this approach may run the risk of regulatory obsolescence in fast-moving labour markets. A related approach has been the development of codes of practice (through tripartite policy forums) identifying factors that should be taken into account in determining who is an employee. The Irish Code which delineates the principal characteristics of employment and self-employment in non-technical language is a prominent example of this approach. South Africa's tripartite national labour advisory council (NEDLAC) is expected to publish a code of good practice on who is an employee during 2006.

Recently, there has been a tendency to relocate that decision to the executive. Executive authorities have been given the power to classify specific categories of workers as employees. These 'deeming' provisions both allow for the status of specific groups of workers to be clarified (without the necessity for expensive litigation) or for an outward expansion of the boundaries of labour law, either generally or in respect of a particular set of rights. This marks a departure from past practice where administrators have been given the powers to exempt particular categories or employers or workers from the application of the law and could use this to effect deregulation. Administrative expansion offers the prospect of a swifter response to changing labour market practices than the legislative route. It also offers the potential for more nuanced categorisations of workers than may be achievable in laws of general application. However, in some countries it could raise issues of the appropriateness of assigning essentially legislative functions to a Minister. The effective exercise of these powers would also require adequate information about the types of employment relationships. The ILO Reports on the scope of the employment relationship have emphasised the need for the scope of labour law to be regularly reviewed and, where necessary, adjusted to keep in line with labour market changes.[32]

---

[31] See M. Linder, 'Dependent and Independent Contractors in Recent US Labor Law: An Ambiguous Dichotomy Rooted in Simulated Statutory Purposelessness' (1999) 21 *Comparative Labour Law & Policy Journal* 187, and P. Benjamin, 'An Accident of History: Who is (and Who should be) an Employee in South African Labour Law' (2004) 25 *Industrial Law Journal* (SA) 787.

[32] See, most recently, *Report V(1): The Employment Relationship* (International Labour Conference, 95th Session, Geneva, International Labour Office, 2005), available at: http://www.ilo.org/public/english/standards/relm/ilc/ilc95/pdf/rep-v-1.pdf.

7. AN ETERNAL TRIANGLE?

Davies and Freedland argue that the key feature of triangular employment relationships is that the 'task side of the employment relationship is not outsourced, but only the recruitment, dismissal and employment functions'.[33] As the previous discussion indicates, the labour broker or 'temporary employment service' has become the primary mechanism for informalisation in South Africa.

In South Africa, a temporary employment service is defined as an organisation that provides or procures employees for a client and retains the responsibility for paying those employees, irrespective of the period of employment. If the criteria of procurement and payment are present, the TES is the employer, with the client having a default liability (joint and several) in the event of non-compliance with statutory duties.[34] Very significantly, this default liability does not apply in respect of dismissal. Nor does it apply to all statutes: the 'client' employer remains responsible for meeting the obligations of an employer in terms of occupational health and safety legislation.

On the one hand, this default liability has encouraged more responsible contracting patterns. However, the lack of any limitations in respect of the duration of contracts has allowed employers to use the vehicle of the temporary employment service permanently to outsource recruitment and employment functions. The lure has been to deprive employees of employment security. Because the decision to terminate is conveyed from client to employment service it falls outside the employment relationship. Put another way, the client's decision not to continue using a particular worker will always provide a justification for the TES to terminate the employee's services. A clause intended to facilitate the supply of temporary staff has therefore become an omnibus clause enabling permanent triangular employment of workers who are without any security of employment.

According to the ILO, the challenge in respect of triangular (externalised) employment relations lies 'in ensuring that employees in such a relationship enjoy the same level of employment protection traditionally provided by the law for employers that bilateral relationship, without impeding legitimate private and public business initiatives'.[35] In the highly-charged debate in South Africa as to the future direction of labour law, there are two distinct responses to the emergence of TESs (or labour brokers as they are more commonly called).

---

[33] P. Davies and M. Freedland, 'Changing Perspectives Upon the Employment Relationship in British Labour Law' in Barnard, Deakin and Morris, above n 22, 129, at 141.

[34] S 198 of the *Labour Relations Act* 66 of 1995 and s 82 of the *Basic Conditions of Employment Act* 75 of 1997.

[35] *Report V(1)*, above n 32.

One response is found in a policy paper circulated within the ruling African National Congress (ANC) which argues for the introduction of a two-tier labour market, in which businesses with fewer than 200 employees would be exempted from much (exactly how much is not specified) of labour law.[36] The ANC policy paper rightly identifies the proliferation of labour brokers as one of the unintended consequences of the post-apartheid Labour Relations Act and the Basic Conditions of Employment Act. It argues that companies outsource the 'hassle factor' in employment contracts to labour brokers. The solution to this problem it proposes is to reduce the burden that labour law places on employers, thereby encouraging direct employment. An unintended consequence of labour regulation, the paper argues, is to 'distort jobs that in the absence of the legislation might be permanent positions'. What this approach ignores is that in the absence of the labour law it proposes rolling back, these jobs would not be permanent. This type of deregulatory approach does no more than level the playing field at the lowest level. Its failure to look more closely at what aspects of labour law may be creating rigidities prevents it from offering a constructive solution.

On the other hand, the Department of Labour's research concludes that the rise of labour broking has been a response to the absence of an appropriate regulatory framework for labour brokers, who at this stage are not even required to register with the Department. What are the boundaries between the legitimate use of TESs and their abuse? In the most extreme cases where an employer seeks to 'disguise' its personnel department as a TES, the courts will be entitled to lift the corporate veil between client and employment service. However, any revision of statute law will have to seek to identify appropriate boundaries between the legitimate use of TESs and their abuse. It will have to be investigated whether this can be achieved by limiting the duration for which employees can be employed by TESs. It is suggested that the employees of labour brokers should have the same unfair dismissal protection as other employees. Where the worker is genuinely temporary, there will always be a justifiable reason for the termination based on the client's operational requirements. Where this is not the case there is no reason why the client should not have to justify the termination on the normal grounds.

However, the regulation of TESs cannot be seen in isolation from broader debates about the appropriateness of particular aspects of labour law. Presently, employees in South Africa receive the full gamut of protection from the outset of their employment. The Code of Good Practice on Dismissal allows a dismissal to be justified on 'less compelling grounds' during an initial probation period of 'reasonable duration'.[37] This approach has the hallmarks of a political compromise, rather than a rational attempt

---

[36] African National Congress, above n 6.
[37] 'Code of Good Practice: Dismissal', Schedule 8 to the *Labour Relations Act* 66 of 1995.

to provide guidance to employers as to how they should assess the employee's performance during an initial probationary period.

One solution may be to limit the rights of all employees to unfair dismissal protection during an initial period of six months. During this period, as in many other jurisdictions, employees would be limited to protections against dismissals violating fundamental rights, such as protection against dismissal or victimisation. This would create the space in which genuine temporary employment services could operate. However, trade unions are likely to be persuaded to support such an approach only if it is accompanied by a mechanism that prevents employers replacing or 'turning over' employees at the end of the six-month period.

8. INTERNATIONAL LABOUR STANDARDS AND THE BOUNDARIES OF LABOUR LAW

Labour law theory is grappling with the growth of supra-national legal systems and institutions. The potential and pitfalls of supra-national laws as a vehicle for enhancing labour protection have been debated at length elsewhere.[38] This chapter focuses more narrowly on the potential impact of the ILO's extensive body of conventions on the debate on the boundaries of labour law. I argue that there is a need for a careful scrutiny of all conventions of the ILO to determine which of these are intended to impose obligations on ratifying states in respect of all workers and which have application only to employed persons more narrowly defined.

This scrutiny applies to the entire body of ILO international instruments, including the eight core conventions incorporated into the ILO's Declaration on Fundamental Principles and Rights of Work. In Southern Africa, the SADC Charter of Fundamental Rights adopted in August 2003 requires SADC members to ratify and implement the eight core ILO conventions encapsulated in the Declaration.[39] The African Growth and Opportunity Act (AGOA), passed by the US Congress in late 2000, provides duty-free access for certain products from African countries that meet qualification criteria that include 'making continual progress towards establishing . . . protection of internationally recognized worker rights'.[40]

---

[38] See, eg, K. Klare, 'The Horizons of Transformative Labour and Employment Law' in J. Conaghan, R.M. Fischl and K. Klare (eds), *Labour Law in an Era of Globalisation: Transformative Practices and Possibilities* (Oxford: Oxford University Press, 2002), 3.

[39] This requires the ratification of 8 conventions dealing with the Abolition of Forced Labour: Freedom of Association, Collective Bargaining, the Elimination of Discrimination and Child Labour.

[40] Title of the Trade and Development Act 2000, 19 usc 3271ff. Kalula, above n 22, at 281–4. This clause was apparently included to obtain the support of the AFL–CIO for the legislation. AGOA qualification has contributed to labour law reform processes in a number of African countries including Kenya, Tanzania, Uganda, Nigeria and Lesotho.

This has been interpreted as a requirement to comply with the conventions that comprise the Declaration.

What is the significance of these international standards for defining the boundaries of labour law? Convention 87 of 1948 (Convention concerning Freedom of Association and Protection of the Right to Organise), for instance, guarantees the right of 'workers and employers, without distinction whatsoever' to establish and join organisations of their own choosing without previous (state) authorisation. The Freedom of Association Committee of the Governing Body of the ILO has held that the criterion for determining whether this right covers persons is not based on the existence of an employment relationship and that self-employed workers in general should enjoy the right to organise.[41] Similar language is found in the Right to Organise and Collective Bargaining Convention (No 98) which applies to 'workers'. Another one of the core conventions, Convention 100 on Equal Remuneration, promotes 'equal remuneration for men and women workers for work of equal value'. Likewise, there is no provision in Convention 111 on Discrimination (Employment and Occupation) that limits its application to persons employed in terms of contracts of employment.

The broad scope of these, and many, other conventions is consistent with the ILO's mandate to protect all workers.[42] At the same time, the application provisions of Conventions reflect an appreciation of the variations in the appropriate scope of particular aspects of labour protection. Thus, the highly influential Termination of Employment Convention (158 of 1982) applies to 'employed persons', indicating that protection against unfair dismissal is limited to employees. The Protection of Workers' Claims (Employer's Insolvency) convention (173 of 1992) applies only to employees. On the other hand, the very extensive body of conventions on topics of occupational health and safety tends to apply to all workers. The scope of recent instrument such as the Maternity Protection Convention (183 of 2000) reflects current concerns about the boundaries of labour law and requires ratifying countries to provide protection for all women workers 'including those in atypical forms of dependent work'. This would require ratifying countries to ensure that the forms of maternity protection specified in the Convention are extended to women engaged in dependent work beyond the confines of an employment contract.

---

[41] *Freedom of Association* (4th edn, Geneva, International Labour Office, 1996), 51.

[42] See G. Minet, *Coverage of Contract Labour by International Standards* (Geneva, unpublished, 2001). Minet cites an article by Morellet, a former legal adviser of the International Labour Office, 'Legal Competence of the International Labour Organisation' (1933) 16 *The Annals of the American Academy of Political and Social Science* 49, in which it is argued that the ILO was given a broad competence in respect of all workers to allow it to adapt itself to the evolution of society.

What can be read into the different terminology defining the scope of these conventions? It is suggested that the differing fields of application of conventions open up the potential for the Declaration and other conventions to be used as a basis for arguing that international law may require countries to extend aspects of their labour law to workers other than employees. A very strong argument can be made that those conventions that apply to 'workers' or whose application is not expressly restricted to 'employees' or 'employed persons' create obligations on ratifying countries to grant appropriate protections to all persons engaged in the labour market, irrespective of their contractual arrangements. The precise content of this obligation would depend on which conventions a country has ratified and a construction of the application clauses of those conventions.[43]

The dominance of conventional notions of the employment relationship in labour discourse means that in all likelihood many countries are not complying with such a construction of the obligations they have accepted under ratified conventions. How many countries extend protected rights of organisation, protection against discrimination or pay equity as far as the relevant conventions require? While employee-likes and self-employed workers may have a freedom to organise, few—if any—have the protections from discrimination or retaliation for exercising these freedoms as are provided to employees under labour legislation.

Declaration compliance and monitoring of compliance with ratified conventions may provide a means for pressing for labour law reform in countries where labour law is still confined to employees as conventionally understood. In addition, these arguments could provide a basis for the reinterpretation of legislation in countries such as South Africa, where ratified conventions form part of domestic law or are a recognised aid to statutory interpretation.

9. COUNTERING THE NEW INEQUALITY

Informalisation produces new forms of inequality. The South African Department of Labour's research referred to above shows that the wages of workers in externalised employment are significantly lower than those employed in the firms which they supply with goods or services.[44]

In sectors with minimum wages,[45] employees will be entitled to receive at least the minimum rate. However, where this is not the case, anti-discrimination or wage equity legislation may be the primary legal mechanism

---

[43] I do not propose to deal with the separate debate concerning the nature of obligations that the Declaration of Fundamental Rights places on countries that have not ratified conventions forming part of the Declaration.

[44] Department of Labour, n 23 above.

[45] Sectoral minimum wages may be set by collective bargaining through representative bargaining councils or by minimum sectoral determinations made by the Minister of Labour.

available for redressing these new forms of inequality. In South Africa, unfair discrimination is prohibited by two statutes: the Employment Equity Act, which applies to employees, and the Promotion of Equality and Prohibition of Unfair Discrimination Act (PEPUDA), applicable to the rest of society. The former Act also requires employers employing more than 50 employees to implement affirmative action in respect of the employment of blacks, women and disabled persons. In one area, the boundary is shifted: employees supplied to a client by a temporary employment services for an indefinite period or a period in excess of three months are treated as employees of the client for the purpose of affirmative action measures. However, other than this one exception, there are no obligations in respect of affirmative action in respect of the hiring of non-employee contractors. There is no obligation to pay similar wages to employees engaged through a temporary employment service even if they perform the same work as employees on the employer's core staff.

The shifting varieties of work do raise a question as to the application of laws promoting equality to workers falling outside the traditional definition of an employee or engaged in externalised work. Presently, employers who engage some of their workers through triangular employment relationships are able to offer differential remuneration without violating anti-discrimination and wage equity laws. It is suggested that outsourcing aspects of the employer's personnel functions by establishing triangular employment relationship should not justify paying differential wage rates to workers whose work is for the benefit of the same enterprise. However, such an extension of wage equity will certainly require legislative amendments.

Legal notions of equality impose obligations on employer and in societies with enforceable Bills of Rights such as a South Africa, the state as well. The definitions adopted in labour law are often reflected in other legislation. This can lead to employees having greater rights than other categories of workers. Thus, insolvency legislation in South Africa creates a preferred claim for wages and other benefits owed to workers, while there is no similar preference for other categories of workers. It is difficult to justify this form of differentiation between employees and other workers, and in a country such as South Africa where legislation must comply with the principle of equality enshrined in the Constitution this type of provision is liable to be struck down as unconstitutional. Likewise, the government's promotion of economic transformation through a preferential procurement system includes the promotion of employment equity and skills development targets in respect of employees but not other contractors.

South African law has barely had the chance to grapple with the massive inequalities—in and out of the workplace—that are the legacy of apartheid. However, it will now have to take measures to ensure that an increasing informalised and unprotected labour market does not erode the gains that have been made and exacerbate the unsustainable levels of inequality that are such a dominant feature of the society.

10. SOCIAL SECURITY

A significant theme in the future of labour law debates is the need for labour law to engage with social security. For instance, Silvana Sciarra suggests that a European labour law could address the need for new forms of protection for those who have never been in the labour market or those who are in marginal employment.[46]

Any discussion of this issue must take into account the differing borders between labour market regulation and social insurance. In countries with comprehensive social security systems, forms of social insurance such as unemployment insurance and workers' compensation for occupational injuries and diseases, may be provided as part of a package of social security benefits guaranteed to citizens irrespective of employment status. In countries without comprehensive social security, worker's compensation and unemployment insurance tend to be provided to employees. Labour statutes either establish state-run contributory schemes or require employers to insure themselves through private providers. This is common in Anglophone Africa, constituting something of a 'Commonwealth' model.

In societies with high levels of unemployment the incorporation of these worker benefits in a universal social security may lead to a significant dilution of benefits for workers. For this reason, reforms of this type may be opposed by trade unions. In Zimbabwe, for instance, the establishment in the 1980s under the ILO orthodoxy of the time of a comprehensive social security system led to a very significant decrease in benefits such as worker's compensation.

South Africa's workplace-based social safety net consists of a mixed economy of statutory funds and contractual schemes. Participation in the statutory unemployment insurance fund and the worker's compensation fund is compulsory, but restricted to employees. Since the 1980s, collective bargaining has driven a process of creating widespread coverage in the formal sector of contractual provident, retirement and health insurance funds. This significant 'social wage' element coupled with the cost of contributions to statutory funds is cited as a significant reason for employers cutting back on their workforce or using sub-contractors.

How can labour law engage with the social security systems to extend forms of protection to those who currently work outside the social safety net as well as to ascertain whether the protections of protected workers

---

[46] S. Sciarra, 'The Making of EU Labour Law and the Future of Labour Lawyers' in Barnard, Deakin and Morris, above n 22, 201, at 207.

should be adjusted to provide more appropriate benefits? At the most modest level, existing contributory schemes could be expanded to cover those who work but are not currently regarded as employees. This might extend coverage to 'employee-like' workers. A further expansion would allow the self-employed to participate, either voluntarily or a compulsory basis, in a scheme such as workers' compensation.

The post-apartheid modernisation of social insurance legislation has not led to the reconstruction of the categories of benefits. The Unemployment Insurance Act of 2001 provides unemployment, maternity and illness benefits to employees. The Act's scope was extended to high wage-earners as well as to include domestic workers, which has resulted in some 600,000 private employers registering with the Fund. The Act's extension to public service employees is still under discussion. A new system for collection of contributions by the taxation authorities coupled with the inclusion of higher-paid workers has moved the Fund in a comparatively short period from being in deficit to having a significant surplus, raising the issue of whether additional benefits could be provided.

Despite its updating, the Act still reflects its apartheid-era origins as a Fund catering for the limited requirements of a historically privileged workforce not seriously threatened by unemployment.[47] The Act has been criticised by the leading text on social security for its failure to provide benefits for the partially employed, the failure to provide measures to integrate and reintegrate the partially employed and failure to provide measures to promote employment.[48]

Those who become self-employed or establish their own businesses lose their coverage. Employees who resign may not claim benefits under the Act. While this was introduced to stop abuse and has resulted in a significant decline in claims, a consequence is that employees who leave employment to undergo further education or training cannot claim benefits. Any voluntary change in status disqualifies an employee from receiving benefits. Employees who opt to become self-employed lose their accumulated benefits in respect of future periods of total or partial unemployment. In theory, even retrenched employees who choose to set up a business may lose out on benefits because they are no longer work-seekers.

These restrictions hamper job mobility and are a disincentive for employees to undergo training that may enable them to become self-employed. The expansion of benefits, whether on a voluntary or compulsory basis, requires investigation. A concept of employment insurance which allows persons to draw on accumulated rights at times of transition or insecurity may provide a framework within which benefits can be realigned to the realities of the

---

[47] *Transforming*, above n 16, at ch 5.
[48] M. Olivier, N. Smit and E. Kalula, *Social Security: A Legal Analysis* (Durban, Butterworths, 2003), 458.

contemporary labour market, allowing employees to draw on these benefits to improve their employability. This raises the potential linkages between social security and labour laws aimed at enhancing employability. Traditionally, these two policy goals have been pursued in relative isolation by discrete sections of labour departments. Traditional unemployment insurance has only encouraged job-seeking by penalising employees who do not actively seek work, while skills development laws have concentrated on employees in formal employment. These internal boundaries within labour law have prevented the development of effective forms of protection and promotion. This linkage and the issues it raises concerning the boundaries of labour law are developed in the next section of this chapter.

11. LABOUR PROMOTION

Labour market regulation plays a 'labour promotion' function of labour law through its contribution to improving the employability of workers and the aggregate labour supply. Labour promotion can be seen as covering supply side regulation in areas such as immigration, training and social security aimed at creating or sustaining 'human capital'. Labour promotion aims at creating workers who are able to function in the market. [49] Labour laws seek to promote the employability of individuals through national and sectoral schemes by provide training and skills development for employees and work-seekers as well as providing mechanisms for placing persons in work. In South Africa there is the simultaneous existence of a skilled labour shortage and unskilled labour surplus. It has been argued that this points to the importance of adhering to a policy framework that emphasises the need both to enhance economic growth and ensure that the characteristics of the suppliers of labour match those in demand by growing sectors.[50]

In SADC countries, for instance, outdated apprenticeship laws from the colonial era continue to exist side by side with modern legislation establishing sectoral vocational training authorities. In South Africa legislative provisions for developing skills are largely restricted to the formal employment sector. Despite its broader labour market and labour promotion functions, South Africa's Skills Development Act is focused on the formal employment sector and utilises the same definition of employee as other labour statutes. Learnerships (a modernised form of the apprenticeship) provide a flexible

[49] C. Arup, J. Howe, R. Mitchell, A. O'Donnell and J.-C. Tham, 'Employment Protection and Employment Promotion: The Contested Terrain of Australian Labour Law' (Working Paper No 19, Centre for Employment and Labour Relations Law, University of Melbourne, Apr. 2000), available at: http://www.law.unimelb.edu.au/celrl/assets/Working%20Papers/celrl-wp19.pdf.

[50] H. Bhorat, 'Labour Market Challenges in Post-Apartheid South Africa' (paper presented at the Annual Labour Law Conference, Sandton, South Africa, 2004).

framework for skills development by employees and by new entrants into the workforce. There are simplified conditions of employment and significant tax incentives for employers who engage learners.

Employers are required to pay a skills levy equivalent to 1 per cent of their wage bill in respect of employees.[51] Likewise, learnerships are posited on the existence or establishment of an employment relationship. Other workers and unemployed persons may take part in skills programmes. However, research has shown that there are severe difficulties in providing skills development programmes within the informal sector. There is significant public spending (through tax-breaks) on employers who engage learners, but no equivalent subsidisation of unemployed or self-employed persons who seek to enhance their skills.

In unregulated work outside the boundaries of traditional labour law, the burden of employment security and maintaining employability is shifted onto the employee alone.[52] The application of the conventional boundary of labour law to the arena of labour promotion exacerbates the inequalities between the formal sector and the rest of the economy. However, the extension of these schemes across the range of current working forms will require the development of new models for facilitating access to training.

12. CONCLUSION

The effective extension of labour law's protective potential involves the questioning of three conventional boundaries. The exploration of the boundary between employees and other workers is necessary to determine what protections are appropriate for different categories of workers. The expansion of protection to more contingent categories of workers raises the second boundary, that between labour law and other bodies of law such as social security. These two issues have received extensive attention. In this chapter, it is argued that the challenge of extending effective protection for all workers, particularly those in informalised and vulnerable work, requires the interrogation of a further set of boundaries. These are the internal divisions within labour law and administration, such as that between social insurance schemes such as unemployment insurance and skills development programmes. Legislative schemes spanning these two areas may offer the most effective mechanisms for protection of workers during transition phases in their working life and skilling them for entry or re-entry into the labour market.

---

[51] *Skills Development Act* 97 of 1998 and *Skills Development Levies Act* 9 of 1999. Employers who develop a workplace skills plan may claim 50% of their levy back.

[52] J. Rojot, 'Security of Employment and Employability' in R. Blanpain (ed.), *Comparative Labour Law and Industrial Relations in Industrialized Market Economics* (8th edn, Deventer, Kluwer, 2004), 380.

After 1994 South African labour law was debated and reconstructed one statute at a time. The challenge of regulating a changed labour market increasingly points to the points of potential intersection between the different statutes and to the shortcomings of the models inherited from the past. The remaking of labour law to adapt to these changes will require debates with a broad focus that seeks to adjust the body of labour law to the changed reality that it must now regulate. This will require the development and acceptance of a definition of employment that accommodates the full diversity of the contemporary labour market.

10

Protecting the Worker in the Informal Economy: The Role of Labour Law

KAMALA SANKARAN*

Indian society is like a mountain, with the very rich at the top, lush Alpine pastures where skilled workers in the biggest modern industries graze, a gradual slope down through smaller firms where pay and conditions are worse and the legal security of employment means less, a steep slope around the area where the Factories Act ceases to apply . . . , a plateau where custom and the market give poorly paid unorganised sector workers some minimal security, then a long slope through casual migrant and petty services to destitution.[1]

1. THE INFORMAL ECONOMY IN INDIA

CUTTING ACROSS AGRICULTURE, mining, manufacture and the service sectors, the informal economy in India accounts for 92 per cent of the workforce, with over 350 million persons working in the informal economy.[2] The rate of growth of employment is higher than that of the

* Reader, Faculty of Law, University of Delhi, India. I am grateful for the comments received from T.S. Sankaran and Professor Upendra Baxi on an earlier draft of this chapter.

[1] M. Holmstrom, *Industry and Inequality: The Social Anthropology of Indian Labour* (Cambridge, Cambridge University Press, 1984), 319.

[2] Employees are considered to have informal jobs if their employment relationship is, by law or in practice, not subject to standard labour legislation, taxation, social protection or entitlement to certain employment benefit: Informal Sector Statistics, Ministry of Statistics and PI, available at: www.mospi.nic.in. According to the UN definition, the informal sector comprises private unincorporated enterprises (enterprises owned by individuals or households that are not constituted as separate legal entities independent of their owners) and for which no complete accounts are available that would permit a financial separation of the production activities of the enterprises. In addition they must produce at least some of their goods and services for sale or barter, the employment size of the enterprise must be below a certain minimum and the enterprise should not be registered under specific national legislation.

formal economy. The informal economy is also a major contributor to national income, accounting for over 65 per cent of the GDP. The sheer size of this sector coupled with its diversity in terms of varieties of working arrangements and employment relationships poses a challenge to policy makers.

Employment security and income security are major deficits with the bulk of those in employment relationships and the millions who work as own account workers. In the latter category, the majority do not employ any regular hired help and rely on unpaid family workers; of those employing workers (12 per cent of the total of such own account enterprises), over 92 per cent employ three persons or fewer.

Persons working in the informal economy often have precarious conditions of work.[3] The vulnerability of those working in the informal economy (often referred to as the unorganised sector in the literature in India[4]) gets compounded by the fact that they are mostly unprotected. Many of the laws do not apply to those who work here. The laws that do are poorly enforced, and most are unable to access the rights accorded to them in the law.

The challenge is to extend and to enforce the laws that apply to the formal economy to this segment of the workforce, and to create conditions in order that these rights can be accessed. Labour laws[5] in India have various exclusion mechanisms that leave out many of those in the informal economy from their coverage.[6] Labour laws often apply only to certain sectors of the economy, or in certain cases to what is interpreted judicially to be an 'industry'. The labour laws variously determine minimal levels of

---

[3] For vivid accounts of the conditions of those working in the varied informal economy of India see Government of India, *Report of the National Commission on Labour* (New Delhi, Ministry of Labour, 2002), J. Bremen, *Footloose Labour: Working in India's Informal Economy* (Cambridge, Cambridge University Press, 1996), B. Hariss-White, *India Working: Essays on Society and Economy* (Cambridge, Cambridge University Press, 2004), R. Dutt (ed.), *Organising the Unorganised* (New Delhi, Vikas Publishing, 1997).

[4] Those who work in regular jobs in sectors such as the government, local bodies, large-scale manufacturing, transport, banks, services and shops and establishments are termed the formal or organised sector. This accounts for just around 10% of those employed in India. (The sector is organised; the expression organised is no reflection on whether workers are organised into trade unions nor does it reflect high trade union density.) It is sometimes felt that the categories of formal and informal are too broad to capture the kinds of relationships that exist in the continuum. For a survey of the informal economy in India see Government of India, *Shramshakti: Report of the National Commission on Self-Employed Women and Women in the Informal Sector* (New Delhi, Ministry of Women and Child Welfare, 1988), *Report of the National Commission on Rural Labour* (New Delhi, Ministry of Labour, 1991) and *Report of the National Commission on Labour*, above n 3.

[5] The distinction followed in some countries between employment law and labour law is not maintained in this chapter.

[6] Certain laws such as the minimum wage law apply to the informal economy.

employment as necessary conditions for their applicability and so exclude the vast numbers of smaller establishments. This, coupled with definitions of workers based on a functional or remunerative criteria, excludes certain categories of workers such as those in domestic work, those in managerial or supervisory levels or those earning above a certain ceiling, result in limiting the coverage of labour laws. As a result many of the labour laws apply to a small proportion of the workforce. Thus, although an enterprise could be covered under the labour law due to its size or sector (and thus be part of the formal economy), one could still have several persons employed within such enterprises who would be outside the scope of the law due to the nature of the work they perform or other exclusionary criteria.[7] The problems of poor enforcement also account for the limited application of the labour laws.

In this chapter, I examine the legal possibilities and constraints in extending the labour law to certain categories of persons working in the informal economy but who do not appear readily to fall within an employment relationship, and argue that there is scope to bring some additional sections of the informal economy workforce within the scope of the labour law. I also focus on what the role of the state should be in regulating employment relations, the changes that are needed in the labour law, how remedies are accessed in the labour laws and how the justice delivery system should be re-designed, keeping in mind the vulnerabilities of those in the informal economy. In the next section I outline some of the initiatives that are presently under consideration in India to provide protection for vulnerable sections of the informal economy, whether or not they fall within the employment relationship; whether these two categories can be treated on par in the law, and the questions this raises about the boundaries of labour law and its relationship with universal rights based on citizenship.

---

[7] It is thus possible to talk of informal employment in a formal enterprise. The Government of India, for instance, defines informal employment as informal jobs both in informal and formal enterprises and in households. Employees are considered to have informal jobs if their employment relationships are, by law or practice, not subjected to standard labour legislation, taxation, social protection or entitlement to certain employment benefits. For further details, see www.mospi.nic.in and http://millenniumindicators.un.org/unsd/sna1993/glossform.asp?getitem=632. In any event, not being protected by the law is not the only feature of informality. As the ILO Report notes, 'These different groups have been termed "informal" because they share one important characteristic: *they are not recognised or protected under the legal and regulatory frameworks. This is not, however, the only defining feature of informality. Informal workers and entrepreneurs are characterised by a high degree of vulnerability.* They are not recognised under the law and therefore receive little or no legal or social protection and are unable to enforce contracts or have security of property rights': *Decent Work and the Informal Economy* (Geneva, International Labour Office, 2002), 3, available at: http://www.ilo.org/public/english/standards/relm/ilc/ilc90/pdf/rep-vi.pdf.

2. EXPANDING THE SCOPE OF THE EMPLOYMENT RELATIONSHIP

The employment relationship is understood as the contract between the employer and the employee, with terms of employment being determined between the parties mutually. Collective *laissez faire* has not been the predominant motif in the labour relations in India. A high level of state intervention and regulatory initiative had until recently been widely accepted as necessary to bring about social justice. This had been perceived as being necessary even in the more organised sectors of the economy characterised by higher levels of unionisation and union power. Yet paradoxically, legal intervention in the form of extending the coverage of labour laws relating to social security or conditions of work has been significantly absent in the more unorganised sectors of the economy that have very low levels of unionisation and weak bargaining positions of workers. The opening up of the economy and the challenges of a globalising world have led to serious cleavages in India about the need to have 'less' or 'more' of labour law, particularly with respect to labour law reforms for the *formal* economy. While for decades the collective bargaining systems of the developed countries of the 'West' were held up by many within India as models for us to emulate, today, the Chinese model with what many in India perceive to be its chief virtue—limited labour regulation—has become a leading *mantra*.[8] It is in this context that creating regulatory systems for the informal economy is being discussed in India.

The understanding that process-based labour rights (such as the principles in the ILO Declaration on Fundamental Principles and Rights at Work), that ensure 'voice' and participation for employees in the employment relationship on an equal footing with the employer, assumes that the law acknowledges their employee/worker status as a precondition for them to draw upon these rights. Establishing this status under the law appears to be an even more fundamental principle for those working in the informal economy than claiming the rights flowing from employment. This aspect appears to parallel what some scholars have noticed to be an aspect of modern (as contrasted to contemporary) human rights, viz., its exclusion of those perceived to be less than 'human' such as slaves, colonised people and women, and therefore the importance of a preliminary struggle to be recognised as human before claiming human rights.[9] Extending the ILO's fundamental principles to the

---

[8] See for instance the views of the employers' organisations that appeared before the Second National Commission on Labour who felt that, 'China had liberal labour laws, and not rigid labour laws as in India . . . that India could attract FDI or improve the performance of its industries only if Indian labour laws were "liberalised" as China had done': *Report of the National Commission on Labour*, above n 3, at 197.

[9] See, for instance, U. Baxi, *The Future of Human Rights* (New Delhi, Oxford University Press, 2002) and U. Baxi, 'From Human Rights to the Right to be Human: Some Heresies' in U. Baxi (ed.), *The Right to be Human* (New Delhi, Lancer International, 1987), 185.

informal economy would therefore need as a pre-requisite examination of the ways to bring those working in it within the contours of the law, particularly labour law.

Labour law treats the relationship between the employer and employee as essentially a bilateral one, even if there be areas where the terms and conditions of employment are not determined mutually and the law sets the standards. This is particularly the case with respect to minimum wages, termination payments, social security and safety and health issues. However, for many workers in the economy, employment is of short duration, with many changes of employers, coupled with a definite powerlessness to demand and access the rights that flow from employment or the law. Contracts of employment in the informal economy are typically unwritten. The employment relationship is often difficult to prove in a court of law. Wage slips are not provided, wages are often in kind, and the employers do not maintain registers and records, even though they may be required to do so. If there are multiple employers or frequent changes of employers, as in the case of casual workers, the problems only increase. In such cases, the bilateral nature of the employment relationship needs to be examined. Apart from provisions of the law that mandate certain minimum conditions of employment, the role of the state/regulating authorities may require to change, and they may need to adopt a more active role in monitoring the employment relationship. It is to understand the possible nature of such an enhanced role of the state/regulating authorities that some experiments with the employment relationship are worth noting.

A. Creating Tripartite Boards to Regulate Employment Relationships

There are a large number of head load workers or *mathadi/hamal* workers (who lift parcels/goods in the markets across India). They are casual workers who enter into contracts with traders for carrying and loading heavy goods and parcels. This is one of the better unionised sections of the informal workforce and they agitated for regularisation of the ad hoc employment relationship they had with individual traders. As a result, in some states in India, laws have been passed to regulate the employment relationship for this section of the casual workforce in the informal economy. The law requires all existing workers and potential employers to be registered with an autonomous tripartite regulating board or authority; subsequently all employment has to be routed through this regulating authority. Wages are collected from employers and paid by the board. The regulation of employment is no doubt a cumbersome process and involves a tripartite arrangement instead of the bilateral employer–employee arrangement. It has also introduced in some senses a closed shop, since unregistered workers find it impossible to lawfully obtain employment and 'permanent' registered head load workers have been known to auction off their 'right to get employment'. The employers too lose their prerogative to determine who will be employed by them. The advantage of this kind of regulation of employment is that records are maintained of short–term sporadic employment and if social security benefits are to be provided, the employer's contribution (and there may be multiple employers for each worker in the course of even a year) can be easily tracked. This regulatory system has formalised work patterns of an earlier informal arrangement, and delivers greater protection to the workers; yet it has also created a further underground/shadow market in the informal economy. For all practical purposes, the tripartite authority becomes an employment regulator, not a contractor, since it does not employ the workers, while the employer establishes an employment relationship with the head load worker and exercises control over the employee. Could such a regulatory model be scaled up across diverse sectors and regions of the informal economy? For those who believe there is already 'too' much of law in labour matters (and the number is growing in the liberalisation period), the board would replace enforcement by the state with a tripartite body. It is this form of limited regulation via a board that is being considered for intermittent or casual employees or self–employed workers in the informal economy, that we will consider in the next section.

B. A Pro-active Labour Law?

The labour law dealing with those in the informal economy certainly needs to go beyond merely indicating the rights and duties of the parties in the contract of employment. The law has to address how the contract of employment would be proved and questions of burden of proof discharged. For example, where there is an allegation of non-payment of minimum wages or other payments, the burden of proof may need to be shifted to the employer. The law also needs to address how workers can enforce their rights if power is so skewed against them. The right to legal aid as a necessary component of the legal framework has often been mooted. There is also need to focus attention on whether a legal system that waits passively for an aggrieved person to access his/her rights would be suitable when dealing with the informal, economy and how justice delivery can become more pro-active, and whether the state too should be liable when any rights violation is brought to book since it also reflects on poor enforcement.

The boundaries between labour law and the rights flowing from constitutional law or human rights jurisprudence also need to be looked at more closely. To give some examples, non-payment of minimum wage could be presented as a case of forced labour, since it is often poverty alone that compels a person to work at wages below minimum wage. Similarly wrongly violation of one's livelihood (a far broader term than the right against wrongful termination), which would cover self-employed persons also, can be treated as a violation of a person's liberty or right to a dignified life. Re-working many of the rights flowing from labour law as constitutional or human rights is not merely a conceptual exercise. It has often been found that presenting labour law violations as violations of constitutional or human rights has made redress easier and swifter. The latter category often has priority to judicial time and, at least in the Indian system, allows direct access to the higher judiciary. Some of these courts have diluted rules of standing, and not just trade unions but non-governmental organisations and persons acting *pro bono* can also appear for the parties. This is an important consideration when unionisation rates are very low among those working in the informal economy, and where membership based organisations may not exist. Citing violation of a constitutional right also permits one to include the state as a party. Creating multiple avenues for redressing rights violations may become necessary if we are to develop a viable regime for the informal economy.

A necessary condition to be fulfilled in most laws before they become applicable is that a person must be 'employed'. There are laws such as the law governing trade union registration which deliberately use the expression 'engaged in an industry' that permits self-employed persons to register trade unions. Thus the well-known Self Employed Women's Association (SEWA) is a trade union registered under the Trade Unions Act 1926 of India. As in other countries there is a rich body of case law that elaborates what is meant by the term employed and there are tests to determine whether an employment relationship exists, and who is an employer and who an employee. However being brought into an employment relationship is not an unmitigated virtue. For instance, for those who work in bonded or forced labour conditions such as migrant workers, who are obliged to work with a particular contractor because of a petty advance taken by them, the employment relationship and the implicit notion of freedom of contract within this relationship often hides their bondage and how 'unfree' they are.

A part of the employment in agriculture and more so in construction—the two largest sectors for employment—is through the system of labour contractors and sub-contractors or jobbers. The practice of labour suppliers arose during the colonial period. Much of the indentured labour sent from India to work on plantation in the Caribbean, Africa, present-day Sri Lanka and south east Asia was mobilised by labour contractors.[10] A sizeable proportion of the internal migration follows the same pattern. Today,

---

[10] Once employed by a contractor, leaving the job meant arrest and prosecution.

in many of the large construction firms, the main contractor may have grown into an agency, yet the chain of sub-contractors they rely upon to create these pathways of migration continue to be individuals who have personal links with the workers. The (sub)contractor is usually a local person, belonging to the same social stratum and often the caste as that of other workers in his 'gang', who agrees to bring labour from rural areas to work in other places during the harvest season, or to work in brick kilns or construction sites or even in urban manufacturing units.

C. Dealing with Triangular Relationships

The old practice of engaging contract labour has resulted in considerable judicial decisions and legislation on this point. The question that was asked in early cases was whether the contractor or jobber (and not the worker employed by him) could be treated as a worker of the user enterprise or not. A leading case decided in 1957 which laid down some of the determinative tests of what constitutes an employment relationship dealt with this matter.[11] The case arose in the salt industry of Gujarat, where gangs of workers brought by a jobber prepared salt under the supervision of the salt factory. Applying a traditional control and supervision test, the court held that the mere fact that the person in question was allotted a plot of land to make salt by working himself together with workers employed by him would not take away from his workman (employee) status.[12] The person was free to employ labour, and determine their hours of work and wages. The person was obliged to sell the salt only to the factory. The work was controlled by the factory. He was paid by the factory for his work, and he in turn could pay the workers employed by him. In short all the necessary indicia of being employed were fulfilled and the person (whom we may perhaps also call a jobber) was held to be employed by the factory. Performance of personal service seemed to be the clinching factor for holding that such persons were employed by the factory and were not independent contractors. That they were employers too in their own right seemed to have been a minor consideration.

Interestingly enough the question was never raised whether the workers employed by the jobber were employees of the main factory or not. One reason for this was the presence of trade unions among such jobbers (*agarias*), who were perceived and also saw themselves as working under

---

[11] *Dharangadhara Chemical Works Ltd. v State of Saurashtra* [1957] I LLJ 577 (SC).
[12] Subsequent cases have considerably broadened the test of employment beyond the control and supervision aspect.

the supervision of the factory which allotted salt pans to each gang to man-ufacture salt. The presence of a trade union among the jobbers and their greater social status permitted them to challenge their case in the courts and get the relief they required, which the labour employed by them could not do. The focus of attention has shifted these past few decades and the position of the contract labour has come in for attention.[13] Yet some implications that flow from the case law discussed above need to be examined further.

Accepting that an employee can also simultaneously be an employer opens up interesting possibilities to expand the scope of the employment relationship. Could own account workers who employ persons themselves be brought into an employment relationship with the buyer of their goods or services? Several own account workers are economically dependent on a single buyer for selling their services or goods. Such linkages between the formal and informal economy have been well documented in recent years. (There are of course a large number of own account enterprises that sell their goods or service in the market and that are not confined to selling their goods to a single user; I am not focusing on this category for the present.) Relationships between the seller of goods and services and the smaller enterprise are treated as commercial relationships. However, where the linkages are deeper, for instance where raw materials are supplied by the buyer, specifications provided and work done according to the schedule determined by the buyer, can this relationship be transformed into an employment relationship? Can the work be considered as being performed under the 'control and supervision' of the buyer? The case of the *beedi* (hand-rolled cigarettes) in India seems to broaden the scope of an employ-ment relationship. Decided cases have taken the view that supply of raw material (even if presented as a sale of tobacco and leaves) to workers work-ing at home (perhaps with the assistance of others, including that of family members) and the right of rejection of the end product by the eventual buyer, constitutes adequate supervision to transform this apparent commer-cial relationship to an employment relationship.[14]

Critical to such a view was to hold that all that really changed was the place of employment, from the factory to the premises of the *beedi* worker,

---

[13] The Report of the Royal Commission on Labour (1931) has documented the role of the jobber in the Indian labour market. The present-day system of engaging contract labour through a contractor may perhaps be distinguished. While the jobbers of old themselves worked on the job, contractors today are often outsiders who are mere labour suppliers. See for instance, Holmstrom, above n 1, at 53.

[14] See, for instance, *Birdhichand Sharma v First Civil Judge* [1961] 2 LLJ 86 (SC) and *VP Gopal Rao v Public Prosecutor Andhra Pradesh* [1970] 2 LLJ 59 (SC). Later cases relating to other sectors include *Employers in relation to Punjab National Bank v Ghulam Dastagir* [1978] 1 LLJ 312 (SC) and *Mahila Griha Udyog (Lijjat Papad Kendra) v Ratnamala D Koken* [1996] Lab IC 644.

and that continuous supervision at the workplace was replaced by supervision at the final stage of manufacture, seen in the right of unilateral rejection of poor quality goods. The risks of production—of wasted materials and time—was borne by the worker, but that did not take away from the relationship as being characterised as an employment relationship between the person working and the buyer. This has now been incorporated in the law, with the *beedi* workers law holding that sale-purchase agreements between factory owners and home workers would be treated as an employment relationship. Can such a development be extended in other areas where commercial contracts are involved? In the case discussed above, the employer was the supplier of raw materials and a guaranteed buyer of the finished products, and thus took on the traditional risks of an employer.[15] Similar factors need to be present in other commercial contracts constituting a production chain, as otherwise extending the employment relationship through the value chain would remain doubtful.[16]

D. Dealing with Child Work within the Home

The transformation into an employment relationship discussed in the case of *beedi* workers seems to be unaffected by the fact that the home worker would most likely have used other family help (including child work) in the production of the *beedis*. Could other members of the family, or in an extended case those employed by such a home worker, be treated as employees of the eventual buyer? This would involve, first, treating the home worker in a dual capacity as an employee and as an employer, somewhat similar to the case of the gang leader/individual contractor that we noticed above. Secondly, it would also require us to establish the triangular relationship not dealt with in that case. Alternatively, if the home worker is not to be thought of as employing her family in her work, the family labour must be deemed to be permitted by the principal employer, and it thus become a bilateral and not a triangular employment relationship between

---

[15] In another leading case the Supreme Court held that tailors who took pre-cut cloth from a tailoring establishment and finished it at home according to specifications, and who worked for other tailoring establishments simultaneously, were in an employment relationship and were not independent contractors. See *Silver Jubilee Tailoring House v Chief Inspector of Shops and Commercial Establishments* [1973] 2 LLJ 495 (SC).

[16] In 2002 the Supreme Court held as unconstitutional a provision under the Kerala Fishermen's Welfare Act 1985 which levied a burden on fish dealers for contributing to the welfare fund set up under the law. The court held, '[t]he burden of the impost may be placed only when there exists the relationship of employer and employee between the contributor and the beneficiaries of the provisions of the Act and the scheme made thereunder: see *Koluthara Exports Ltd. v State of Kerala* 2002 (2) SCC 459.

the principal employer and other members of the family who worked on the goods. This would of course mean that the number of employees in home-based industries would increase and quality of the employment relationships (ie whether it be voluntary or forced, discriminatory across age or sex) would also have to be considered.

Economically active children who perform (unpaid) work within the household present a challenge to labour law. Dealing with child labour, the ILO has clarified that the term 'does not encompass all work performed by children. . . . Child labour does not include activities such as helping out, after school is over and school work has been done'.[17] On the other hand, work that is hazardous for the child should be treated as child labour and prohibited. However, laws in countries like India do not treat child work within the household as child labour.[18] As a result much of the work performed by children in the informal economy (given the large size of the own account segment that uses only family labour) would not fall within the prohibited category of child labour even if the work were hazardous. The reason is the ambivalent attitude to bringing the household within the scope of labour law. Paid domestic work thus is outside labour law in countries like India, though the law on home workers in the *beedi* industry treats home workers as employees. The definition of employee under the *beedi* law defines employee as '. . . any person . . . working with the permission of or under an agreement with the employer or contractor or both'. It is well recognised that home workers frequently use the labour of children within the homes to complete their work. One of the reasons is that home workers are usually paid on a piece rate basis. Studies show that only if a person works 10–11 hours will a home worker be able to earn something approximating an eight-hour time rated minimum wage. (To meet the required number of person-hours, all members of the family have to work. There is a need of course to carry out scientific studies in order for the piece rated wage to correspond to what a diligent worker working for eight hours with a lunch break would earn.) Given this, can one claim that children or other adults of the family work 'with the permission' of the employer in the case of home work? I think this can be argued, and one could establish an employment relationship between members of the family and the employer in the case of homework where piece rates are fixed absurdly low. Making explicit the employment relationship would entitle unpaid family workers not only to get a wage in their own right but would also entitle them to benefits accorded to employees.

---

[17] *A Future without Child Labour: Global Report under the Follow-up to the ILO Declaration on Fundamental Principles and Rights at Work* (International Labour Conference, 90th Session, Geneva, International Labour Office, 2002), 9.
[18] See for instance the Child Labour (Prohibition and Regulation) Act 1986.

Extending the argument to create an employment relationship between the home worker (as employer/contractor) and other members of the family as her employees seems problematic. Like the 'wages for housework' debate, examining the patriarchal family and the role of head or parents *vis-à-vis* children and their 'right' to claim unpaid work from members would require the examining of the sexual division of labour within the family not only for women in the household but also with regard to children. This also raises the question of forced labour, but I do not want to pursue this line of argument further. Alternatively, focusing on the need for the piece rated wage to have a rational nexus to a time rated wage would reduce the pressure on family members, particularly children, to work alongside the home worker. In any event, if child work which is part of the unpaid family labour is to be treated as part of the employment relationship between the child and the home worker or the child and the main employer, it would require removing the present exclusion clause governing child work within the household and bringing such work within the employment relationship.

3. INCREASING PROTECTION AGAINST VULNERABILITY: SHOULD EMPLOYMENT MATTER?

The idea of universality of basic human rights stands at odds with the limited access to labour rights available to workers, particularly for those working in the informal economy in developing countries. The limitation in the coverage of labour law is one factor behind this exclusion from protection. Another is the nature of labour law itself. What are the kinds of rights that labour law ensures? Do these include only the 'basic human rights' mentioned in the ILO Fundamental Principles or do they go farther, and cover issues of right to work, social security, health, wages, in short the whole set of social rights included in notion of decent work?[19] Should labour law cover only those within employment relationships (howsoever broadly defined) or should it cover all those who work for their livelihood? These questions become important in countries such as India where those working in the informal economy constitute the majority of the working population, and do not readily fall into an employment relationship, yet are in desperate need of protection. This section argues for the need to complement labour law with universal entitlements based on citizenship or residence to effectively protect those working in the informal economy.

---

[19] I have in mind the distinction made by some that the core conventions of the ILO alone merit being called 'labour rights', while those relating to wages or conditions of work which are specific to the degree of development of each country should be referred to as 'labour standards'.

The entitlement to benefits/welfare measures such as access to health care and old age benefits offered by the state is seen as an attribute of citizenship or residence in several countries. However, claims to similar benefits that flow from a person's employment/working relationship are often based on a weaker foundation. The rights could be limited by the capacity of the employer to finance such benefits. Some benefits like social security benefits may be contributory in nature, and in that sense limited by the capacity of the employee to contribute. These benefits could be further hedged in by other eligibility criteria, such as a minimum period of employment or nature of work performed. Where it is difficult to establish the employment relationship, such as for workers in the informal economy, access to these rights located in labour law virtually vanishes. To what extent, then, should labour law serve as the vehicle for delivering benefits to persons who work in the informal economy and those who do not fit into the conventional employer–employee relationship? Would the distinction between labour rights and standards have any place in conceptualising the scope of labour law? Should the self-employed in the informal economy who do not have the features of being 'economically dependant' be covered under social security schemes covering other employees or not? These are matters agitating policy makers, trade unions and organisations working among the informal sector in India where there are plans to begin a (contributory) social security scheme for the more than 300,000,000 workers in the informal economy.

Many of the ILO standards apply both to employees and workers at large. Yet it is clear that these two categories are not identical. This does not however mean that the level of benefits and protection enjoyed by these two categories of working people cannot be identical. For example, the ILO Convention on home workers does not treat home workers recruited through an intermediary as employees of the principal employer; yet the standards dealing with homework establish that the rights and benefits applicable to home workers need be comparable with those of regular employees. In India, too, the law dealing with contract labour does not establish workers employed by a contractor as employees of the principal employer. (Yet there have been cases where the court has 'lifted the veil' and declared them to be direct employees of the principal employer.[20]) However according to the rules made under the law dealing with contract labour, there is to be parity, not only of rights and benefits, but also of wage rates with regular employees of the principal employer (user enterprise). There is a power with the government to abolish the practice of contract labour where there is perennial use of contract labour. However, once employment

---

[20] See, for instance, *Hussainbhai v Alath Factory Employees' Union* [1978] 2 LLJ 397 (SC).

of contract labour is abolished it does not entitle the contract labour to be absorbed as employees of the principal employer, presenting a dilemma to the contract labour who wish to be directly employed by the principal employer.

In recent times there have been initiatives in India to offer the same level of social security benefits to self-employed workers who cannot be brought into employment relationships as those enjoyed by employees in the informal economy. By enacting an umbrella law that covers both those employed and self-employed in the informal economy, similar levels of rights are sought to be delivered. And since many persons in the informal economy move from the category of employed to self employed and back again frequently (seasonal migration in agriculture is one example), there is a need to deal with both these categories in one single law in order for these to be uniformity in rights for all those who work and for the 'portability' of benefits.

In the past few years several government appointed commissions have looked into the matter.[21] One common feature of many of the proposals is to have a board/fund that will register employers, workers and the self-employed that will not only lay down minimum terms of employment but that will also operate and deliver the social security benefits. However, given the 300,000,000 plus persons we are talking about and the diversity of this sector, it may require state-level and industry-level boards. There have also been debates about the level of rights and benefits that can be extended.

4. CHOICE OF BENEFITS AND THEIR FINANCING

Rights that correspond to the core conventions of the ILO are considered *relatively* inexpensive or 'cost less' to the employers, and the state would of course be the obvious choice for such extension. Rights to organise, against discrimination, forced labour and against use of prohibited forms of child labour could well be extended to those in self-employment also. These rights correspond often with constitutional provisions in many countries and human right provisions and can be universally made applicable irrespective of whether one is or is not in an employment relationship. To give

---

[21] The National Commission on Labour, above n 3, proposed an umbrella law for the unorganised sector workers (broadly defined) and the setting up of a central board to deal with employment, social security and welfare issues. Trade unions working among the informal economy workers have suggested several drafts in the last couple of years. In 2004 the government appointed a National Commission on Enterprises in the Informal and Unorganised Sector which also has a mandate to examine how best to provide social security and protection for workers in these sectors.

an example, boycott of vendors based on religion or gender or the compulsion to enter into commercial contracts or into certain trades and occupations for customary reasons of caste or ethnicity can be dealt with in the law. This would no doubt circumscribe the freedom to contract or to transact based on one's property rights, but it would be justified on the grounds of public policy.

Laws that cast a financial burden on the employer, such as social security and welfare legislation, pose a greater problem with regard to the extent to which they can be extended to the self-employed. Just as labour law can provide for minimum conditions of employment for those in employment relationships dealing with aspects of safety, health and hours of work, the law could provide at least a meta-right to those in self-employment by directing the state to keep considerations of livelihood promotion of this section as a central part of their policy formulation. Matters of livelihood promotion would include access to common property resources and proper zoning laws that keep the interests of street vendors and hawkers in mind.[22] In the case of the self-employed working in the informal economy the financial burden of social security and welfare benefits poses a problem. To expect the self–employed worker to bear the full insurance costs of these benefits (and being expected to pay both the employed and the employer's contributions, because that is how many of the insurance schemes are set up), when most of them are earning well below the minimum wage levels is not feasible. Instead of a general tax burden on the population to finance social security benefits, one option could be to impose a tax on each industry that would bear the cost of the workers related with that particular industry. This is one option being seriously considered in India currently. The idea is to have several industry/employment-related boards for delivering social security benefits and welfare benefit. Workers—both those in employment relationships and the self-employed—would be registered and contribute to these schemes with some of the corpus coming from a specific cess[23] imposed on that industry (in lieu of the employer contribution, in the case of self-employed workers). A certain amount of cross subsidisation across industries would have to take place, given the differing sizes of these industries, and their economic capacity to contribute.[24]

---

[22] For an example of such an initiative to provide legal cover to the interest of livelihood promotion for the self employed in the informal economy see the draft Unorganised Sector Workers (Conditions of Work and Livelihood Promotion) Bill, 2005 prepared by the National Commission on Enterprises in the Informal and Unorganised Sector, available at: http://www.nceuis.nic.in.

[23] In India, such specific levies are imposed by law on the industry concerned. See, e.g., the Beedi Workers Welfare Cess Act 1976 and the Building and Other Construction Workers Cess Act 1996.

[24] It of course needs to be considered whether multinational corporations with their deeper pockets should contribute relatively more than other enterprises within the same industry.

The nature of the social security benefits that should be provided for those in the informal economy also varies across sections. The traditional limbs of social security covering specific contingencies found in the ILO standards may not be relevant, since these are based on reduction in the income earning capacity of the insured worker. Many have argued that such an approach is based on a presumption of a near lifetime of employment, with social security providing the safety net for the occasional period when a person is unable to earn an income. Asset security, security against natural disasters and ability to upgrade one's skills may be more meaningful aspects while designing a social security scheme for the informal economy. The flexibility to deal with each sector has to be a part of the structure envisaged for the regulation of the informal economy.

By stopping well short of universal coverage, these provisions could well be considered to be labour standards and not general welfare or social assistance provisions. Yet since the maximum that could be achieved by such state- and industry-supported financing is limited social security benefits, there is need to complement this with social assistance schemes and public health measures which target the population at large and of which those in the informal economy constitute nearly 50 per cent.

11

Ways and Effects of Deconstructing, Protection in the Post-socialist New Member States*—Based on Hungarian Experience

CSILLA KOLLONAY LEHOCZKY**

THERE WAS A kind of 'end of the world' feeling in the eyes and in the voice of a senior and distinguished teacher of languages in the largest Hungarian university when she came to ask for my legal advice: she had been confronted with the alternative: to become an 'entrepreneur' providing teaching services to her former students through a contract between the university and her 'enterprise' or lose her job. The university—due to serious budget cuts—decided to offer formerly free language tuition as a paid service to the students and to shift the business and employment risk of the activity to the previous teachers by requiring them to form small private companies with which the university would contract for the services. The teacher insisted that she had been a faculty member, a public employee of a state university, for about a quarter of a century and she found it an absurd idea to be a university teacher as a private entrepreneur. She could hardly believe that there was nothing in the law books that would have prevented the university from making such a move.

---

* After more than 15 years of changes we still have terminological problems. When naming these countries both 'post-socialist' and 'post-communist' are used and both are correct, as much as they underline a different feature of the previous regime. The term 'post-socialist' refers to the pre-1989 economy that was based on socialised property and central planning, whereas denoting them as 'post-communist' indicates that the political regime in the past was based on the monolithic power of the communist-party.

** Professor of Law, Central European University, Budapest, Hungary.

This case might illustrate the scale of the proliferation of contractual relationships replacing employment in Hungary predominantly for cost saving and risk avoiding purposes.[1]

This 'reorganisation' of teaching activity was preceded by contracting out cleaning, security and maintenance services, and followed by converting even secretaries and administrative staff members into 'independent contractors', in the latter case through a similar solution: the employee formed (or joined) a partnership or a limited liability company and continued performing the same activities within the legal framework of services provided by the company. The intensity of such contracting out is no less in private companies or in other state services. For example, the operation of small post offices of the Hungarian Mail Service was put out to tender and the employees, if they wanted to keep their jobs, had the 'opportunity' to bid for their workplaces.

The fall of the communist regimes has brought about, not surprisingly, the fall of the over-important and all-encompassing domain of labour law in the post-socialist countries. However, the range and intensity of the process have been worrying and naturally resulted in academic and political debates as well as legislative steps. This chapter will first give a summary presentation of the historical background, explaining the fervour for abandoning the restrictions of labour law. In part 2 it will overview the effects of the economic and political changes to the position of the labour force, as a result of the strong prioritisation of contractual freedom and private entrepreneurship. Part 3 makes an inventory of the judicial and legislative reaction to the release of 'contractual freedom'. Finally the chapter will summarise the conclusions that follow from the described developments as well as the potential future tendencies and processes.

1. HISTORICAL BACKGROUND

While there is a strong re-contractualisation drive as well as a move to escape from labour law in the whole developed world, the same process in the Central–East European (CEE) countries has a special dynamic that cannot be understood without understanding the position of labour in the imminent past of these countries.

---

[1] We could add a further lesson to this story: the employee in the anecdote succeeded in achieving that, as an exception, she could retain the 'dignifying' position (as she thought it) of a public employee because she was really excellent and the university did not want to lose her. The lesson is that the weaker the bargaining position of an employee is, the bigger chance there is to be converted from employee into a kind of 'entrepreneur'.

The economy was entirely in the hands of the totalitarian states and the position of workers could be approximated to that of 'citizens' or 'state subjects' as a result of the almost complete 'de-contractualisation' of their status. The forms and intensity of the total subordination of economy to the monolithic political power varied from country to country and also changed by time, permitting Hungary to establish its special prelude to the post–1989 developments.

A. The Decreased Role of Contract: The 'Status' of the 'Socialist Worker'

Contract did not play much role during the decades of the socialist era, either in setting the terms of the employment relationship or in shaping the rights and duties of people in general. The state was based on centralised national property and people were legally prevented from owning property beyond personal needs. Consequently, private business transactions—besides elementary contracts of everyday living—were not a standard part of life. Transactions of economy and commerce were executed almost exclusively between parts of the nationalised property[2]—let alone that these 'contracts' were more the fulfillment of administrative decisions than the results of autonomous negotiations. Satisfaction of everyday needs also was closer to rationing and distribution by public administration (free or at a nominal price) than obtaining goods from the market.[3] Therefore waiting lists and the discretionary power of administrations in allocating goods and services played a bigger role than the rule of the market (even if people were formally concluding 'sale' contracts when finally getting access to the needed goods, or, as to housing, 'rent contracts'[4]).

The socialist legal vocabulary did not use 'employee' for those working in an employment relationship. The general term was 'worker'.[5] This was not a mere terminological preference: a 'worker' had a status stipulated by law, in contrast to a contractual relationship established by the autonomous negotiation and agreement of the employer and employee. Furthermore, being an 'employee' is only one (albeit decisive) dimension of the existence

---

[2] Private entrepreneurship—within the restricted property and employment boundaries—accounted for about 5–6% of the national economy. Collectivised agricultural property did not permit more individual contracting either, although in the last period of the regime its members were permitted to do very small scale private farming and freely to sell the products from it—in line with the cautious trials with market reforms in Hungary.

[3] On the other hand goods considered 'luxury' goods were dissuasively highly priced (when available at all), while they were also frequently subject to rationing and distributing decisions.

[4] Understanding of that economy is greatly helped by János Kornai's famous work, *Economics of Shortage* (Amsterdam, North Holland, 1980), 306–9, describing 'soft budget constraint' as a main source of the permanent excessive demand.

of a person. Being a 'socialist worker' was an overall status before the state, that encompassed practically all areas of the life of the person, contained a broad scale of entitlements and obligations encroaching into the private life:[6] and all kinds of social security benefits besides increased job-security. The 'worker's status' was closely attached to, and hardly distinguishable from, 'citizenship'[7].

Working conditions were tightly regulated—levelling wage policy through centrally set levelled wages (rather nominal than real), uniform, generous benefits, homogeneous norms governing rights and duties at the workplace, work procedures and disciplinary rules, leaving hardly any margin for the parties to negotiate about anything. The structure of employment was similar to the hierarchical state–citizen relationship, rather than to a contractual bond. The Constitution equated the status of 'workman' with 'citizen': not only implicitly by the general, interchangeable use of the two words, but also by the explicit setting of workplace duties (caring for social property, observing workdiscipline) as citizens' duties.[8]

In summary, rights and duties of people—inside and outside the workplace—were connected to the status of the 'worker participating in building up socialism'—in the phraseology of the time. The term was also a caution to the people as to what qualified persons eligible for benefits and distribution. The expression, especially in the light of Article 2 of the Constitution, establishing that 'Hungary is the State of workers and working peasants',[9] also implied a warning of exclusion from distribution (as happened in practice) and even the threat of restriction to a limited status if someone abandoned this position—ie by becoming an 'idler' or parasite (unless the 'non-working' status occurred for acceptable reasons, such as inability to work or other kind of hindrance).

Nonetheless, the formal concept and institution of the contract was widely used throughout the socialist era. The Roman law traditions (that came to Hungary and to a number of CEE countries through the transmission of

---

[5] The vocabulary had strong ideological fetishisation in the communist regime. 'Peasant-worker' was still an acceptable class, nevertheless a somewhat lower category, similarly to the distinction between 'workman' and 'clerical employee', also with the coded meaning of first and second rank 'worker'.

[6] Housing, childcare, holiday resorts, organised cultural events were naturally available through the workplace, while various activities in leisure time were expected, obtaining a passport or studying depended on the employer etc.

[7] 'Socialist citizenship', of course, distinct from the legal-moral content that is attached to this word in a democratic society.

[8] See Art 9 (2) and (3) of the Hungarian Constitution (Act XX of 1949) as they were in force until April 1972.

[9] The expression—used throughout the Soviet block—meant that peasantry, even if not *employed,* could have a status assimilated to that of 'workers' as much as they were working in socialist co-operatives; however, anyone outside this category was a non-worker, therefore a potential 'parasite', who did not deserve the same status as 'workers'.

Austrian and German law) played a role in preserving the form.[10] This 'contract' was rather a technical-administrative instrument organising socio-economic relationships than an institution of autonomous negotiation, while maintaining some appearance of autonomy of the 'parties'.[11]

Although workers were employed pursuant to a 'labour contract', this contract was primarily formal rather than being an expression of the mutual agreement of the parties. As mentioned above, terms and conditions of employment were regulated in every detail by centrally set laws, leaving only a very small margin for the parties to negotiate. As the doctrine of that time had it: the contract of employment meant 'freedom in the choice, constraint in the terms'.[12] It has to be added, though, that not even choosing a partner was entirely free. Varying greatly from country to country and changing with time (earlier years were tougher than later from the late 1960s), several norms limited the freedom of both parties. Mandatory placement of new graduates as well as tight rules of termination of employment for both parties (exclusive list of permitted causes of termination), sanctioning departure from the norm[13] and the wide power of the employer to transfer an employee not only within the establishment but also to another employer questioned even the freedom of 'choosing the party'.

The huge number of administrative norms regulating workplace life (not even 'law' in the true sense) was labelled 'labour law' and elevated to high importance. As an early 1960s legal history textbook taught: 'with the victory of the socialist revolution commercial law, the in-house law of the old ruling class had to disappear, whereas labour law, the law of the new societies based on labour elevated to dominant role'.[14] The self-confidence and absurdity of such a statement may show how much the ideological and political infiltration into law magnified artificially the imaginary (never real) importance of labour law.

The political glory created around labour and labour regulations by the socialist regime explains the controversial attitude of both legislation and academia towards labour law after the shift. Before turning to the result of

---

[10] While on the one hand Roman law (civil law) traditions were condemned and intended to be outlawed by some enthusiastic communist-party committed legal theorists, in fact they remained a basis for the theory and regulation of the Soviet era. See G. Hamza, *Az európai magánjog fejlődése* [*The Development of European Private Law*] (Budapest, Nemzeti Tankönyvkiadó, 2002), 232 ff, and *Die Entwicklung des Privatrechts auf römischrechtlicher Grundlage* (Budapest, Andrássy Gyula Deutschsprachige Univ. Budapest, 2002), 167 ff.

[11] In Hungary the concept and function of contract could recover some of its real meaning in the wake of the gradual (and fluctuating) economic liberalisation and market oriented measures in the last two decades of the socialist era. See below here, in sect. 2B.

[12] I. Kertész, *A fegyelmi felelősség* (Budapest, Akadémiai Kiadó, 1966), 43.

[13] Employees could lose a part of their annual vacation and were taking the risk of mandatory placement if they left their employer in an unlawful manner.

the political changes, a Hungarian peculiarity—individual contracting opportunities within the collective property, having a role in the post-socialist developments—is worth a look.

B. Reforms of the Socialist Economy: 'Intrapreneurship' as a Combination of Employment with Entrepreneurship

Hungary experimented with market-type reforms from the late 1960s, trying to combine, even if on a limited scale, institutions of the market (eg competition, economic interest, market price) with the state owned, centrally planned national economy. There were three waves of these reforms—in the late 1960s, in the mid 1970s and from the early 1980s.[15] The first two trials faded away (and than re-started) mainly as a result of the weakening or rising political support within the communist leadership, not independently of domestic and international economic and political processes.

The reforms opened wide the idea and practice of secondary employment popular both among employees for the extra income it brought and among employers for the opportunity to manipulate staff and wage limitations. In order to escape from the restrictions of vigilant (and always changing) regulations the dominant practice from secondary employment switched to non-employment types of secondary engagements. The legal qualification remained obfuscating throughout the decades (up to now) and merged under the elastic and puzzling name of 'other relationship aimed at work performance'—indicating that it was similar to employment, however, other than those falling under the Labour Code.

The third and last desperate attempt to revitalise the insolvent state's socialist system started in the 1980s and was channelled into the 1989 overthrow of the regime. Catchwords of this last series of reforms drummed into us 'entrepreneurial spirit' and 'entrepreneurship' as required and assumed attributes on the part of the workers in the state enterprises—being in part the explanatory basis (whether true or false) of transferring the control of state enterprises from the central authorities to the state enterprises themselves (by creating governing bodies there).

---

[14] Ö. Both, A. Csizmadia, L. Hajdú, P. Horváth and K. Nagyné Szegvári, *Universal Legal History* (Budapest, Texbook Publishers, 1984), 489.

[15] For more on the reform see J. Kornai, 'Comments on the Present State and the Prospects of the Hungarian Economic Reform' (1983) 7 *Journal of Comparative Economics* 225, J. Kornai, 'The Hungarian Reform Process: Visions, Hopes and Reality' (1986) 24 *Journal of Econ Literature* 1687 at 1691, L. Csaba, 'The Recent Past and the Future of the Hungarian Reform: An Overview and Assessment' in R. Clarke (ed.), *Hungary: The Second Decade of Economic Reform* (London, Longman Group UK Limited, 1989), 13.

The provisions, adopted in 1981, permitted private economic activity of individuals on a scale that was unprecedented in that time East European countries.[16]

The new forms were forerunners of the post-1989 variety of legal forms of engaging labour, as much as they were non-employment forms of engaging labour mainly added to the existing employment relationship, or, in some cases, even replacing it. Employees of the same employer, forming autonomous *quasi*-business companies (similar to partnerships) of two to 30 members could contract to work for their employer for an extra fee, performed at the sites of the employer and using its facilities. The aim was better utilisation of state property through the private initiative and the use of the increased time employees were ready to spend at the workplace in the hope of higher income. (It is important to add that the decades of state socialism were characterised by permanent shortages of labour as well as administrative restrictions on hiring new labour.[17]) In spite of the emerging practical legal problems deriving from the operation of the new forms, these new initiatives of '*intrapreneurship*'[18] were proliferating rapidly and became popular among both employers and employees.[19]

In summary: emerging flexibility, speeding up from the 1980s, was seen in Hungary as an achievement under central control and as a reasonable and gainful alternative to the inefficient typical employment. The alternative and flexible forms of engaging in work remained an auxiliary activity, supplementing the secure, modestly paying full-time employment in the state sector of the economy—thereby investing both.

2. THE BACKLASH OF THE PAST IMPINGING ON POST-SOCIALIST LABOUR LAW

The need for re-drawing the boundaries of what is called labour law has arisen under different circumstances and by entirely different dynamics in the post-socialist countries than in the Western market economies. While labour law has carved out a part from the domain of contract law where the freedom of contract of the weaker party has been guaranteed by legislative intervention, still within the domain of private law and preserving the

---

[16] Governmental Decree no 28/1981, on 'Economic Work-Communities'.

[17] See Kornai, above n 4.

[18] 'Intrapreneurship' was one of the novel and at a time very fashionable ideas of the late 1970s and early 1980s worldwide within managerial sciences, aimed at inventing new methods able to bring about higher efforts and greater efficiency from employees. In substance these goals—although under entirely different circumstances—were not much different from the Hungarian efforts in the 1980s.

institution of contract, socialist labour law has been established as a separate branch of law, closer to public law, replacing the contract between the parties by central regulation imposing duties upon the parties and lacking the domination of mutuality and the exchange character.

The collapse of state socialism has brought about a radical setback in the position of workers. This was in part a result of the objective facts of economic regression and necessary restructuring; in part it was a result of subjective reasons, deriving from the controversial and politically tinted position of labour law under the two opposing political regimes. The collapse of the socialist regime brought about a backlash of the past, trying to turn everything that was an attribute of the fallen regime into its opposite. The setback has been connected to the celebrated revival of contractual freedom, accompanied by a re-contractualisation of labour law and a conspicuous imbalance between employee and employer.

A. The Economic Background

The 1989–1990 revolutions have been followed by deep economic recession throughout the region. The restructuring of the wasteful socialist industry, the collapse of COMECON,[20] that was previously the main market for socialist goods resulted in immense fallback of production. The privatisation, the closing down of big strongholds of the 'workers' class' maintained for political reasons through huge subsidies were naturally accompanied by the shedding of labour and a resulting imbalance in the labour market. Demand dramatically shrank,[21] and the enormous surplus of labour was aggravated by the fact that it had never before been confronted with the phenomenon of unemployment: unemployment rates jumped from zero to 12 per cent by 1992[22] and was rising until 1994, reaching 13 per cent before its peak.

Such a vast discrepancy between labour supply and demand always weakens the position of workers. The early 1990s' situation in the post-socialist countries has been aggravated by the fact that the whole of society,

---

[19] An obvious advantage of this matching of the state sector economy with private initiative was that it was *open*, while in Hungary and in practically all socialist economies there was a firm practice, a kind of hidden economy working on the workers' own account during working hours, on the employer's premises and using its resources. See M. Lackó, 'The Hidden Economies of Visegrád Countries in International Comparison: a Household Electircity Approach' in L. Halpern and C. Wyplosz (eds.), *Hungary: Towards a Market Economy* (Cambridge, Cambridge University Press, 1998), 129.

[20] Council for Mutual Economic Assistance, the economic organisation of the Soviet Bloc countries (abbreviated also as CMEA).

[21] GDP fell by close to 20% between 1990 and 1992, the profits in the non-financial corporate sector turned into negative, wages were cut significantly: L. Halpern and C. Wyplosz, 'The Hidden Hungarian Miracle' in Halpern and Wyplosz, above n 19, at 3.

[22] *Ibid.*

in particularly employees, was unprepared to cope with that scale of unemployment. The defencelessness of workers was further aggravated by the desperate need of the economy to attract capital investments and to find buyers for the huge tracts of state property—while practically the whole of Central and Eastern Europe (CEE) was on sale—in itself created a social and political atmosphere prioritising employers' interests over employees' interests.[23]

A further objective factor was, not only in Hungary but all over in the CEE countries, the dramatically weakened position of the trade unions in part by their political discreditation, fragmentation and rivalry.

B. Backlash of the Past and the Restoration of Contract

The objective factors weakening the position of labour have been associated with subjective reasons created by the specific circumstances of the transition.

The fall of the communist regime caused an allergic reaction to nearly all phenomena associated with the past—not only in politics, economics and law, but also in culture, family and social relations, and education.[24] Since the system which had collapsed was based on collective property the main thrust of the changes was to reinstate private property and the freedom of private property. The past exaggeration of collectivism provoked over-emphasised individualism, as an important ingredient of a democratic society.

The almost uncritical rejection of anything that was considered a value in the past has been the most intensive in the economic area, and especially in the field of labour law. Paternalism and lack of freedom in the past inflated the significance of market freedoms in general. The lack of a clear set of values and enthusiasm for the new market freedoms frequently led to the

---

[23] A further, general feature of the transitional market was immaturity, with acts that could rather undermine than build the moral and mutual trust—impacting first of all on small and medium sized enterprises (as well as on their employees), whose capital power was relatively small.

[24] Just to illustrate the atmosphere all over the region and in particular in Hungary: not only did the Russian language become discredited and unfavoured but Russian culture as such; royal family members became popular and came back to politics; serious efforts were made to rehabilitate Nazis or collaborators of the Nazis because they fought against the communist (Soviet) power, and were executed by the communists; nearly funny anecdotes emerged about re-allocations of artistic monuments, re-naming of public places as well as allergic rejection of the use of the red star in any form, eg on the label of Heinecken bier. See also on this issue this author in 'European Enlargement: A Comparative View of Hungarian Labour Law' in G.A. Berman and K. Pistor (eds.), *Law and Governance in an Enlarged European Union* (Oxford, Hart Publishing, 2004), 209 at 211–13, and in 'The Significance of Existing EU Sex Equality Law for Women in the New Member States: The Case of Hungary' (2005) 12 *Maastricht Law Journal* 467.

toleration or even celebration of unscrupulousness and the misuse of economic power as long-needed entrepreneurship. The idea of the freedom of contract in general and that of the employment contract in particular was popular within the whole population in the early 1990s: there was a hope that they would bring about good organisation, efficient management and the reward of hard and good quality work replacing the domination of mediocrity and inefficiency through levelling wage policies.

The ardour for increased contractual freedom raised the issue of the 're-assignment' of labour contracts back to the Civil Code[25] and thereby practically suppressing labour law—the 'favourite child' of the communist regime—or at least moving it to the periphery.[26]

At the same time the effective legislative steps were tamed by political considerations: the priority goal of maintaining social peace and creating a social consensus about the new system of labour law regulation. Dependent on the activity and organising-bargaining capacity of the various social groups in the CEE countries, this taming effect varied in form and content in the different post-socialist countries. Functioning tripartism, established on the ruins of the past corporative system of industrial relations,[27] assisted in exerting a balancing effect, though clearly to a limited extent.[28] The new Labour Code of 1992[29] basically succeeded in bringing labour legislation in line with the requirements of the private market economy[30] and reduced the

---

[25] See J. Radnay, 'A munkajog és a polgári jog kapcsolata' ['The Link between Labour Law and Civil Law'] in G. Bánrévi, G. Jobbágyi and C. Varga (eds.), *Justum, aequum, slautare* (Budapest, Osiris Publishers, 1998), 242; T. Prugberger, 'A munkajog és a polgári jog kapcsolata a jogdogmatika tükrében' ['The Link between Labour Law and Civil Law in the Mirror of Legal Doctrine'] (2000) XVII *Tomus* 211.

[26] The dispute started within the framework of a thorough amendment of both the Civil Code and the Labour Code of Hungary—and neither of these major legislative works has been finished. Consequently the question is still open.

[27] This particular phenomenon, characteristic of the CEE countries in the process of abandoning state-controlled economy necessarily by the state itself, has been called 'transformational corporatism'.

[28] L. Héthy, 'Political Changes and the Transformation of Industrial Relations in Hungary' in J. R. Niland, R. D. Lansbury and C. Verevis (eds.), *The Future of Industrial Relations: Global Change and Challenge* (London, Sage, 1994), at 317.

[29] Act XXII of 1992 on the Labour Code, in force from 1 July 1992.

[30] By abolishing lots of bureaucratic prescriptions, generalising the concept of employer, abolishing a part of the barriers to terminating employment, guaranteeing trade union freedom and separating trade union activity from the necessary information and consultation system. It principally changed the system of termination of employment in two important respects. First, the previous broad scale of socially indicated limitations and prohibitions on termination was radically cut, and only a few restrictions were retained as to private employment (a longer list of protected situations remained in force, however, as to public employees). Secondly, financial compensation for the loss of a job—formerly unknown—was introduced. Mandatory redundancy payments—after completion of a threshold year of service—were enacted, fixed term employment contracts could be 'bought off' prematurely by payment of lost wages, and, last but not least, among the principal changes, financial compensation in lieu of reinstatement as a consequence of unlawful termination became possible.

previous bureaucratic rigidities, while still maintaining a floor of rights through the Labour Code.[31] The provisions on the individual employment relationship—following the German *Günstigkeitsprinzip* as a pattern— have been characterised by the so-called 'one sided permissivity'. The norms are mandatory and no departure to the detriment of workers is permitted, unless explicitly provided otherwise by the Labour Code itself,[32] whereas departure in favour of the employee is possible as a rule.

C. Employers' Practices: 'Flexibilisation' as Entrepreneurial Freedom

In spite of the relatively moderate liberalisation of labour law, the re-contractualisation of employment relationships went far beyond the mere abolition of the impediment of central regulation of wages and benefits and had a devastating effect on working conditions. The concepts of 'autonomy' and 'freedom' of de facto dependent workers proved more endemic and more difficult to reveal and unmask in countries where entrepreneurship has been glorified as a victory over communist type dependence.

The combined effect of the threat of unemployment and of the supportive political spirit around proprietary and entrepreneurial freedom has been joined by the 'quasi-state authority' of the employer inherited from the past when the state-employer represented state power over workers. These together created tremendous divergence of negotiating power between the parties and brought workers into an ultimately helpless position. Hence, the management succeeded in stretching, evading or even openly violating the rules unpunished and gradually developed an unusual level of flexibility in employment. In this process the employers could also confidently rely on the uncertainties and overload of the courts,[33] as well as on the moral and social support surrounding the 'new ownership' and condemning 'socialist workmanship', identifying the latter with inefficient, lazy work. All these exacerbated the tight objective economic reasons already silencing aggrieved workers.

---

[31] Eg the provisions on justified reason for ordinary termination and prohibiting it during sickness, the restrictions on fixed term contract, the duty of reinstatement in the case of unlawful termination as well as some norms on the rights of trade unions.

[32] If departure to the detriment of the workers is explicitly permitted, in most cases this is possible only by collective agreement and not by individual agreement—thereby becoming an incentive for collective bargaining.

[33] As a step towards the rule of law, the ability to go to the court in legal disputes of a citizen was opened wide. At the same time, the budget of the courts was not proportionately increased, which resulted in cases stretching on for years. The delivery of justice was particularly high in labour matters where the former first instances of workplace labour arbitration committees were abolished.

'Internal' flexibility—that is, the extension of the unilateral managerial prerogatives within the framework of an employment contract in order to adjust labour force availability to the changing needs of the management—has affected all possible dimensions of work: time, workplace, scope of activity and wages.

Temporal flexibility has grown most widely. According to a survey undertaken in 2001, at least one form of temporal flexibility (shift-work, overtime, week-end or holiday work, night work and part-time work[34]) was affecting two thirds (67 per cent) of the total labour force examined, while 50 per cent of workers worked under the most irregular circumstances, and also close to half (48 per cent) worked evening shifts.[35]

Spatial flexibility (working from home, having a mobile workplace, working abroad and working occasionally outside the contractual workplace) also applies to one third (33 per cent) of the labour force. Since the surveyed forms are also mixing contractual and unilaterally ordered flexibility, it cannot reflect the effect of the 2001 amendment of the Labour Code that increased employers' ability to order employees to work out of their contractual workplaces from two months to 110 working days per year[36]), working in some form of spatial flexibility.[37]

Wage flexibility imposed on workers in the name of contractual freedom proved one of the most ominous inventions by employers. Since only the very low national minimum wage (about US$ 280 per month for 2005) is mandatory under the Labour Code, the labour contract frequently stipulates only the mandatory minimum wages and the rest of the real payment (frequently the main part of the remuneration) is provided by a 'flexible wage' (or 'mobile wage') that depends on the fulfillment of further preconditions prescribed by the employer. Not infrequently the supplement is paid to the employee as 'presence remuneration', not paid for days of absence. Such an arrangement, while being within the limits of permitted contractual freedom, can prevent employees from taking sick leave, annual vacations or any time off (like for parental duties) to which they are entitled by law.

---

[34] Of course, such simply definable flexibility can cause terminological difficulties: what intensity of irregular work (here once a week: in strict terms, once a month in lose terms) qualifies someone as a night-worker, weekend worker or overtime worker? The forms of flexibility chosen for the survey are, from a legal point of view, mixing contracted flexibility (part time) with unilaterally ordered flexibility. In the case of other flexibilities the criteria are even more complex to define for a scientific survey.

[35] E. Sík and I. Nagy, *The Forms of Flexibility (FF) in Contemporary Hungary (Country Report)* (Budapest, TÁRKI, 2002), 4–5, available at: http://www.tarki.hu/adatbank-h/kutjel/pdf/a074.pdf.

[36] Act XVI of 2001, in force from 1 July 2001. The amendments have been adopted with reference to the transposition of the posted worker directive—'smuggling in' provisions that were not required by the *acquis*. At the same time this amendment was stopping the use of the opportunity of hidden agency work in the form of posting workers to other employers.

[37] Cf. above n 35, at 4.

Flexibility of the form of the contract also applies to about one third (31 per cent) of all employees, of whom—worryingly—more than one tenth of the total surveyed workforce (11 per cent) had no contract at all, 9 per cent were self-employed, 7 per cent were employed for a fixed term and the rest were sustained by mixed forms, such as casual work and agency work;[38] however, supposedly these latter forms of employment have increased in the wake of the 2001 legitimisation of temporary agency work.

The statistical data show that the two groups of workers in which flexibility is most frequent are the lowest (poorly educated, remote areas, low-prestige jobs, low wage earners) and the highest (highly educated, high-income workers) groups of the sample examined. There are, of course, differences, for example while within temporal flexibility workers with the highest education represented the biggest group among those working evening shifts, part-time work was the highest among the lowest educated.[39] Similarly, within spatial flexibility telework is rather characteristic of employees with higher education; home-working and mobile jobs are more frequent among those with lower education. Regarding contractual flexibility the lower groups prevail, with the exception of multiple jobs, that is, an attribute of the higher groups, in particular of high income groups.[40]

This correlation may lead us to an important conclusion: while the various forms of flexibility are imposed on the worker and, even if it brings some advantage for the worker, it mainly brings gains for the employer. The data suggest that the lower groups have more flexibility; there seems to be at the same time a segment of strongly-positioned workers (highly educated, high-income persons) with considerable flexibility that might be presumed voluntary.

The growth of the forms of flexibility confronts both the legislature and judiciary with the question of reasonable need for and limits of intervention into the freedom of the parties in flexibilising their relationship. In looking for answers to such a question the separation of voluntary and imposed flexibility might be decisive, while hard to measure.

3. CONSOLIDATION: LEGISLATIVE CHANGES AND SHAPING OF NEW PRACTICES

After the first wild years of the sweep of liberalisation and exploitive practices, by ending the privatisation process, adjusting regulation to the shaping

---

[38] *Ibid.*, at 5. Cf. too: A KSH Jelenti, Gazdaság és Társadalom [National Statistical Office Reports: Economy and Society] (2004) 39, according to which in 2003, out of the 3,922,000 active population, 2,753,000 had employee status.

[39] *Ibid.*, at 9–10.

[40] *Ibid.*, at 18.

(existing) markets and, last but not least, by the regulatory obligation to bring laws into compliance with the *acquis communaitaire* the laws also brought about a consolidation of the labour markets.

A. Legislative Changes

The pressure on the legislature to stop the releasing process and resulting chaos was multiple and differentiated. While it aimed at limiting the vigour of employers' shifting to non-labour law forms of employment, it tried to provide with protection and support those who had been exposed to such forms beyond their control.

The legislative steps—adopted in Hungary mainly between 2001 and 2004 and showing efforts to protect working persons from the employers' inventive flexibilisation as well as to formalise and make more visible the hidden, informal economy—can be subsumed under four headings regarding the approach to the new forms of employment:

—legitimise and regulate emerging new forms of employment;
—extend basic labour law protection to non-labour law areas;
—prohibit and discourage false self-employment;
—inspect and sanction the observation of the rules.

1. Legitimisation and Regulation of New Precarious Forms of Employment

Regulation and at the same time legitimisation have been particularly relevant to the emerging new forms of employment at the borderline of labour law. These forms were primarily temporary agency work and telework. These forms, gaining ground from the mid 1990s, emerged first as specific (flexible) application of existing norms on secondment, outworking and home-working. Nevertheless the precarious character of such engagement was soon revealed and a question emerged: whether to prohibit them or to regulate them as specific forms of employment. By regulating them in the Labour Code[41] and obliging agencies to establish an employment relationship with temporary workers, the legislature has provided basic guarantees and minimal standards for employees and at the same time granted security to the placement agencies which were previously on the verge of violating

---

[41] Chapter X/A on Telework of the Labour Code, in force from 1 May 2004, and Chapter XI on Agency work, in force from 1 July 2001 and considerably amended in November 2005, inserting equal treatment requirements, and assigning the user-employer as legal employer in abusive cases as a measure intended to prevent such use of the new legal forms.

labour rules and thereby facing the threat of sanctions. A thorough 2005 amendment of the relevant provisions has increased the guarantees, especially in cases of longer-term employment (equal treatment with employees of the user-employer and automatically establishing employment with the user-employer in most cases of violation of the rules).

On the other hand, a few special kinds of employment that have been considered as a typical departure from traditional employment have been regulated and legitimised as non-employment forms of using labour. These borderline activities were considered by the legislature to be irregular and closer to independent contractorship, and received special regulation: this was so with the relationship of business agents (market promoters), private security guards and some categories of artists, journalists and professional athletes. The special regulations guaranteed special employment as well as social security and taxation status to these groups—trying to remove them from the 'grey' part of the economy. In these cases the special circumstances of the activity supposedly justified the departure from labour law employment. While the exercise of these professions in most cases indeed offered and also required a considerable amount of independence and autonomy of the worker, the automatic legitimisation of the avoidance of labour law has lacked differentiation and protection in cases of clearly dependent labour.

2. Extension of Protection to Non-labour Law Areas

Some core protection attached to labour law employment and established for vulnerable situations has been extended to workers in other relationships when the worker is, or might be, in a dependent situation, even if not in the form of subordinate labour. The extended forms of protection are: social security, safety and hygiene, prohibition of child labour, equal treatment, and entitlement to unemployment benefit.

The extension of social security coverage to 'independent contractors' has been one of the very first measures in re-regulating social security, as a remedy for the previous discriminatory measures regarding any 'non-socialist' (ie other than employment in the state sector) type of work under the communist regime. The prohibition of child labour and the prohibition of discrimination both were extended to the so-called 'other relationship aimed at work performance'[42] in the early 2000s. Similarly, the law on labour safety and hygiene covers 'all organised forms, regardless of the organisational form or proprietorship'.[43]

---

[42] Art 72/A of the Labour Code, Art 5(d) of Act CXXV of 2003 on Equal Treatment and Equal Opportunity.
[43] Act XCIII of 1993 on Labour Safety and Hygiene, art 9.

As a clear acknowledgement of the 'intermediate' position of 'self-employed' persons between dependent employees and (truly) independent contractors was the establishment of a limited version of unemployment allowance, called 'entrepreneurs' allowance' and available for those who worked previously as individual entrepreneurs (self-employed) or members of an associate form of undertaking.[44]

3. Prohibit and Disfavour Forced Self-employment

While the consistent case law of the labour courts has for decades, limited the freedom of the parties in choosing the title of their contract an amendment of the Labour Code was adopted in 2003, explicitly prohibiting the choice of a type of contract that would 'limit or prevent the application of provisions aimed at the protection of just interests of the employee'. It also added—enshrining the consistent basis of the case law of the courts now in the words of its Labour Code—that the type of the contract has to be evaluated irrespective of its title, with respect to all circumstances of the case, with special regard to the preliminary negotiations of the parties, their declarations, to the character of the work performed, and to their mutual rights.[45] This amendment only made explicit in the law books what has long been firmly established in the case law, serving much more a political than legal purpose: the intention of the amendment was to caution employers as well as to fulfill an election campaign promise of the governing socialist party to tame employers' practices converting employees into forced independent contractors. Consequently the change in the law, beside having a temporary 'restraining' effect, did not much change (and did not help) the dilemmas of the courts in the interpretation of more and more complex cases.[46]

Another small measure, intended to prevent the escalation of non-labour law employment forms, is found in the Employment Act: job opportunities available for the unemployed (recently: jobseekers) cannot qualify as 'appropriate' and thus establish a duty of the jobseeker to accept a job if the offered job is not in the legal form of labour law employment.

4. Increasing Inspection and Punishments

Parallel to the substantive regulations encouraging employers and employees to find the correct legal forms for their relationship, the regulations on

---

[44] Arts 44 to 46, as in force from 1 Jan. 2005, of Act IV of 1991 on Promotion of Employment and the Assistance to the Unemployed (referred to as Employment Act further on).

[45] The 2003 amendment to the Labour Code enacting this qualifying norm as Art. 75/A was the fulfillment of a prior promise made in the election campaign by a left-wing government (showing the social importance of this issue).

[46] See sect. B below on the case law of the Labour Courts.

inspecting and sanctioning the observance of the various regulations have tightened. Inspection and collection of social security dues has been transferred to the tax authorities with very wide authority (close to that of the criminal prosecution authorities), and both labour and tax inspectors have received the right to punish employers who report their employees in the wrong category.

While the Constitutional Court has declined to find a violation of the Constitution in the right of labour inspectors to qualify the title of a contract,[47] there seems to be a real controversy about the increased intensity and rigour of the sanctions. There are two interests to be served by the actions of the authorities, two intertwined problems, that should be separated. One is the observation of the statutory rights of dependent employees to protection in employment, eminently, protecting them from risks that are beyond their control, whereas the other is the legitimate interest of the state in collecting its dues (taxes and social security premiums) so as to cover its expenses. In the game of hide-and-seek, strong, frequent and tough inspections by both tax inspectors and labour inspectors, in both open and hidden collaboration between them,[48] this divergence between the two legitimate goals or interests can distort the context as well as finding the right answers.

B. Post-socialist Uncertainties and Typology in the Case Law of the Courts

Uncertainty about values and lack of experience with market economies have created a fluctuating and mixed case law of the labour courts. On the one hand courts tried to maintain the past case law that had been broad, sophisticated and well established. The case law—as in most European countries—has been consistent in assessing a contract independently from the title chosen by the parties, merely and entirely on the basis of the real circumstances of the relationship. Relying on a combination of primary and secondary attributes, using the right of the employer to give instructions (and the subordination based on it) as an ultimate test—'*differentia specifica*'—of employment the courts moved into two directions. First, they tried to restrict the new freedom of the parties in choosing the type of their contract.

Three types of cases—reflecting the dominant practice in the Hungarian labour market—come to the court, and, in spite of some unevenness in the

---

[47] Decision no 28/1998.
[48] Eg tax supervision lasts for weeks, while tax inspectors are working at sites of employers for weeks. If they find an invoice from someone they thought was an employee who was co-operating with them throughout this period, they have to alert the labour inspection organs to the fact that the ostensible employee is actually an independent contractor.

case law, a more-or-less harmonised response by the courts can be detected corresponding to the dominant characteristics of the cases, ascribing the will of the parties to one or other type of contract (irrespective of the title used by them).

The three groups can be called: sequential, supplementary and autonomous incidence of labour law and civil law contracts.

In the first group of cases, when there is a chronological relationship between the employment relationship and the civil law contract, the courts are mostly finding continued employment. In these quite frequent cases of Hungarian practice an existing employment relationship is terminated, usually by agreement (ie without any notice period, without any severance pay) and following the termination the parties conclude a civil law contract whereby the former employee, either as an 'individual entrepreneur' or as the internal member (with unlimited liability) of a limited partnership, undertakes the same duties that were previously performed under the employment contract. In such cases the courts typically decide that both contracts—the one terminating the employment as well as the one establishing a civil law relationship—were false, for want of a real intention to accept any of the declared legal effects, therefore the former employment continues.

The second group consists of cases where the labour law employment is supplemented by a second contract for independent services. In the typical case the parties conclude the employment contract at the minimal wage (or just above) and the bulk of remuneration comes through a civil law contract where the services to be provided are identical or tightly connected to the tasks to be performed within the employment contract. Under the supplementary contract the employee gets the 'real' compensation for the job even if the performance requirements (the services to be provided) seem to be clearly and separately determined for both contracts. The courts in these combined cases typically merge the duties and compensation and subsume both considerations under the employment contract. That is, for example, in a case of lawful termination of employment, under the heading of 'backpay', the employee becomes entitled not only to the meagre wages from the employment but also to the more generous remuneration deriving from the private law contract.[49]

Of course in each of the two above groups it can happen that, contrary to the typical circumstances, the two contracts are for different activities that may justify the different and separate qualification of the contracts.

---

[49] Case no 49.Mfv.27643/2001 of the Capital Court of Budapest, as appeal court in the case of a radio programme editor, who was employed under an employment contract as well as under a civil law contract for work, where—in a dispute about the lawfulness of the termination of the contract—the total remuneration has to be considered as a part of the employment contract.

The third group of cases is the largest, where there is an autonomous private law relationship and there is neither an accompanying nor a preceding employment linked to the civil law agreement. In assessing these cases the courts are apparently struggling with the dilemma of maintaining the old case law, or adjusting it to the new—increased—amount of general market freedom. The most frequent dilemma is generated by cases when the contract for work is established purely between companies, no private individual is a signatory party to the contract, but nevertheless, the worker asserts the conclusion of an employment contract and submits a claim for lost wages. In such situations the courts are divided: some decisions exclude, as a principle, the establishment of employment between two companies. However, there are opposite decisions. In a case when the first instance Labour Court declined the claim of a newspaper editor that the contract between her and her husband's limited partnership on the one hand and the employer on the other should be qualified as and employment contract, the higher court invalidated the decision and instructed the first instance court to analyse the real elements of the relationship—eminently the subordination and control, in combination with the other elements—regardless of the signatory parties and the form of the contract and, if it were to find that it was rather a subordinate relationship, to award the back-pay for unlawful termination with regard to the fee contracted between the two companies. Interestingly, however, the court added, that the calculation of the amount has to take into consideration that the contract fee was to be paid for two persons, not just the worker.[50]

4. LOOKING FOR FAIR WAYS OF OPENING UP THE BORDERS OF LABOUR LAW

A. Freedom and Fairness in Contract

Contract is about exchange; about exchange that is not only free, but also fair. This has been unequivocally emphasised by both the common law and continental law theory and case law and, indeed, in spite of that most authors attribute the emergence and crystallisation of the idea to the eighteenth to nineteenth centuries, its roots go back as far as the ancient times as Aristotle's justice theory. Rectificational (transactional) justice requires everyone to be in the same position (or as close as possible) after the action (transaction) as before.

The priority given to justice over freedom turns freedom into an instrument serving the fairness of the contract; therefore it is functional only if

---

[50] Capital Court of Budapest case, no 59 Mf.630.572/2004/4.

fulfills this role. This approach helped contract to 'survive' and triumphantly remains the main organiser of economic relationships through the eras (mainly in the middle years and second half of the twentieth century), when state intervention, form-contracts and public interest limitations signalled the end of the institution of contract.

Before 1989 for half the world—state-communism or communism—there was no freedom; equity (social juistice) was promised in exchange. For the other half—called the market economy or capitalism—there was freedom; social justice as a primary goal was given up in exchange. As a result of the political division of the world, freedom and equity—the two sides of 'fair contracting' (or contracting at all)—appeared as opposites, while the competition between the regimes encouraged efforts at reconciliation and convergence.

The fall of the communist regime replaced the slow (and uncertain) process to *détente* and suddenly brought the former two halves of the world together. However, this merger could not be accompanied by the merger of 'freedom' and 'equity'. The totalitarian communist regimes discredited state intervention and the promotion of 'social justice' by administrative-statutory means, and they have become associated or even identified with economic inefficiency and with a threat to freedom (and not just to political freedom). The remaining political bias and the simultaneous acceleration of the globalisation process have resulted in the triumphant ascendancy of 'freedom', no longer hindered by competition from an opposite political order.

This distributional effect (economic polarisation) of the shrinking and weakening legislative intervention is only one of the hazards raised by the imbalance and growing gap between 'freedom' and 'equity'. Another, and perhaps more damaging, effect is the inability to influence risk allocation by risk regulation (accompanying an activity, raised by a decision) should be with the actor who has control over the activity or makes the decision. Unregulated 'freedom' is further dissociated from 'equity' by permitting controllers of means and resources to transpose the risks of their actions to parties with no control over those factors, while pocketing the 'price' of risk bearing. Shifting the physical and economic risk of a business to the labourers depending on it without giving them any real controlling power over their physical and economic conditions is only one manifestation of that trend.

In summary, threats to contract by limitations and state intervention are in the past; it seems now that untamed 'freedom' would endanger the contract and freedom to contract. In the name of free competition there is no real competition in the world, just as in the communist countries in the past where there was no equity—in the name of equity.

The regulation of the use of labour can be put on an equal basis of freedom and equity if the simple rule of fair exchange is observed. Fair exchange—requires the producer or service provider to pay the total cost, without externalising any part of it, for the resources used whose price is collected in the price of the product or service. What is a fair exchange, fair price when human labour is used as one of the 'resources', and what is the total cost of the labour used (without shifting any part of it to others) would take us into much debated and never resolved questions of economics that is far beyond the scope of this chapter. However, two things are significant elements of the labour law discourse relevant here. First, the changed composition of 'price' and, secondly, the changing amount of 'risk' linked to the different types of contract.

B. The Costs to be covered by the 'Fair Price' of Labour

When taking into consideration the biological, intellectual and social needs of a worker—as elements of the costs that the 'fair pay' has to compensate—two features of current labour may show the ways to invent new approaches or new solutions. The first is the changed role and changed nature of knowledge and the second is the changed relationship between family and work.

1. Work and Learning

The issue of 'life long learning' is a matter of joint interest of the employer and the employee. While increasing the knowledge of the employee or the future employee (and the two are less and less separated[51]) is a personal interest, it is also an interest of the employers (of the imminent employer using the actual knowledge and—if one may say that—of the class of employers, who would and may in the future take the use of the knowledge of this or other workers). For this reason it is not unjust if this 'investment' (acquiring and utilising it) is under joint control, or is jointly financed.

Working hours in the majority of the developed world—if the rules are observed—are not excessive. In Europe, the weekly working hours are in general no more than 40,[52] and in some countries even fewer.[53] Many workers, mainly highly qualified, work more than the permitted maximum hours, and they do this without being told to and paid overtime. They do this voluntarily, if and to the extent that their work provides them with autonomy and self-fulfilment. Thus, one could say that it is not so much the number of hours worked but more the content and conditions of the work

---

[51] This directly follows from the idea of 'active security' of Alain Supiot's vision of the future of work: A. Supiot, *Beyond Employment: Changes in Work and the Future of Labour Law in Europe* (Oxford, Oxford University Press, 2001), 198ff.

[52] At any rate it cannot be more than 48 hours a week, including overtime: Div. 2003/88/EC, art. 6(b).

[53] France is at the other extreme, with its 35-hour working weeks.

that matters in the division between 'work' and private activity. Similarly, part of the increased leisure time can and should be invested in the enhancement of the worker's marketable knowledge. This portion of time can be under the joint control of the employer and the employee, thereby creating a kind of 'time' that is neither working time nor leisure time, requiring 'contribution' from both parties to its gainful utilisation. There are already rudimentary forms of the combination of learning and work where the flexibility needed by the employee is expressed in the reasonable waiver of workplace rights and vice versa, when the employer rewards studies by additional benefits, working hour arrangements, and financial support. Further elaboration, as well as inventive new solutions combining inside and outside employment methods, offers a form of fair and free arrangement of flexibilisation of employment.

2. Work and Family

In the classic employment relationship the 'responsibility' of the employer for the family of the employee covered fair wages (meaning family wages) and—perhaps, in later periods—fair social security. Beyond that, not even rest periods or holiday vacations were provided with respect to the family, solely with respect to the physical recovery of the employee. Although obviously the employee had a family that needed not only money but also care, the structure was based on the fact that someone, standing behind the worker (as a connection between the worker and the family), took care of family chores. By definition, the worker was a male, who could be purely a 'worker', and saved from anything connected to the family, because there was the 'mother', who by definition was not a worker, or, if worker, too, then a 'working mother' in atypical relations.[54]

The progress of gender equality in the labour market, however, restructured the picture: both the non-working mother, and family wages have disappeared from the former classical employment relationships. Employers have the advantages (in wages and also in the spill-over effect of atypical female working conditions to the core, male labour) of this progress, therefore it seems timely and justified that they do not extract this gain from compensation of labour. Instead, they fairly pay the 'price' of the 'reproduction' of the labour force that includes the needs of families and children in labour costs, if no longer in family wages, then in working arrangements that are

---

[54] From the mountains of literature on this topic, I think the 'classic' by F. E. Olsen, 'The Family and the Market: A Study of Ideology and Reform' (1983) 96 Harvard Law Review 1497, might be mentioned here; however, this is the core issue of the 'socially created' gender. See also on this topic, J. Conaghan and K. Rittich (eds.), Labour Law, Work and Family (Oxford, Oxford University Press, 2005).

adjusted to the fact that the workers are also parents, and there is no longer a person (a cover) standing between the worker and the family, freeing him from family chores. The expression of the joint interest and responsibility of the working parents and the workplace for the family also can facilitate the finding and elaboration of mutually agreeable, voluntary and fair flexible working arrangements. At the same time the elaboration of statutory ways of promoting the reconciliation of workplace and family life in today's society is a responsibility of the state like controlling working time or healthy and safe working conditions.

C. Fair Allocation of Risk and Control

Contract is not only about payment, but also about risk. Who bears the risk of the non-execution of the contract, the risk of damage, the risk of changing market relations? The fairness of the contract encompasses the fair allocation of the risks as well.

In traditional employment the risks as well as the control of the worker do not extend beyond his personal working capacity and job performance. The conditions of successful performance—material, financial and also personnel conditions (the working environment)—and the use of the product of the work are beyond the control of the employee; they are 'provided' for him or her. Consequently, the risks following from decisions regarding either the working conditions or the economic operation of the establishment (economic loss for poor contracting, workplace accidents due to inappropriate materials, appliance or irresponsible co-workers etc.) are to be borne by the organiser and decision maker, who is the employer, the bearer of the residual risk and gain, consequently the ultimate controller of the working conditions. These are expressed in the guaranteed wage, vicarious liability of the employer for damage, the excess remuneration for working under unusual conditions or overtime, or not working at all for technical or organisational reasons, etc.

To the extent that control over the conditions shifts to the worker it is appropriate that he or she takes over a proportionate amount of risk. (For example, the proportion between guaranteed wage and bonus for successful operation may change in the case of executives, overtime pay does not apply in cases of free use of working time etc.)[55]

In the process of flexibilisation, especially regarding the legal form of the contract, unfairness and therefore a violation of the market freedom enters the relationship when the employer's stronger negotiating power distorts

---

[55] The same is to be applied in cases of employee participation rules the details of which go beyond the scope of this chapter.

the balance of risk and control, and shifts more hazard to the worker than he or she can control. On the other hand, the tight labour law regulations should loosen and give way to flexible arrangements in situations where the control and autonomy of workers and labour service providers brings conditions under their control, and the additional risk undertaken in exchange for flexible conditions is felt justified, whether against less or more income, that is, indifferent in this respect.

Risk without control is either mere gambling or simply serfdom—leading to desperation, whereas control without risk (or at least the 'risk' of liability) leads to recklessness. For this reason the healthy condition of the market and, the restoration of fair competition require that no employer may have more control than is proportionate to the risk it bears.

It seems that the boundaries of labour law will, indeed, dissolve and open doors to private life and autonomous activity of workers, giving up the past, simple model that is based on one basic pattern. As long as exchange on the market and also labour market is based on fair dealing, free for both parties—that means that what is used is entirely paid for, and that risk and control remain in correspondence—no amount of flexibilisation can harm workers and undermine the policies and doctrine of labour law. Rather, it can promote the successful and creative assimilation of individuals into the permanently re-arranging market, and will bring about enriching solutions, challenging doctrinal tasks—and a radical development of the labour laws.

12

National and European Public Policy: the Goals of Labour Law

SILVANA SCIARRA*

1. MARKET RATIONALITY AND THE EMERGENCE OF EUROPEAN SOCIAL POLICIES

IN THE EUROPEAN tradition labour law was built on specific values, typical of each national legal order and yet comparable to one another in a functional perspective. After the Second World War, the legal foundations of the discipline were laid down while pursuing the search for democracy, a search which in itself justified the defence of national traditions.

Legal values, especially when enshrined in national constitutions, were not extraneous to the strengthening of social movements, active even before formal organisations came into the picture. National traditions contributed to determining the structures and the functions of collective organisations.

The 'public' relevance of labour law was ascertained by the combination of individual and collective guarantees, notwithstanding the private nature of collective organisations. Thus the notion of 'autonomy' of collective bargaining, developed in some countries, contributed to clarifying the public policy goals to be pursued by the discipline. In countries like Italy, Germany and Sweden, to mention only a few examples, no legislation on minimum wages was deemed necessary and the matter was left entirely to collective agreements and to their 'autonomous' role. Such a development of autonomous private orders confirms that, at least in some countries, the combination of legal and voluntary sources may enhance the function of labour law in setting minimum standards.

However, such a function was defined along the lines of the dominant model of subordinate employment relationships and consisted in the allocation of individual and collective guarantees to the weaker party. The

* Jean Monnet Professor of European Labour and Social Law, University of Florence, Florence, Italy.

emancipation of weaker parties in contracts of employment significantly embodied the evolution of labour law.

Especially in the continental European tradition, pursuing a fair balance of powers between the two contracting parties was an achievement running in parallel with the expansion of fundamental rights and freedoms in national constitutions. Such a 'national' coherence can be shaken and possibly weakened whenever fundamental principles governing contracts of employment are confronted with a 'European' coherence, lacking the same constitutional embedding.

This chapter aims to examine a possible tension between national and supranational lawmaking in the European Union (EU). The intention is to investigate whether, because of this tension, labour law is slowly and yet inescapably changing and adjusting its goals. In particular, attention will be paid to exploring whether at national level we are witnessing a fragmentation of employment contracts, occurring in parallel with—or perhaps as a consequence of—a re-organisation of legal and voluntary sources.

Before we examine some examples which will be proposed later in this chapter in order to illustrate these preliminary remarks, a few words must be said on sources of European law.

Tracing back the history of European Directives in the social field, we are reminded in a recent analysis that in the 1970s there was no 'harmonisation upwards',[1] but a simple attempt to bring closer procedural rights by imposing on the employer the duty to inform and consult workers' representatives. The relevant Directives in those years were the ones structurally related to economic circumstances—collective dismissals, transfers of undertakings, insolvency—having an impact on enterprises and on the 'safeguarding' of employees' rights.

One could argue that in those days the choice of Article 100 (now Article 94) of the Treaty of the European Community (TEC) as a legal basis for the adoption of social measures did not ostensibly shake labour law's ground rules within national legal orders.[2] Yet, ever since the early days of the European Community, an intellectual challenge was launched. It had to do with the possibility of combining labour law measures with market rationality and produce effects both at a national and at a supranational level.

In the late 1980s the need to establish uniform standards of protection inspired secondary legislation on health and safety. Over the years, such legislation has remained a corner stone of European labour law. Even the most sceptical observers of the achievements made in European social policies

---

[1] B. Hepple, *Labour Laws and Global Trade* (Oxford, Hart, 2005), 200.

[2] Art 100 (now Art 94) provides for the approximation of laws which 'directly affect the establishment or functioning of the common market'. On historical developments and on the interpretation of changes in the Treaty legal basis see S. Giubboni, *Social Rights and Market Freedom in European Constitution: A Labour Law Perspective* (Cambridge, Cambridge University Press, 2006).

cannot be little the importance of the slow and yet continuous construction of health and safety legislation as a solid legal pillar on which fundamental workers' rights could securely rest, despite the apparently narrow legal basis in the Treaty (Article 118, now Article 137 TEC) and in the face of qualified majority voting in the European Council.

Together with legislation on equality between men and women, later followed by legislation banning discrimination on all grounds, health and safety legislation represents a confirmation of the 'public' connotation of labour law at a supranational level, similar to what national traditions had pursued.

When procedural rights to inform and consult are combined with the safeguarding of employees' rights—as in the Directives on collective dismissals and transfers of undertakings—the purpose of labour law is once more characterised by the introduction of standardised rules. Limits set by national legislatures to discretionary managerial choices cannot be lower than the binding minimum standards set at a supranational level and originated in market rationality.[3]

The current centrality of the Directive on transfers of undertakings[4] must be explained against the spreading phenomena of industrial restructuring and mass redundancies currently taking place in Europe.[5] This Directive confirms the goal of 'safeguarding' the rights of employees in all such events occurring to undertakings. The underlying philosophy, inspired by Article 100 (now Article 94) TEC as a legal basis, rather than favouring managerial plans for liberalisation or externalisation of productive activities, is, as previously underlined, to harmonise protective measures.

As for the Directive on collective dismissals,[6] it may suffice to mention that issues related to the selection of workers to be dismissed have given rise to different solutions in national legislation. While leaving ample space to employers' economic freedom, it proved important to guarantee respect for objective and non-discriminatory criteria, as well as the principle of proportionality in measures to be adopted.[7]

---

[3] For example, in the UK supplementary legislation was introduced to comply with the duty to inform and consult employees' representatives on matters of redundancies and transfers, following the ECJ's ruling in Cases C–382/92 and 383/92 *European Commission v United Kingdom* [1994] ECR I–2435 and 2479. Comments in S. Deakin and G.S. Morris, *Labour Law* (4th edn, Oxford, Hart, 2005), 864ff.

[4] Council Directive 2001/23/EC of 12 Mar. 2001 on the approximations of the laws of the Member States relating to the safeguarding of employees' rights in the event of transfers of undertakings, businesses or parts of undertakings or businesses [2001] OJ L/82/16, consolidating Directives 77/187/EEC and 98/50/EC.

[5] See T. Edwards, 'Corporate Governance Systems and the Nature of Industrial Restructuring' (European Foundation for the Improvement of Living and Working Conditions, 2002), available at: http://www.eiro.eurofound.eu.int/about/2002/09/study/tn0209101s.html.

[6] Council Directive 1998/59/EC of 20 July 1998, [1988] OJ L/225/16 modifying Directive 75/129 EEC, [1975] OJ L/98/29.

[7] See, for a national example, A. Perulli, 'Razionalità e proporzionalità nel diritto del lavoro' (2005) 27 *Giornale di diritto del lavoro e di relazioni industriali* 17, dealing with the concept of rationality, central to the case law of the Italian Constitutional Court in all such matters.

Other Directives characterised by a more trans-national connotation—
among them Directives on European Works Councils (EWC) and on
Workers' Involvement in European Companies[8]—rather than pursuing uniformity, aim at establishing equivalent standards in Member States.[9]

It is worth noting that information and consultation must represent the
minimum requirement if an agreement on workers' involvement is to be
reached.[10] The EWC Directive introduces the principle of equal treatment
among workers affected by different legislation in different Member States,
not 'geared to the transnational structure of the entity which takes the decision'.[11] In both examples the procedural rights at stake are thought of as
measures to limit and counterbalance managerial decisions and to do so in
an integrated market.[12]

One striking difference in comparing the evolution of EU law with national
labour law is that at a European level voluntary sources do not accompany
or strengthen the development of public policies. Despite the dynamic role
played by the social partners according to Title XI TEC, a supranational system of collective labour law is still incomplete. The inability of European
social partners to conclude and enforce binding collective agreements should
be signalled as one of the deficiencies within the EU legal order.[13]

Procedures provided for in Article 138 TEC—consultation of the social
partners by the European Commission before proposing legislation in the
social field and the possibility that the social partners can themselves take
the initiative, trying to reach an agreement at the European level—have so
far given rise to so-called framework agreements. They were then transposed
into Directives, following the social partners' requests addressed to the
Council. Directives regulating part-time work and fixed term contracts of
employment were generated by this procedure and will be mentioned later.

Levels of law making in the EU legal order are so closely related to each
other that the borders of domestic labour law, especially in some areas of

---

[8] Council Directive 94/45/EC of 22 Sept. 1994 on the establishment of a European Works
Council or a procedure in Community-scale undertakings and Community scale groups undertakings for the purposes of informing and consulting employees [1994] OJ L/254/64; Council
Directive 2001/86/EC of 8 Oct. 2001 supplementing the Statute for a European company with
regard to the involvement of employees [2001] OJ L/294/22.

[9] A recent analysis in X. Blanc-Jouvan, 'Les Limites d'un droit européenne du travail' in
P. Birks and A. Pretto (eds.), *Themes in Comparative Law* (Oxford, Oxford University Press,
2002), 229.

[10] Directive 2001/86/EC, above n 8, recitals 6 and 8.

[11] Directive 94/45/EC, above n 8, recital 10.

[12] The transnational nature of the duty to inform is underlined by the ECJ in Case C–349/01
Betriebstrat der Firma ADS Anker GmbH v ADS Anker GmbH [2004] ECR I–6803.

[13] A. Lo Faro, *Regulating Social Europe. Reality and Myth of Collective Bargaining in the
EC Legal Order* (Oxford, Hart Publishing, 2000). The European Commission has now opened
the floor for discussion in the proposal for the Social Agenda to cover the years untill 2010,
where reference is made to 'an optional framework for transnational collective bargaining at
either enterprise level or sectoral level': Communication from the Commission on the Social
Agenda, Brussels, 9 Feb. 2005, COM(2005)33 final, 8.

the discipline, appear uncertain, as if they were merging into European strategies or, in some cases, as if they were conditioned by European targets.

The picture is even further complicated by the legal nature of different European acts and procedures and by the intersection of obligations to be fulfilled by Member States, in compliance with EU law.

Furthermore, fundamental values inspiring national and supranational legal systems are constantly coming closer, according to an unfinished and yet continuous process of constitutionalisation taking place in the EU.[14]

While not expecting to address all these issues in detail, the discussion that follows is based on the understanding that the history of European social policies is in itself an explanation of the complex mechanisms assisting national and supranational law makers. It is, at the same time, a sign of the continuity of a profitable, albeit at times critical, dialogue among national and supranational institutions.

2. *IUS COGENS, IUS DISPOSITIVUM* AND THE ROLE OF EU LAW

In the most significant European traditions the evolution of labour law at national level coincided with the fulfilment of public policy objectives.

The French doctrine of *ordre public* and *ordre public relatif* or *social*,[15] the Italian notion of *inderogabilità*,[16] applied both to law and collective agreements, and the British doctrine of restraint of trade all rest on the assumption that private parties should not depart from legal standards, unless specific and exceptional powers to do so were granted to them.[17] This limitation of contractual freedom indicates a specific function of labour law and underlines its dominant connotation: measures to protect the weaker party in private contracts are a matter of public policy.

This terminology is coherent with concepts developed in private international law. In the 1980 Rome Convention on the law applicable to contractual obligations 'mandatory provisions' in employment contracts are those

---

[14] C. Joerges, 'What is Left of the European Economic Constitution' (2004) 13 *European University Institute Working Paper Law* No 2004/13 (San Domenico, EUI 2004), available at: http://www.iue.it/PUB/law04-13.pdf; O. De Schutter and P. Nihoul (eds.), *Une Constitution pour l'Europe: Reflexions sur les transformations du droit de l'Union européenne* (Brussels, Larcier, 2004).

[15] J. Pélissier, A. Supiot and A. Jeammaud, *Droit du Travail* (22nd edn, Paris, Dalloz, 2004), 119ff, dealing with the complex interchange between law and collective agreements was separate sources of regulation, both inspired by the principle of *favor* towards workers.

[16] R. De Luca Tamajo, *La norma inderogabile nel diritto del lavoro* (Naples, Jovene, 1976); M. D'Antona, 'L'autonomia individuale e le fonti del diritto del lavoro' in B. Caruso and S. Sciarra (eds), *Opere* (Milan, Giuffrè, 2000), 117ff.

[17] M. Freedland, 'Ius Cogens, Ius Dispositivum, and the Law of Personal Work Contracts' in Birks and Pretto, above n 9, at 165ff. For an inspiring comparative approach see Lord Wedderburn, 'Inderogability, Collective Agreements, and Community Law' (1992) 21 *Industrial Law Journal* 127.

referred to 'public policy rules' of national law (Article 6),[18] constructed on the principle of objectively applicable law. It is noteworthy that the European Commission is considering the Europeanisation of this source, trying in such a way to combine existing European law with broader principles governing contracts.[19] For contracts of employment this will imply coming to terms with notions of mandatory provisions as means of guaranteeing binding minimum standards.

Models of protection have been repeatedly revised when discussing changes and adaptations in labour law. In the current discussion, as will be underlined further on, 'new' weaker parties enter contracts of employment; they impose a new definition of entitlements to be recognised to them, in order to respond to uncertainties in the continuity of occupations and in the adequacy of remuneration.[20]

The argument developed in this chapter is that respect for core legal principles in non-standard employment contracts should be presented to national legislatures as the main road to follow when re-designing the purposes of labour law. This choice, while being characterised by continuity with previous legislative options, would also leave ample space for a new definition of contractual duties and obligations.

The characteristic of the current discussion, which is also relevant to the arguments put forward in this chapter, is that blurring the divide between *ius cogens* and *ius dispositivum*, rather than remaining an exceptional prerogative of collective parties and an expression of collective interests, is becoming a recurring option. Furthermore, collective agreements may leave space for individual derogations and consequently expand the role of *ius dispositivum*. The lack of objective principles governing all such new and unlimited individual options could in perspective deeply affect the goal of labour law.

An excessive weight put on the individualisation of employment contracts may be the consequence of a much looser interrelation among law and collective agreements, unlike in previous European experiences, whereby collectively agreed standards were focused to the relevant choices made by legislators in order to establish mandatory principles governing contracts of employment.

At the present stage in the evolution of labour law, several reasons may cause a less strict coordination among levels of collective bargaining and lead to an uncontrolled proliferation of standards to be enforced in individual employment contracts. Decentralised agreements often become autonomous

---

[18] Art 6, dealing with the contract of employment, constitutes an exception with regard to the principle of free choice of the law applicable (Art 3).

[19] Commission of the European Communities, Green Paper on the conversion of the Rome Convention of 1980 on the law applicable to contractual obligations into a Community instrument and its modernization, Brussels, 14 Jan., 2003 COM(2002)654 final.

[20] A parallel debate is taking place among scholars in European private law. See Study Group on Social Justice in European Private Law, 'Social Justice in European Contract Law: a Manifesto' (2004) 10 *European Law Journal* 653.

sources of regulation, irrespective of what has been agreed upon at a more centralised level. It may also happen that workers entering non-standard employment contracts are not covered by collective agreements at all.

The differentiation of working conditions, considered an essential feature of flexible firms, may cause turmoil in defining the main purposes of labour law. Standardisation, one of the traditional aims pursued by this legal discipline, may itself follow the multiplication of employment contracts and result in fragmenting minimum legal standards.

In this unsettled scenario the notion of most favourable treatment, namely the standard that should not be attacked by pejorative derogations brought about by *ius dispositivum*, becomes controversial. Comparisons among different sources—be they European and domestic, legal and voluntary, or even collective agreements at different levels—produce uncertain results and may give rise to solutions, not reflecting the original internal coherence of national legal orders.

Such a new triumph of *ius dispositivum* follows—and in a sense favours—the fragmentation of employment contracts, without generating a new solid framework of labour rights. Some examples will illustrate this analysis.

A. Working Time: The Fundamental Right to Health and Safety

Directive 2003/88 on the organisation of working time, based on Article 137 TEC and concurrent with Directive 89/391 on the protection of workers' health and safety,[21] constitutes a landmark in the construction of European *ius cogens*.

Its transposition proved controversial in several Member States. A wide discussion is open on derogations from the law agreed upon in collective bargaining, in some cases allowing individual 'opting out' in contracts of employment. In such cases *ius dispositivum* becomes the guide in orienting supranational public policy and in influencing national legislative choices.

Furthermore, in the final provision of the Working Time Directive (Article 23) we encounter a so called non-regression clause, drafted in an ambiguous way. While maintaining that 'minimum requirements' must be complied with, it is acknowledged that 'in the light of changing circumstances' Member States have the right to develop different regulatory strategies. This clause too has given rise to controversial understandings at national level.

[21] Directive 2003/88 EC of the European Parliament and of the Council of 4 Nov. 2003, concerning certain aspects of the organisation of working time [2003] OJ L/299/9 consolidates all amendments made by Directive 2000/34/EC of the European Parliament and of the Council to Council Directive 93/104/EC. Directives on working time are interrelated to Council Directive 89/391/EEC of 12 June 1989 on the introduction of measures to encourage improvements in the safety and health of workers at work [1989] OJ L/183/1. It is important to underline that minimum requirements provided for in Directive 2003/88 apply to all workers as defined in Art 3a of Directive 1989/391 on health and safety.

Member States made use of their prerogatives and gave extensive interpretations—both in legislation and in collective bargaining—of the derogations first included in the 1993 Directive, now in Article 17 and 18 of Directive 2003/88. The Commission is now proposing to modify such a Directive, to try and solve the remaining tensions between national and European law.[22]

The notion of working time and the purposes of the Directive for the protection of workers' health and safety are also central to some recent rulings of the European Court of Justice (ECJ). The case law developed by the Court, while confirming the standing role of *ius cogens* in the interpretation of EU law, adds further emphasis to the need to improve existing legislation, while safeguarding its overall coherence.

For the main argument developed in this chapter it is useful to reflect upon the leading criteria adopted by the ECJ.

In *BECTU*[23] the ECJ pointed its attention towards the protection of health and safety, ruling on Article 7 of Directive 93/104, dealing with paid annual leave. This decision was welcomed with enthusiasm by commentators as one of the first cases in which the Advocate General made a reference to the Nice Charter of fundamental rights. To quote an interesting recent development, it had an impact on a 2003 Greek law, granting this fundamental right to workers employed on fixed term contracts, regardless of the length of employment.[24]

Jaeger[25] deals with questions related to a doctor employed by a hospital and required to work 'on call' for part of his working time. The emphasis is put on the unconditioned principle set out in the Working Time Directive, fixing a maximum of 48 hours per week, including overtime, and on the related interpretation of whether on-call duty should be considered working time.

[22] See the Commission's draft proposal on the modification of the Working time Directive(COM (2004)607 final, 2004/0209 COD) and the critical opinion adopted by the European Economic and Social Committee (SOC 2004 CESE 527/2005). This proposal was forwarded to the European Parliament (EP) and the Council on 22 Sept. 2004. The EP gave its opinion at first reading on 11 May 2005, proposing a series of amendments. See now the Amended Proposal presented by the Commission, COM(2005)246 final, 2004/0209 COD).

[23] Case C–173/99 *The Queen v Secretary of State for Trade and Industry, ex parte Broadcasting, Entertainment, Cinematographic and Theatre Union (BECTU [2001] ECR I–4881)*. Comments in G. Ricci, 'BECTU: An Unlimited Right to Annual Paid Leave' (2001) 30 *Industrial Law Journal* 401f; see also S. Sciarra, 'Market Freedom and Fundamental Social Rights' in B. Hepple (ed), *Social and Labour Rights in a Global Context* (Cambridge, Cambridge University Press, 2002), 95. *BECTU* inspires in several passages the Advocate General's Opinion in Cases C–131/04 and C–257/04 *C.D. Robinson-Steele v R.D. Retail Services Ltd; Michael Jason Clarke v Frank Staddon Ltd; J.C. Caulfield, C.F. Caulfield, K.V. Barnes v Hanson Clay Products Ltd*, judgment of 27 Oct. 2005, not yet reported.

[24] S. Yannakourou, 'Country Study on Greece: Final Report', *The Evolution of Labour Law in the European Union: 1992–2003* (Employment and Social Affairs General Directorate of the European Commission), in *The Evolution of Labour Law (1992–2003)*, vol. 2: National Reports, OOPEC, Luxembourg 2005, 223, also available at: http://europa.eu.int/comm/employment_social/labour_law/docs/ell_el_en.pdf.

[25] Case C–151/02 *Landeshauptstadt Kiel v Norbert Jaeger* [2003] ECR I–8389, is a preliminary ruling brought by a German court, dealing with a doctor employed by a hospital in the city of Kiel.

This principle, central in the Court's reasoning, has given rise to differing interpretations at national level. Attempts to combine the protection of a fundamental social right with enhanced flexibility at the place of work may endanger 'public policy' objectives. In ruling that time spent on on-call duty is part of working time, the Court wants to limit the scope of derogations provided for in the Directive and make them apply only 'to what is strictly necessary in order to safeguard the interests which those derogations enable to be protected'.[26] Therefore, the adequacy of rest periods must be such to allow the persons concerned to recover from fatigue, but also have a 'preventive' function in reducing risks affecting health and safety.[27]

It is of crucial importance to state, as the Court does in *Jaeger*, that the notion of working time cannot be 'unilaterally' determined by Member States, since individual rights 'stem directly' from the Directive.[28]

In *BECTU* and in *Jaeger* the Court expressly states that fundamental social rights are not subject nor subordinate to economic considerations. This statement may be taken as a sign of the positive—although limited—results achieved by reforming the Treaty and expanding the legal basis, as well as by adopting the Nice Charter as a solemn declaration.

In *Pfeiffer* the ECJ states once more that, in order to protect workers' health and safety, legal limits to working time, weekly maximum hours and rest periods must be respected. It adds that not even a collective agreement can fully guarantee that, in entering individual employment contracts, the weaker party is made fully aware of the consequences deriving from derogations.[29]

The arguments of the Court are very relevant in a labour law discourse. The Court seems to suggest that a public policy goal pursued in the law cannot be diminished or imperilled by voluntary sources. It recalls the notion of weaker party in the contract of employment since the individual worker may be lacking all necessary information in order freely to accept or refuse minimum requirements, different from the ones provided for in the Directive. A 'social right, directly conferred on the employee by the directive' cannot be 'relinquished' through individual derogations, unless the employee is made fully aware of all implications.[30]

Pfeiffer underlines that, when the Directive is sufficiently precise and unconditional, national courts have an obligation to give a consistent interpretation

---

[26] *Ibid.*, at 89, recalling the leading Case C–303/98 *Simap* [2000] ECR I–7963.

[27] *Ibid.*, at 92.

[28] *Ibid.*, at 59.

[29] In Case C–397/01 *Pfeiffer v Deutsches Rotes Kreuz, Kreisverband Waldshut eV* [2004] ECR I–8835, a preliminary ruling brought by a German court, dealing with Red Cross workers, the argument was whether a collective—sector or plant agreement—can derogate from the limit of maximum daily working time. Notions of *Arbeitsbereitschaft* or duty time, *Bereitschaftsdienst* or on-call time and *Rufbereitschaft* or stand-by time are derived from case law and may therefore give rise to different interpretations.

[30] *Ibid.*, at 82ff. The issue of individual consent for derogations is also dealt with in Case C–303/98 *Simap*, above n 26, a leading case in this field. See J. Fairhurst, 'SIMAP—Interpreting the Working Time Directive' (2001) 30 *Industrial Law Journal* 236. A principle

of national law, namely to interpret it 'in the light of the wording and the purpose of the Directive concerned'.[31] Such an obligation implies that national courts, in order to ascertain the centrality of the fundamental social right to health and safety, must address the coherence of German law on working time 'as a whole', including references to voluntary sources.

Notwithstanding this very powerful statement, the Working Time Directive, lined up with other European Directives in the field of social policies, attends with new emphasis to issues of national diversities within the European legal order, leaving ample space for manoeuvre to national legislators. This mechanism of multi-level policy making explains the development of parallel systems of norms within one legal order. It also represents a constant intellectual challenge for domestic labour law.

However, in its numerous judgments the ECJ draws a clear picture of what the hierarchy of sources should be like, in order to guarantee full enforcement of fundamental social rights. The 'cogent' function of such rights should orient the choices of social partners in collective agreements and limit, whenever possible, individual derogations *in peius*.

B. Flexible Employment Contracts: The Fundamental Right to Equal Treatment

In the Framework Directives on part-time and fixed-term work[32] a new key is proposed to unlock difficulties in the law making process. As previously indicated, these Directives are the result of procedures provided for in the TEC in order to involve the European social partners in the law making process. Consensus reached by representatives of management and labour at a supranational level should provide a solid ground in combining the quest for flexible employment contracts, possible tools to fight unemployment and create new employment opportunities, and respect for national preferences.

of transparency is recalled in the Advocate General's opinion in Cases, C–131/04 and C–257/04, above n 23, with regard to individual employment contracts and collective agreements lacking precise information on compensation for periods of annual leave not taken by the beneficiaries.

[31] *Pfeiffer*, above n 29, at para 113. See the annotation of this case by S. Prechal in (2005) 42 *Common Market Law Review* 1445ff. The author underlines how the novelty in this case is considering consistent interpretation 'inherent in the system of the Treaty' (at 1452 and at 1461) and indicating that such an interpretation should apply not only to Directives, but to Community law in general. *Pfeiffer* and the principle of consistent interpretation with regard to the regulation of working time are referred to by the Advocate General in Cases C–131/04 and C–257/04, above n 23, underlining (at point 44 of the Opinion) its importance in disputes between individuals.

[32] Council Directive 97/81/EC of 15 Dec. 1997 concerning the Framework Agreement on part-time work concluded by UNICE, CEEP and the ETUC [1997] OJ L/14/9; Council Directive 99/70/EC of 28 June 1999 concerning the framework agreement on fixed-term work concluded by ETUC, UNICE and CEEP [1999] OJ L/244/64.

A common minimum standard, consisting in the principle of equal treatment among comparable workers, is imposed. A powerful constitutional principle is thus combined with non-binding indications on policies to be adopted by Member States, in order to remove obstacles impeding the full development of flexible employment contracts.[33]

One can argue that the Directives in question, because of this combination of regulatory techniques in the same legal source, have introduced a most critical element of irrationality within national legal systems, despite the consideration paid to domestic labour law internal coherence.

Furthermore, both Directives include a non-regression clause, namely the indication that implementation of the Directives should not 'constitute valid ground for reducing the general level of protection afforded to workers'.[34] This clause has a double message for national legislatures: an indication not to lower existing standards and, at the same time, respect for national parliaments taking legislative initiatives.

The question, relevant for the arguments developed in this chapter, is whether the interpretation of 'valid ground' for lowering existing standards should be inspired by the overall coherence of national legal orders or be based on European standards. National legal systems are grounded on binding constitutional rights and freedoms; European law puts forward in both Directives the principle of equal treatment. These are two parallel ways to ascertain the public policy goals of labour law.

National legislatures could go as far as insinuating that, in compliance with the non-binding policy indications present in both Directives, they were free to enter new regimes in the regulation—or re-regulation—of both employment contracts and even to lower existing standards, if this measure was deemed necessary for reaching a high level of employment and fulfilling a European objective.

Such instrumental use of EU law may deeply influence labour law and its public policy goals. The fundamental right to equal treatment is a matter of

---

[33] See Directive 97/81/EC, above n 32, 5(a) ('Member States . . . should identify and review obstacles of a legal or administrative measure which may limit the opportunities for part-time work and, where appropriate, eliminate them') and Directive 99/70/EC, above n 32, 5 (on measures to prevent abuse in using successive fixed-term contracts). The latter is formulated in a more prescriptive way than the previous one, since it requires 'objective' reasons to be adopted and the adoption of criteria to interpret when fixed term contracts should be regarded as successive

[34] A similar expression is used in Art 23 of the Working Time Directive, as previously indicated. In Case C–144/04 *Mangold v Rüdiger Helm*, Opinion of 30 June 2005, Advocate General Tizzano proposes (point 54ff) a classification of the non-regression clauses. Some Directives include them in the opening 'whereas'; others incorporate them in the text. There is no unanimous opinion on the legal relevance of the latter clauses, regarded by some commentators as binding principles and by others as merely political indications. An analysis of non-regression clauses is in U. Carabelli and V. Leccese, 'Interpretive Dilemmas Posed by Favor and Non-Regression Clauses: Harmonisation through Improving Protection or "Race to the Bottom" of Labour Conditions?' in *International Legal Essays in Honour of Jo Carby-Hall* (Patrington, Barmarick, 2006) 139.

public policy, an example of national and European *ius cogens*. Measures introducing differentiated treatment for part-time and fixed term workers should therefore be considered illegal. One could propose the idea that if legislation was adopted in breach of the equal treatment principle, national courts could refer cases to the ECJ in preliminary ruling procedures.

In *Mangold*,[35] a preliminary ruling originating in a German court, the ECJ was required to look at the Directive on fixed term contracts and at Directive 2000/78 on equal treatment. The question was whether legislation providing for unlimited fixed term contracts for elderly workers was discriminatory on the basis of age. The origin of the German law not requiring objective reasons for recourse to fixed term contracts is to be found in the urgency to promote employment, as advocated by a governmental Commission asked to look into specific proposals.[36]

This law could arguably be considered among measures adopted by national legislatures in order to remove obstacles to the introduction of more flexible conditions, as phrased in the 'soft' guideline present in the Directive and addressed to Member States. The potential breach of a fundamental right needs to be balanced against a non-binding European employment policy: whereas the former is a matter of public policy both at national and supranational level, the latter is a response by a national legislature, framed within a broad European plan to fight unemployment. Moreover, the latter is the expression of a state's sovereignty in selecting priorities and in choosing legislative solutions.

The principle of equal treatment among comparable workers, a binding principle for national judges, must, in the case of fixed-term contracts, be correctly enforced by evaluating the objective criteria according to which fixed-term workers entered into their contracts. Similarly, violation of the same principle could be the result of incomplete or lacking national measures 'to prevent abuse' in a disproportionate use of successive fixed-term contracts, as stated in clause 1 of the Framework Agreement. All such criteria must be observed, even when enforcing employment strategies.

In *Mangold* Advocate General Tizzano argues that it is the general principle of equality, implemented by the ECJ even before the adoption of Directive, 2000/78 to be recalled in order to measure the non-compliance of national legislation with European law.[37] Infringement of the non-regression clause is, on the contrary, difficult to interpret, since the legal measures

---

[35] Case C–144/04 *Mangold v Rüdiger Helm*, decided on 22 Nov. 2005, not yet reported.

[36] U. Preis and M. Gotthardt, 'Fixed-Term Work in Germany' in B. Caruso and M. Fuchs (eds.), *Labour Law and Flexibility in Europe: The Cases of Germany and Italy* (Baden Baden and Milan, Nomos and Giuffrè, 2004), 126.

[37] Above n 34, at 83–4 and at 99ff of the Opinion. It is interesting to recall that the request of the national court based on cl 5 of the Framework Agreement of fixed term contracts is not acceptable according to the Advocate General, since no reiteration of contracts occurred in the case under scrutiny. The case appears to be an example of 'strategic' litigation, since the reference to the ECJ originated soon after the stipulation of a single fixed-term contract.

under scrutiny must be framed within broader policies aiming at facilitating employment for categories of workers potentially at risk of exclusion from the labour market. In all such matters states' sovereignty becomes a priority and the interference of the Court may be inappropriate.

In *Mangold* the Court implies that the non-regression clause—Article 8(3) of the Directive—cannot be interpreted as a limit to the adoption of legislation justifying fixed term contracts, as tools for the promotion of employment. It finds, however, that the right not to be discriminated against on the ground of age is violated under German law and that it should be the task of national courts not to enforce legislation infringing such a fundamental right.

This reassuring statement on the role played by Directive, 2000/78 bringing about broad grounds for banning discrimination, indicates, however, that the principle of non-discrimination among comparable workers provided for in Article 4 of the Directive, on fixed term contracts is not relevant in the Court's reasoning.

The difficult point to raise, therefore, is whether a similar ground for preliminary ruling procedures can be found in national legislation on fixed-term contracts dealing with other 'objective' reasons inspiring managerial decisions and justified on the ground of merely productive and organisational reasons.

To make a further step forward, it should be argued that the correct enforcement of organisational rules at the place of work must represent the essential precondition for a full guarantee of the fundamental right to be treated equally. Managerial discretion—as in the case of non-objective reasons leading to fixed term contracts—should therefore be held contrary to the principle of equal treatment among comparable workers. Such an interpretation of the fundamental right in question could open the way to preliminary ruling procedures, since the Directive sets out the employer's obligation to give reasons for the stipulation of fixed-term contracts.

Some examples of recent national legislation expanding considerably the margins of managerial prerogatives will be analysed further in section 3. This analysis will once more underline that in the current academic discussion in Europe, as well as in policy making, tests for labour law internal coherence are constantly multiplied, as if we were looking into a kaleidoscope. Even when European law is inspired by respect for national traditions, it still requires of national interpreters and legislatures the reorganisation of their priorities and the search for new solutions.

Meanwhile, looking at the broad spectrum of European sources analysed so far, we can try to draw some conclusions.

In an integrated and completed single market, the impact of *ius cogens* is visible and less controversial in areas falling within a traditional purpose of labour law. This is the case of legislation on health and safety and on working time, defined along the lines of labour law's 'public' function. The same is true for the fundamental right to equality.

However, even in these areas a significant differentiation in standards of protection can occur and require a correction in the balance of powers within individual contracts of employment. The ECJ is well aware, in this regard, of the everlasting necessity to guarantee fundamental social rights in a very broad perspective.

In the development of both national and European labour law coherence, the European Directives linked to employment policies—as in the example of fixed term contracts—disclose new purposes of the discipline, in between the fulfilment of policy objectives and the guarantee of fundamental rights.

Rather than aiming at retaining the 'autonomy' of labour law,[38] legislation framed within employment policies shows constant intersections with other disciplines and is profoundly affected by economic constraints in national budget laws. National legislatures—and in some cases national social partners—are thus constantly reminded that incoherent solutions may shake the ground rules of labour law and alter its function.

3. CONTESTED TERRAINS IN NATIONAL AND EUROPEAN LABOUR LAW

A comparative analysis of recent labour law reforms adopted in Member States of the EU reveals that a variety of employment contracts occupy a new large territory, the borders of which remain uncertain.[39] The goal of labour law is split between old loyalties and new demands. In this broad general trend, the language adopted by national legislatures may, at times, seem to mimic the non-legal jargon adopted in European soft law, especially in the European Council's decisions on employment guidelines, addressed to Member States.[40] Concepts such as 'modernisation', 'employability', 'adaptability' may lead to discretional interpretation of the means of compliance with EU law.

[38] P.L. Davies and M.R. Freedland, 'Employees, Workers, and the Autonomy of Labour Law' in H. Collins, P. Davies and R. Rideout (eds.), *Legal Regulation of the Employment Relation* (London, Kluwer, 2000), 267.

[39] S. Sciarra, *The Evolution of Labour Law (1992–2003) Volume 1: General Report*, OOPEC 2005, a study based on national country studies in 15 Member States, also available at: http://europa.eu.int/comm/employment_social/ labour_law/docs/generalreport_en.pdf, S. Sciarra, *The Evolving Structure of Collective Bargaining in Europe 1990–2004: General Report* (Research Project Co-financed by the European Commission and the University of Florence, 2005), based on national country studies in 25 Member States and in candidate and acceding countries, available at: http://www.unifi.it/polo-universitario-europeo/ricerche/collective_bargaining.html. I acknowledge in the following footnotes the work of all national *rapporteurs* involved in both these projects, but I am responsible for the interpretation I offer in comparative terms.

[40] D. Ashiagbor, 'The European Employment Strategy and the Regulation of Part-Time Work' in S. Sciarra, P. Davies and M. Freedland (eds.), *Employment Policy and the Regulation of Part-Time Work in the European Union* (Cambridge, Cambridge University Press, 2004), 35. For an historical approach to employment policies under Title VIII TEC, see S. Sciarra, 'Integration through Coordination: the Employment Title in the Amsterdam Treaty' (2000) 6 *The Columbia Journal of European Law* 209.

I described elsewhere the 'soft law environment' in which this new European style flourished and was cultivated.[41] All non-legal notions adopted in that environment have undoubtedly influenced the shaping of national priorities and indirectly affected the purposes of labour law.[42] In some cases an assumed compliance with European law may have facilitated the adoption of national legislation lowering normative labour standards.

In most national legal systems the regulation of non-standard contracts of employment has been the result of a slow and often contested process. The notion of atypical worker is no longer useful to describe the fragmented environment of non-standard contracts, all characterised by a new asset of bargaining powers and a new definition of contractual obligations. Rather than attempting to return to the *status quo ante,* such an equilibrium can be re-constructed in non-standard employment contracts, confirming and, when necessary, expanding the role of fundamental rights and principles.

The most complex issue is how to measure legislatures' full compliance with fundamental rights, when no 'technical' standards—as in health and safety legislation—nor procedural obligations—as in the duty to inform and consult workers' representatives—can assist interpreters and judges. The right to dignity, to mention one example, could be subject to different evaluations in non-standard contracts. So would be the right to social security for economically dependant workers, not eligible to full entitlements.[43]

Measuring standards in legislation on 'flexibility' can result in a paradox. When flexible measures are at stake, the purpose of labour law should be to limit recourse to 'traditional' guarantees, in view of expanding managerial discretion. Even the adaptation of existing normative standards may not be an easy task. Flexible contracts may lack essential elements that traditionally qualify subordinate employment. For example, there may be no continuity of work to be performed; inclusion in work organisation may be temporary, and so may be the presence in the same place of work.

---

[41] S. Sciarra, 'New Discourses in Labour Law: Part-time Work and the Paradigm of Flexibility' in Sciarra, Davies and Freedland, above n 40, at 22, with references to the White Paper on Governance and its impact on domestic debates. A very articulate and critical analysis of the White Paper and of its influence on OMC is in A. Andronico and A. Lo Faro, 'Defining Problems: Open Method of Coordination, Fundamental Rights and Governance' in O. De Schutter and S. Deakin (eds.), *Social Rights and Market Forces: Is the Open Coordination of Employment and Social Policies the Future of Social Europe?* (Brussels, Bruylant, 2005), 41.

[42] A similar concern inspires some of the reflections of the previously mentioned group of private law specialists. See 'Social Justice in European Contract Law: A Manifesto', above n 20, at 671, where attention is paid to the fact that 'the laws and other governance techniques regarding market relations cannot be constructed and revised in isolation from other developments in techniques of European governance'.

[43] The opening section of the 2001 Nice Charter is entitled Dignity. This fundamental right is thoroughly analysed by Alain Supiot in drawing the conclusions of the research carried on by a working party set up by the ILO in 2003. See *Standards Related Activities and Decent Work: Prospects in the Field of Social Security. Final Report of the Group of Experts* (forhcomitng in *Droit Social* 2006).

In dealing with individual employment contracts, labour law's purpose in the European legal tradition has been—and still is—to measure the equilibrium of powers established by legislation and in some cases by collective agreements, whenever they depart from the law.

In order to verify whether recent legislation is abandoning 'public policy' options, which have, in the past, shaped and clarified the role of labour law within national and supranational legal orders, it is suggested that comparative labour law research should investigate which minimum standards best exemplify the function of *ius cogens* in non-standard contracts.

Especially in the European civil law tradition individual employment contracts are means by which subordinate employees become an active part of production systems. Entering an employment contract freely means for the employee purging the notion of subordination of all negative implications.[44] Rather than being subordinated to the employer's unlimited powers to organise and to discipline, the individual employee is connected with other employees within a 'place of work', defined by clear organisational rules.

This *'contrat bizarre'*, a privileged point of observation in discussing the general theory of contracts,[45] was born over and over again, in order to be adapted to different and more individualised requirements and to meet the demands of both contracting parties.

At the European level, duties to inform and consult individual employees, dealt with in Directive 2002/14,[46] were a tentative and yet significant response to the ongoing differentiation of employment contracts and to the spreading of informality and casualness in the setting up of employment relationships. In this regard it has been suggested that 'contractualisation' becomes a new technique in labour law.[47] In this context the purpose of labour law is expanded, since it should 'anticipate' and 'prevent'[48] all those measures which may drastically affect individual employees, as in cases of restructuring or other threats to employment. In rediscovering the role of individual contracts of employment, the abovementioned Directive imposes obligations on the employer, which should limit recourse to arbitrary and non-transparent decisions. All these very different theoretical and practical approaches to employment contracts are like magnifying glasses through which we can observe some embryonic anomalies in non-standard contracts. In the following sections an attempt will be made to classify some of their prevailing features.

---

[44] L. Mengoni, 'Il contratto individuale di lavoro' [2000] *Giornale di Diritto del Lavoro e di Relazioni Industriali* 181.

[45] This is the fascinating expression used by G. Lyon-Caen, 'Défense et illustration du contrat de travail' [1968] *Archives de philosophie du droit* 69.

[46] Directive 2002/14/EC of the European Parliament and of the Council of 11 Mar. 2002 establishing a general framework for informing and consulting employees in the European Community [2002] OJ L/80/29.

[47] A. Supiot, 'Un faux dilemme:la loi ou le contrat?' [2003] *Droit Social* 60.

[48] As in recital 8 and 10 in Directive 2002/14 EC, above n 46.

A. The Goals of Labour Law in Agency Work

The dispersal of discretionary prerogatives in the exercise of managerial powers is observed in the recent evolution of labour law in the EU. Whenever national laws correct the existing distribution of powers within employment contracts, the result is the loss of a balance among contracting parties. The rationale behind such legislative choices is indicated in the changing nature of production and in the need management has to act quickly, in order to control the volatility of work organisation and respond to market demands.

Agency work is the most suitable example at this regard. The user company's discretionary powers coincide with the expansion of economic and organisational options in restructuring or downsizing business activities. The choice not to enter employment contracts and to stipulate instead a commercial contract with a temporary work agency imposes a thorough redefinition of the goals of labour law.

If we look at working conditions, solutions adopted at a national level are varied. Agency workers can be paid less than comparable workers employed by the user company.[49] They receive 100 percent of salary from the agency, after 18 months of being employed, even if not working for the user company.[50] Agencies pay them minimum wages applicable by the user company, unless a separate agreement covers the agency sector, as often happens.[51] Collective agreements covering agency workers in Austria deal with the amount of the allowance to be granted to agency workers in periods of no work. During such periods agency workers must be available during normal working time, for us to a maximum of 38.5 hours per week. There is an ongoing obligation to work for the agency at any time the latter so requests.[52]

A recent Italian reform[53] provides a whole list of activities for which open-ended contracts can be stipulated between the user company and the agency. Temporary agency work, the other option provided for in Italian law, can take place whenever 'organisational, technical and productive' reasons are put forward by the user, even within the user's 'ordinary' production process.

In both cases collective agreements have wide margins for manoeuvre. For open-ended contracts collective agreements can expand the list of activities, thus expanding recourse to agency work beyond the letter of the law. In temporary agency work collective agreements can set quantitative limits to the user company, thus partially limiting managerial prerogatives.

---

[49] See M. Fuchs, 'German National Report' in *The Evolving Structure of Collective Bargaining*, above n 39.
[50] See B. Nystrom, 'Swedish National Report' in *ibid*.
[51] See N. Bruun, 'Finnish National Report' in *ibid*.
[52] U. Runggaldier 'Austrian National Report' in *ibid*.
[53] D Lgs 276/2003, Art 20. See B. Caruso and L. Zappalà, 'Italian National Report' in *The Evolving Structure of Collective Bargaining*, above n 39.

In the Dutch system, agency workers are entitled to an increasing number of rights, even to enter an open-ended contract, after being employed for a certain number of weeks. This 'phasing legislation' has been beneficial for an estimated 30 percent of agency workers, entitled to training and even to enter a pension scheme as well as being represented on the agency's works councils.[54]

The impossibility so far to reach an agreement on the Draft European Directive in the controversial field of temporary work,[55] introducing among other measures the provision of equal treatment, leaves national legislatures free to apply very different models of regulation.[56]

One should not forget, however, that a significant impulse to the spread of temporary agencies came after the abolition of national public monopolies in placement services.[57] Market rationality inspires the flourishing and expanding industry of agency work, whereas labour law rationality has not yet been able to express its own regulatory principles. This is why positive integration should be enhanced in this field as a further contribution to the efficient functioning of an integrated market.

Minimum standards potentially applicable to this employment contract range from the principle of equal treatment with the user company's comparable workers to the granting of some form of authorisation to agencies, thus ascertaining the 'public' function assigned to private economic actors.

Furthermore, the introduction of a scheme of joint liability for both the agency and the user would keep alive labour law and its public policy goals even in a trilateral relationship.[58] Minimum standards should also include rights to fair remuneration and to health and safety.[59] It is suggested, following the Dutch example and similar solutions in other countries, that the right to training should be thought of as a binding minimum standard, one that would best qualify the 'public' function played by agencies in labour markets.

---

[54] J. Visser, 'I contratti di lavoro flessibile' (2005) 27 *Giornale di Diritto del Lavoro e di Relazioni Industriali* 142; E. Sol, 'Targeting on Transitions: Employment Services in the Netherlands' (2001) 22 *Comparative Labour Law and Policy Journal* 97.

[55] Proposal for a Directive on working conditions for temporary workers, COM(2002)149 final, 2002/0072 (COD), Brussels, 20 Mar. 2002.

[56] The only legal source—not to be forgotten—is based on Art 118a and is EEC Directive 91/383 [1991] OJ L/206/1 on the protection of health and safety for workers with a fixed duration or a temporary employment relationship, which also provides for the user company's duties to inform workers on risks they face and also on training necessary to avoid them.

[57] Case C–111/94 *Job Centre Coop. ARL.* [1995]; Case C–55/96, *Job Centre Coop. ARL* [1997] ECR I–7119.

[58] The principle of joint liability is advocated in comparative labour law. See L. Corazza, *'Contractual integration' e rapporti di lavoro. Uno studio sulle tecniche di tutela del lavoratore* (Padua, Cedam, 2004).

[59] The 2001 Finnish Employment Contracts Act refers to EEC Directive 91/383, n 56 above, for shared responsibility of the user company and the agency with regard to health and safety.

B. Jobs on Call, Part-Time Work, Fixed Term Contracts

Employers' discretionary prerogatives are significantly expanded when employment contracts are characterised by the uncertainty of some essential elements, such as the duration of working time, the distinction between work and non-work, and the right to be informed in due time of changes in working conditions. We witness all these elements in various new employment contracts, such as jobs on call, zero-hours contracts and some exceptional forms of part-time contracts.

A complete novelty for the Italian legal system is represented by the introduction of '*lavoro intermittente*', dealt with in the recent labour market reform.[60] This contract of employment can be described as an extreme form of part-time work, whereby the employer can, in a very discontinuous way, request that work be performed in areas of production indicated by collective agreements.

The contract of employment must be stipulated in writing, with all necessary indications of the details of the parties' obligations. If workers declare their availability even when work is not requested, an indemnity for this non-working time is due. Refusal to work can only occur in case of illness or any other serious impediment. In such cases of refusal to work for legitimate reasons, workers lose their indemnity. In all other cases, refusal to work may lead to the termination of the contract for just cause and will also imply the payment of compensation for damage caused to the employer. This latter provision paradoxically inverts the purposes of labour law, holding the worker—in this case truly a weaker party—liable for damages, as if, despite his discontinuous position, he was an essential and permanent part of the work organisation.

In 'on call' employment contracts and, as we shall see, in the regulation of part-time work we find one of the most controversial contents of the new Italian reform, particularly because of the significant unbalance created within individual employment contracts, characterised by an unusual disparity in the exercise of bargaining powers.[61]

Jaeger, the ECJ's ruling previously quoted, does not provide an easy analogy. In that case the definition of a 'job on call' is related to a contract including on-call duties among other obligations.

In the unstructured employment contract provided for workers 'on call' the main obligation, the one which most qualifies the contract, is to be available in periods of non-work. The weaker party's expanded obligations must be balanced against an almost unlimited exercise of managerial prerogatives,

---

[60] D Lgs 276/2003, above n 53, Attuazione delle deleghe in materia di occupazione e mercato del lavoro, di cui alla legge 14 febbraio 2003, n 30 [Decree introducring Measures on Employment and the Labour Market], Gazzetta Ufficiale n 235, 24 October 2003 arts 33-40.
[61] G. Boni, 'Contratto di lavoro intermittente e subordinazione' (2005) 1 *Rivista italiana di diritto del lavoro* 113.

since no objective criterion must assist the choice to 'call' in order to receive the work required.

Unlike in traditional subordinate employment, the non-continuous correlation to a work organisation makes the position of such workers paradoxically more dependant on the employer's initiatives. However, the ECJ ruling in a case of work on demand argued that it falls within the part-time Directive, despite the difficulty of finding a comparable worker and of enforcing in such a way the principle of equal treatment.[62]

It is difficult to say which minimum standards would contribute to establishing a different equilibrium of bargaining powers. The right to information can certainly be thought of as an essential precondition in view of creating a fair balance. Such a right would enable workers to plan work and non-work, both for reconciling family life and for seeking other occupations.

The right to a minimum wage is undoubtedly of a constitutional relevance. In 'jobs on call' a potential difficulty may rise if the required periods of availability are scattered in such a way along working days as to make the search for extrawork impossible. The absence of whatsoever guarantee in this employment contract could potentially lead to a violation of the right to dignity.

The new regulation of part-time work, introduced in the framework of the already mentioned reform of the Italian labour market, represents another example of restriction in a traditional labour law goal and of parallel expansion of managerial prerogatives.[63] In the legislation pre-dating the 2003 reform collective bargaining played a role in dealing with various modalities of entering part-time work and also in approaching rather complex and controversial issues, such as over-time work. The most representative unions had in this field quite a large variety of options to intervene, even derogating from the law, and were regularly informed by the employer of number of employed part-time workers and of the amount of over-time.

The so-called '*clausola elastica*' or elastic clause allowed the employer unilaterally to modify the modalities of part-time work, provided that there was a collective agreement indicating recourse to such a clause. This clause represented a compromise between collective guarantees and managerial prerogatives. Individual workers could, however, ask not to observe such a clause, if they produced evidence of the impossibility of accepting the employer's unilateral decision on the organisation of working hours. The employer had to give at least 10 days' notice and to provide for an increase in remuneration. Health and family reasons, as well as the need to work elsewhere on a different contract of employment or even as self-employed, were accepted.

---

[62] Case C–313/02 *Nicole Wippel v Peek & Cloppenburg GmbH & Co. KG*. [2004] ECR I–9483, at 62.

[63] D Lgs 276/2003, above n 53, Arts 46ff, modifying, but not completely replacing, previous legislation on part-time.

'Elastic clauses' are now in force even in the absence of collective agreements. This implies that individual workers' consent is required. Dismissals for refusing to consent are still illegal, but this measure does not in itself suffice to bring bargaining powers into a reasonable balance. The right to exit 'elastic clauses', a measure which could provide further options to workers, has been repealed.

Even the regulation of 'supplementary' work has changed. A previous role of collective agreements, thought of as 'filters' for the admissibility of such additional work, seems reduced by recourse to individual consent.[64]

Individual guarantees are still visible, just as they were in previous legal regulation of part-time work. For instance, a refusal to work part-time cannot by itself be ground for dismissal. This does not imply that justified dismissals for objective reasons should not occur. Furthermore, the transformation from a full-time into a part-time contract is always done in writing, at the worker's request and with the assistance of a union representative. Part-timers have the right to apply for full-time jobs, should the employer decide to hire new workers. Recent collective agreements have intervened in the so-called 'consolidation' of supplementary work, namely when recourse to it is persistent. These examples show interesting ways to counterbalance managerial prerogatives and to set limits to discretionary reasons in the recourse to part-time contracts.

In the regulation of part-time work across Europe we find examples of imaginative solutions, whenever this employment contract can be beneficial to certain groups of workers and become a choice, rather than an imposition.

In Germany legislation originating in the 'Alliance for Work' favoured the move into part-time contracts for workers over 55 years of age. The opportunity to offer new jobs to younger people was combined with a slow transition from active working life into a reduced work load, before retirement. Compensation is offered by the employer to the pension fund as if workers' salary were equal to 90 percent and a reimbursement of such sums to employers who can prove to have hired registered unemployed persons having undergone and completed their training.[65] A similar measure was adopted in Austria, granting an allowance to employers for old age part-timers.[66]

There are also cases, such as in Sweden and in the Netherlands, in which this employment contract is more strictly linked to voluntary choices of

---

[64] Collective agreements are, however, intervening on these matters, indicating in some cases the full liberalisation of recourse to supplementary work; in others indicating 'objective' criteria, such as an increase in production, preparation of inventories, shipping of goods, training of newly hired employees, and so on.

[65] U. Zachert, *The Evolution of Labour Law in Germany and Austria 1992–2002*, in *The Evolution*, above n 24, 145, also available at: http://europa.eu.int/comm/employment_social/labour_law/docs/ell_de_at.pdf; Caruso and Fuchs, above n 36; Maximilian Fuchs, 'Germany: Part-Time Work—a Bone of Contention' in Sciarra, Davies and Freedland, above n 40, at 121.

[66] U. Runggaldier 'Austrian National Report' in *The Evolving Structure of Collective Bargaining*, above n 39.

individual workers and associated with parental leave legislation or with other leave related to the life cycle.[67]

These are all examples in which, rather than measuring labour standard, theoretically guaranteed by the principle of equal treatment, one should be looking for legal and voluntary sources privileging workers' choices, in line with the fundamental right to reconciliation of family and working life.

Another example to be quoted is legislation on fixed term contracts.

In the 2001 Italian reform, which also transposed EC Directive 1999/70,[68] the main intention was to expand significantly recourse to fixed term contracts. Instead of following the previous technique of exemplifying binding cases in which such contracts could be legally stipulated, the current option is to do so whenever 'technical, productive, organisational and substitutive' reasons occur. In choosing to offer a generic and ample definition, the legislature takes the risk of creating a potentially contentious terrain around this interpretation, since employers should not be exempt from the duty to give reasons for their decisions.

If we return to the previously mentioned non-regression clause, we can maintain that the Italian reform has significantly reduced the limits (and therefore lowered the standard) previously set for recourse to fixed-term contracts.[69] Furthermore, no indication is given for the obligation, present in the Directive, to set a limit on the maximum number of renewals of fixed term contracts. It remains to be seen whether national courts will be able to refer cases to the ECJ on the basis of the non-regression clause.

The 'soft' style adopted by the European legislator is controversial even in other countries. In Greece the Presidential Decree transposing the Directive introduced a long list of exceptions allowing successive fixed term contracts. Due to a widespread recourse to such employment contracts particularly in the public sector, not corrected by the Decree, the Commission acted formally against the Greek government. Meanwhile, taking a very interesting initiative, some national courts have ruled repeatedly for the transformation of such contracts into open-ended ones, without referring cases to the ECJ.[70] One court, on the contrary, referred the case to the ECJ in order to clarify when national judges should be obliged to interpret national law in conformity with EU law. Fixed term contracts, in fact, were stipulated even before the final deadline for the transposition of the

---

[67] See E. Verhulp, 'Dutch National Report' in *ibid*.

[68] D Lgs 368/2001 was the first labour law reform adopted by the newly elected centre-right administration, with the open dissent of the largest Italian confederation CGIL.

[69] A complete commentary on the Italian Decree is in L. Zappalà, 'Fixed Term Contracts in Italy' in Caruso and Fuchs, above n 36, at 114–15.

[70] Yannakourou, above n 24, at 41. The most recent Presidential Decree has been considered in compliance with European standards; therefore no infringement procedure was started.

Directive into national law and during the extended time required by Greece for fulfilling its obligation.[71]

We can try to draw some conclusions by references made both to the enforcement of fundamental rights and to the 'soft' legal framework of the European Employment Strategy.

Part-time work has been presented in some countries as a leading example of 'instrumental use'[72] of the Directive, particularly of the Article (5 (1) (a)) which imposes on Member States an obligation to identify and possibly remove all obstacles to recourse to part-time employment. It is on the basis of such Article that some of the interpreters justify all possible changes in national legislation, even those downgrading existing levels of legal guarantees.

The debate is also open on the compatibility of such measures with the non-regression clause in the Part-time Work Directive, followed by a caveat indicating that Member States and social partners, 'in the light of changing circumstances', should not be limited in their 'right' to adopt different provisions. This truism, which confirms Member States' sovereign legislative powers, finds a boundary in the principle of non-discrimination between comparable full-time workers.

As for fixed-term contracts, the non-regression clause has, so far, been interpreted with caution, possibly because of its ambiguous formulation in relation to the concrete sanctions provided for in the Directive against abuses in the stipulation of such contracts. The choice of sanctions, we are reminded in a recent case, must be left entirely to national judges, who must come to their decisions in full respect for the final aim of the Directive, namely to avoid abuses in recourse to fixedterm contracts.[73]

The role of fundamental rights is thus ascertained as a limit to all deregulatory policies which may imperil the full enforceability of the principle itself. The difficult comparison among legal standards and the equally difficult evaluation of what should be deemed to be less favourable treatment must be left to national judges, steeped as they are in the traditions of each legal system.

---

[71] Case C–212/04 *Konstantinos Adeneler et al.*, Opinion of Advocate General Kokott, 27 Oct. 2005. At 45 Kokott makes reference to her own opinion in *Wippel* (above n 62), maintaining that the obligation of consistent interpretation is enforceable when the Directive comes into force, even if not transposed.

[72] A. Lo Faro, 'Italy: Adaptable Employment and Private Autonomy in the Italian Reform of Part-time Work' in Sciarra, Davies and Freedland, above n 40, at 156; B. Caruso, 'Riforma del part-time e diritto sociale europeo: verso una teoria dei limiti ordinamentali' [2003] *Diritti lavori mercati* 301, also available at www.lex.unict.it/eurolabor/riurca/presentazione. For the UK see C. Kilpatrick and M. Freedland, 'The United Kingdom: How is EU Governance Transformative?' in Sciarra, Davies and Freedland, above n 40, at 299.

[73] Case C–212/04 *Konstantinos*, above n 71, at 64 ff and at 80 of the Advocate General's Opinion (above n 71).

C. Derogations in Collective Agreements

Signs of changes affecting the purpose of labour law are visible also in collective bargaining, in as much as they expand the margins of pejorative derogations from minimum standards.

In Germany a debate is open on the so-called 'opening clauses' in sector collective agreements. Because of such clauses collective parties at plant level exercise their discretion to depart from terms and conditions of employment, including pay, agreed at the national level by employers' associations and trade unions.[74] This scenario alerts trade unions to exercise control over decentralised agreements concluded without their participation in negotiations.

In Italy collective agreements can expand to 12 months the reference period for the calculation of 'average' working time for 'objective or technical reasons, or reasons pertaining to work organisation, as specified in the collective agreements'.[75]

Different examples can be put forward, in order to prove that a balance between legal and voluntary sources can still be maintained. The notion of 'semi binding law' is also noteworthy. Danish legislation implementing the Working Time Directive is addressed only to employees not covered by collective agreements.[76]

In a different legal context, solutions adopted in Ireland are equally not invasive of collective parties' autonomy. The Labour Court can issue binding recommendations on pay and working conditions, if one of the parties refuses to enter negotiations and to follow voluntary procedures.[77]

In France the 2004 *Loi Fillon* introduced a majority principle to allow derogations at plant level both from the law and from standards agreed upon at sector level. The organisations signatory to such agreements must prove to have gained consensus among the majority of workers they represent. In order to introduce derogations there must be either a majority of unions signing or no opposition from the majority. Such alternative criteria are dealt with in national agreements and made binding by a ministerial decree.

It is worth underlining that, unlike in the previous *Auroux* reforms allowing derogations mainly in the field of working time, the *Loi Fillon* leaves only four subject areas untouched by this new technique. Apart

---

[74] Fuchs, above n 49.

[75] D Lgs 66/2003, art 4.4, transposing the Working Time Directive, n 21 above.

[76] N. Bruun and J. Malmberg, *The Evolution of Labour Law in Denmark, Finland and sweden 1992–2003*, in The Evolution above w.24, 82, also available at: http://europa. eu.int/comm/ employment_social/labour_law/docs/ell_da_fi_sv.pdf. The threat of a Commission infringement procedure forced the Danish legislature to implement by law measures already enforced in collective agreements. The latter do not in the Danish system have an *erga omnes* effect.

[77] Industrial Relations (Amendment) Act 2001. See A. Kerr, 'Irish National Report' in *The Evolving Structure of Collective Bargaining*, above n 39.

from minimum wages, job classifications, complementary systems of social protection, funds for professional training, all other subjects can be subject to derogations.[78]

4. CONCLUDING REMARKS: THE SEARCH FOR CORE PRINCIPLES IN NON-STANDARD EMPLOYMENT CONTRACTS

This chapter has addressed issues of coherence in recent labour law developments, so as to indicate how critical the dialogue among national and supranational law-makers can be. The goals of labour law have been framed within the tradition of 'public policy' objectives, comprehensively followed by legislatures and courts both at national and supranational level. In trying to balance fundamental social rights with market freedoms, attention has been paid to the role of core principles in non-standard contracts of employment.

If we take an historical perspective on European social policies, we notice that harmonisation of minimum standards, the most recurrent regulatory technique in the social field, did not lead to the disregarding of workers as 'persons'.[79] It is less evident that other techniques, alternative to harmonisation, will provide clear-cut responses to unanswered questions of social justice.

Accomplishing an equilibrium of bargaining powers in employment contracts can be regarded as a most significant outcome of labour law. That equilibrium is constantly undermined by legislation departing from the protection of weaker parties and therefore ignoring situations of objective imbalance between contracting parties. Managerial prerogatives are expanded because of new market pressures. They may take the way of new commercial transactions, moving productive activities outside the firm; they may opt for fragmenting employment contracts within the firm. The argument developed in this chapter is that all such new options available to the employer must be accompanied by new ways of balancing powers within a contractual framework.

The spread of non-standard contracts of employment at a time of declining harmonisation in EU law should awaken new attention in labour law scholarship and suggest a return to critical and at the same time innovative interpretations.[80]

---

[78] Pélissier, Supiot, and Jeammaud, above n 15, at 956–7.

[79] The ILO has stressed the centrality of this point in launching the project on Decent Work. See *Decent Work: Report of the Director General to the 87th session of the International Labour Conference* (Geneva, International Labour Office, 1999).

[80] An example is the notion of 'extended category of contracts' analysed in innovative terms by M. Freedland, *The Personal Employment Contract* (Oxford, Oxford University Press, 2003). The author confirms the centrality of contract law in employment law 'by refocusing on this different and enlarged contract type, the personal employment contract'. See in particular the Conclusions at 519.

Core principles in the laws governing employment contracts should be enforceable especially when there is a departure from traditional schemes of contractual obligations.

The right to professional training, for example, can easily be adapted to different individual needs and should be accompanied by the right to information. Both rights may represent an opportunity to respond to workforce reductions, or to expand workers' opportunities in improving the content of their jobs. They may also be functional in moving from one job to another or to consolidating a precarious working position.

Core principles should be built in terms of open opportunities for workers, adaptable to non-standard contracts and useful in redistributing powers in the uneven structure of individual employment contracts.

Particularly in the still undefined terrain of economically dependant work,[81] core principles should not be constructed as protective measures, but rather as entitlements for guaranteeing economic support in different fields. One can think of the accession to pension funds or to special credits from banks; the guarantee to enter social security schemes and to benefit from special allowances or training facilities in moving from one job to the other; the entitlement to pregnancy leave, parental and care leave and access to care facilities for children.[82]

In the most consolidated and widespread European tradition, labour law aimed at creating support mechanisms in order to let weaker parties emerge from their state of dependency and develop into 'persons', even within the constraints of employment contracts. It is suggested that this tradition be continued in the territory of non-standard contracts and even beyond subordinate employment, in the field of economically dependant work.

---

[81] G. Davidov, 'Who is a Worker?' (2005) 34 *Industrial Law Journal* 57.
[82] I have developed these ideas in Sciarra, above n 39, at sect V2.

IV

Identifying the Employer and Determining its Responsibilities

13

The Complexities of the Employing Enterprise

PAUL DAVIES* AND MARK FREEDLAND**

1. INTRODUCTION: RECONSIDERING THE IDEA OF THE EMPLOYER

Here come the new boss. Same as the old boss.

(Old saying)

I met a man upon the stair;
I looked again, he was not there.
He was not there again today.
Oh how I wish he'd go away!

(Traditional, anon.)

FOR LABOUR LAWYERS, we suggest that the mysterious man of the poem, who is not there and should go away, is, like the subject of the old saying, none other than 'the employer'. This chapter will argue that some of the difficulties which attend the whole debate about the personal scope of employment law can best be resolved, or at least understood, by questioning and de-constructing not, as is traditional, the concept of 'the worker' or 'the employee', but rather that of 'the employer', especially in the context of the contract of employment.

Our main line of argument will therefore consist of suggesting that the debate about the personal scope of employment law might benefit from being approached from an unfamiliar perspective, indeed initially a counter-intuitive one. The normal course of debate about the personal scope of employment law takes place primarily within a paradigm of bilateral

* Cassel Professor of Commercial Law, London School of Economics, United Kingdom.
** Professor of Employment Law, University of Oxford, United Kingdom.

employment relations or contracts between a worker and an employer. The problem about personal scope is perceived primarily or even solely as one of designating the appropriate category of workers to be included within the scope of legislation governing the employment relation. The primarily and traditionally appropriate category is that of dependent employees, in English law those with contracts of employment.

That category is traditionally distinguished from and contrasted with that of independent contractors, who are primarily and traditionally excluded from the scope of employment, though there are various experiments with the inclusion of semi-dependent workers, and even occasional instances of the inclusion of all workers even if independent. Somehow, but with difficulty, the more modern versions of that discussion manage to accommodate within it various 'anomalous' cases of triangular employment, such as that of labour-only sub-contracting or temporary employment via employment agencies. But, as we have argued elsewhere, the adherence to the contract of employment as a normative category gives rise to a legal analysis of personal work relations in essentially binary terms with which theorists and practitioners of employment law have constantly to struggle, because of its constant and increasing counter-factuality.

That path of discussion remains a most important one, but is now quite well-trodden, at a theoretical level if not at a practical one. On this occasion, we shall try to strike out in a rather different direction by arguing that a tangential but no less important aspect of the problem about the personal scope of employment law might consist not so much in the *binary* analysis of the *worker* as in the *unitary* analysis of the *employer*. We shall suggest that this unitary analysis of the employer is no less deep-seated in employment law than the binary analysis of the worker, certainly no less counter-factual, and probably making as great a contribution to our present difficulties about the personal scope of employment law.

We commence this presumptuous argument by considering, in the remainder of this introductory section, why the unitary analysis of the employer is so firmly entrenched. We continue in our second section by considering challenges to the unitary analysis from within the single enterprise, in our third section by considering challenges to the unitary analysis from situations of network employment; and in a concluding section we seek to link these arguments back into the main theme of this book.

As one of us has recently argued elsewhere,[1] employment law, at least in the UK upon which we shall concentrate, is imbued with the notion of the employer as a single person—in most cases a legal person rather than a human one, but even so the paradigm is strongly analogised to that of the

---

[1] M. Freedland, 'Rethinking the Personal Work Contract' (2006) 58 *Current Legal Problems*, 517.

'master', the male human employer of the servant in master and servant law. So powerful is this metaphor that the employer is still usually designated as 'he' in legislation and in case law, although that attribution of single male human personality is usually as fictitious as is John Doe, the non-existent actor in common law litigation. If we leave aside that particular attribution of male human personality and concentrate simply on the way in which 'the employer' is envisaged as a single indivisible entity, we find that the paradigm is even more universally and strongly entrenched. No black box could be more opaque or firmly shut.

Our contention is that this paradigm normally fictionalises and distorts a more accurate perception of the employing enterprise as a multi-polar organisation; even if it consists of only one nucleus, that nucleus has several atoms and its own internal structure. We may find instances where one human being is in fact and in law the sole employer of another, but they are very far from typical. Even in employment relations where there is in substance a single human employer, as soon as vehicles of corporate or quasi-corporate legal personality are invoked the situation becomes complex, and in some sense multi-polar—a nominal second shareholder becomes involved, or something like that.

Nevertheless, employment law, and especially the law of the contract of employment which, in the UK case at least, forms its conceptual core, the paradigm of the employer as a single indivisible or atomic entity is resolutely maintained, however counter-factual it may be. When a counter-factual paradigm is insisted upon in this way, especially in a juridical context, that is often defended as a matter of 'convenience' or of 'shorthand'—that is to say the fiction is depicted as a conscious and superficial one—but there usually turns out to be an ideological reason for doing so. In this case there are several, operating cumulatively.

First, there is the ideology of master and servant relations and master and servant law. Just as the terminology of 'master and servant law' very long outlived the disappearance of its substance and its pre-industrial and early industrial context, so also did the paternalist ideology of employment as a relationship of loyalty and commitment, moving primarily from a subordinate servant to a superior master. That described the axis of the employment relation, the strength of which depended on that clear identification and characterisation of two individuals, one at each pole of the axis.

Secondly, in the course of the nineteenth century, in a way that was so memorably identified and charted by Alan Fox,[2] that paradigm was, in a development of remarkable subtlety, superficially subsumed into that of

---

[2] A. Fox, *Beyond Contract: Work, Power and Trust Relations* (London, Faber, 1973), 181–90.

contract law and the liberal ideology of freedom of contract which under-pinned it. In that new ideological framework, the employment relation was no less strongly characterised as a bipolar one between two individuals, with the sole difference that they were now represented as being in an axiomatic state of contractual equality with each other.

Next, perhaps somewhat from a tangent, there intrudes in the course of the nineteenth century the emergent ideology of company law, with its cen-tral commitment to the recognition and protection of the unity and integrity of corporate legal personality—a commitment of crucial significance to the development of commerce and industry as enabling the limited liability company to function as a valid actor in the market economy. So company law contributes an ideology in which the limited liability company is asserted to be the exact and full equivalent of the human employer.

However, much of the sustaining ideology for the unity of the employer and the bipolarity of the employment relation comes from within employ-ment law, and not just from the early paternalist 'master and servant' ver-sions thereof. On the contrary, it is not exaggerating to say that the whole of twentieth century labour law had as its ideological core the notion of the essentially bipolar relation between 'the worker' and 'the employer', the lat-ter being the atomised embodiment of 'capital' or 'management'. For the axis between those two poles was the one across which stretched the pre-sumed subordination of the worker and the presumed inequality of bar-gaining power which it was the very function of labour law to re-balance, preferably by the development and deployment of voluntary collective power. The idiom and ideology of re-equilibrating a balance in favour of the worker is a pervasive and dominant one in labour law. The whole construct postulates and requires 'an employer' at the other end of the normative see-saw.

This is not to assert, however, that the idea of 'the employer' as an anti-thetical unity to the worker is confined to the extreme or dialectical ideolo-gies of modern labour law. We find that 'the employer' figures equally strongly, and generally in a virtuous role, as a key actor in the scenarios of welfare capitalism, of welfare state tripartism, and, currently, of competi-tive labour markets regulated by strategies for employment, equality and social inclusion. Those constructs similarly depend upon the designation of 'the employer' as the bearer of an extensive range of social and economic responsibilities for the beneficial conduct and outcomes of employment relations.

It is not, however, the purpose of this chapter to chop away at the ideolog-ical foundations of employment law, but, less iconoclastically, to suggest why the notion of 'the employer' as the simple antithesis to and counterpart of the worker might be over-zealously protected by those ideologies. Nor do we seek to deny that, for some purposes, not investigating too closely the notion of the 'employer' has advantages for the law of the employment relationship.

Thus, we referred earlier to the employer as 'the atomised embodiment of "capital" or "management"'. Simply concentrating on the company as employer permits the law of the personal work contract not to concern itself with whether control of the company is located with the directors (as was typically the case in large companies in the 1950s) or with the shareholders (as may be the case today if institutional shareholders have established substantial holdings in the company) or with some combination of the two. Attaching liability to the 'company' brings home responsibility to the employing enterprise, no matter where its control is located.

In fact our endeavour is, by questioning the conceptualisation of 'the employer' at its margins, both to reinforce the edifice of employment law, and in certain ways to extend its personal scope by bringing certain complex forms of work relations firmly within it. In pursuit of that objective we engage in some re-examination of the concept of 'the employer', first from an internal perspective, looking at hierarchies, and secondly from an external perspective, concentrating upon networks, and also at that point subjecting the notion of 'self-employment' to renewed scrutiny.

2. THE IDEA OF THE EMPLOYER AND INTERNAL STRUCTURES OR HIERARCHIES

A. Dual Role Managers and Workers

In a recent piece of writing[3] we engaged in some de-construction of the concept of the employer in labour law, concentrating upon the situation where a multiplicity of (legal) persons or enterprises are involved as employer. We return to a particular aspect of that set of issues in the next section, but in this second section we reexamine the idea of the employer by looking at it from within the single employing enterprise; our concern is with internal structures or hierarchies within that single employing enterprise. So we are 'splitting the atom' of employment law and representing it as an often complex molecule.

It is of course well-known to employment lawyers that employing enterprises do have an often complex internal organisational structure, which will usually have some sort of hierarchical pattern, but one which may well have lateral and diagonal ramifications within the organisation (as well as outside it; as we have said, we revert to external ramifications later). That is well-recognised, and we would insult the intelligence of employment

---

[3] P.L. Davies and M.R. Freedland, 'Changing Perspectives Upon the Employment Relationship in British Labour Law' in C. Barnard, S. Deakin and G.S. Morris (eds), *The Future of Labour Law: Liber Amicorum Sir Bob Hepple QC* (Oxford, Hart, 2004), 129.

lawyers by alleging otherwise. But employment lawyers, for the reasons we have put forward in the previous introduction, are firmly committed to the view that it is systematically possible to distinguish and designate an inner core, or top slice, of that organisational structure which constitutes 'the employer', and which corresponds exactly to the 'master' in the ideal-type of the employment relation between two human beings.

Our suggestion is that such a simple delineation and separation of 'the employer' is very often difficult and at times impossible. We further suggest that this difficulty is attributable to two closely linked features of the internal organisation or ordering of many employing enterprises, indeed one might say of the *typical* modern employing enterprise. Let us, as a preliminary to elucidating those two features, loosely designate the functions of employing, or the role which we are accustomed to attribute to 'the employer', as 'managerial functions', and so let us also designate those to whom those functions are entrusted within the employing enterprise as its 'managers'.

Using that terminology (not without some detailed caveats and reservations, of course), we may make two crucial observations. The first is that the managers or bearers of employing functions may themselves be constituted as employees of or workers for the enterprise in question and this may even be true for those right at the top of a hierarchical structure. The second observation is that those managerial or employing functions may be distributed widely within an internal organisational structure, and may cascade a long way downwards through its hierarchy; indeed, current organisational practice seems to extend and intensify that dispersal.

Moreover—and this is the metaphysical and transformative nub of the argument—those observations lead on to the further observation that some persons, possibly many persons, within employing enterprises play in varying degrees the dual role of both managers and workers; they figure both as employers and employees. There may of course be a person or persons at the apex of the managerial pyramid who are not employees of or workers for the enterprise in any sense; there will also usually or typically be some workers without any managerial functions; but between those extremes lies a long spectrum occupied by dual role manager/workers. Their importance to the theory and practice of employment law is very great and has been greatly under-stated.

Indeed, the employment practices of large City firms consist to no small extent of negotiating contracts of employment for executive directors and senior managers and then negotiating the compensation payable if these contracts are subsequently unlawfully terminated. Recent governmental proposals further to control the 'rewards for failure' syndrome have concentrated almost entirely on standard contractual techniques, for example, the length of the notice period or contract term, the duty to mitigate loss or the use of liquidated damages clauses. In the ensuing paragraphs we consider some developments in organisational and contractual practice which have contributed to the intensification of this dual-role phenomenon, and then we reflect on the response of employment law to it, and the implications for the personal scope of employment law.

There are a number of factors in past organisational and contractual practice which have contributed to the growth of this role duality, and some factors in current practice which tend to intensify it. The first is a long evolution of the practice of corporate management whereby the directors and senior executives of commercial companies have tended to be accorded service agreements and so to be treated as employees of companies, as well as being, in many instances, officers of the companies concerned. This has almost, if not entirely, reached the point where employment is the dominant paradigm for relations between companies and their chief executives.

A second and perhaps even more long-standing and general historical factor has been that of the vertical integration of production, that is to say the evolution from processes of production by a number of distinct enterprises in a horizontally dispersed pattern of organisation towards processes of production through concentrated and unified elements vertically merged into a single organisation. It is well observed that this evolution, strongly associated with nineteenth century industrialisation and twentieth century Fordism and Taylorism, served extensively to transform independent artisans into dependent workers; less emphasised is the fact that this evolution also operated to extend and enlarge the whole cadre of middle managers, in other words to swell the ranks of the dual-role manager/workers who are the focus of our present argument.

Paradoxically, the more recent reverse trend towards vertical disintegration of production probably further reinforces the size and significance of the contingent of dual-role manager/workers (while at the same time, as we shall see in the next section, often placing them in more complex organisational structures). As Hugh Collins famously argued in the early 1990s,[4] the primary effect of the sort of vertical disintegration of production which became prominent from the 1980s onwards, consisting of various kinds of outsourcing, was to extrude workers from the employing enterprise, often re-casting them as independent contractors outside the scope of employment law. However, as one of us has recently argued elsewhere,[5] there is also a significant secondary phenomenon of fragmentation of production *within* the employing enterprise, whereby units of production are identified within the structure of the firm and are managed and accounted for as partly distinct entities. Where this occurs, the managerial role of those responsible for those distinct entities within the firm is heightened; they are more strongly identified as dual-role managers/workers.

---

[4] H. Collins, 'Independent Contractors and the Challenge to Employment Protection Laws' (1990) 10 *Oxford Journal of Legal Studies* 353.

Strongly associated with this development is a corresponding trend to re-frame the employment relations of many workers, especially but not solely those in managerial positions, so that their situation is in various respects a more entrepreneurial one within the employing enterprise. In various ways, their remuneration and career development become specifically dependent upon the development and exercise of entrepreneurial skills, and their abil-ity to take a business approach to their work situation and to their relations to those around them in the organisational hierarchy. In the ensuing para-graphs we consider how far and how employment law has responded to these developments, and with what implications for the debate about the personal scope of employment law.

B. The Dual Role and the Law of Organisational Liability

As we might imagine, in view of the arguments about ideology which were advanced in the previous section, there has been some reluctance to recog-nise and internalise the idea of the dual-role manager/worker in the legal system at large, in company law, and most particularly in employment law. It is beyond the scope of this chapter to go at all deeply into the topic of corporate civil and criminal liability for the actions or decisions of direc-tors, or managers, who are also employees, but it is worth drawing atten-tion to the notable absence of any real recognition of the dual role of managers in a few different specific situations where organisational liabil-ity for managers/workers has been in question. We begin with the recent decision of the Court of Appeal in the case of *Majrowski v Guy's and St Thomas' NHS Trust*.[6]

The issue here was whether the defendant health authority was civilly liable under the Protection from Harassment Act 1997 in respect of the bul-lying at work inflicted on the claimant by his departmental manger. Given that the Court of Appeal did by a majority find in favour of such liability, thus making an important extension to the protection of employees from bullying at work, it may seem rather carping to criticise the basis on which they did so; but it is nevertheless worth remarking that, although the employee who inflicted the bullying was in a reasonably senior middle management role and therefore a very good example of the dual-role manager/worker, there seems to have been no suggestion that she could have been regarded as an embodiment of 'the employer' so as to make the Trust *primarily* liable for her actions.

---

[5] Freedland, above n 1.
[6] [2005] EWCA Civ 251.

The question was approached entirely as one of *vicarious* liability of 'the employer' for the conduct of one employee towards another, as if the perpetrator and the victim were of exactly comparable status; and the Trust as employer was regarded as 'knowing nothing' of the harassment which had taken place. As the decision and the doctrine which sustained it may yet be rejected by the House of Lords as the highest appellate court, it is perhaps not out of place to express concern that the decision was not buttressed by a demonstrated awareness of the significance of the managerial power which the perpetrator evidently exercised over the victim, and which indeed created the very basis for the harassment which took place.

Indeed, it is curious that British organisational law has not developed its own set of concepts for determining when the organisation (whether corporate or otherwise) is liable, given that the organisation is incapable of acting in law except where the acts of human beings are attributed to it. Generally, for liability extending beyond the acts of the organisation's constitutional bodies (board of directors or shareholders' meeting in the case of a company), reliance is simply placed on the common law doctrines of authority (for contractual liability) and vicarious liability, (for torts), coupled with a marked reluctance to impose any organisational liability at all for crimes involving *mens rea*. Only slowly and intermittently have the courts come to accept that particular statutes might require them to adopt a broader approach. See *R v British Steel plc*[7] (in the area of criminal law) and *Meridian Global Funds Management Asia Ltd v Securities Commission*[8] (in the area of regulatory law). Unlike vicarious liability, the broader approach does not require the identification of an individual manager with whom the organisation can be made jointly liable; and thus it creates scope for holding the organisation liable for inadequate managerial structures where no single individual can be held to be blameworthy. Similar issues arise on the current proposals for an offence of corporate killing to supplement the common law offence of manslaughter by gross negligence.

However, when we move from the sphere of general corporate civil liability into that of employment law, there are some senses in which, despite the ideological antithesis between 'employer' and 'worker' which we identified in the previous section, the dual-role manager/worker is recognised. Thus, although the courts will regard a purported contract of employment between a company and its true sole proprietor as a 'sham' which does not qualify that proprietor as the bearer of employment rights against the company, they seem very willing, in any situation which falls short of that one-on-one fit between the company and its proprietor, to accept the presentation of the

[7] [1995] ICR 586.
[8] [1995] 3 All ER 918.

relationship as a contract of employment despite the primary managerial role of the purported employee.

There does, moreover, seem to be quite an extensive recognition of the dual role of the manager/employee in the now elaborate and rapidly growing body of case-law which concerns on the one hand the fiduciary duties and on the other hand the more broadly conceived obligations as to mutual trust and confidence which apply to employees, whether as duties or obligations owed by them or owed to them. Thus in the sphere of fiduciary duties, we find an emerging recognition of a specially strict regime for 'senior employees' which the Court of Appeal has recently identified, in its important decision in *Item Software Ltd v Fassihi*[9] as sometimes including a duty to confess their own misdeeds, as well as the duty to report the misconduct of other employees which had earlier been developed in *Sybron Corporation v Rochem*.[10]

On the other hand, and no less significantly, the obligations as to mutual trust and confidence which are owed to employees could equally be seen as being specially strongly developed in relation to senior and high-status employees. This trend is almost sufficiently pronounced to produce a distinct genre of the implied obligation for dual-role managers/employees. Such a trend is predictable, if for no other reason, because of the extent to which the implied obligation has taken the form of a duty of parity or equity of treatment *between employees of the same grade or situation*.[11] The development of the obligation of mutual trust and confidence in that lateral dimension is inherently likely to generate a doctrinal sub-set of dual-role managerial or executive employees.

At the same time it has to be observed that this development presents formidable potential difficulties in separating the roles of such employees in order to decide when they are the perpetrators and when they are the victims of breach of the obligation of mutual trust and confidence—nowhere more so than in the foundational case of *Malik v BCCI*,[12] where it was never really satisfactorily resolved who among the managers of the bank were inflicting and who among them were suffering from the corrupt mismanagement of the enterprise which seems to have stigmatised many or all of the managerial employees of the bank in the eyes of potential employers when the bank went into liquidation.

This is the point at which we have to consider how these developments, in the conceptualisation and understanding of 'the employer' in employment law, bear upon the set of issues about the personal scope of employment law. We suggest that there is the following very important link. We have

---

[9] [2004] IRLR 928.
[10] [1984] Ch 112 (CA).
[11] See M.R. Freedland, *The Personal Employment Contract* (Oxford, Oxford University Press, 2003), 223–30.
[12] [1997] ICR 606.

argued that the category of employees actually intersects with the category of persons who constitute the human embodiment of 'the employer', so that there is an extensive category of dual-role manager/worker. Moreover we have argued that there is often, and indeed with increasing frequency, an entrepreneurial quality in the relations of those dual-role manager/workers with the enterprise in which they are employed.

The effect of these phenomena is to create a significant degree of *intermediacy* and of *multi-polarity* in employment relations within the employing enterprise. Cadres of people work within employing enterprises, but in situations of intermediacy between those of 'the employer' and 'the employee' in the traditional paradigm; and those intermediate persons or groups themselves form further focal points for employment relations within the enterprise, transforming those relations into multipolar ones rather than simple bipolar ones.

So this set of developments challenges and disrupts an understanding of employment relations within the enterprise as simple bipolar ones between 'the employer' and a series of dependent and subordinate employees. It focuses attention upon a level of employment relations within the enterprise which cannot satisfactorily be characterised in terms of simple subordination and dependency. This thereby erodes, at a deep and subtle level, not just the simple bipolar antithesis between 'the employer' and 'the worker', but also, and no less momentously, the simple binary distinction between employees and independent contractors. All this tends to de-legitimate the use of that distinction as a basis for drawing the boundaries of employment rights.

This argument will appear to be surprising because of the extent to which, as we have said, employment law is ideologically committed to the bipolar analysis of employment relations within the enterprise. Even to the extent that employment law has *in substance* come to recognise the dual-role manager/worker and multipolar employment relations within the enterprise, it has *in formal terms* not yet really begun to do so. The force of this argument will become more evident when we extend it beyond the single employing enterprise into the wider realm of multi-agency and 'network' employment, as we seek to do in the next section. As indicated in our Introduction, this will also involve bringing the notion of 'self-employment' into renewed question.

3. THE IDEA OF 'SELF-EMPLOYMENT' AND THE MULTI-AGENCY EMPLOYMENT NETWORK

A. The Traditional Binary Divide

As we began to indicate at the close of the previous section, our purpose in re-visiting the concept of 'the employer', and in re-examining it from an internal perspective upon employment relations within the employing enterprise, was, by exhibiting the limits and shortcomings of an analysis of those relations as a simple series of bipolar superior/subordinate ones, to open up to question the binary analysis of all personal work relations as totally divisible into those of employment and those of self-employment, the latter being traditionally treated as beyond the purview of employment law. In this section we pursue that argument from a perspective which is, initially at least, external to the employing enterprise, looking outwards from and beyond the employing enterprise at the relations generally regarded as those of independent personal work contracting or of self-employment.

We suggest that in this sphere too, as in the sphere of intra-enterprise employment relations, employment law has a stereotype of basically bipolar independent personal work relations and contracts, generally regarded as 'self-employment'. This latter stereotype, although viewed as in radical contrast to the stereotype of bipolar employment relations within the enterprise, in fact mirrors or even replicates the other stereotype, and often has the same defect of over-simplification.

For we suggest that independent personal work relations and contracts do not really lend themselves to an *exclusively* bipolar analysis any better than personal employment relations within the enterprise do. Just as the bipolarity of personal employment relations *within* the enterprise is compromised by the existence of dual-role manager/workers, so the bipolarity of personal employment relations *outside* the enterprise (those therefore generally regarded as 'self-employment') is equally compromised by the existence of elaborate multi-agency structures or networks.

We further suggest that the existence of this set of similarities or parallels, between personal work relations viewed as being within the employing organisation (and therefore those of 'employment') and personal work relations viewed as being outside the employing organisation (and therefore viewed as those of 'self-employment'), serves yet further to undermine the supposed binary division between employment relations regarded as basically within the realm of employment law, and relations of 'self-employment' regarded as generally outside the realm of employment law.

All this in our view points up yet further the need to be able to envisage and accept multipolar and multi-agency employment relations and contracts as falling within the realm of employment law, and across the binary divide between the two traditional stereotypes of employment and self-employment. However, that is an argument which needs to be constructed carefully and in stages, as we endeavour to do in the succeeding paragraphs.

Let us start by examining a little more fully the traditional stereotype of independent personal employment relations, the relations in other words of 'self-employment' with which employment law is traditionally not concerned. In these relations, the independence of the worker or personal independent contractor is generally supposed to consist in the fact that he or she makes so many discrete task contracts, possibly with one employer but typically or potentially with so many different employers, that he or she does not thereby enter into any one dependent employment relationship. In this stereotype, the bipolarity or bilaterality of these relations is just as strong as we found it to be in the employment stereotype, the main difference consisting in the multiplicity and discreteness of relations and contracts as opposed to the singularity and greater continuity, and therefore greater dependency, of the relation and contract of employment.

Just as the stereotype of the simple bipolar employment relation may have accurately reflected real and prevailing master and servant relations in an earlier, perhaps pre-industrial, era, so this stereotype too may have reflected equally real and prevalent work relations for independent journeymen and craftsmen in the same era. Moreover there were important connections and similarities, extending into a much more recent period, with the situations of people working on their own (rather than in associations or partnerships) in the so-called 'liberal professions' such as those of medicine or advocacy.

B. New Forms of Vertical Disintegration

It is one thing to believe in the historical accuracy and utility of this stereotype. It is quite another thing, and a much more questionable one, to assume that the recent and current phenomenon of vertical disintegration of production, as considered earlier in this chapter, consists in or brings about a latter-day reversion to that earlier stereotype. This might sometimes be the case; we might for instance be prepared to see the work situation of Mr Lorimer, the film technician, previously employed in-house by the BBC and then working on a freelance basis for many different employers, whose work situation was the subject of the leading tax classification case of *Hall v Lorimer*,[13] as having undergone exactly that transformation.

However, we suggest that this should no longer be regarded as the current stereotype of vertical disintegration of production. Instead, we suggest that vertical disintegration can best be understood, in many situations at least, as involving, not just changes in the situation and defining characteristics of the worker, but also changes in the characteristics and configuration of 'the employer'. Vertical disintegration of production is, as we have indicated, often viewed as extruding the worker from the employing organisation into a situation of self-organisation. But very often vertical disintegration in fact results in the worker being still within an organisation, the

---

[13] [1994] ICR 218 (HL).

difference being that the organisation is a looser and more strongly multi-polar one than that of the single employing enterprise.

In those situations, the internal multipolarity of the employing enterprise which we focussed upon in the previous section has a greatly magnified equivalent in multi-agency personal work structures. The work organisation has disintegrated, but not into completely discrete atoms, as the traditional stereotype might suggest. It is rather that larger, looser multi-nuclear molecules have been formed. In the succeeding paragraphs we will expose and analyse this phenomenon more fully, and will then proceed, in the way that we did in the previous section, to consider what has been the response of employment law to this phenomenon.

A most useful starting point in this respect is the symposium of papers which appeared as special issue of the *British Journal of Industrial Relations* in December 2004, on the topic of 'Changing Contours of Employment and New Modes of Labour Regulation'; and in particular the synoptic introductory paper by Linda Dickens.[14] Dickens describes how the contributors to the conference, of which this symposium was the product, identified and focused upon two broad aspects of change in the nature of employment, the first being the growth of atypical, non-standard or 'flexible' jobs and a growth in self-employment, and the second being 'the rise of networked, boundaryless (sometimes virtual) organisations in which highly skilled, autonomous professional individuals, with occupational or portfolio careers rather than organisational careers, link together with each others to work on a non-hierarchical project basis'.

She remarks upon the way that the first category of change 'is often associated with the growth of "poor work"', while 'the second category of change tends to be linked to the growth of the so-called "new economy", the "wired world" or the "knowledge economy" with generally positive connotations for those knowledge workers employed in high-tech sectors'. As far as the first category is concerned, she is careful to stress her view that there is considerable heterogeneity in atypical work,[15] and that, in quantitative terms, the most important forms of atypical employment are part-time and temporary work, which may be of poor quality, but of course may well not be.[16] Observing those important caveats on her part, we make grateful use of the categorisation which she has set up, even if the fit with 'poor work' and 'high-grade work' is only a loose one.

She also comments that 'cross-cutting the two categories is the growth of small and medium-sized enterprises (SMEs), although these are heterogeneous, varying both within and across sectors'. Accepting, then, that dual

---

[14] L. Dickens, 'Problems of Fit: Changing Employment and Labour Regulation' (2004) 42 *British Journal of Industrial Relations* 595.

[15] *Ibid.*, at 596.

[16] *Ibid.*, at 597.

categorisation of change in the nature of employment, we are suggesting a somewhat more ambitious cross-cutting theme, which is that of the growing multi-agency organisation of personal work relations, of which the growth of SMEs is indeed a part, but only a part, of the story.

So if we begin by considering Dickens' first category of change, that of the growth of frequently though not always 'poor' atypical employment, we can readily observe how strongly that development is associated with the growth of intermediary labour-providing enterprises, such as temporary employment agencies or labour-only or labour-intensive sub-contractors. In many instances, the casual or flexible character of the personal work situation of the workers concerned flows from or denotes, not the *absence* of an employing organisation, but the *complication* of the employing organisation into a multi-agency one, that is to say one which is multipolar across more than one enterprise.

Two incidental observations are important here. First, the intermediary labour-providing enterprises may themselves be very large and important ones, whether as employment agencies or labour-only or labour intensive sub-contractors. Thus in a certain sense enterprises such as Manpower or Group Four have become enormous employing organisations in their own right, with very large and sophisticated organisational structures of their own. Secondly, these labour-providing enterprises, whether large ones or SMEs, often have very highly developed arrangements of co-operation and co-ordination with their client end-users of the labour services in question, so much so that they are effectively in continuing partnership with the end-users in the employment of the workers concerned (whether those workers are regarded as employees or as self-employed casual labour). Both these factors serve further to negate the conception of the world of flexible casual employment as one in which there is an absence of continuing organisational structure for the workers in question.

C. Complex Organisation in the Networked Economy

If we turn our attention to Dickens' second location of change in employment relations, that of the new networked knowledge economy, a similar set of observations may be made. We suggest that in this sphere of the work economy, as in that of atypical flexible work, personal work relations may better be understood in terms of complex multipolar employing organisation than in terms of an absence of continuing employing organisation. The Dickens analysis of this category, in a way that deserves respect as coming from such an authority on employment relations, and which reflects widely held views, stresses the extreme looseness or absence of connectedness between workers and employing enterprises in this sphere, describing the networks as boundaryless and virtual, implying that those concerned are linked together only by the internet.

The exception which is admitted by that analysis, an exception which is almost seen as proving the rule, is to notice the formation of workers into laterally connected teams or groups of professional workers for the purpose of particular work projects. In his contribution to the symposium to which we referred earlier, David Marsden focussed especially on this phenomenon of collaborative work with a team output.[17] The description of such networks by Marsden, and indeed by Linda Dickens in her general overview,[18] suggests that they lack hierarchy. We incline to the view that, although this might occasionally be the case, the more typical position would be that, even if networks involve teams brought together for particular projects, someone must be sitting at the centre of the web co-ordinating these inputs and so creating some element of hierarchy.

In fact, our suggestion is that this particular occurrence of team or project formation, although quite significant in itself, is, or at least will turn out to be, part of a larger phenomenon of formation of complex multipolar personal work organisations in the 'new knowledge economy', in which the links will be diagonal, and even occasionally vertical ones, with employing enterprises, as well as just lateral ones within teams of workers. We start to encounter personal work situations involving 'knowledge workers' which stretch outside and beyond single employing enterprises but, so far from existing in an organisational vacuum traversed only by computer signals, sit within intense structures of self-incorporations, and incorporated or unincorporated consultancies, themselves in complex contractual relations with end-user employing enterprises.

There is one particular reason why we should expect this to occur; it relates back to our discussion of intra-enterprise employment structures in the previous section, where the dual manager/worker role was identified and argued to be of great significance in understanding the nature of 'the employer' as well as of the worker. We suggest that, in what is really a parallel phenomenon, the personnel working in the 'new knowledge economy' will consist not only, perhaps not even primarily, of pure information technology experts, but also or even primarily of professional dual-role workers engaged in managerial or executive functions (and using highly developed IT skills), but doing so on a consultancy basis wholly or partly from outside employing enterprises, rather than from within them as under earlier vertically integrated patterns of production.

We may even speculate that eventually pure IT experts may join earlier generations of heroes of industry, wielders of hammers and drivers of engines, in the lower ranks of personal work hierarchies, leaving this middle and higher

---

[17] D. Marsden, 'The "Network Economy" and Models of the Employment Contract' (2004) 42 *British Journal of Industrial Relations* 659.

[18] Dickens, above n 14, at 595.

ground to consultants in management, regulation and finance who can deploy and draw on those technical IT skills as necessary. That may be far-fetched; the far more real and immediate point is that this part of the personal work economy is likely, even more obviously than are the cadres of dual-role managers/workers located firmly within employing enterprises, to consist of working people with entrepreneurial skills, approaches and inclinations. It is to be expected that such working people, rather than remaining in an organisational vacuum, will themselves contribute to the formation of elaborate personal work structures, and may introduce new SMEs into those structures, thus further adding to their organisational intensity and complexity.

D. The Response of Employment Law

As in the previous section, having thus identified a dynamic of multipolarity in which dual manager/worker roles are very significant, we turn to consider what response employment law has made to these developments, both in general terms and more particularly with regard to the personal scope of employment law. The short answer is that there has been some response, but that it still falls very short of the kind of rethinking of the concept of 'the employer' which we believe to be functionally required. It is useful here to continue to follow Dickens' distinction between the two kinds or locations of change in employment relations, that is to say the growth of, on the one hand, work which is frequently 'poor' work, in flexible, or atypical patterns, and, on the other hand, of work outside single-enterprise organisations in the 'new knowledge economy', which is frequently higher-grade work.

Most of the legal response, especially as regards the personal scope of employment law, has hitherto been in the former location rather than in the latter one. For example, the very valuable study by Guy Davidov, 'Joint Employer Status in Triangular Employment Relationships' which also formed part of the Network Economy symposium[19], concentrates considerably on the situation of temporary agency employment in the weakest sections of the workforce. For a long time, the response in this area to multipolar flexible or atypical work situations was a distinctly negative one; a line of cases from *Construction Industry Training Board v Labour Force Ltd*[20] through *Ironmonger v Movefield Ltd*[21] to *Montgomery v Johnson Underwood Ltd*[22] showed the courts taking the view that a triangular

---

[19] And therefore appears in the special issue of (2004) 42 *British Journal of Industrial Relations* 727.
[20] [1970] 3 All ER 220 (QBD).
[21] [1988] IRLR 461 (EAT).
[22] [2001] ICR 819 (CA).

personal work situation was as such a *sui generis* one, outside the scope of the contract of employment and therefore of most employment legislation. The recent decisions of the Court of Appeal in *Franks v Reuters Ltd*[23] and in *Dacas v Brook Street Bureau (UK) Ltd*[24] have shown a greater willingness to find or imply a contract of employment in such situations, but, far from recognising triangular employment contracts as such, the court insisted in each case on reducing the triangular relationship to a bilateral contract either with the intermediary agency or with the end-user, but not with both.

In the very little case law that is to be found concerning the personal scope of employment law in the 'new knowledge-based economy', something rather similar seems to be occurring. The most important legislative initiative with regard to multi-agency personal work relations has been the extension of the various kinds of legislation concerning discrimination in employment to 'contract workers', treating the legislation as applying between an employed person and a 'principal' whom he or she 'works for' even though that principal is not directly the employer.[25] In *MHC Consulting Services Ltd v Tansell*,[26] the Court of Appeal was willing to include within this 'contract worker' relationship a computer consultant who worked for the end-user insurance company via a specialist employment agency and also via a company into which the worker had incorporated himself.

However, that willingness to move directly along a chain of intermediaries does not itself satisfy the demand for imaginative legal recognition of complex multipolar personal work situations in the network economy which we have identified in earlier paragraphs, and for which Marsden has argued very eloquently and effectively in his contribution to the symposium to which we referred earlier.[27] Perhaps unsurprisingly, there seems to be more inventiveness in the realm of the law of restrictive covenants; thus the unusual and fascinating case of *Dawnay Day & Co Ltd v De Braconnier D'Alphen*[28] construed a covenant against competition in the context of a highly complex employment structure of a team of inter-dealer bond brokers who moved *en bloc* from employment in one finance house into a joint venture, as a team, with another finance house; there was no insistence on artificially simplifying the whole set of arrangements into purely bilateral contracts of employment.

---

[23] [2003] ICR 1166.
[24] [2004] ICR 1437. Compare now *Muscat v Cable & Wireless* [2005] EWCA Civ 220.
[25] For example s 12 of the Disability Discrimination Act 1995.
[26] [2000] ICR 789.
[27] Above n 17.
[28] [1997] IRLR 285 (CA).

Thinking about or hoping for a similarly constructive future response of employment law more generally, and in the personal scope of employment law in particular, to the increasing multipolarity of personal work relations, we proceed in the next and final section to make a general point about the place of the foregoing discussion in the overall theme and concerns of the present book.

4. CONCLUSION: THE IDEA OF 'THE EMPLOYER' AND THE RE-DRAWING OF THE BOUNDARIES OF EMPLOYMENT LAW

If the readers of this chapter have found the re-examination of the idea of 'the employer' interesting, and our arguments about the need to recognise the increasingly multipolar nature of employing organisations persuasive, they might nevertheless be left with two concerns which we shall attempt in this brief concluding section to address. The first such concern may be that re-considering the idea of 'the employer', interesting though it may be, does not have very much to do with the redrawing of the boundaries of employment law, that being very largely dependent on the way we think about the classification of workers and their work relationship rather than upon the way we think about the employer.

The second concern might be that, even if the topic of the conceptualisation of 'the employer' is relevant to the redrawing of the boundaries of employment law, nevertheless our way of considering it has been so largely concentrated upon superior or managerial working people and personal entrepreneurs as to have very little relevance to the ordinary working people who are traditionally and normally regarded as the main subjects of employment law. We shall try to meet those possible concerns by considering how the foregoing reflections about the idea of 'the employer' might have some relevance to a question which has rightly been identified as very important to this symposium as a whole, namely how to draw the boundaries of employment law at the interface with the informal economy.

The extent and nature of this problem for British employment law were starkly revealed by the appalling events in Morecombe Bay in 2003, in which a large group of illegal immigrants working as cockle-pickers were drowned in the notoriously dangerous waters to which they had been taken to work. This produced an outcry about the exploitative employment of workers in these lower depths of a burgeoning informal economy. The regulatory response consisted in the enactment of the Gangmasters (Licensing) Act 2004, which identified as such a certain category of employers of workers harvesting agricultural and maritime crops, required such employers to be licensed, and made it a criminal offence to operate as such without a licence, or to trade with an operator of this kind if that operator is unlicensed.

It is far too early to be able to offer any assessment of the adequacy or effectiveness of this regulatory response, and we would not presume to do so. But there is one aspect of that regulatory response which we might subject to a conceptual and possibly practical critique from the arguments which have been developed in this chapter. Those arguments have been directed towards enlarging the boundaries of employment law (in particular offering further challenges to the binary distinction between employees and independent contractors) by opening up an expansive view of 'the employer' as a potentially or actually highly complex organisation, usually internally multipolar, and often constituted of a multiplicity of agencies. That conception has been contrasted with an artificially narrow conception of 'the employer' which over-equates it with a single (male) human being, the 'master' of master and servant law.

Assessed in the light of those arguments, this new regulatory regime for gangmasters has some negative and some positive features. On the negative side, it could be said that the legislation has been rather too narrowly focussed upon a particular type of 'rogue' employer, when in reality such employers represent the tip of an iceberg of which the larger, less visible part is an elaborately organised and multi-faceted informal labour market, connecting and overlapping with the growing casual, marginal and precariously employed workforce.

As it is, this legislative design of singling out agricultural gangmasters for special regulation presents both technical and political problems. At the technical level, it proves difficult to pin down exactly which kinds of primary or intermediary labour supply contractors count as 'gangmasters' and which do not. Those difficulties are compounded by problems of intersection with the statutory regime for 'employment agencies' and 'employment businesses'. At the political level, there is pressure on the government narrowly to confine the scope of this special regulatory regime, and those wishing to do so can represent the characterisation of 'gangmaster' as a stigmatising one. So at the time of writing the Department for Environment, Food and Rural Affairs is engaged on a consultation on draft Gangmasters (Exclusion) Regulations which would narrow the category in various ways, and the consultation document[29] shows clearly what a complex discussion this involves.

On the other hand, to look as its positive features, this legislation does make some important advances in the technique of regulation of the informal and precarious sectors of the labour market, if only with regard to a narrow part of those sectors. In particular, the creation, by section 13 of the Act, of the offence of entering into arrangements with unlicensed gangmasters

---

[29] See: http://www.defra.gov.uk/corporate/consult/gangmaster-exclreg/consultlist.htm.

for the supply of 'workers or services' by the gangmaster does represent a significant step towards the recognition of responsibility for observance of labour standards on the part of enterprises which are further up the chain of use or exploitation of the services of the workers in question than is the 'gangmaster' upon whom the regulation is primarily focussed. In a small way, and not of course in any contractual sense, this helps to articulate an extended employment relationship between the informally and precariously employed agricultural harvesters and the farmers who contract with the gangmasters, and the processing and marketing enterprises further along the supply chain.

As we said, this is not the place in which to evaluate this whole initiative in depth. But even this brief analysis of it serves, we hope, to support our concluding arguments. For it shows how discussion of the nature of the employing organisation and the distribution of responsibility within it does concern the situation of the disadvantaged worker as much as that of the highly advantaged worker. Moreover it demonstrates the integral importance of that analysis of the employing enterprise or organisation to the whole debate about the personal scope of employment laws. Indeed, we hope to have substantiated our claim that a deepening and reinforcement of the understanding of the employing organisation may do more to optimise the personal scope of employment laws than could in future be achieved by further discussion about where to place the binary divide between 'employees' and other workers, important though that debate has been in its time and place. Here, we suggest, is where the future may lie for the personal scope debate.

14

The Legal Boundaries of the Employer, Precarious Workers, and Labour Protection

JUDY FUDGE*

THE TECTONIC SHIFT in employment relations over the past 20 years has shaken the foundations of the legal architecture of the employment relationship, which in common law countries is conceptualised as a personal and bilateral contract.[1] The employment relationship is among one of 'a handful of key institutions'—'the vertically integrated enterprise, the industrial union, the male breadwinner family and the state as employer and provider of services'—which served as 'the basis on which social policy was reconciled, in an historical compromise, by the mid point of the twentieth century'.[2] Vertical disintegration, the emergence of the flexible firm, and corporate networks undermine one of the pillars supporting the standard employment relationship—the large vertically integrated firm. In Canada, it became the emblematic employer for the purpose of labour law, serving as the anchor for the standard employment relationship.

The fragmentation of the enterprise and the decline of hierarchally organised internal labour markets have led to more complex employment relationships that do not fit with the conception of employment as a bilateral and personal contract. There are a wide range of situations involving, for example, employment agencies, franchising, subcontracting, and labour-only contracting, in which the different functions involved in employing labour have been distributed among a number of different entities. Interconnected corporate

* Osgoode Hall Law School, York University, Toronto, Canada. My thanks go to Valerie Baker and Katherine Zavitz for their research assistance, my colleagues Neil Brooks and Harry Glasbeek for many conversations about statutory interpretation and employers' liability for employment obligations, and the workshop organisers, Guy Davidov and Brian Langille, for the opportunity to present the paper at a workshop called 'Redrawing the Boundaries of Labour Protection' held at the Rockefeller Centre in Bellagio, Italy, 23–27 May 2005.

[1] M. Freedland, *The Personal Employment Contract* (Oxford, Oxford University Press, 2003), 36.
[2] S. Deakin, *Renewing Labour Market Institutions* (Geneva, International Labour Office, 2004), 1–2.

groups rival the vertically integrated firm as a method of organising services and production, and integrated chains of production and distribution have long been the preferred method of organising enterprises in certain sectors.

The changes to how enterprises are organised have resulted in a transformation in, and polarisation of, employment relations. At the high end of the spectrum are the knowledge workers, who are associated with the rise of the 'new economy' and networked organisations.[3] These workers function as entrepreneurs in the boundaryless enterprise, building their own networks which, when linked with their property in knowledge, can invert the relations of power and subordination that have traditionally structured employment. Employed primarily in managerial, professional and technological occupations, these informational workers belie 'the myth of service-sector employment characterised by low skills, low wages, and low stability'.[4] Although they fall outside the standard employment relationship, these workers are not typically considered to be in need of labour protection.[5]

At the other end of the spectrum, are 'precarious' or vulnerable workers, who are associated with the informal economy and subcontracted labour.[6] These workers are poorly paid and employed in atypical and unstable jobs, which more often than not fall outside the scope of collective representation or legal regulation. Initially identified with household labour in small, family enterprises in the developing countries, the informal sector has grown across the world as firms pursue flexible forms of labour, such as casual labour, contract labour, outsourcing, home working, and other forms of subcontracting that offer the prospect of minimising fixed non-wage costs. Guy Standing refers to this process as the 'informalisation' of employment, claiming that 'although the dichotomy of "formal" and "informal" *sectors* has always been misleading, a growing proportion of jobs possess what may be called informal characteristics, i.e., without regular wages, benefits, employment protection, and so on'.[7] In both developed and developing countries this work is performed primarily by women, and in certain countries visible minority workers are over-represented amongst the ranks of

---

[3] L. Dickens, 'Problems of Fit: Changing Employment and Labour Regulation' (2004) 42 *British Journal of Industrial Relations* 595; A. Hyde, *Working in Silicon Valley: Economic and Legal Analysis of a High-Velocity Labor Market.* (Armonk, NY, M.E. Sharpe, 2003); K.V.W. Stone, *From Widgets to Digits: Employment Regulation for the Changing Workplace* (Cambridge, Cambridge University Press, 2004).

[4] Y. Aoyama and M. Castells, 'An Empirical Assessment of the Informational Society: Employment and Occupational Structures of G-7 Countries, 1920–2000' (2002) 141 *International Labour Review* 123, at 146.

[5] However, in a labour market in which knowledge workers are oversupplied, they too are easily transformed into contingent workers who may well be in need of labour protections: see J. Purcell, K. Purcell and S. Tailby, 'Temporary Work Agencies: Here Today, Gone Tomorrow?' (2004) 42 *British Journal of Industrial Relations* 705.

[6] J. Fudge and R. Owens, 'Precarious Work, Women, and the New Economy: The Challenge to Legal Norms' in J. Fudge and R. Owens (eds.), *Precarious Work, Women and the New Economy: The Challenge to Legal Norms* (Oxford, Hart, 2006).

[7] G. Standing, 'Global Feminisation through Flexible Labor: A Theme Revisited' (1999) 27 *World Development* 583, at 585.

precarious workers.[8] It is precisely these workers who are considered to be in need of labour protection.[9]

How enterprises are structured determines which entity bears the responsibility for employing labour and the attendant employment-related obligations and, thus, is of critical importance to determining the scope of labour protection. There is a close relationship between precarious work, labour protection, and vertical disintegration, especially the expansion of various forms of subcontracted labour and labour market intermediaries.[10] The blurring of organisational boundaries affects not only which entity bears the responsibility for legal obligations owed to employees in different legal contexts, but also equity in employment conditions.[11] However, identifying the employer in situations in which responsibility for employment has either been divided amongst a number of entities or outsourced to dependent businesses is a problem given the prevailing conception of the employment relationship as a bilateral and personal contract.

Canadian courts have been developing techniques for addressing the problem of attributing employment-related responsibility amongst multiple employing entities.[12] There are also provisions in employment and labour-related legislation that deal with aspects of the problem of identifying the employer in specific contexts, such as a sale of a business or undertaking. However, so far, the approach developed by courts (and legislatures) to the problem of attributing responsibility for the obligations of employment in situations involving multiple-employing entities is *ad hoc* and haphazard. It is not clear what approach courts are taking to this issue from one legal context to another or the extent to which contractual norms will be used to interpret remedial legislation.[13] Sometimes courts use a functional approach to impose responsibility on a group of entities for employment-related obligations.[14]

---

[8] K. Sankaran, 'The ILO, Women and Work: Evolving Labor Standards to Advance Women's Status in the Informal Economy' (2002) 3 *The Georgetown Journal of Gender and the Law* 851; Standing, above n 7; Fudge and Owens, above n 6.

[9] *Meeting of Experts on Workers in Situations Needing Protection (The Employment Relationship: Scope)—Basic Technical Document* (Geneva, International Labour Office, 2000), available at: http://www.ilo.org/public/english/dialogue/ifpdial/publ/mewnp/.

[10] C. Becker, 'Labor Law Outside the Employment Relation' (1996) 74 *Texas Law Review* 1527; G. Davidov, 'Joint Employer Status in Triangular Employment Relationships' (2004) 42 *British Journal of Industrial Relations* 727; Freedland, above n 3; *Report V: The Scope of the Employment Relationship* (International Labour Conference, 91st Session, Geneva, International Labour Office, 2003); F. Raday, 'The Insider–Outsider Politics of Labour-Only Contracting' (1999) 20 *Comparative Labour Law & Policy Journal* 413.

[11] H. Collins, in this volume; J. Earnshaw, J. Rubery, and F. Lee Cooke, *Who is the Employer?* (London, Institute of Employment Rights, 2002), 2.

[12] Freedland (above n 1, at 39) uses the term 'employing entities' in order to disrupt the simple personalisation of the employer with a human being.

[13] See, eg, *Lian J. Crew Group Inc.* (2001), 54 OR (3d) 239 (Cumming J), which is discussed in Part 2 of this chapter.

[14] *Husky Oil Operations Ltd. v M.N.R.* [1995] 3 SCR. 453, especially Iacobucci J's dissent at paras 130, 194, which is discussed in Part 2.

At other times courts invoke a contractual analysis to limit attributions of responsibility for employees to the employing entity with which the worker has a contract.[15]

This chapter focuses on how and where the legal boundaries of the employer are drawn for the purposes of ascribing responsibility for employment-related obligations owed to precarious workers, and does so from two perspectives. The first is conceptual and general and the second is empirical and specific, and it is designed to illustrate the failure of adjudicators, especially courts, to grapple with the conceptual problems of attributing responsibility for employment-related obligations in integrated enterprises. Drawing on the work of scholars in England,[16] the first part examines the conceptual framework for attributing responsibility for employment-related obligations, focusing on the conception of the employment relationship as a personal and bilateral contract and the equation of the employer with the corporate form. It explores how economic and legal models of the firm reinforce a conception of the employer that bears little resemblance to how employing functions are organised, and emphasises the practical consequences of this conceptual framework by showing how firms are able to externalise the responsibility for, and risks of, employing workers' services in their enterprises. The second part illustrates why the boundaries of the employer are so difficult to draw in practice, using Canada to illustrate the complexity of the legal terrain. It then focuses on how the legal boundaries of the employer are drawn in situations involving subcontracting.[17] How responsibility for employment-related obligations is attributed in subcontracting situations is crucial for determining the scope of labour protection. Reflecting upon the Canadian example, the chapter assesses the capacity of the courts to adopt a functional approach to identifying the employer for employment-related obligations, and offers some suggestions about how the boundaries might be redrawn.

1. CONCEPTUALISING THE EMPLOYER

A. Employment: A Personal and Bilateral Contract

According to Mark Freedland, it is employment's master and servant roots that shape its characterisation as a personal and bilateral contract.

---

[15] *Société Place des Arts des Montréal v. I.A.T.S.E. Local 56* [2004] 1 SCR. 43, which is discussed in Part 2.

[16] H. Collins, 'Ascription of Legal Responsibility to Groups in Common Patterns of Economic Integration' (1990) 53 *Modern Law Review* 731; S. Deakin, 'The Changing Concept of "Employer" in Labour Law' (2001) 30 *Industrial Law Journal* 72; Freedland, above n 1.

[17] The discussion is confined to Ontario and Quebec to illustrate the problems and solutions.

While this characterisation fits with situations in which a human employer personally directs an employee, it bears little resemblance to situations in which the employee is employed in a large bureaucratic network, subject to many sources of direction and authority, and in which the employee's contract is with a corporation and not a human being. Yet, despite the change in employment relations and enterprises, the conceptual framework for the relationship has remained intact. Freedland explains its durability; the continued rationalisation of contractual employment in bilateral and personal terms from the nineteenth century onwards has crucially depended upon regarding the legal corporate person, the incorporated company, as the direct equivalent of the individual human employer or master.[18]

Although equating the corporate employer with the human master resolves the conceptual problem, 'it imposes a wholly oversimplified vision of the institutional organization of the employment relationship'.[19] Moreover, it attributes at a deep level the 'human personality of the master' to the 'legal company in constructing the contractual conception of the corporate employer'.[20] The complex multilateral relationship between people within a work organisation is equated with a simple bilateral relationship between an employee and an employer. This legal equation, or fiction, receives support from R. H. Coase's economic model of the firm, which is often invoked to explain the employment relationship. This reliance on Coase's theory of the firm to explain the employment relationship is not surprising, given that he invoked 'the legal relationship normally called that of "master and servant" and "employer and employee"' to verify that his concept of the firm fit in 'with that existing in the real world'.[21]

---

[18] Freedland, above n 1, at 37.

[19] *Ibid.*, at 37. Freedland uses *Nokes v Doncaster Amalgamated Colleries* [1940] AC 1014 (HL) to illustrate this point. The House of Lords concluded that the contract of service was too personal to be assignable from one company to another which was operating the same mine in the same manner without the knowledge and agreement of the employee concerned. This case is often cited as one that protects employees, because the conceptualisation of the contract of employment as personal meant that the coal miner who absented himself from work escaped criminal liability under the Employers and Workman Act 1875 for breaching his contract of service. It continues (mistakenly) to be invoked by Canadian courts under the guise that it is helpful to employees, when, in fact, its impact is the opposite. For example, in *Stone v H.J. Hotels Ltd. Partnership Ltd.* (2001), 12 CCEL (2d) 229, the New Brunswick Court of Appeal rejected the argument that the provision in the employment standards legislation that transfers the employment relationship between seller and purchaser when a business is sold gave the employee who was dismissed a cause of action against the purchaser employer on the ground that the purchaser had not employed the employee. The Court stated at 224: 'Simply put, the law is not willing to perpetuate the belief that employers are entitled to create a marketplace in which workers may be bought and sold as was done in this Province in the first half of the nineteenth century. . . . Accordingly, the law does not permit an employee to be transferred from one employer to another, unless the existing contract of employment is terminated and replaced with a new contract between the employee and the new employer.'

[20] Freedland, above n 1, at 37.

[21] R.H. Coase, *The Firm, the Market and the Law* (Chicago, ILL, University of Chicago Press, 1988), 53; Coase (at 54) quotes F. R. Batt, *The Law of Master and Servant* (London, Sir Isaac Pitman & Sons, 1927), 6, for the proposition that it is '[t]his right of control or interference,

The legal conception of employment relationship reinforces the economic model of the firm and vice versa; as Mark Freedland so nicely puts it, 'not only does the bilateral and individual contract model keep Coase's black box firmly shut, but it also writes a fictitious description on its lid'.[22] Freedland looks inside the box and identifies four functions that make up the idea of employing workers or being an employer: (1) engaging workers and terminating employment; (2) remunerating and providing them with other benefits; (3) managing the employment relationship and the process of work; and (4) using workers' services in the process of production or service provision.[23] He also complicates Coase's simple notion of the firm by explaining how the different functions related to employing labour 'may be exercised together by or within a single employing entity, or they may be exercised separately by different employing entities'.[24]

Coase's theory of transaction costs provided an account of why relations of production would be organised either through a firm or by a market, and offered a rationale for the growth of the vertically integrated firm and the expansion of the standard employment relationship. In order to minimise the costs of discovering prices and negotiating contracts, the entrepreneur enters into contracts that provide the authority to direct, and it is this authority that constitutes the firm. Vertical integration substitutes hierarchy for the price mechanism and authority for market incentives. Although never universal, after the second World War the vertically integrated firm rose to dominance over other forms enterprise and 'influenced the larger culture of everyday life itself'.[25] To a large extent labour law was based upon this model. The large vertically integrated firm with an internal labour market provided support for the standard employment relationship, and the employment contract became the platform for legislation, and the key governance mechanism, linking the enterprise to the welfare state.[26]

The legal fiction of the personal and bilateral nature of the relationship was sustained by the rise of the legal corporate person and vertically integrated firm. When production was organised within large vertically integrated corporations and most employees had a standard employment

---

of being entitled to tell the servant when to work (within the hours of service) and when not to work, and what to do and how to do it (within the terms of such service) which is the dominant characteristic in the relation and marks off the servant from an independent contractor.'

[22] Freedland, above n 1, at 46.

[23] *Ibid.*, at 40.

[24] *Ibid.*, at 40.

[25] W.W. Powell, 'The Capitalist Firm in the Twenty-First Century: Emerging Patterns in Western Enterprise' in P. DiMaggio (ed.), *The Twenty-First-Century Firm: Changing Economic Organization in International Perspective* (Princeton, NJ, Princeton University Press, 2001), 33, at 39.

[26] S. Deakin, 'The Many Futures of the Contract of Employment' in J. Conaghan, R.M. Fischl and K. Klare (ed.), *Labour Law in an Era of Globalization* (Oxford, Oxford University Press, 2002) 177, at 178.

relationship, equating the employer with the corporation for the purposes of employment-related obligations made sense. There was a fit between the firm for reasons of corporate governance and the firm for reasons of labour law in situations in which 'the productive relations are controlled and directed within one capital unit'.[27]

The growth of complex economic organisations that function as quasi-firms suggests that there are other efficient ways of reducing transaction costs.[28] The boundaries of the firm have proven to be quite porous, 'making it difficult to know where the firm ends and where the market or firms begins'.[29] There has been a growing reliance on relational contracting and cooperation between firms at the expense of organising activities within the firm. These emerging organisational forms have combined with older, pre-Fordist, organisational forms—especially subcontracting and employment agencies—to blur the traditional boundary of the firm.[30] Collins argues, that 'contrary to many theories of the firm, . . . efficiency considerations permit employers considerable discretion in determining the forms of contractual relations through which labour is acquired'.[31] There is no necessary fit between how an enterprise is organised and its corporate structure. This disjuncture is not surprising, given that the corporate form concentrates on suppliers of capital (shareholders' interests); it has to do with financial claims on assets and income streams, and is not directly interested in the relations of production and the integration of labour.[32]

B. Externalising Employment Responsibility

The bilateral approach to the employment relationship has a difficult time dealing with situations in which several entities share the functions involved in employing labour. The legal starting point does not begin by holding each of the entities jointly and severally responsible for the employees; instead, it searches for a contract with an employer as the basis for ascribing employment-related obligations. Only the employer with whom the employee has a contract is liable for employment-related obligations and risks. The legal conception of the employment relationship as a personal and bilateral contract allows (and, perhaps, invites) firms to shift the risks associated with

---

[27] Collins, above n 16, at 732.

[28] *Ibid.*, at 734.

[29] Powell, above n 25, at 58.

[30] A. Supiot, *Beyond Employment: Changes in Work and the Future of Labour Law in Europe* (Oxford, Oxford University Press, 2001), 18.

[31] H. Collins, 'Independent Contractors and the Challenge of Vertical Disintegration to Employment Protection Laws' (1990) 10 *Oxford Journal of Legal Studies* 353.

[32] S. Deakin, '"Enterprise Risk": The Juridical Nature of the Firm Revisited' (2003) 32 *Industrial Law Journal* 97.

employing labour. Instead of retaining the services of workers directly, firms can resort to various forms of intermediaries in order to have work performed.

Collins calls this the capital boundary problem; 'where the work is organised through numerous separate legal entities rather than a single firm, the limits of legal responsibility set by reference to the boundaries of capital units establish the conditions for potential injustice'.[33] This is because the owners and directors of enterprises are free to organise the activities of the enterprises as they see fit, either through vertical integration within one corporate entity or via external contracting. An enterprise can be organised in order to avoid statutory employment-related obligations like pay equity, health and safety, and severance pay, or minimise its exposure to judgement. Vallée describes practices such as subcontracting and the use of employment agencies as the externalisation of the responsibility linked to the status of employer. The problem with these practices is that:

> It becomes difficult to identify the real beneficiaries of the wealth produced by someone's labour, and to determine who should be responsible for the risks related to this labour. For example, in a production network where the dangerous work is subcontracted or entrusted to employees from a placement agency, the enterprise that gives out the work is the beneficiary of this labour but it is not this enterprise that assumes the risks. The real beneficiary of the wealth produced by the workers does not, in the final analysis, assume the costs related to the protection of these workers.[34]

The traditional bilateral model of employment and the tendency to equate the employer with the corporation allows firms to shift the responsibility for, and the risks of, employing labour to other smaller, less stable firms. Ultimately, these risks are borne by some of the most vulnerable groups of workers.[35] Subcontractors are much more susceptible to failure than larger firms are, and the division of the workforce into core and peripheral components tends to entrench segmented labour markets and undermine equity in employment.[36]

This problem has not escaped the attention of the International Labour Organisation, where it appeared before the International Labour Conference in 1997 and 1998 in the form of discussions on 'contract

---

[33] Collins, above n 16, at 736.

[34] G. Vallée, 'What is Corporate Social Responsibility?: The Case of Canada' (2005) 47 *Managerial Law* 20, at 30.

[35] P. Davies and M. Freedland, in this volume; D. Grimshaw, M. Marchington, J. Rubery and H. Willmott, 'Introduction: Fragmenting Work Across Organizational Boundaries' in M. Marchington, D. Grimshaw, J. Rubery and H. Willmott (eds), *Fragmenting Work: Blurring Organizational Boundaries and Disordering Hierarchies* (Oxford, Oxford University Press, 2005), 1.

[36] Collins, above n 11; Earnshaw, Rubery and Cooke, above n 11; Supiot, above n 30, at 191.

labour'.[37] In the draft convention, the term 'contract labour' applied to work performed for a user enterprise by workers who did not have an employment relationship with the enterprise, and included workers provided to the user enterprise by subcontractors or intermediaries as well as workers who performed the work on the basis of a direct contractual relationship.[38] Significantly, it provided that contract workers should be guaranteed equal treatment with employees of the user enterprise and, where the contract labour is used mainly for the purpose of denying labour law or social security rights, that the contract workers should be treated as employees of the user enterprise. Another provision was joint (or secondary) responsibility on the part of the user for certain obligations owed to workers by the subcontractor.

The Contract Labour Convention proved to be very controversial; the meaning of the term 'contract labour' was especially contentious. The Worker Vice-Chairperson pointed out that it 'can mean different things', including subcontracting, outsourcing, privatisation (contracting out of public services), labour-only contracting, contracting in which involves the use of temporary work agencies, staff leasing agencies, dispatching agencies and other enterprises supplying contingent workers, and certain kinds of homework, and atypical work such as temporary work and self-employment.[39]

The Conference failed to adopt an instrument for contract labour, as Employer Members noted their 'implacable opposition to the adoption of any instrument on contract labour whatsoever'.[40] As a compromise, 'workers in situations in need of protection' became the focus of attention, and a meeting of experts was convened and research commissioned. In 2003, the International Labour Conference held a general discussion on the scope of employment and, in 2005, the ILO issued a report on the employment relationship, in preparation for the adoption of a recommendation at the 2006 Conference. During this process, attention shifted at the ILO from contract labour in general to triangular employment arrangements in particular.[41]

---

[37] For a discussion of the recent history of the ILO's attempt to regulate subcontracted labour see E. Marín, in this volume.

[38] *Report of the Committee on Contract Labour* (Provisional Record, International Labour Conference, 86th Session, Geneva, International Labour Office, 1998); Raday, above n 10; L.F. Vosko, 'Legitimizing the Triangular Employment Relationship: Emerging International Labour Standards from a Comparative Perspective' (1997) 19 *Comparative Labour Law & Policy Journal* 43.

[39] *Report of the Committee on Contract Labour*, above n 38, at para 14.

[40] *Ibid.*, para 13.

[41] Triangular relationships occur when the employees of a provider work for a user: *Report V(I): The Employment Relationship* (The International Labour Conference, 90th Session, Geneva, International Labour Office, 2005), 13, available at: http://www.ilo.org/public/english/standards/relm/ilc/ilc90/pdf/repvi.pdf.

2. MULTIPLE EMPLOYING ENTITIES AND ATTRIBUTING EMPLOYMENT-RELATED RESPONSIBILITY

A. A Complex Legal Landscape

Identifying the employer for the purposes of employment and labour-related responsibilities in situations outside a simple and straightforward bilateral employment contract can be very complex. There are two main sources of this complexity: the freedom of entrepreneurs to structure their business enterprises as they see fit and the plurality of different legal contexts and legal norms that make up the broad field of employment and labour law.

The entrepreneur is free to determine the organisational structure of the business enterprise, giving her or him considerable freedom in law and practice to determine a firm's boundaries. An enterprise can be organised as a large vertically integrated firm, through a series of contracts with independent firms, or through a number of subsidiary corporations that correspond to different aspects of production. How a firm is structured can also determine how the labour force will be integrated into the organisation—whether directly as employees, as independent consultants, through employment agencies, or labour subcontractors.

Even though the entrepreneur has the initial freedom to organise the business enterprise, the parties' agreement does not simply dispose of the issue of identifying the employer. A legal determination of employer status can arise in a number of legal contexts for a range of different purposes, and this legal pluralism adds complexity to attributing responsibility for employment-related obligations in situations in which there are multiple employing entities.

Labour regulation occurs at different levels and is multi-dimensional, serving a variety of instrumental goals and responding to different normative concerns.[42] Moreover, in Canada, a variety of institutions administer

---

[42] M. Freedland, 'The Role of the Contract of Employment in Modern Labour Law' in L. Betten (ed.), *The Employment Contract in Transforming Labour Relations* (The Hague, Kluwer, 1995), 17, at 24, identifies two levels at which norm making or contracting takes places within work relationships. The executory level is concerned with the basic exchange of services for remuneration, while the relational level is more focused on security of expectations. For workers these are expectations about income and employment security and occupational health and safety, while for employers they centre on how to insure that workers' activities will help achieve employers' goals. With a view to creating categories that reflect current socio-legal practice and that have common characteristics in respect of their extension to categories of workers, some researchers and scholars have attempted to identify these dimensions of labour regulation. There are, at least, three dimensions of labour regulation: social justice, economic exchange and governance, and social wages or revenue. See H. Collins, 'Regulating the Employment Relation for Competitiveness' (2001) 30 *Industrial Law Journal* 17; G. Davidov, 'The Three Axes of Employment Relationships: A Characterization of

the different dimensions of labour regulation, and several are involved in adjudicating whether or not an entity should be legally responsible for employment-related obligations. Given the diversity of goals in the different dimensions of legal regulation and the different institutions involved in making decisions, it is not surprising that the attribution of responsibility for employment-related obligations depends upon the legal context in which the case is situated. In Canada, who the employer of an employment or temporary help agency worker is depends upon the context in which the question is put, the jurisdiction in which the question is posed, the legal test invoked, and the factual circumstances involved. This creates a high degree of uncertainty regarding the legal liability of client firms for workers provided through temporary help agencies. According to Lamer CJ in his 1997 majority decision of the Supreme Court of Canada in *Pointe Claire v Quebec*, this is because 'the tripartite relationship does not fit very easily into the classic pattern of bilateral relationships. . . . The traditional characteristics of an employer are shared by two separate entities—the personnel agency and its client—that both have a certain relationship with the temporary employee'.[43]

Labour law has developed a range of techniques to ensure that firms do not structure their enterprises to avoid the costs, or shift the risks, of employing labour. There are a number of statutory devices designed to expand both the traditional conception of an employer as a unitary entity and the employment relationship as bilateral contract. Typically, they do so by lifting corporate veils and ignoring privity for specific purposes in specific contexts. The next section explores how these different devices have been used in the context of subcontracting in Ontario and Quebec.

B. Subcontracting

The practice of subcontracting, in all of its varieties, is not only crucial to determining the effective scope of labour protection; it provides a good example of how discrete and varied the legal treatment of employment-related responsibilities is. Both the Civil Code in Quebec and the common law in the rest of Canada start from the position that, barring de facto management of the subcontractor by the principal, the legal and financial

---

Workers in Need of Protection' (2002) 52 *University of Toronto Law Journal* 357; P. Davies and M. Freedland, 'Employees, Workers, and the Autonomy of Labour Law' in D. Simon and M. Weiss (eds.), *Zur Autonomie des Individuums* (Baden-Baden, Nomos Verlagsgellschaft, 2001); S. Engblom, 'Equal Treatment of Employees and Self-Employed Workers' (2001) 17 *International Journal of Comparative Labour Law and Industrial Relations* 211; J. Fudge, E. Tucker and L. Vosko, *The Legal Concept of Employment: Marginalized Workers* (Ottawa, Law Commission of Canada, 2002).

[43] *Pointe Claire (City) v Quebec (Labour Court)* [1997] 1 SCR 1015, 1055.

independence of the subcontractor prevents the establishment of a direct legal link between the principal and the subcontractor's employees—which is the basis for imposing employment-related responsibilities. Nor is recourse to subcontracting prohibited by Canadian or Quebec labour law, although some aspects of subcontracting are regulated.

In particular, Quebec is much more willing than its common law counterparts to impose joint and several liability in subcontracting situations when it comes to matters relating to economic governance. The minimum standards legislation provides that '[a]n employer who enters into a contract with a subcontractor, directly or through an intermediary, is responsible jointly and severally with that subcontractor and that intermediary for the pecuniary obligations fixed by this act or the regulations'.[44]

By contrast, in Ontario, minimum standards legislation does not directly impose joint and several liability on users and subcontractors. Instead, it imposes joint and several liability on separate legal entities only if they are related or associated and the intent or effect of the arrangement is to defeat the intent and purpose of the legislation.[45] This has been described as a 'deep-pocket' provision designed in the case of insolvencies to hold companies, individuals, firms, syndicates, or associations carrying on related activities, businesses, works, trades, occupations, professions, projects, or undertakings, accountable as one 'employer'.[46] However, even though the wording of the provision is broad enough to capture subcontracting arrangements, it has been given a much narrower interpretation—one that emphasises common control, ownership, and management amongst the employing entities, and not simply functional integration.[47]

Recently, the Ontario Superior Court emphasised the need to establish something more than functional interdependence between businesses in order to establish a common employer amongst related entities and impose joint and several liability. In *Lian J. Crew Group Inc.*,[48] a union representing garment workers sponsored an application by a home worker who was owed wages and vacation pay from a garment subcontractor for the certification of a class action on behalf of home workers. Not only was the procedure for enforcing the Employment Standards Act novel, so too was the claim that the retailers of the garments produced by the home workers were

---

[44] Labour Standards Act, SQ 1979, SQ 1994, s 95.

[45] Employment Standards Act 2000, SO 2000, s 4.

[46] Employment Standards Act 2000, Policy and Interpretation Manual, (Toronto, Thomson Carswell, 2004).

[47] In the context of a labour-only contracting agency that provided two truck drivers to a client manufacturing company over a period of years the referee refused even to consider whether the agency and client firm were common employers on the 'ground that there was simply no evidence of the kind of relationship contemplated by section 12': *Eaton Yale Ltd. (c.o.b. Commander Electrical Equipment)*, [1998] OESAD No. 234 (Randall), affirmed in *Global Driver Services Inc. v Fallon* [1999] OJ No 4786 (Ont Sup Ct J).

[48] (2001), 54 OR (3d) 239.

common employers of the home workers and, thus, jointly and severaly responsible for their wages and vacation pay. The argument was that the retailers did not take sufficient steps to minimise the risks of subcontractors' non-compliance with Employment Standards Act obligations *vis-à-vis* home workers and that their participation in an industry with well known and continuing problems in respect of compliance constituted an arrangement which had the effect of indirectly defeating the purpose of the Employment Standards Act.

It is useful to explore the Court's reasoning in some detail, since it exemplifies the difficulty in extending liability outside a narrow bilateral contractual framework even in the context of remedial legislation. Referring to recent Supreme Court of Canada decisions, Cumming J characterised the Employment Standards Act as 'a check on unbridled market forces' designed to protect 'non-unionised employees and immigrant workers'.[49] He also concluded that it was 'reasonable to foresee that there are ESA compliance problems with some suppliers' subcontractors in the garment industry'.[50] Despite these findings, he dismissed the certification application on the ground that it did not reveal a cause of action. According to him, the earlier cases interpreting the statutory provision did not consider a 'situation involving one business which has no direct contract with another business, operated by a subcontractor'.[51] Distinguishing between a vertically integrated business and a vertically integrated industry, Cumming J interpreted the statutory provision as limited to the former:

> In the absence of intervention by legislation or regulation, businesses have the freedom of action to determine the type and extent of the particular business activity carried on, as seen to be in their own self-interest.... The fact that there is a known chain of supply and pyramid of businesses within the overall garment industry, such that it can be said there is a vertically integrated industry, is in itself of no adverse legal consequence to the retailer. [52]

The absence of any direct contractual or financial relationship between the retailers and the subcontractor was critical to the Court's finding that the businesses were not related and, thus, not jointly and severally liable for the employment standards obligations owed to the home workers. Cumming J was also concerned with the implications of finding vertically integrated industries to be common employers. He pointed out that if a subcontractor completed work for several retailers and the retailers were considered to be common employers of the subcontractor, each retailer would be jointly and severally liable for all of the wages not paid by the subcontractor no matter

---

[49] *Ibid.*, para 36.
[50] *Ibid.*, para 52.
[51] *Ibid.*, para 47.
[52] *Ibid.*, paras 69–71.

which retailer's garments the particular workers had produced.[53] However, the implication of the interpretation the Court provided is that home workers, not retailers, continue to bear the clearly foreseeable risk of subcontractor failure. The problem of a retailer's liability for the unpaid wages of workers regardless of the garments produced could be resolved amongst retailers through indemnification provisions. Joint and several liability would provide retailers with an incentive to ensure that subcontractors complied with employment standards legislation.[54] In fact, there is a long history of using joint and several liability between manufacturers and contractors in the garment industry to ameliorate widespread, and often exploitative, subcontracting arrangements.[55] This is why Quebec imposes joint and several liability between principals and subcontractors for labour standards such as minimum wages and overtime. Moreover, the ILO Convention on Homework specifically provides that principals be held responsible for wages and other payments owed by contractors to home workers.[56]

Until very recently, another big difference between Quebec and Ontario had to do with how successor employer provisions in collective bargaining legislation, which transfer collective agreements and union representation rights when undertakings and businesses are sold, treat subcontracting arrangements. These provisions are designed to address the lack of fit between the corporation and the enterprise, and to protect collective bargaining rights, and they are administered by specialised labour boards or labour courts.

In Quebec, the successor employer provisions were interpreted broadly so that subcontractors were bound both by the collective agreement and by the union certificate, which requires that the employer recognise and bargain with it exclusively. The Quebec labour court adopted a functional interpretation which emphasised a set of tasks or functions as the basis for transferring bargaining rights. Even more significantly, the Quebec labour court did not require that there be a direct contractual relationship between the predecessor and successor employers for the successor employer provision to apply. This meant that cases of building-services contracting—a form of labour-only subcontracting in which cleaning, security, janitorial, and/or

---

[53] *Ibid.*, para 67.

[54] D. Weil, 'Public Enforcement/Private Monitoring: Evaluating a New Approach to Regulating the Minimum Wage' (2005) 58 *Industrial & Labour Relations Review* 238.

[55] B. Goldstein, M. Linder, L.E. Norton and C.K. Ruckelshaus, 'Enforcing Fair Labour Standards in the Modern American Sweatshop: Rediscovering the Statutory Definition of Employment' (1998–99) 46 *UCLA Law Review* 983; ILGWU and INTERCEDE, *Meeting the Needs of Vulnerable Workers: Proposals for Improved Employment Legislation and Access to Collective Bargaining for Domestic Workers and Industrial Homeworkers* (Toronto, ILGWU & INTERCEDE, 1993).

[56] Sankaran, above n 8.

cafeteria services are provided to buildings—were caught by successor rights. Unions were able to hold on to their representation rights and collective agreements as subcontractors changed, even though there was no legal relationship between the subcontractors.[57]

By contrast, in Ontario it was much more difficult to establish successor rights in the context of subcontracting. Not only was the instrumental approach, which emphasised the essence of the undertaking (land, equipment, employee skills, and licences), dominant in determining a sale of a business, it was (and is) necessary to establish a legal relation between the seller of the business and its purchaser in order for the latter to be liable for the employment obligations accrued by the former.[58] What this means is that in the vast majority of cases, service contracting—where all that is provided by the contractor is labour and not capital—falls outside the scope of successor provisions, and the workers lose their unions and their collective agreements when the service contract is retendered.

Since the late 1980s, the treatment of subcontracting under successor rights provisions in labour relations statutes in Quebec and Ontario has increasingly converged, with the Supreme Court leading the way in pushing Quebec towards Ontario. In 1988, the Supreme Court of Canada brought the interpretation of Quebec's successor employer provision in line with the jurisprudence in the rest of Canada by requiring both that there be a direct legal relation between the contractors and that the undertaking be understood in an organic sense.[59] The effect of the first requirement was to respect privity between the employing entities in the interpretation of the successor employer provisions, even though the legislation did not require a direct legal relationship between the employing entities. By requiring a contract between the employing entities as a basis for ascribing employment-related responsibilities, the decision effectively took building-service contracting outside the scope of successor employer provisions.

This brief review of how courts have interpreted remedial provisions in employment standards and collective bargaining legislation in the context of subcontracting arrangements suggests that the courts' tendency is to

---

[57] G.W. Adams, *Canadian Labour Law* (2nd edn, Aurora, Canada Law Book, 2004), paras 8–23, 8-40-8–41.

[58] *Ibid.*, at 8-13; J. Sack, C.M. Mitchell and S. Price, *Ontario Labour Relations Board Law and Practice* (3rd edn, Markham, On, Butterworths, 1997), 6.17–17. For a brief period in Ontario—1992 to 1995—the successor rights provisions specifically covered building service contractors: Adams, above n 57, at 8–23.

[59] *Syndicat national des employes de la Commission scolaire regionale de l'Outaouais (C.S.N.) v Union des employes de service, local 298 (F.T.Q.)* [1988] 2 SCR 1048. The Quebec Labour Code, RSQ c–27 was amended after this case to expand the definition of successor employers (see Adams, above n 54, at 8–40 discussing SQ 1990, c 69, s 2), and subcontracting arrangements were captured by it (see *Ivanhoe Inc. v TUAG, section locale 500*, [2001] 2 SCR 566; *Sept-Iles (Villes de) v Quebec (Labour Court)* [2001] 2 SCR 670). In 2003, the provision was amended to place subcontracting arrangements outside its scope, SQ 2003, c 26, s 2.

invoke traditional conceptions of liability to limit the ascription of employment-related obligations and responsibilities. The requirement of a contractual basis for liability has been imported into remedial provisions that seek
to expand the scope of employment-related obligations beyond the traditional confines. The problem is, as Craig Becker put it, that 'contemporary
law is marked by a disjunction between theories of rights and duties based
on privity of contract between employer and employee and new forms of
work relations that disrupt this model of employment by increasingly inter-
posing intermediate employers between the entities of labor and capital'.[60]
Moreover, as the example of the garment industry indicates, a contractual
basis for liability does not fit well with some old forms of work relations
either.

C. Formalism versus Functionalism

Canadian courts have been unwilling to depart from the traditional basis
for ascribing employment-related obligations—a direct, and preferably contractual, relationship—between the employers and employees, even in the
context of triangular employment relationships and integrated enterprises.
They are also inclined to treat the legal form of the corporation as defining
the employer. Although courts are prepared to ignore the form and look at
the substance of the relationship in order to determine which entity bears
employment-related responsibilities, they are unwilling to impose joint and
several liability in the absence of direct control (typically ownership or
management) between the employing entities. Courts start from the premise that employers are free to structure their enterprises in order to contract
out the responsibilities of employment. They take a formalistic approach to
identifying the employer, and this has a conservative impact on the interpretation of remedial legislation.

It is not at all surprising that courts (and the legal system for that matter)
would respond to the problem of attributing employment-related obligations in subcontracting situations by simply adapting the bilateral contractual approach. The legal system's traditional response to newly emerging
economic relationships is to 'seek to apply established legal principles to
them, and then gradually to adapt these principles'.[61] The ideal of the rule
of law, according to which the ordinary courts are to have the final say as
to the validity of legal decisions, exerts institutional pressure for consistency
and coherence across different areas of law. Courts attempt to establish
consistency in principles and concepts across legal fields, since it is the

---

[60] Becker, above n 10, at 1534.
[61] D. Marsden, 'The "Network Economy" and Models of the Employment Contract' (2004)
42 *British Journal of Industrial Relations* 659.

capacity of the legal system to provide an internally consistent and comprehensive approach to social relations that is the source of its legitimacy.[62] In the realm of economic relations, courts default to traditional conceptions of contract and the corporation for attributing responsibility for risks and obligations.

Is it possible for courts to develop 'an understanding of how particular rights and liabilities are to be allocated when the traditional functions and the assumptions of certain social and economic risks are divided among a number of different entities'?[63] Can courts develop and apply a functional approach that appreciates, on the one hand, the complexity of employing entities, and, on the other, the policy goals of different legal contexts? In Canada, as in the United Kingdom, where fiscal considerations such as social insurance contributions and tax are involved, legislation that trumps contractual allocations of obligations and risks is justified on the ground that third parties are involved.[64] In Saskatchewan, for example, the workers' compensation legislation provides that principals are liable for any contributions that contractors are required to make on behalf of their employees. It also permits the principal to be indemnified by the contractor for such sums. Iacobucci J of the Supreme Court of Canada characterised these provisions in the following way:

> The strength of the fund is thus key to the viability of the workers' compensation system. In turn, the financial integrity of the Workers' Compensation program depends on an effective means of ensuring that sufficient monies are paid into the Injury Fund. . . . This is accomplished by holding principals liable for the unpaid dues of contractors because, from the perspective of the workers, both contractors and principals are 'employers'. Moreover, from the point of view of rudimentary economic analysis, both gain from the surplus value of the workers' labour. . . . [These] provisions . . . further the policy choice to shift losses for unpaid premiums from the Board and workers to principals. Workers' compensation legislation strives to visit the costs of industrial disease, death and injury on the employer community which exposes its workforce to those risks. An attempt is made to spread responsibility for those costs amongst multiple employers engaged in a single project.[65]

---

[62] A. Woodiwiss, *Social Theory after Post-Modernism: Rethinking Production, Law, and Class* (London, Pluto Press, 1990).

[63] Deakin, above n 16.

[64] *Ibid.*

[65] *Husky Oil Operations Ltd. v Minister of National* Revenue [1995] 3. SCC 453, para 130. The interpretation of this provision arose in a situation in which the principal challenged its constitutionality on the ground that the off-setting stepped into exclusive federal jurisdiction over bankruptcy because the effect of the provision was override the bankruptcy priority system by letting the Workers' Compensation Board obtain funds before the secured creditors. The majority of the Court, with Iacobucci J and three others dissenting, declared the provision unconstitutional and inoperative.

In the context of social welfare legislation that imposed joint and several liability on principals and contractors for contributions to fund a public insurance scheme, the Supreme Court of Canada was willing to trace the extraction of surplus value through the production chain as the method of defining the boundaries of employment-related obligations.

By contrast, in a paradigmatic context involving economic governance—the regulation of industrial sanctions—the Supreme Court took a formalist, and not a functional, approach to the question of who is responsible for employment-related obligations. In *Société de la Place des Arts de Montréal (SPA) v IATSE Local 56*,[66] the SPA (an entity created by statute to operate a business for the diffusion of performing arts and to administer a performing arts complex) decided, during a strike by its unionised stage hands, to get out of the business of providing stage technicians to its tenants. When the tenants (five performing arts groups operating out of the performing arts centre operated by the SPA) directly employed stage technicians during the technicians' union's on-going strike against the SPA, the union brought proceedings under the Quebec *Labour Code* against the SPA 'for utilizing, in the establishment where the strike or lock-out has been declared, the services of a person employed by another employer or the services of another contractor to discharge the duties of an employee who is ... on strike or locked out'. In separate legal proceedings, the Labour Tribunal and the Superior Court agreed that the SPA was in violation of the *Code*'s provision restricting the use of replacement workers by letting the tenants hire personnel to offset the inconveniences brought about by the strike. These decisions were upheld by reviewing courts until they reached the Supreme Court of Canada. On behalf of unanimous Court, Gonthier J allowed the appeal:

> In my view, the approach adopted in the courts below effectively conflates the SPA and its Tenants into a single undertaking whose acts are attributable solely to the SPA. This analysis risks losing sight of the fact that the SPA and its Tenants are distinct legal persons. The various activities of the SPA and its Tenants are economically interdependent, yet they remain activities engaged in by several juridically distinct entities. Likewise, the economic risks assumed by these entities, and the benefits gained by them, are attributable to each entity individually according to the tasks each undertakes and the business choices each has made. While a functional, rather than formalistic, approach is undoubtedly desirable in labour law matters, one must not take this approach so far as to ignore the actual legal and economic structure of complex organizations like the Place des Arts.[67]

Gonthier J characterised the SPA's decision to amend its contracts with its tenants to require them to provide their own stagehands as 'engaging the

[66] [2004] 1 SCR 43.
[67] *Ibid.*, para 20.

right of enterprises governed by the [Labour] Code to go out of business, either completely or in part'.[68] Thus, he found that the SPA was not utilising the stagehands. He also went on to add 'that the SPA's new pared-down business model was in line with practice elsewhere in the industry, whereby producers supply their own stage technicians rather than rely on the ones provided by their landlords. This fact is not, on its own, decisive. Yet it gives further weight to the view that the SPA had genuinely shut down and withdrawn from the technical services side of its business'.[69] This reasoning (which was endorsed by a unanimous Supreme Court of Canada) suggests that courts are unlikely to upset contractual allocation of risks and obligations when it comes to matters directly related to economic governance, even when contractual relations have been restructured specifically to avoid labour-related obligations.

Moreover, when confronted with situations in which responsibility for employment-related obligations must be attributed among a number of integrated entities, courts are prepared to go only as far as to adapt the bilateral model, not to develop a new basis for imposing liability. They shy away from imposing joint and several liability on multiple employing entities and justify their caution in developing legal doctrine or interpreting statutes in terms of their institutional role. In *Pointe Claire*, Lamer J noted the lack of fit between the Quebec *Labour Code* and triangular employment relationships, and stated, 'when faced with such legislative gaps, tribunals have used their expertise to interpret the often terse provisions of the statute. In the final analysis, however, it is up to the legislature to remedy those gaps. The Court cannot encroach upon an area where it does not belong'.[70] However, the problem with this analysis is that it does not acknowledge the extent to which the courts create the problem in the first place by continuing both to insist on a conception of the employment relationship as a personal and bilateral contract and to treat the corporate form as sacrosanct.

3. CONCLUSION: DRAWING NEW BOUNDARIES

Ascribing responsibility for employment-related costs and risks tests the limits of a contractual analysis of employment. Conceptually there is a lack of fit between the traditional binary and personal conception of the employment contract in which the employer is conceived of as a unitary entity and

---

[68] *Ibid.*, para 28.

[69] *Ibid.*, para 33. The legality of any attempt by the union representing the members who lost their jobs when the SPA went out of the technical side of its business is controversial.

[70] *Pointe Claire*, above n 43, at para 21. See also *Lian Crew*, above n 13, at para 72 for similar reasoning.

the actual range of complex ways in which labour is employed in enterprises that are often composed of several entities. More importantly, the insistence on privity and separate legal corporate personality as a basis for liability creates a number of normative and distributive problems. Although employees have little say in how enterprises are organised and employment relations are structured and, thus, have little input into how risks are distributed amongst entities in the enterprise, they bear the consequences of how those risks are distributed. Moreover, the current legal basis for ascribing employment-related obligations operates as an incentive to firms to externalise their responsibility for employing labour. For these reasons several commentators suggest that there is a need to go beyond contract and the corporate form, and they advocate a relational and functional approach to ensure that those who benefit from employing labour bear the social and economic costs and risks related to that labour.[71]

Different techniques can be used to draw the boundaries of responsibility for employment-related obligations.[72] One suggestion is to redefine the 'employer' and move it away from the idea of the corporation to bring it closer to the notion of an enterprise as an economic unity with a physical presence.[73] Since collective bargaining law is concerned with the coordinating role of management within the process of production and organisation of services, the idea of the enterprise is a better fit with the purpose of labour law. Another proposal is to adopt a functional approach that recognises multiple employers for different purposes. Deakin identifies coordination, risk and equity as different bases for ascribing responsibility for employment-related obligations in different contexts.[74] Users would be responsible for health and safety and equality-related obligations, whereas providers would be liable for payroll taxes. In this way, different entities would be severally responsible for different obligations. On the other hand, it is possible simply to ignore intermediaries in certain situations and attribute responsibility to the entity that uses the employees' labour as the only employer. Alternatively, joint and several liability for employment-related obligations is a method of dealing with the problem of ascribing responsibility in situations involving complex employment relationships and multiple employing entities. Davidov advocates joint and several liability for users and providers in triangular employment relationships when it comes

---

[71] Collins, above n 16; Deakin, above n 16; Vallée, above n 34.

[72] P. Davies and M. Freedland, 'Changing Perspectives Upon the Employment Relationship in British Labour Law' in C. Barnard, S. Deakin and G. Morris (eds.), *The Future of Labour Law: Liber Amicorum Bob Hepple QC* (Oxford, Hart, 2004), 129, at 141–5; D. Grimshaw, M. Marchington, J. Rubery and H. Willmott, 'Conclusion: Redrawing Boundaries, Reflecting on Practice and Policy' in Marchington, Grimshaw, Rubery and Willmott, above n 35, 261, at 279–80.

[73] Deakin, above n 32; Vallée, above n 34.

[74] Deakin, above n 16.

to labour protection.[75] He claims that this allocation of responsibility is not only simpler than a functional approach, but that it is more responsive to democratic deficits and economic dependency experienced by employees. Contract compliance is yet another method of ensuring that principals are responsible for employment-related obligations owed by subcontractors; one of its virtues is that it can be used in situations in which the principal has no direct relationship with the subcontractors' employees.[76] Which technique for attributing employment-related obligations is selected will depend not only upon the specific legal context, but also upon the institutions, agents and norms in different national and regional labour markets.

Where the boundaries of responsibility for the social costs and economic risks of employing labour will be redrawn is linked to the capacity of the employment contract to continue to function as the primary platform for governing employment relationships, and this is an open question. However, in surveying the terrain of legal regulation and mapping possible boundaries of responsibility it is important to triangulate based on the following considerations. First, the empirical and practical reality is that there is a multiplicity of employing functions and a great deal of complexity and diversity in how enterprises obtain and utilise labour. Secondly, there are a range of different legal contexts that engage different dimensions—social justice, economic governance and social welfare—of labour regulation. Thirdly, labour is not simply a commodity to be bought and sold, but is embodied in human beings with aspirations and agency. What is required is a functional approach to identifying the employer that is designed to ensure that precarious workers are included within the scope, and enjoy the benefits, of labour protection.

[75] Davidov, above n 10.
[76] Becker, above n 10; Earnshaw, Rubery and Cooke, above n 11; Weil, above n 54.

15

Multi-segmented Workforces, Comparative Fairness, and the Capital Boundary Obstacle

HUGH COLLINS*

IMAGINE THE FOLLOWING case: three nurses with similar qualifications who work the same shifts together on a hospital ward discover that they receive different pay and other benefits and that they enjoy different measures of legal rights. The differences result from the separate identity of their employers. One nurse is employed by the hospital trust that operates the hospital as a whole, another is supplied by a private sector employment agency, and the third by a public sector nurses' bank for casual work.[1] Each employer has offered different terms for what is essentially the same work. Is there anything wrong with that?

When considering similar questions in the 1990s,[2] I emphasised the extent to which the core employer, in this case the hospital trust, had determined and controlled the outcome of the disparity in benefits and legal rights of the workers. Using techniques of vertical disintegration the core employer could outsource employment obligations and responsibility for labour standards to other employing entities such as subcontractors. Typically the employees of the subcontractors received inferior pay and benefits, and often incidentally lost many employment law rights. My argument was that employment law should pierce the veil of the formal separation between the employing entities produced by vertical disintegration, and should hold the core employer responsible for fair wages and compliance

---

* Professor of English Law, London School of Economics.
[1] NHS professionals in an in-house agency that offers improved pay and employment conditions for bank nursing, using call-centres to match supply to need for short-term cover, effectively competing with private sector temporary employment agencies: Department of Health, *Investment and Reform for NHS Staff: taking forward the NHS Plan* (London, Feb. 2001). See also J. Purcell, K. Purcell and S. Tailby, 'Temporary Work Agencies: Here Today, Gone Tomorrow?' (2004) 42 *British Journal of Industrial Relations* 705, at 720.

[2] H. Collins, 'Ascription of Legal Responsibility to Groups in Complex Patterns of Economic Integration' (1990) 53 *Modern Law Review* 731.

with other labour standards. In the above example, on this argument, the hospital trust might be held responsible for any unlawful discrimination or lack of compliance with labour standards, not only for direct employees, but also for the temporary and casual nurses. In presenting that argument it was acknowledged that it needed to overcome a crucial problem that the law does not usually hold one employing entity (the core employer) responsible for the actions and contractual relations of another (the subcontractor), a problem which I called the capital boundary problem.

That line of argument concerning ascription of responsibility in employing organisation networks remains fruitful and controversial,[3] and is explored more thoroughly in the chapters by Judy Fudge[4] and Mark Freedland and Paul Davies[5] in this volume. In this chapter, however, I consider a different approach to the issue of unfairness in the outcomes produced by vertical disintegration of employing entities. Here the argument concerns claims of comparative fairness between workers. It examines the potential scope of a claim that two workers who are performing similar work should receive the same benefits even though their employers are different legal entities. This comparative fairness claim does not rely on an argument that, despite the formal separation of legal entities, in economic substance the dominance of the core employer remains, so that the shadow of vertical integration can be invoked to justify holding the core employer responsible for labour standards. Instead, the comparative fairness claim simply asserts that it should be regarded as wrong that two workers performing similar work should be paid differently or enjoy different levels of legal protection. The difficult issue for the comparative fairness claim is to determine its scope: in what circumstances should it be permitted to succeed?

In the past, labour laws in many countries applied an extensive scope to the comparative fairness principle. Commonly employers were required to apply the going rate of pay to everyone in an industrial sector or everyone performing a particular kind of job. This industrial sector regulation was usually linked to collective bargaining. In the United Kingdom and many other countries, that pattern was replaced by the internal labour markets of

---

[3] Eg G. Davidov, 'Joint Employer Status in Triangular Employment Relationships' (2004) 42 *British Journal of Industrial Relations* 727.

[4] J. Fudge, 'The Legal Boundaries of the Employer, Precarious Workers, and Labour Protection'. In that essay she explores in particular the concept of joint liability between two or more employers for breach of labour standards, a potentially fruitful idea that is not explored in my work.

[5] P. Davies and M. Freedland, 'The Disintegration of the Employing Enterprise and its Significance for the Personal Scope of Employment Law', in which the 'multipolar' nature of employing organisations corresponds to the second type of segmentation discussed in this chapter. My chapter also uses some of the terminology and concepts including 'employing entity' and 'personal work contract' developed in M. Freedland, *The Personal Employment Contract* (Oxford, Oxford University Press, 2003).

large businesses and the public sector, in which the employer applied (or purported to apply) the principle of equal pay for work of equal value. Here the comparative fairness principle could be invoked inside the organisation, as in claims for equal pay, but not so readily outside the organisation between separate businesses.[6] With the decline of internal labour markets in recent years, that toehold of the comparative fairness principle has been progressively eroded, yet the principle is still invoked in such cases as discrimination against part-time workers.

Having considered further the qualities, scope and strengths of comparative fairness arguments in labour law, this chapter examines their application to two kinds of segmentation in the workforce. The issue in each case is to consider the extent to which the comparative fairness standard persists and can be made to operate as a regulatory standard for labour law. The first type of segmentation considered is the use of non-standard forms of employment such as part-time, fixed term and casual work. The second type of segmentation, as in the example of the nurses, concerns workers within a single productive undertaking who have contracts with different employing entities. In conclusion, it is observed that, whilst for the former kind of segmentation the comparative fairness standard has usually been preserved, albeit with controversial modifications, for the latter the differentiation of employing entities or capital units appears usually to block its application. The boundaries between capital units often rather artificially prevent the application of the comparative fairness standard to workers engaged in a common productive network.

1. THE STRUCTURE OF COMPARATIVE FAIRNESS STANDARDS

'Every worker has the right to fair and just working conditions.' So it is said in nearly every declaration of social and economic rights.[7] But what is meant by just and fair in these bold assertions of rights? These general declarations about fair and just working conditions contain at least two conceptions of fairness. One conception tries to specify some baseline conditions, such as maximum hours of work or minimum wages, beyond which there is automatic unfairness. A second concept of fairness relies on

---

[6] In the case of equal pay, for example, in general comparators employed by different employers cannot normally be used, though some exceptions exist: eg where one employing entity is controlled directly or indirectly by the other and where common terms of employment fixed by a collective agreement are observed in both employing entities (Equal Pay Act 1970 s 1(6)(c)).

[7] Eg Revised European Social Charter 1996 of the Council of Europe, Art 2, declares the right to just conditions of work, which provides for limits on working hours and the right to an annual paid holiday, and Art 4 declares the right to fair remuneration, which specifies that it requires remuneration at a level that will give workers and their families a decent standard of living and that men and women should receive equal pay for work of equal value.

a comparative assessment rather than a fixed standard: men and women should be treated equally, whatever the standard or measures adopted; or full-time and part-time workers should be treated proportionately the same.

The problem with baseline conditions of fairness is that it is hard to reach agreement on where to draw the line. International declarations often go no further than to insist that there should be a limit on the hours of work, but do not specify where that limit should be fixed; or, if a substantive standard is determined, numerous derogations and exclusions will be permitted by the convention; or again, the promulgated standard may be framed in an open-textured rule, such as the right not to be unjustly dismissed, thereby avoiding detailed specification of mandatory standards.

In contrast, the comparative conception of fairness is precise in form but indeterminate in substance. In the case of equal pay, for instance, the rule is precise that whatever standard is applied to men should also be applied to women, but that standard remains wholly indeterminate. There are two further crucial differences between these two conceptions of fairness in international standards. The comparative conception of fairness is applicable only between specified groups, such as men and women in the equal pay example, and its scope will also be limited by reference to a criterion that determines the relevant employing entities. This latter criterion might refer at one extreme to all employers in a particular industrial sector, or at the other extreme be confined to comparisons between employees of a single employer.

Equal pay claims are unusual types of comparative fairness claims because they impose a strict term by term comparison. It is more common for comparative fairness claims to impose a more flexible standard. The test may require an employer to offer terms that, viewed as a whole, are no worse than the comparator, thus permitting some disadvantageous terms mixed with others that are clearly superior.[8] Under such a test, for instance, the exclusion from the employer's occupational scheme (a disadvantage) might be off-set by higher weekly wages or longer paid holidays (an advantage). This looser comparative formula can be expressed in various ways,

---

[8] Eg the Australian innovation of workplace agreements: 'An agreement passes the no-disadvantage test if it does not disadvantage employees in relation to their terms and conditions of employment. Subject to [other qualifications in other sections of the legislation], an agreement disadvantages employees in relation to their terms and conditions of employment only if its approval or certification would result, on balance, in a reduction in the overall terms and conditions of employment of those employees under: (a) relevant awards or designated awards; and (b) any law of the Commonwealth, or of a State or Territory, that the Employment Advocate or the Commission (as the case may be) considers relevant': Australian Workplace Relations Act 1996, Part VIE, s 170XA(1) and (2). B. Creighton and A. Stewart, Labour Law: an Introduction (3rd edn, Sydney, Federation Press, 2000), 167–8. See for the application of this provision R. Mitchell, R. Campbell, A. Barnes, E. Bicknell, K. Creighton, J. Fetter and S. Korman, 'What's Going on with the "No Disadvantage Test"? An Analysis of Outcomes and Processes under the Workplace Relations Act 1996 (CWLTH)' (2005) 47 *Journal of Industrial Relations* 393.

such as 'no less favourable over-all',[9] or 'no disadvantage on balance',[10] or, as in Spain where the general legislation provides that although individual contracts of employment should be determined by the agreement of the parties, the parties cannot agree 'to the detriment of the employee terms of employment that are less favourable or contrary to legal requirements or relevant collective agreements'.[11]

It is also common for the comparative fairness standard to have a more complex structure in which the comparison establishes the foundation for a claim but then the claim may be defeated by reference to the defence of proportionality. In other words, although the claimant succeeds in establishing a difference that appears unfair on its face, when the reason for the difference is examined in greater depth, it is defensible on the ground that it serves a legitimate purpose and is a necessary and appropriate measure for the employer to use in the pursuit of that purpose. That is the basic structure of indirect discrimination claims. The defence of objective justification has been interpreted in European law to require the application of a proportionality test: the alleged unfair term had to serve a legitimate purpose or real need, and the use of the term had to be necessary and appropriate for the achievement of that legitimate purpose.[12] The same structure of comparison followed by the possibility of objective justification applies to other European Directives regulating employment conditions, as in the cases of fixed term work and part-time work.[13]

2. THE CHALLENGE TO COMPARATIVE FAIRNESS CLAIMS

The presence of comparative fairness arguments in legal regulation is a distinctive hall mark of labour law. In most other fields of law a comparative fairness claim would be regarded as irrelevant, or even improper.

---

[9] 'Where the service provider recruits new staff to work on a local authority contract alongside staff transferred from the local authority, it will offer employment on fair and reasonable terms and conditions which are, overall, no less favourable than those transferred employees. The service provider will also offer reasonable pension arrangements': Office of the Deputy Prime Minister, Local Government Act 1999: part 1 Best Value and Performance Improvement, Annex D of ODPM Circular 03/2003, 13 Mar. 2003. The circular goes on to explain that a comparison of terms should be as a package, in the round, and that the aim is to provide flexibility to the contractor whilst excluding changes 'which would undermine the integrated nature of the team or the quality of the workforce' (para 8).

[10] See above n. 8.

[11] Art 3.1 Estatuto de los Trabajadores; cf R. Rebhahn, 'Les clauses générales dans le droit du travil européen' in S. Grundmann and D. Mazeaud (eds.), *General Clauses and Standards in European Contract Law: Comparative Law, EC Law and Contract Law Codification* (The Hague, Kluwer Law International, 2005), 85.

[12] Case 170/84 *Bilka-Kaufhaus GmbH v Weber von Hartz* [1986] ECR 1607 (ECJ).

[13] Directive 99/70, Annex [1999] OJ L 175 143; Directive 97/81, Annex cl 4.1 [1998] OJ L 149; see text below at n 17 and 18.

Provided that the outcomes of different contracts in the market have not been affected by coercion, the lack of a competitive market or some other kind of market failure, it is usually assumed that the contracts cannot be impugned for unfairness. Thus in my original example, provided that the nurses could have obtained work from any of the three different employing entities, it is up to them to select which package of terms suits them best. Having made their choice, they cannot turn round, it could be said, and complain that someone else has made a superior choice. From this market-oriented perspective the example of the nurses does not seem to differ from a case where an energetic consumer goes to the market to buy fruit and manages to discover a bargain at one stall, whereas another less assiduous purchaser does not look at that stall and ends up paying a higher price. The good fortune of the energetic consumer does not seem to be unfair on the less assiduous purchaser; on the contrary, the energetic consumer appears to have reaped a just reward for his effort.

Yet a persistent characteristic of labour law has been that it has often rejected that simple market-forces argument in favour of upholding claims of comparative fairness. The use of such claims has not depended upon a suggestion of some kind of market failure. It has not been a requirement, for instance, that it be shown that the worker was unaware of the difference in pay and conditions at the time of entering into the contract of employment. Such a requirement of a defect in information is often regarded as essential to justify interventions in other types of market transactions such as consumer credit. In labour law, however, there is a tradition of accepting a more direct standard of comparative fairness as a ground for intervening in the labour market (though defects in information may also justify interventions).

That tradition of accepting comparative fairness arguments seems to have been grounded on two institutional features of the labour market. The first was the use of multi-employer collective bargaining to establish terms and conditions for a particular economic sector. This mechanism permitted comparative claims for equivalent terms and conditions of employment between employers. Examples in the United Kingdom of this comparative fairness process in the context of sectoral bargaining could be found in Fair Wages clauses in government contracts that require contractors to pay wages at the standard rate,[14] the establishment of minimum wages and conditions for a sector by means of enforceable orders of Wages Councils,[15] and techniques for the extension of collectively agreed terms and conditions to workers employed by employers who were not parties to the collective

---

[14] Fair Wages Resolution 1946 (now abolished); for comparisons with the USA (Walsh Healey Public contracts Act 1936) and France, see O. Kahn-Freund, *Labour and the Law* (2nd edn, London, Stevens, 1977), 158–60.

[15] Wages Councils Act 1959 (now abolished); Agricultural Wages Acts 1948 and 1949.

agreement.[16] The second institutional feature was the use of internal labour markets within larger businesses, under which rates of pay and other benefits were fixed by reference to administrative rules of the organisation that claimed to provide a fair system of remuneration. Within an internal labour market it became possible to make claims of comparative fairness, as in the case where equal pay claims could rely on the fact that the jobs had been rated as equivalent under a job evaluation scheme. Similarly, other instances of the legal application of the comparative conception of fairness, as for example in the comparison between full-time and part-time workers, rely as well on the notion that an employer should have a payment scheme that can be objectively justified by the kinds of criteria used in job evaluation schemes, and should not be simply a response to the vagaries of supply and demand in the external labour market.

It is well-known that government policies and employers' managerial strategies designed to derigidify labour markets in the name of improving competitiveness and reducing unemployment have greatly diminished the impact of sectoral bargaining and internal labour markets on pay and conditions. To the extent that these labour market institutions have been replaced in order to link pay more closely with external labour markets, the shift in payment systems renders the application of the comparative fairness standard much harder. In other words, once the employer disclaims a commitment to an internal labour market or to paying the collectively agreed standard rate, but instead insists that pay should be related to individual performance or should be fixed by market forces, it becomes harder to justify the application of the comparative conception of fairness.

Paradoxically, however, that same shift also creates stronger demands from representatives of workers for the adoption of a comparative fairness standard in legislation. For example, in a period when all nurses working on the hospital ward were employees of the health authority and their terms of employment were fixed by a collectively agreed internal labour market scheme, the rules of the employer's organisation effectively secured at least some ostensible standard of fairness in pay between different nurses. Once the hospital trust decides to use on a systematic basis nurses from agencies whose terms of employment are not governed by the internal labour market, unjustified and perhaps unjustifiable differences in pay begin to emerge, to which the likely response from workers is a demand for legislation or some other effective action to impose a comparative conception of fairness on employers. It is no accident therefore, I suggest, that legislation endorsing a comparative conception of fairness, such as the part-time workers and the fixed term employees directives in Europe, has been introduced

---

[16] Terms and Conditions of Employment Act 1959, s 8; Employment Protection Act 1975, Sched 11 (now both repealed). For comparisons with European countries and the Australian Awards system, see Kahn-Freund, above n 14, at 140–9.

at precisely the same time as employers have been dismantling internal labour markets and rejecting sectoral bargaining.

Those developments create an interesting tension. On the one hand, the plausibility of claims for a test of comparative fairness diminishes as terms and conditions are fixed less by reference to labour market institutions and more by reference to external market forces. On the other hand, the perceived need on the part of workers for enabling legally enforceable comparative fairness claims increases as the employer no longer routinely applies the standard automatically by observing sectoral rates or rules of an internal labour market. A contemporary challenge for labour law is to try to devise ways of responding to the call for enabling legally enforceable claims for comparative fairness in the context of the new, relatively inhospitable, terrain of payment systems that have abandoned to a significant extent the notion that they are determined by objective considerations that are not simply the ebb and flow of market forces.

3. MULTI-SEGMENTED WORKFORCES

As noted earlier, comparative fairness claims require the identification of specified groups for comparison and are limited to a particular locality, such as a single employing entity or an industrial sector. In addressing the challenge for labour law described above, the contested issues typically focus on those two problems: the relevant groups for comparison and the appropriate scope of the locality. Employers and their representatives will argue that the groups should be narrowly conceived and the locality strictly confined, whereas workers and their representatives argue for the opposite point of view in order to give comparative fairness arguments greater bite. This section examines critically how these issues have been resolved in connection with two kinds of segmentation in the workforce.

A. Non-Standard Workers

The first type of segmentation concerns all those workers who are non-standard in the sense that they do not work under a permanent (open-ended) contract of employment, and their terms of employment are not governed by the rules of an internal labour market applicable to permanent staff or core employees. These non-standard workers are likely to include fixed-term, temporary, casual, and part-time workers. This group also extends to workers who may not easily be classified as employees under a contract of employment, because, despite 'employee-like' aspects of the working arrangement, such as a measure of control exercised by the employer, the form of the contract puts them into the category of self-employed independent contractors.

Here the comparative fairness argument insists that it is appropriate to make comparisons between standard employees and these other groups of workers, despite the fact that their forms of employment differ in important respects.

We have already observed that European directives envisage the application of the comparative fairness standard between various groups of workers, either defined by reference to the protected groups under the anti-discrimination laws (sex, race etc.), or by reference to contract form (part-time, fixed term). Consider, for instance, clause 4(1) of the framework agreement on fixed term work:

> In respect of employment conditions, fixed-term workers shall not be treated in a less favourable manner than comparable permanent workers solely because they have a fixed-term contract or relation unless justified on objective grounds.[17]

A similar non-discrimination principle applies to part-time workers:

> In respect of employment conditions, part-time workers shall not be treated in a less favourable manner than comparable full-time workers solely because they work part-time unless different treatment is justified on objective grounds.[18]

In all these examples the comparative fairness standard adopts a complex structure. Having established a detriment through a comparison, there is then a second stage of the enquiry: the potential for the employer to justify the difference in contract terms on 'objective grounds'. These objective grounds are not defined in the Directives, though the General Considerations listed in the preambles to the Directives indirectly suggest some relevant factors. In the case of part-time work these legitimate purposes might include such matters as whether the arrangement contributes to a desirable balance between flexibility and security, and whether it affords the workers a better work-life balance. These goals indicate the type of legitimate purpose for which an employer might discriminate against a fixed term worker or a part-time worker, but under the test of proportionality the employer still has to demonstrate that the unfavourable discrimination was appropriate and necessary in the circumstances.

The legal construction of suitable groups for comparison proves more complex than appears from this brief description of the legislation. In a typical case part-time workers may differ from full-time workers to some extent with respect to the skills that they bring to the job and in the tasks assigned to them. The terms of the contract may reflect these differences in various ways, so that even ignoring the disparity in hours of work the contracts of the part-timers are probably not identical to those of the full-time workers.

---

[17] Directive 99/70, above n 13, Annex.
[18] Directive 97/81, above n 13, Annex, cl 4.1.

Should these differences preclude any comparison on the ground that the workers are not employed on the same type of contract, as required by the Directive,[19] or simply lead to the conclusion that the differences should be reflected in the proportional difference in pay and conditions? The Directive would lose much of its impact if either minor differences in terms other than hours or slight differences in the type of work actually performed were sufficient to preclude the application of the comparative fairness standard. In the United Kingdom, the implementing regulations increased that risk of preventing application of the comparative standard by excluding comparisons where it is reasonable for an employer to treat workers in a particular group as different on the ground that they have a different type of contract.[20] That risk has diminished as a result of purposive interpretation by the courts aimed at protecting the position of part-time workers, as in the permitted comparison of full-time and part-time fire-fighters despite the fact that full-time workers carried out additional functions to that of fighting fires and usually had additional qualifications and skills.[21]

Furthermore, even when suitable groups have been identified, the question whether one group suffers a disadvantage can also be contested. This issue arises with respect to the consequences for legal rights arising from differences in the terms of the contracts enjoyed by member of the segmented workforce. Consider, for instance, the legal right to claim unfair dismissal in the UK. In the field of sex discrimination law, it was decided that a disproportionate exclusion of women from the legal right arising from the application of longer qualifying periods for part-time workers amounted to indirect discrimination.[22] Here the comparative disadvantage in legal rights arising from part-time work was measured by reference to a comparative fairness standard. In contrast, in relation to fixed-term work designed to terminate after 51 weeks, that is, one week before the employee qualifies for

---

[19] *Ibid.*, Annex, cl 3: 'The term 'comparable full-time worker' means a full-time worker in the same establishment having the same type of employment contract or relationship, who is engaged in the same or a similar work/occupation, due regard being given to other considerations which may include seniority and qualifications/skills.'

[20] Part Time Workers (Prevention of Less Favourable Treatment) Regs 2000, SI 2000/1551, reg 2(3)(d) (as amended). See C. Kilpatrick and M. Freedland, 'The United Kingdom: How is EU Governance Transformative?' in S. Sciarra, P. Davies and M. Freedland (eds.), *Employment Policy and the Regulation of Part-time Work in the European Union* (Cambridge, Cambridge University Press, 2004), 299, at 322–8.

[21] *Mathews v Kent and Medway Towns Fire Authority* [2006] UKHL 8, [2006] ICR 365(HL).

[22] *R v Secretary of State for Employment, ex parte Equal Opportunities Commission* [1994] ICR 317 (HL); the application of a comparative fairness standard in principle to the qualifying period for full-time workers was also accepted in case C–167/97 *R v Secretary of State for Employment ex parte Seymour-Smith* [1999] ECR I–0623, [1999] ICR 447 (ECJ), though the claim for indirect sex discrimination was not ultimately successful: *R v Secretary of State for Employment ex p Seymour-Smith & Perez (No 2)* [2000] ICR 244 (HL).

a claim for unfair dismissal, the practice of using such contracts was held not to amount to disadvantageous treatment of fixed-term employees compared to permanent (open-ended contract) employees.[23] The court rejected the view that it was unfair to design contracts of employment in a way that deliberately and effectively excluded employment law rights (provided that such measures were not expressly made unlawful by the legislation itself). But the effect of the decision was that whereas permanent employees would acquire the legal right through the effluxion of time, provided that they were not dismissed earlier for reasons of incapacity or redundancy, the fixed-term employee could never obtain the right, no matter how much her services were needed and valued. The puzzle here is that, if being a fixed term employee as opposed to a permanent employee is not to be regarded as a disadvantage in itself, does it follow that any consequential disadvantages with respect to entitlements to legal rights are themselves also not to be regarded as relevant disadvantages for the purpose of making the comparison? That conclusion was rejected in the context of claims for indirect sex discrimination, though the burden of establishing an objective justification for the difference in legal entitlements was pitched fairly low.[24]

In the context of this kind of segmentation, however, the most significant restriction on the comparative fairness standard concerns the limitation on the categories of permitted comparisons. The question is whether the groups for comparison might be extended. For example, could a comparison be drawn between the terms of the permanent staff of the core employer and those of employee-like dependent contractors, that is persons who, though notionally in business on their own account, have only one client, perform work personally, and effectively fall under the managerial control and direction of the core business? The underlying issue here is whether the special favour shown by labour law to the comparative fairness standard applies only to employees with contracts of employment or whether the personal scope or protective effect of the comparative fairness principle should extend to persons who contract to perform work personally regardless of the legal form of the transaction.

B. Multi-employer Segmentation

The second type of segmentation concerns workers who do not work directly for the core employing entity, but work for another employer or contractor. This employer or contractor has the core employing entity

---

[23] *Webley v Department for Work and Pensions* [2004] EWCA Civ 1745, [2005] ICR 577, (CA).
[24] See cases cited above in n 22.

as a client, but the legal relationship of the individual worker is with the contractor rather than the client. As in the original example of nurses, into this category fall various groups including temporary agency workers, workers on some kinds of secondment, and employees of subcontractors. In these instances of segmentation there are multiple employers for the workforce. In this context the application of the comparative fairness standard encounters not only the difficulty discussed above of the differences presented by the variety of contracts for personal service, but also the difficulty of defining the locality for an appropriate comparison. Since the same undertaking or capital unit does not directly employ the workers, it seems harder to apply the comparative fairness standard. The blunt response of any employer is simply that it has no control over what other employers may pay their workers and that it is none of its business.

One response to that view is to suggest that the comparative fairness standard should apply within a multi-employer entity that is effectively partially integrated in its production system in the sense that productive activities require intense co-ordination and cooperation without, however, ownership or direct control. In other words, an acephalous network architecture between the employing entities should suffice to bring the workers within the framework of a comparative fairness test. On this view workers of different employers who are working alongside each other and who are subject to coordinated managerial direction should be able to appeal to a comparative fairness standard, regardless of whether or not one employer can effectively control the conduct of the other. Even where workers are not physically contiguous but where their activities for their different employers are coordinated, as in the case of a component supplier to a manufacturer operating under a continuous replenishment of stock system, it should be possible in principle to advance such a claim for comparative fairness on the basis of the network architecture that links the multi-employer entity. In other words, although the workers may have contractual exchange relations with separate employing entities, their integration into a productive operation that has coordinated managerial direction should suffice to permit the application of the comparative fairness standard. On this view of the potential reach of comparative fairness arguments within networks of employing entities, it should be straightforward to permit comparative fairness claims between temporary workers and permanent staff where the temporary workers are supplied in the correct numbers and quality through a coordinated mechanism between the core business and the agency supplying labour.

This suggested application of the comparative fairness standard to multi-employer productive organisations has so far been resisted in most employment law measures. The comparative fairness standard has predominantly been understood in European law as being confined to comparison within a single employing entity.[25] More precisely, the ECJ has determined that the comparative standard of fairness should be applied only where the terms of employment are determined by a 'single source'.[26] A single source is usually regarded as a single employing entity or capital unit, though an associated group of companies would amount to a 'single source', even though technically the employees would be employed by different legal entities such as subsidiary companies.[27] Similarly, if a collective agreement applied to both groups of workers, that agreement would be regarded as a single source, even though the workers had different employers. Comparisons across employers by reference to collective agreements are also permitted in connection with discrimination against part-time and fixed term workers. These Directives provide that if there are no suitable workers for comparison in the same establishment, the comparison should be made by reference to the applicable collective agreement or, where there is no applicable collective agreement, in accordance with national law, collective agreements or practice.[28] On the other hand, even though workers may all be technically employed by a single legal entity such as the state, if effective determination of terms and conditions has been delegated to separate divisions or departments, the existence of a common employer in law does not satisfy the 'single source' test, which looks rather at the reality of wage determination.[29] The fundamental justification for this restriction of comparisons with a 'single source' lies in the argument that one employer has no control over the working conditions offered by another employer and that, therefore, it would be unfair to permit comparisons between the working conditions offered.

Let me illustrate this conceptual limit of a 'single source' on the scope of the comparative fairness standard with the decision of the European Court

[25] Some Member States of the EU envisage that agency workers should have the right to parity of terms with employees of the core business under certain conditions: D. Storrie, *Temporary Agency Work in the European Union* (Dublin, European Foundation for the Improvement of Living and Working Conditions, 2002), 21–3; for a wider comparative survey, including the use of the comparable fairness principle in Israel, see Davidov, above n 3, at 731–6.

[26] Case C–320/00 *Lawrence v Regent Office Care Ltd* [2002] ECR I–7325, [2003] ICR 1092 (ECJ). This case concerned the contracting out of the public sector to a private contractor of a school meals service, and the rejected comparison was between the transferred employees of the private contractor and some retained employees in the public sector.

[27] Employment Rights Act 1996 s 231: 'For the purposes of this Act any two employers shall be treated as associated if—(a) one is a company of which the other (directly or indirectly) has control, or (b) both are companies of which a third person (directly or indirectly) has control . . .'. For discussions of the concept of 'associated employer' in UK law, see H. Collins, 'Associated Employers' (1989) 18 *Industrial Law Journal* 109; Collins, above n 2; P. Davies and M. Freedland, 'The Employment Relationship in British Labour Law' in C. Barnard, S. Deakin and G. S. Morris (eds), *The Future of Labour Law* (Oxford, Hart, 2004), 129, at 138–40.

[28] Directive 97/81, above n 13, Annex, cl 3; Directive 99/70, above n 13 Annex, cl 3.

[29] *Department for Environment Food and Rural Affairs v Robertson* [2005] EWCA Civ 138, [2005] ICR 750 (CA).

of Justice (ECJ) in *Allonby v Accrington and Rossendale College*.[30] A college of further education, which employed both full-time and part-time teachers, decided for financial reasons to terminate the contracts of employment of all of the 341 hourly paid, fixed term, part-time teachers, but then to re-engage them through an agency. The part-time teachers registered with an agency called Education Lecturing Services as self-employed workers. They were then sent on assignment to the college, and the college paid a fee to the agency for their services. In turn the agency negotiated a fee with each teacher for each assignment and paid that fee as remuneration. The effect of this arrangement was that the teachers' remuneration was reduced, and in particular they lost membership of the state's contributory pension scheme created for teachers in further education because they were no longer employees of the college. By this route the college reduced its labour costs. In effect, the college avoided the legal requirements introduced by the Part-time Workers Directive and the Fixed Term Employees Directive.

One cannot but note with a wry smile this pristine example of regulatory back-firing: a Directive designed to improve the position of part-time workers had the effect of reducing the teachers' pay and eliminating all their statutory rights based upon continuity of service and their status as employees as opposed to independent contractors. To achieve that outcome, it is true that the employer had to dismiss these workers and probably pay compensation for redundancy (the case was settled out of court, so the issue of whether they were redundant and the level of compensation was not litigated). But that one-off expense of compensation for dismissal was presumably far less than the recurrent savings in labour costs by means of out-sourcing to an agency. Given the fees charged by the agency, there may have been little saving in terms of ordinary wage costs, but no doubt there were much greater savings to be found from such items as the avoidance of the contributory pension, the avoidance of paid leave obligations such as maternity leave, and lower employer taxes. In addition, the college almost certainly avoided the risk of incurring liabilities under other statutory employment rights, such as the right to claim unfair dismissal. If a part-time teacher proved unsatisfactory, the college could merely notify the agency that her services were no longer required without dismissing her itself.[31]

The gender composition of these part-time fixed term teachers provided the basis for a claim for sex discrimination. Of the 341 dismissed teachers, 110 were men and 231 were women. The retained lecturers of the college were roughly equally divided between men and women. The applicant, who

---

[30] Case C–256/01 [2004] ICR 1328(ECJ).

[31] There cannot be complete certainty about this in the light of the observations in *Dacas v Brook Street Bureau (UK) Ltd* [2004] EWCA Civ 217, [2004] ICR 1437(CA) regarding a possible implied contract of employment with the client.

was a dismissed part-time teacher now performing much the same job as before but through the agency, claimed that the dismissals of the part-time workers amounted to indirect sex discrimination, and that the college, by denying the applicant benefits granted to retained salaried workers, was discriminating against her as a contract worker on the ground of her sex. Those issues were not referred to the ECJ, but remitted for further consideration to a domestic employment tribunal for resolution.[32] The difficult legal issues referred by the English Court of Appeal to the ECJ were, first, whether, under Article 141 EC, the directly effective treaty provision on equal pay, the agency was required to pay the applicant equally with a male lecturer permanently employed at the college, and, secondly, whether her exclusion from the occupational pension scheme constituted unlawful sex discrimination.

On the first issue, the ECJ held that Article 141 was inapplicable to the circumstances because the differences in pay could not be attributed to a 'single source', which was responsible for the difference. In this case of an agency worker, neither the college nor the agency was solely responsible for the difference in pay. On the contrary, the college independently determined the terms of employment of the male full-time comparator, and the agency separately determined the remuneration of the assigned workers. The fact that the level of fee paid by the college to the agency indirectly influenced the amount the agency paid to the teacher was insufficient to make the college or the agency a single source to which the difference could be attributed.

On the second issue regarding membership of the pension scheme, the same reasoning about the absence of a single source of the discrimination prevented any straightforward claim against the agency. But there was an indirect claim available against the agency, based upon unlawful discrimination contained in the Teachers' Superannuation (Amendment) Regulations 1993 with respect to the condition that required all members of the state's occupational pension scheme to be employees of an employer of teachers in the further education sector. The ECJ observed that Article 141 applied to persons who were 'workers', not merely to employees working under a contract of employment. According to the ECJ, in European law a worker is a person who, for a certain period of time, performs services for and under the direction of another person in return for remuneration. While the concept of a 'worker' in European law is therefore restricted to circumstances in which there is a relation of subordination with the person who receives the services, it is possible for the equal pay principle to apply to a person who is classified as an independent contractor by national law, if this independence is notional and disguises what is in reality an

---

[32] [2001] ICR 1189(CA).

employment relationship.[33] In this particular case, the agency teachers were subject to the control of the college and the fact that they could choose not to take a particular assignment offered by the agency was irrelevant. Given that Article 141 applied to these agency workers, the applicant could then establish an equal pay claim by demonstrating that the exclusion of workers who were not employees from the pension scheme had a disproportionate adverse effect on women. If there was no objective justification for this exclusion, the claim for equal pay should succeed. Where legislation is not in conformity with Article 141, it must be regarded as invalid for all purposes, including the admission of a claim based on Article 141 against a private employer.[34] Thus this claim could be brought against the temporary employment agency as the undertaking responsible for paying the remuneration of the worker and the employer who complied with the invalid exclusion of workers from the statutory pension scheme.

This decision illustrates the limits placed on the scope of the comparative fairness standard in the context of vertical disintegration. With respect to the first claim, the doctrine that the difference in pay must be attributable to a 'single source' restricts comparisons to a single undertaking that effectively controls the terms of employment of both workers subject to the comparison. The fact that the agency and not the college determined the applicant's rate of hourly pay was the decisive fact against the possibility of making a valid comparison with an employee of the college. In other words, the argument that the shadow of vertical integration still determined terms of employment for employees of subcontractors was rejected both on grounds of principle and in fact. But the court does not address fully the comparative fairness claim which insists that the scope of comparisons does not have to be fixed by reference to an employing entity, but might instead involve comparisons between workers performing similar jobs, especially if, as in this case, they were working contiguously in a coordinated and cooperative productive activity. The single source doctrine effectively limits the scope of comparisons to a single employer, a single collective agreement, or, as in the second claim, a single piece of legislation, whereas comparative fairness claims can in principle be used to cross these barriers. An alternative test for the scope of the comparative fairness principle appropriate to this case might have focussed instead on the coordinated work activity of the full-time and part-time teachers combined with a closely linked network between the employers in their arrangements for labour supply and personnel management.

---

[33] For arguments that a similar test of dependency should apply in UK law for the concept of worker see G. Davidov, 'Who is a Worker?' (2005) 34 *Industrial Law Journal* 57.

[34] Case C–171/88 *Rinner-Kuhn v FWW Spezial-Gebäudereinigung GmbH & Co KG* [1989] ECR 2743 (ECJ).

In reaching these conclusions, the ECJ was clearly tempted to revise or qualify its doctrine that applications of the equal pay principle, and I would add the comparative fairness standard, should be limited by the requirement of a 'single source'. The strength of the teacher's claim to permit a comparison was assisted by three principal factors. First, the use of agency workers was a transparent device to circumvent EC legislation designed to protect part-time workers for the purpose of saving labour costs, and the court was no doubt reluctant to endorse this subversion of legislative policy. Secondly, there was the historical point that before the dismissals of the part-time teachers they were able to make the necessary comparison. Thirdly, there was the compelling factual circumstance that in practice little had changed in the workplace: the part-time teachers taught the same courses, according to the same timetable, alongside the same colleagues, at the direction of the same managers, in the same workplace. The sole significant change was the form of the contract under which they provided their services.

Nevertheless, these considerations were ultimately overridden by the perceived difficulty in principle of holding one employer liable for not treating its workers the same as another employer treats its workers. That difficulty seems to act as a barrier even in legal systems that seek to improve the position of temporary agency workers. Measures such as requiring the agency worker to be treated as a permanent employee after a certain period of time,[35] or forbidding discriminatory treatment of the agency worker or employees of contractors in comparison to the treatment of employees,[36] still maintain the principle of a single source of the discrimination, albeit sometimes providing an effective, though indirect, route towards the implementation of the comparative fairness standard in the workforce.[37] These measures do not embrace the comparative fairness standard but rather implement minimum standards of fairness. Even for workers who are not their employees or direct contractors, these measures require a business to establish safe conditions of work and not to engage in discriminatory behaviour. These rules might be extended, as Davies and Freedland suggest,[38] to other minimum standards, such as the right not to be unfairly

---

[35] Eg, France.

[36] Eg, Sex Discrimination Act 1975 s 9; Race Relations Act 1976 s 7; Disability Discrimination Act 1995 s 12: see S Deakin, 'The Changing Concept of the Employer in Labour Law' (2001) 30 *Industrial Law Journal* 72, at 76–7. These anti-discrimination laws apply to an employing entity (the principal) even though it is not the employer of the victim of discrimination, if the victim provides work for the principal, which seems to mean that to some extent the victim works under the instructions of the principal: *Harrods Ltd v Remick* [1998] ICR 156(CA); *O'Shea (CJ) Construction Ltd v Bassi* [1998] ICR 1130 (EAT).

[37] Eg, an agency worker succeeding in a claim for discrimination against the user or client when she was not permitted to return to her posting after maternity leave, though the formal ground of the decision was that she was treated less favourably than a male agency worker would have been: *Patefield v Belfast City Council* [2000] IRLR 664 (N I CA).

[38] Davies and Freedland, above n 27, at 143.

disciplined or dismissed. But the application of the comparative fairness standard across capital boundaries seems to run up against an impenetrable barrier.

As we have noted, the comparative fairness standard contests the implications of government policies aimed at derigidifying labour markets. The single source doctrine supports those policies by enabling different employers to bargain with employees for their own wage scales regardless of those paid by other employers. Although the comparative fairness standard has never of course tried to suppress all pay differentials between employers, it is likely to contest its disapplication to cases such as *Allonby* where the groups of workers are working alongside each other under coordinated and cooperative managerial control provided by linked employers. The question is whether an alternative to the single source doctrine might be developed that permits a comparative fairness standard to be applied where the workers of different employers contribute to a productive activity according to coordinated managerial direction from the cooperating employers in a network.

A similar extension of the comparative fairness standard has been used in connection with public sector workers who are transferred by an outsourcing arrangement to a private sector contractor. Where a contractor wins a competitive tender to supply a service and takes on the existing workforce from either the public authority or a first generation contractor, it is obliged either under the Acquired Rights Directive[39] or UK government rules[40] to continue to apply the same terms and conditions to the transferred workforce. Over the course of time, however, this contractor may need to hire recruits to replace transferred workers who leave. Since these new joiners have not been connected to the transfer in any way, they are not protected by rules about the transfer. Nevertheless the contractor for the public service is now obliged to employ the new joiners on broadly similar terms to those of the protected transferred employees under a comparative fairness standard. These rules also apply to subcontractors of the contractor, so that employees of those subcontractors, or at least new joiners, have to be treated comparably with public sector workers who are working alongside them. In this example, the trigger for the application of the comparative fairness standard is the fact that the employees are working alongside each other within a productive network of employers, and the fact that it is a multi-employer entity does not preclude comparisons. This principle could therefore serve as a template for a replacement of the single source doctrine, in order to permit a wider application of the comparative fairness standard in the context of this kind of segmentation of the workforce.

---

[39] Art 3.1 of Directive 2001/23 on the approximation of the laws of Member States relating to the safeguarding of employees' rights in the event of transfers of undertakings, businesses or parts of undertakings or businesses [2001] OJ L 82 16.

[40] Office of the Deputy Prime Minister, above n 9.

It should always be remembered, however, that although the scope of the comparative fairness standard could be extended by this replacement of the single source doctrine by a network concept, successful claims would still have to overcome any objective justifications for differences in treatment of workers presented by employers.

4. TOWARDS A NETWORK CONCEPT

Patterns of multiple segmentation in the workforce of a particular business undertaking have undermined the practice of using an internal labour market to set legal standards of comparative fairness between different groups of workers. In the absence of the organisational rules producing fair differentiations in pay and benefits, workers have responded by seeking legal avenues for restoring those comparisons, either by using old laws for a new purpose, as in the case of equal pay claims, or by pressing for new laws, as in the case of the EC directives on part-time work, fixed term contracts of employment, and in the so far failed attempt to secure a directive on temporary agency workers.[41] We have observed that despite the competitive pressures that induced employers and governments to seek to diminish the significance of internal labour markets, the moral force of the comparative fairness standard still provides a compelling basis for mandatory standards of justice in the workplace. Where the application of the comparative fairness standard has been blocked in European law has been in the context of the form of segmentation that involves multi-employer undertakings or productive organisations.

The effect of this blockage seems to be to induce employers to prefer this technique of vertical disintegration to other forms of segmentation of the workforce in their quest for various kinds of 'flexibility' and greater efficiencies in the use of labour. In other words, an employer is likely to achieve those goals more effectively by sub-contracting and the use of agency workers than by introducing more variety in the terms of employment of its own employees.

To avoid those incentives and to secure the application of a comparative fairness standard what may be required is a replacement of the 'single source' doctrine. A comparative fairness standard still requires some definition of the locality to which it should apply, but it need not be confined to a single employing entity. As well as notions of a single source, it should be possible to apply comparative fairness standards to a locality defined by a workforce that is united through its co-ordinated management direction in

---

[41] European Commission, *Amended Proposal for a Directive of the European Parliament and the Council on Working Conditions for Temporary Workers*, COM2002/701.

the pursuit of a common endeavour, whilst not necessarily being comprised of a single employing entity. The development of such a network concept to govern the scope of the comparative fairness principle will certainly not prove simple and uncontroversial. The key to such a concept is not to permit the scope of contractual exchange relations to establish boundaries for the application of the comparative fairness standard, but rather to place reliance on managerial co-ordination between the business aimed at achieved the goal of the whole network of employers. This network approach differs from the argument that a core employer should remain responsible for labour standards, even for employees of subcontractors, because there remains a shadow of vertical integration despite the formal separation of employing entities owing to the dominant economic control of a core business. It is not necessary to argue that one employer remains in reality in control of wages and conditions under the network concept, for it suffices that that there is intense co-ordination and cooperation between employing entities without the need to demonstrate that one effectively dominates the other. Without such an evolution in legal doctrine towards a network concept to determine the scope of the comparative fairness standard, labour law stands to risk a diminution of the effectiveness of one of its traditional principles for justifying regulatory interventions in the labour market in the face of the increasing complexity of patterns of vertical disintegration within employer entities.

V

International and Institutional Solutions

16

The Employment Relationship:
The Issue at the International Level

ENRIQUE MARÍN*

O N THE SUBJECT of the debate surrounding the boundaries of labour law, it is useful to look at certain aspects of recent discussions and studies undertaken by the ILO on the employment relationship, and at the possibility of the adoption of an international Recommendation in this area.

1. BACKGROUND

The question of the employment relationship has, in one way or another, been under discussion in the ILO for more than a decade.

Since the 1950s, the ILO has been aware of the growing phenomenon of the lack of protection for a large number of workers, in particular, employees of subcontracting enterprises. Discussions eventually took place during the International Labour Conferences (ILC) of 1997 and 1998 (at its 85th and 86th Sessions, respectively) on 'contract labour'. At the 1997 ILC, a discussion was held on private employment agencies, touching on the situation of workers employed by such agencies. During the latter discussion, the Private Employment Agencies Convention (No. 181) and the Private Employment Agencies Recommendation (No. 188) were adopted. However, against the usual practice of the ILC, no instrument on contract labour was adopted, highlighting the extent to which the subject could be misunderstood and how controversial it was.

* Labour Law Specialist, Infocus Programme on Social Dialogue, Labour Law and Labour Administration, International Labour Office. Although based on the work of the ILO, this chapter is a reflection of my personal view on this issue. I would also like to thank my colleagues for their valuable assistance: Catherine Di Maio and Rita Natola for the translation of this chapter into English, and the final editing, respectively.

Other debates have since taken place at the ILO, including a Meeting of Experts on Workers in Situations Needing Protection in 2000, and a discussion on the employment relationship at the 2003 ILC, during which ideas were aired and allowed to take shape. Furthermore, 39 national studies were prepared between 1999 and 2001. On the basis of this experience, the ILO is currently preparing for a new discussion and for the possible adoption in 2006 of a Recommendation on the employment relationship.[1]

This chapter's objective is to identify some main lines of thought which follow from the work already carried out by the ILO, particularly the abovementioned report. The latter constitutes an international perspective on the subject of the scope of the employment relationship and thus on the wider subject of the boundaries of labour law.

In reality, the debate in the ILO did not deal directly with the boundaries of labour law as such. However, it did refer to a crucial aspect linked to the boundaries of protection at work within the framework of an employment relationship, while acknowledging that these boundaries were neither static nor permanent.

The international perspective offers some elements to contribute to a common understanding of the issue of the lack of protection for dependent workers and certain categories of workers, including women, and indirectly to the issue of the boundaries of labour law. After a long process of research and debate, some clarifications—beyond problems of terminology and the specificities of different legal systems—have been reached concerning the terms of reference of the problem, the most important concepts, and the repercussions of this situation. The international perspective also highlights the potential effects that a national policy on the employment relationship, founded on an international profile and action, may have on the search for balanced, equitable and progressive solutions to improve the law, its observance and practical application.

These diverse points will be developed around two main themes: the lack of focus and the necessary refocusing of the employment relationship; and a possible international response to this refocusing of the employment relationship.

2. THE LACK OF FOCUS AND THE REFOCUSING OF THE EMPLOYMENT RELATIONSHIP

When the delegates at the 1997 International Labour Conference started discussing the possibility of adopting new international instruments on

---

[1] For further information on this work, see *Report V(1): The Employment Relationship* (International Labour Conference, 95th Session, Geneva, International Labour Office, 2005). See also the ILO website where the above report and other relevant documents on the employment relationship can be accessed, at: http://www.ilo.org/public/english/dialogue/ifpdial/ll/er.htm.

'contract labour', it became apparent that the subject under discussion was not clear. Although the expression used in English (contract labour) was apparently self-explanatory, in fact it was ambiguous and was understood differently by different persons and from one language to another.

As such, under 'contract labour' the following categories of workers, amongst others, were discussed: falsely self-employed workers; workers originating from subcontracting enterprises; and workers originating from employment agencies (while another Commission—Private Enterprise Agencies—was also discussing these workers), without a common denominator being found. Nevertheless, it was proposed to give to those different categories of workers, who were not well defined in prior discussions, rights *similar* to those enjoyed by salaried workers.

Likewise, legislative texts, as well as specialised literature and the media, often employ different terms to refer to those categories of workers without protection or whose employment situations offer no protection, eg, 'contractual', 'precarious', 'informal' (casual), or 'external' workers etc. In addition, often related to the discussions of these categories of workers are the terms 'subcontracting enterprises', 'employment agencies', 'workers' cooperatives', 'franchisers', 'new enterprises created with transferred workers', and 'outsourcing'.

Faced with the problem of numerous categories of workers, it has become absolutely crucial to define its terms of reference. In this respect, there has been a certain consensus over the years at the ILO, even though the employers' group have always taken a critical stance.

A. The Terms of the Problem

The 1997–1998 ILC discussion on workers in diverse situations, such as those described above, dealt with the fact that they were actually dependent workers without the protection of an employment relationship, in law or in practice. This conclusion consequently oriented future discussions towards the subject of the employment relationship or the law pertaining to it.[2]

---

[2] The evolution of the discussions at the ILO is crucial for its member states, workers and employers, but it can also be used as a reference for an academic study on the boundaries of labour law. Such a study could also contain definitions of the terms of reference of the problem, identification of sectors where workers are actually protected, as well as an inventory of the problematic areas or thresholds where the non-protected workers can be identified. In doing so, the question of what alternatives exist for labour law to encompass these workers can be better approached. It would also be useful to examine the relationship between labour law and other juridical branches concerning labour, such as civil law, commercial law and public service law.

It was noted by the ILO that:

1. The employment relationship was a universal notion and a current issue: there exists in all countries a legal relationship between employer and employee, founded on a similar basis;
2. The lack of focus of the employment relationship is a universal problem: in almost all the countries studied there are dependent workers who do not have the same protection as salaried workers;
3. National situations are both diverse and dynamic.

The first two points lead us to reflect on the necessity and the practicability of international action. The third point raises the question of whether an international instrument could be flexible enough and could be used as a framework to suit different situations in different countries.

B. The Universality of the Employment Relationship

In the course of the ILO's work and discussions it became apparent that the notion of the employment relationship (as a relationship between employer and worker, for paid services, and under certain conditions) could be found globally with basic similarities.

In addition, the studies carried out by the ILO highlighted the fact that work within an employment relationship continues to be the dominant situation in many countries, despite recent changes which have taken place in the world of work and enterprises.[3] Moreover, it has been noted in industrialised countries and in some Central European countries that the employment relationship is not just predominant but is durable. Furthermore, it appears that countries which have stable employment relationships are characterised by steady economic progress, which proves once again that 'employment protection is not incompatible with economic progress'.[4] On the other hand, in countries with a less structured sector and high unemployment, the situation is different. But even in these countries, salaried

---

[3] In the case of France, for instance, a recent report deals with the feeling of insecurity of salaried workers which affects a large number of workers, but does not question the employment relationship as such. See Conseil de l'emploi, des revenus et de la cohésion sociale, *La sécurité de l'emploi face aux défies des transformations économiques*, Rapport no 5 (Paris, CERC, La documentation Française, 2005), available at: http://www.cerc.gouv.fr/rapports/rapport5cerc.pdf.

[4] P. Auer and S. Cazes, 'The Resilience of the Long-Term Employment Relationship: Evidence from the Industrialized Countries' (2000) 139 *International Labour Review* 379. See also S. Cazes and A. Nesporova, 'Labour Market Flexibility in the Transition Countries: How Much is too Much?' (2001) 140 *International Labour Review* 305.

workers often represent a significant proportion of the workforce, and the laws which cover them invariably serve as a point of reference for the level of protection given to other workers.

It is clear, in any case, that the best legislative labour protection is awarded within the framework of an employment relationship, but this does not exclude the existence of limited protection for independent workers as well.

On this note, the report submitted to the Meeting of Experts in 2000[5] based on the results of the national studies raised the possibility of developing basic protection for all workers beyond fundamental protection. Not only is this basic protection justified by itself, but it makes it feasible to give some immediate protection to workers currently in limbo between dependent and independent work. By the same token, this newly afforded protection can discourage attempts to disguise the employment relationship.

Basic protection for all workers already exists in international law and in the legislation of several countries. A number of ILO instruments,[6] in addition to international labour declarations and constitutional provisions, are addressed to workers without distinction.

The subject of the boundaries of labour law can be approached by visualising the concentricity of the current situation in international law and in the legislation of several countries. They have in fact an inner circle of basic protection covering all workers (including independent workers) within the limits of what is considered employment and not private or business activities; and an outer circle of extended protection, again within the limits of the employment relationship.

---

[5] *Meeting of Experts on Workers in Situations Needing Protection (The Employment Relationship: Scope)—Basic Technical Document* (Geneva, International Labour Office, 2000), available at: http://www.ilo.org/public/english/dialogue/ifpdial/publ/mewnp/.

[6] In particular, the expression 'workers without distinction' can be found in the Freedom of Association and Protection of the Right to Organise Convention, 1948 (No 87), Art 2. However, other ILO instruments are also applicable to all workers, including Conventions concerning: (a) fundamental human rights at work (e.g. the Forced Labour Convention, 1930 (No 29), the Equal Remuneration Convention, 1951 (No 100), the Abolition of Forced Labour Convention, 1957 (No 105), the Discrimination (Employment and Occupation) Convention, 1958 (No 11), the Minimum Age Convention, 1973 (C 138) and the Worst Forms of Child Labour Convention, 1999 (No 182); (b) protecting 'persons' or 'workers' (e.g. the Human Resources Development Convention, 1975 (No 142), the Workers with Family Responsibilities Convention, 1981 (No 156), and the Vocational Rehabilitation and Employment (Disabled Persons) Convention, 1983 (No 159); (c) regulating activities or processes at the workplace (e.g. the Benzene Convention, 1971 (No 136), and the Asbestos Convention, 1986 (C 162); and (d) instruments on the employment of children an young persons (e.g. those already mentioned and many others on minimum age, night work and medical examination of young persons). Furthermore, some instruments are specifically applicable, also, to the self-employed (e.g. the Social Policy (Basic Aims and Standards) Convention, 1962 (No 117), the Rural Workers' Organisations Convention, 1975 (No 141), the Labour Administration Convention, 1978 (C 150), and the Safety and Health in Construction Convention, 1988 (C 167). For further details, see G. Minet, *Coverage of Contract Labour by International Labour Standards* (Geneva, ILO, Internal Document, 1999).

C. The Universality of the Problem

The national studies and the work carried out by the Meeting of Experts in 2000, followed by discussions during the 2003 ILC, have all highlighted the fact that the lack of labour protection of a large number of dependent workers is universal and has become even more commonplace over the last two decades. These workers can be those who are not recognised within an employment relationship and who consequently lack the accompanying protection, or they can be wage earners who are in a complex 'triangular' employment relationship due to the fact that they are linked to an employer who, in turn, provides services for a user. The lack of protection in this case could occur if it is unclear who the real employer is, what the workers' rights are, or who is responsible for these rights.

In the work of the ILO, the following different situations concerning the lack of protection are mentioned: the 'disguised' employment relationship; the 'ambiguous' employment relationship; and the complex 'triangular' employment relationship.[7]

It is important to stress that the lack of employment protection erodes the very base of national and international labour law, from the moment that the employment relationship is set aside.

The work of the ILO has also highlighted this phenomenon's negative repercussions which go beyond individual and private employers' and workers' interests to constitute a social and political problem which affects not only workers and their families but enterprises, the state and society in general.[8] This public aspect of this question alone should suffice in ensuring that the

---

[7] 'Disguised employment occurs when the employer treats a person who is an employee as other than an employee so as to hide his or her true legal status ...

... An ambiguous employment relationship exists whenever work is performed or services are provided under conditions that give rise to an actual and genuine doubt about the existence of an employment relationship ...

'... In the case of so-called triangular employment relationships [...] the work or services of the worker are provided to a third party (the user) . . .': *Conclusions Concerning the Employment Relationship* (Geneva, International Labour Office, 2003), no 7–9, available at: http://www.ilo.org/public/english/dialogue/ifpdial/ll/er_conc.htm; *Provisional Record No 21: Report of the Committee on the Employment Relationship* (International Labour Conference, 91st Session, Geneva, International Labour Office, 2003), at 53, available at: http://www.ilo.org/public/english/standards/relm/ilc/ilc91/pdf/pr-21.pdf., also included in *Report V(1)*, above n 1, at 73. See also, at the same web address, *Report V: The Scope of the Employment Relationship* (International Labour Conference, 91st Session, Geneva, International Labour Office, 2003), 26, 29 and 39.

[8] In reference to employees with fixed-term contracts, the CERC report states at 21 that many of them 'have difficulty in obtaining bank loans or mortgages because of their status, as the banks and lenders' aim is to cover any event of non-repayment or nonpayment due to the risk of unemployment at the end of their contract'. Imagine the situation becoming even more dramatic when these workers are employed by private employment agencies or by successive subcontractors or, even worse, when the fact that they are employees is brought into question. See also *Report V*, above n 7, at 6–13.

employment relationship is not discussed solely in the interests of those directly concerned.

The findings of the ILO in this area were based at the outset on the abovementioned descriptive studies of specific national realities, with particular attention to certain sectors and categories of workers: taxi and lorry drivers; construction workers; garment sector workers; sales assistants in large department stores, supermarkets and hypermarkets; and private security companies.[9] Although they were not exhaustive, the studies also provided insight into the problem of the lack of protection in the way it affects women. The findings of these studies were upheld by the experts' and delegates' statements at the International Labour Conference.[10]

In specialised literature or in the media, these problems are often principally associated with new technologies or with 'new forms of work', as though the expression 'employment relationship' is obsolete or inappropriate for these new situations. However, studies show that authentic, duly protected employment relationships exist in traditional as well as in new employment situations. Dependent employment also exists which is either 'disguised' or 'ambiguous' in both the high-tech sectors and in the traditional sectors, and as much in new employment as in traditional employment. Enterprises also exist where traditional and new employment coexist, protected or not. Dependent, unprotected employment is even integrated into large national or transnational enterprises. No workplace is immune to this phenomenon. Thus, both protected employment relationships and unprotected employment are universal, either because of a lack of focus in legislation, or because of a lack of respect for or misapplication of the law. Moreover, the type, frequency and intensity of the problems vary depending on the country, or even within countries.

D. Regulation of the Employment Relationship in Comparative law: Uniformity and Diversity

Regarding the global character of the employment relationship, there is not only the fact that this legal notion and the problems around it are found everywhere. The universality of the employment relationship can also be appreciated in comparative law, where it is a common issue, often constructed on similar terms, although significant variants exist depending on the specific juridical tradition under study. This fact is borne out in the ILO report which took into consideration the legislation of more than 60 countries with different juridical traditions from different regions of the world.[11]

---

[9] *Ibid.*
[10] *Provisional Record No 21*, above n 7.
[11] *Report V(1)*, above n 1, ch II.

Legislation may contain references to the employment relationship itself and the scope of it, but it can also include provisions tending to facilitate the determination of the existence of an employment relationship.

Legislation in some countries identifies substantial characteristics of the employment relationship and highlights the criteria or the factors distinguishing it, such as dependence, subordination, direction, control, or the fact that workers offer their services for another person, ie the employer.

However, there exists other legislation which defines the employment relationship in a purely descriptive manner and, in some cases, in a roundabout way. Such legislation simply states that the employment relationship is one that exists between employer and employee, without explaining its specificities. In countries with this form of regulation it is left to the corresponding case law to detail the standard in concrete cases, having recourse to 'test' cases.

The same situation occurs concerning the parties to the employment relationship. In some countries the legislation defines employer and employee, often in the same terms that are stated in the definition of the employment relationship, or which complete it. However, in countries which have 'descriptive' definitions, the law states in practical terms that an employer is the person who employs an employee, and an employee is the person who works for an employer.

In connection with the criteria which define the employment relationship, some countries also resort to specific indicators to assess whether such a relationship exists or not.

Often, judges elaborate these indicators, but they can also be included in the law, as in the case of South Africa, or they can result from dialogue between the interested sectors, as in Ireland.

Nevertheless, independently of the way the employment relationship is defined, and from the official criteria used to define it or even the indicators used, it appears that the idea of the employment relationship is similar and functional worldwide. It is precisely this universal common understanding of the employment relationship which allows for comparisons to be made between the legislation of different countries and enables us to base our reflection of labour law boundaries on concrete facts.

To establish the existence of an employment relationship—regardless of how it is defined—gives rise to the problem of the scope of personal application of its regulation.

In general, legislation on the employment relationship is applicable to salaried workers, even if some categories of workers or workers of certain categories of enterprises (in particular small and medium-sized enterprises) are excluded, or if some laws create special status for a particular category of worker. The trend has been towards an expansion of the scope of the application of the law. For example, this trend has materialised as clauses which also cover homeworkers, in countries where they were previously outside the scope of application of the law (Chile) or where there was a need to reaffirm that they were within the scope of application of the law (as in Finland and in Australia). On the subject of homeworkers, some laws specify that dealings of buying and selling of raw materials and processed goods between the same two persons can constitute an employment relationship.

With the intention of making protection for salaried workers more effective, many countries have simplified in their legislation the form of the employment relationship and provided measures to assist workers in proving the existence of such a relationship between them and their employer. The most outstanding point of these measures is probably the general recognition of the principle of the *primacy* of fact. According to this principle, the existence of an employment relationship depends first and foremost on the actual terms of the relationship between employer and worker, and not on the name they give to their contract. In some countries, this principle and the need to protect workers even gave way to a presumption that for an employment relationship to exist, it was sufficient to prove that one person provided services for another, unless the employer was able to prove otherwise.

The question of the scope of protection at work is often treated in relation to the lack of substantial rights for workers. However, the lack of protection as a matter of procedure is just as important in practice where the competence of the labour courts is limited to conflicts concerning the employment relationship. As such, dependent workers who are deemed to be without such a relationship may not have access to labour courts either.

The work of the ILO refers to the figuratively named 'triangular' relationship, although in these situations the bilateral relationship between employer and employee should not be called into question, and consequently the employee should be entitled to protection. However, the presence of a user poses questions such as the true identity of the employer and the possible responsibilities of the user *vis-à-vis* the worker's rights. Moreover, a preliminary question could even be asked: whether the apparent triangular relationship is in fact 'triangular', or whether the apparent user is in reality the employer.

At first this issue seems obvious and in some way dated. However, a recent judicial decision in the United Kingdom reminds us that this is still a current question. The decision concerned a person who was registered with an employment agency and assigned to work as a cleaner at a council-run hostel for people with mental health problems. After several years of service and following an incident at the hostel, the person was withdrawn from the centre at the behest of the council. The agency then informed her that they would no longer be finding work for her. The person had been put in a curious position which ended up dividing the opinion of the courts: she had been registered by the agency under a 'temporary worker agreement' which made it clear that its provisions 'shall not give rise to a contract of employment' between the agency and the worker, or the worker and the client. Having lodged a complaint for unfair dismissal, the following decisions were made: (a) a first instance tribunal found that, in the absence of a contract of employment, she had not been employed by the agency or by the council; (b) the Employment Appeal Tribunal held that she had been employed by the agency, because of its considerable control over her and the mutuality of obligation between the agency and the worker; (c) the Court of Appeal decided that a contract of service could be implied between the council and the worker if there had been an 'irreducible minimum of mutual obligations for a contract of service'. Thus, the Court of Appeal held that the Employment Tribunal had erred in holding that she was not an employee of the council because there had been no express contract between her and the council and, as such, the Tribunal had failed to address the possibility that there was an implied contract of service between the applicant and the council.[12]

The theme of triangular relationships is of great importance as this type of employment relationship represents a serious challenge for labour law today due to their proliferation—even at international level—and their capacity to generate diverse and dynamic forms of work where the conditions and responsibilities are established only with great difficulty. When the triangular relationship is not efficiently regulated the workers in question remain outside the protection of labour legislation or are poorly protected.

The comparative examination showed a relatively minor legislative development in triangular relationships, with sharp contrasts between countries. Moreover, existing legislation is not always efficient.

There have also been declarations from enterprises, as well as framework agreements between large enterprises and international union organisations, concerning triangular employment relationships although they seem to be, in general, at a preliminary stage.

E. Refocusing the Employment Relationship

Although the problem of the lack of focus in the employment relationship is universally acknowledged, it is interesting to highlight the efforts which have been made in many countries to adapt and adjust the scope of the legislation, to which we can add the important judicial decisions and agreements, such as the abovementioned framework agreements.

---

[12] *Dacas v Brook Street Bureau (UK) Ltd* [2004] EWCA Civ 217, and M. Rubinstein, 'Highlights' (2004) 33 *Industrial Relations Law Reports* 345, at 358–60.

In general, legislation confines itself within the traditional boundaries of the employment relationship as it stands in each country. However, some national provisions seem to step outside these limits.

French labour legislation for example, due to the economic dependence of certain categories of workers, assimilates them to the category of wage earners. Such is the case of salespersons who are supplied with goods exclusively or quasi-exclusively by one industrial or commercial enterprise only; or those who receive orders or goods to be processed on behalf of one industrial or commercial enterprise only, in premises supplied or agreed to by the enterprise or industry and at rates imposed by them; or the non-salaried managers of branches of processing industries.[13] On this subject, the French Court of Cassation recognised—in three separate rulings of the same date and concerning the same transport company—that the protection of labour legislation covered three franchised workers who worked in the distribution sector in accordance with a contract established by the franchisor, who should have been given copies of signed contracts with the clients. The Chambre Social stated that once the conditions established under Article L781–1 of the legislation were met, they were hence deemed applicable regardless of the contract's statements, without there being any need to establish the existence of a subordination link.[14]

The 2004 Portuguese labour legislation has, in turn, partially widened its scope of application to economically dependent workers. In fact, Article 13 renders the legislation's principles, notably in the area of laws relating to human rights, equality, non-discrimination, and safety and health at work, applicable to comparable contracts (*contratos equiparados*), that is to say, contracts whose object is the supply of services without judicial subordination but in economically dependent situations regarding the activity's beneficiary.

Italian legislation has already made great headway in search of adequate protection for workers who carry out 'coordinated and continuous' work, especially those workers who are independent with no subordination links, and are better recognised as 'parasubordinates'. The law dated 4 February 2003 anticipates the adoption of provisions for the 'protection of the worker's dignity and safety, and in particular, cover for maternity, ill health, and misfortune, as well as safety at the workplace, and within the framework of collective interests'.

Hence, comparative law shows, on the one hand, the existence of a stock of common notions and rules, or even of a common direction based on the employment relationship, and, on the other hand, the differences from one country to another in the way the employment relationship is regulated,

---

[13] France, ss L.781–1, L.782–1 of the Labour Code.
[14] Rulings Nos 50105034, 35 and 36 of 4 Dec. 2001. See *Libération*, 28 Jan. 2002, and [2002] *Droit Social* 162–3, quoted in *Report V*, above n 7, at 64, n 42.

countries which are determined by their own traditional legislation, the evolution of individual employment relationships, or social and economic circumstances. The lack of protection on a national level is also variable. In certain countries, the deficiencies are principally in the legislation itself, whilst in others lack of respect for and uneven application of the legislation are among the most serious problems. The coexistence of similarities and differences between the countries confirms the need for and viability of an international response, but at the same time, it indicates that such a response must be extremely supple and that its main goal should be its orientation.

3. THE POSSIBLE INTERNATIONAL RESPONSE: A RECOMMENDATION

Successive debates at the ILO helped to air ideas and prepare the way for the adoption of an international standard on the employment relationship. In 2003, the Conference Commission was in favour of this response to complement and support the responses that should be given by the member states at the national level.

The idea is this: the member states share the same problems—the lack of protection for workers who are in fact employees but are not recognised as such, and workers linked by triangular relationships which are not adequately regulated. The Commission therefore requested that governments develop a national policy framework, in consultation with their social partners, which would assess and address the various issues relating to the scope of the employment relationship. Such a policy should have as its goals: to provide workers and employers with clear guidance concerning the employment relationship, in particular the distinction between dependent workers and self-employed persons; to provide effective appropriate protection for workers; to combat disguised employment; and to provide access to appropriate resolution mechanisms to determine the status of workers. In a conclusion which specifically concerned the boundaries of labour law, the Commission declared that this national policy should not interfere with genuine commercial or independent contracting.[15]

This last point, which had already been mentioned in the 2000 declaration of experts, answers the employers' reiterated position that regulating the employment relationship could interfere with free commercial activities and in particular with independent employment.

However, the ILO reports explicitly distinguish between an employment relationship, as flexible as it is, and a civil or commercial relationship established to engage the services of a person outside the employment relationship.

---

[15] *Report V(1)*, above n 1, § 17, 75.

Of course, this crucial distinction leads us to ask the questions: what are the boundaries between them? what is an employment relationship? what constitutes a civil, commercial or other kind of relationship?

National action alone is not sufficient to approach a problem of this magnitude. This was clear to the Conference in 2003 and to the 2004 Governing Body Session from the moment the point was included on the agenda to prepare an international instrument. Many member states will not be in a position to undertake efficient action by themselves, nor will they be willing unilaterally to undertake measures in this regard without assurance that other member states will do the same. Thus, concerted action with the assistance of the ILO could prove to be more long lasting, viable and more efficient, equal and productive.

In its conclusions, the Employment Relationship Commission detailed the form that the international response should take, and its contents.

The conclusions of the Commission were oriented mostly towards the adoption of an international labour Recommendation, although several governmental delegates were in favour of an international labour Convention.

An international labour convention is an instrument likely to be ratified and, consequently, able to create obligations upon member states, as outlined in the ILO's Constitution. On the contrary, a Recommendation is an instrument which contains only directions for the member states.[16]

A Recommendation can be of significant value and impact despite the fact that its application would be purely voluntary on the part of the member states. This may well be the case in the area of employment relationships where there are important similarities but also a lot of diversity between national situations, with important changes taking place.

A. A Policy

The problem concerning the employment relationship, as it currently stands, cannot be dealt with through an international instrument which will obligate member states to define it in some way, by developing certain presumptions or other ways of proving it, or by imposing obligations, in the case of triangular relationships, on the employer and the user. At this stage, there are no elements from the international debate justifying the formulation of definitions, presumptions or obligations which are universal and yet adaptable to the specific situations in different countries. Similarly, the revision of law highlights important differences in the legislation of different

---

[16] See ILO Constitution, Art 19.

countries, in the way it is approached and its technical aspects, although some similarities may exist. On the other hand, the main problem in some countries is probably that of a lack of respect for or a lack of application of the law, and, consequently, the priority in these countries would be, more than legislative reform, setting up or reinforcing existing mechanisms to apply the law, and improving access to the judicial system.

Experience has shown that the practices of enterprises utilising labour are flexible and diverse. For this reason isolated legislative or administrative measures will not be sufficient. Sustained political action would be preferable, in particular one that can be formulated and re-examined depending on the particular needs of the country. From this point of view, the discussions on the employment relationship during the 2003 ILC, and in particular the opinions of the government representatives, convey a clear understanding of the importance of the problem and the need to tackle it via a long-term policy.

B. Mechanisms

Such a long-term policy should be formulated with the help of a transparent mechanism of observation of the realities of labour in consultation with the social partners. This procedure will allow governments to adopt efficient measures to clarify and adjust the scope of legislation, as dictated by the particular conditions in each country. In this way, a possible Recommendation should provide governments with a procedural approach for tackling the employment relationship problem.

The normal practice in treating legal problems is to propose concrete legal or administrative solutions, such as legislative reforms or the improvement of mechanisms for the application of the law. However, on this issue, such standard actions under discussion in this chapter may not be sufficient. In many countries, the lack of protection for dependent workers is a daily occurrence. Workers often have no alternative but to work without protection, or not work at all, to accept their situation, or to assume by themselves the difficult and discouraging task of asking for justice from the authorities in charge of upholding the law.

Nevertheless, some recent experiences point towards a different kind of action, similar to that proposed for the Recommendation.

In South Africa, for example, the legislative reforms in 1995–1997 were deemed to have exacerbated the problem of the lack of protection for workers. In particular, many wage earners were 'converted' to independent employees. This was the case of one worker in a contractor enterprise specialising in the manufacture and installation of fitted cupboards. He had been persuaded to resign and was later taken on by the same enterprise as an independent worker. In a revealing decision, the labour court stated that the worker's new contract was a sham, noting that the worker carried out tasks that were an integral part of the service performed by the entrepreneur. The recent evolution in this country has been witness to intense and productive tripartite debate, resulting in the adoption of labour law reform in 2002. This reform contained provisions which were intended to clarify the scope of application of the law (with indicators and a presumption). Furthermore, the minister was authorised to adapt the scope of labour law and to classify any category of workers as employees for the purpose of labour legislation. But what is especially important is that, from a procedural point of view, this reform had been the subject of tripartite consultations and dialogue on different levels, and had the support of the National Economic Development and Labour Council (NEDLAC) and the Millennium Labour Council (MLC).

In Ireland, the difficulty in distinguishing between dependent and independent workers was addressed during the 2000–2002 national negotiations between the government and the employers' and workers' organisations concerning the Programme for Prosperity and Fairness (PPF). The decision was taken to create a tripartite working group to tackle the questions relating to workers' status (Employment Status Group). This group then produced a set of indicators to distinguish between employees and the self-employed. It was also decided to introduce these indicators as a code of practice and not embody them in a law (in South Africa, it was the law which required the NEDLAC to prepare and publish a similar code of practice).

The 2005 ILO report also mentions the experience of the Canadian Committee of Experts (created in Quebec in 2002) in preparing a report, finalised in 2003, on the need for social protection of persons in non-traditional work situations. The Committee's competence covered a widespread group of workers which did not quite coincide with that which interested the employment relationship commission. But the creation of this Committee, its form of work and its report is a good example of what steps could be taken, amongst others, towards the formulation and application of a policy specifically in the area of the employment relationship.

C. Measures

A possible, Recommendation on the employment relationship can be used to orient the member states in determining suitable measures to adopt according to their country's specific needs in the context of workers' protection.

The 2005 ILO report and the 2003 ILC conclusions contained suggestions on the content of the possible Recommendation. However, the decision on this belongs solely to the constituents who, according to the Standing Orders of the Conference, have two opportunities to express their views. First, the governments answer the questionnaire included in this report. To do this, they are invited to consult with the most representative employers' and workers' organisations (they are obligated to do this if they have ratified the Tripartite Consultation (International Labour Standards) Convention, 1976 (No. 144)). The Office will then prepare a draft Recommendation based on these replies, to be submitted to the Conference in 2006.[17] Secondly, the draft will be the subject of debate during the Conference in a tripartite context, after which the constituents will make their decisions concerning the adoption of the Recommendation.

4. CONCLUSION

After a long process of discussion and research, the ILO has arrived at a certain consensus on the terms of reference of the problem of non-protection of numerous dependent workers. It has been established that the lack of focus of labour legislation and its defective observance or application leave a margin of uncertainty surrounding the employment status of such workers who could in fact be linked by an employment relationship which is not apparent. However, reservations from the employers' group remain.

Taking into account the global character of both the legal notion of the employment relationship and the problem of non-protection of dependent workers, the ILO put this issue on the agenda for the possible adoption of a Recommendation on the employment relationship.

The ILO experience and its concern for standard-setting action at the international level, while taking into account national differences, can also contribute to the debate on the scope of labour law. This scope can be viewed as two concentric circles. The outer circle concerns the systematic protection of employees; its boundaries are the same as those of the employment relationship framework. The work of the ILO does not take a precise position on these limits but rather promotes the adoption of a national policy on the employment relationship. The ILO also suggests a methodology which allows countries to define the employment relationship and indicates the criteria, indicators and proofs of the existence of an employment relationship. The inner circle is of more restricted protection and refers to the scope of labour law in reference not only to employees but to all workers without distinction. For a comprehensive approach to the issue of protection of workers and a broader discussion of the boundaries of labour law, the situation of workers who are not dependent and basic protection for all workers remains to be examined.

---

[17] The draft recommendation will be available in early 2006 at the ILO website, at the address mentioned above, n 7.

17

The Employer and the Worker: The Need for a Comparative and International Perspective

JEAN-CLAUDE JAVILLIER*

FROM A COMPARATIVE and international point of view, we need to have real and complete knowledge of what is happening in labour relations and labour law, linking the definitions and methods with contexts and practice. In the industrialised countries, many academics specialised in labour law point to a growing crisis and even to the elimination of current traditional protection for workers. Seen from Geneva and the ILO, it is not always easy to find a common language and have a clear and objective picture of what is happening in law and in practice around the world—even on one particular continent or region. We need to avoid developing new theories or conclusions, which are linked mainly or only to one specific context such as, for example, developing countries and the post-industrial relations system.

The definitions of employer and worker, and of enterprise and employment, are at the heart of evolution or revolution in the field not only of labour law and industrial relations, but also of social security. From a geopolitical as well as from a legal point of view, there is no longer any such thing as a 'closed' world. More than ever, we need to learn from each other, taking into account not only the European and the (North) American experience, but also the African, Arabic and Asian and Central and South American ones. Every country and every system of law uses concepts deeply rooted in its own history, culture and society. The legal concepts regarding both individual and collective labour relations have been broadly developed by legal experts as well as by legal practitioners. These concepts are

* Senior Adviser, International Institute for Labour Studies, ILO, Geneva. The views expressed by the author are not necessarily those of the ILO, an institution he is proud to serve. It is hoped that these views will contribute, in a necessarily modest way, to the consensus between employers, workers and governments to provide sustainable answers to the increasing challenges facing labour and social security law.

regarded as commonly accepted and well adapted. As always a comparative and critical view is vital and can help one face new challenges in an increasingly globalised economy. Employer and employee or worker (depending on the country) are basic concepts in labour and social security law as well as in various industrial relations systems. It could even be said that without employers and workers there would be no labour and social security law, now or in the future. And also no way of structuring industrial relations. The ILO is based on the existence and action of employers, workers and their organisations, promoting their own interests and strategies. Freedom of association is based on the full respect of the distinction between employers, workers and the state. However, there are several and very different technical ways to make use of (not only from a labour law point of view) these concepts. They do not have the same practical impact, being dependent on the economic and social context. In some countries, labour and social security mean little beyond a contract of employment between an employer and a worker which is at the very heart of legal subordination. The practical content of subordination can vary significantly. The border between the subordinated and independent worker has to be considered carefully as a function of the economic context and the scope of the rule of law.

Moreover, we have to remember that employers and workers have different views and strategies concerning labour law and social security, depending on their country, industry, legal system, culture and economic background. There are clearly different ways of reconciling productivity and protection, freedom and regulation. We can agree on the fact that boundaries between disciplines are either far less important, or far more complex, than they were during the nineteenth and twentieth centuries, both in law and in other technical areas.[1] In other words, the links between different branches of the law must be taken into account more seriously. The interaction between labour and social security law, company law, tax law, environmental law and consumer law seems to be increasing in daily life.[2] The concepts now have to be placed in a different perspective. It is also true that the human rights perspective has far more practical impact than previously, at national as well at regional and international level. But this perspective cannot be the only one for a labour lawyer, because it does not necessarily include all the technical content of labour issues.

---

[1] A lawyer cannot ignore the important developments taking place in science. Ethics also require reflection on the boundaries between topics in open societies which are increasingly under different influences and pressures.

[2] This seems especially true when considering the best way to obtain the effectiveness and efficiency of any rule and regulation. In many situations, it seems that to obtain the result, the best incentives or sanctions have to be found with the help of another discipline. Linking disciplines is one of the most important tasks for lawyers, from a theoretical as well as from a practical point of view.

From a comparative and international viewpoint, especially in the perspective of ILO action and influence, we need to take great care when discussing the scope of labour law and the impact of its classical basic concepts. In addition, we have to be wary of situations where prevailing conditions might lead some distinguished scholars (mostly in industrialised countries) to speak as prophets and announce the 'end' of labour law and social security.[3] It can be true that subordination has changed in relation to culture and technology in western (post-)industrialised countries. But even in this context, 'new' technologies result in an increase in some aspects of subordination workers' daily lives.[4] They also have an impact outside traditional labour relations, including on some major aspects of private and family life. Less subordination in the traditional legal way and more control in the new technical way. However, we need to have far greater knowledge and a fresh view of the definitions of worker and employer. The empirical approach is of the greatest importance (see section 1).

Nevertheless, labour and social security law, as a unique body and system,[5] is often questioned from both theoretical and practical points of view. There are other concepts and methods (that are not necessarily new) to be created and used than lawyers in industrialised countries might think, bearing in mind the always dual (employer/worker, subordination/freedom, blue collar/white collar, individual/collective) and actively conflictual (class/interest) concepts at the origins of labour law. Even in industrialised countries, new concepts and different categories emerge and are promoted in order to obtain more efficient social protection and easier adaptation to economic competition. As regards the dogmatic perspective (see section 2), one has to determine how the increasing pressure for adaptation and competition can be linked to a framework of protection and security. Do we need to re-examine the basic definitions and the traditional status given to labour and social security law? Do we need to reconsider the methods used to implement as well as to interpret labour and social security law?

The conclusion of this chapter describes the work of the International Labour Organisation (see section 3) and shows that progress can be achieved by implementing current standards, using comparative labour and

---

[3] One should perhaps consider that in some countries (more than in others?) legal experts are more accustomed to such broad and radical views. In this respect, France could rank as one of the leading countries. On a regular basis, distinguished legal scholars publish papers stressing the approaching end of labour law. The favourite expression is 'Should labour law be burned?'. The question remains whether the French favour *la réforme (reform), la révolution (revolution)*, or more radically *le bûcher* (the stake) or *la guillotine*.

[4] Computers and mobile phones offer the best and the worse examples regarding individual freedom and privacy.

[5] If considered as such. Everybody knows the difference in approach regarding the existence of such a discipline. Even in countries where there is a consensus on the existence of labour and social security law, the current debate centres on the relationship between labour law and employment law, and between work and activity.

social security law, as well as promoting a decent work strategy. The linkage between all these elements is of primary importance. Various and difficult challenges lie ahead, but there are also great opportunities for employers, workers and governments. We need to have a truly universal approach, a serious perception of the diversity of the situations, and a common will to understand each other. In no way should we consider a national or regional approach as universal. A globalised economy does not bring uniformity. Reconciling local and global means starting with realities and conditions of work on the ground for people in daily ('real') life. Employers and employees, who work in such different situations, and governments, need to find their own way of injecting new dynamism into the employment relationship. We also need to use the decent work concept in a concrete way to promote innovative solutions, especially if the traditional labour and social security perspective has too limited an impact.

1. THE EMPIRICAL APPROACH

It is always very dangerous to speak of realities without sufficient knowledge of what they are and how they are evolving, especially in an age of rapid technological progress and legal change. Governments need to have a real picture of labour relations as well as of the employment situation. In other words, several indicators are needed;[6] statistics play a vital role.[7] However, they must be well understood and used. Precise definitions are required of employer, enterprise, worker and self-employed person. Obviously, the definitions are not exclusive to labour and social security law. They have significant application in tax law and environmental law, among others. There is always a danger of thinking in a closed world. Those in their own 'small world' have the impression that only one definition applies; that there is a unique status for the creation and use of a technical definition. Even in law, we know that the same definition can have different meanings depending on the discipline and even on the law to be implemented.

Statistics are invaluable to measure the relative importance of a phenomenon or a new development. When comparing situations between countries,

---

[6] The way indicators are built is obviously of vital importance. We should ask those working in different contexts to build their indicators around the way they work and want to build an employment relationship. We need to make greater use of a capability approach when considering what Amartya Sen has developed: see A. Sen, 'Work and Rights' (2000) 139 *International Labour Review* 119.

[7] A lawyer would add: even if statistics are not (entirely) reliable. There is always a tension regarding issues related to the statistical perception of the implementation of law. The danger increases if there is a dominant quantitative approach on the way law (and perhaps every question) functions in society. Various elements of law cannot be determined from this point of view. This has to be explained clearly to all non-lawyers and especially to economists.

we need to take in account the many differences that exist. Even though the ILO has played an important role in the drawing up of the methodologies used by statisticians on labour issues, it is not so easy to compare situations and developments around the world. Would things change if labour lawyers developed a greater degree of practical understanding between themselves on definitions such as employer/worker? Or for 'self-employed'? We are always discovering how different a definition and the way it is used can be in labour law. There will be no common understanding if we cannot explain the exact meaning of a technical concept. This is particularly true when preparing a legal instrument at international level, even if, to reach consensus, we always need to maintain a certain degree of ambiguity on limited legal issues. Those who helped develop standards at national, regional and international levels know the delicate balance between what has to be precise and what has to be implied but not explicitly written or even said. This is the art of the unspoken which plays so important a role in law as well as in diplomacy.

We also need a sociological perspective when speaking of realities and development in law. Employer and employee, enterprise and employment, contract of employment and self-employment have very different meanings in the real world, depending on the context, especially the economic and technological context. The lawyer always has to have concepts and categories in mind, and has to take into account how people work in 'real life'. It is of the greatest importance to look at how these citizens perceive the law, especially labour and social security law. For example, the lack of implementation of some, if not all, of the provisions of an act or a labour code has to be carefully screened. What are the elements that cause ineffectiveness? Many reasons have to be taken into account such as, for example, the complexity of the rules, the resistance of employers (individually or collectively), the weakness of the state, especially the absence of a labour inspectorate, the difficulty for employers and/or workers to take legal action, as well as a poor sentencing record on violations by courts. Obviously the employers' and workers' points of view can differ sharply on that topic in any country. But we have learned from the sociology of comparative labour law that the lack of implementation of core labour conventions and especially violations of freedom of association and the right of collective bargaining, as well as discrimination, plus weaknesses in the industrial relations system, affect the organisation of labour relations based on the employer and worker concept, Theories can be developed on the diversity of situations relating to the self-employed. We know that in developing countries many of those working in the informal economy would love to be fully recognised as employers and/or workers. In many countries, people organise in order to escape the black or grey legal area. The absence of rule of law makes provision of benefits impossible. Many would like to act as employers or to work as salaried women and men. But their enemies have names: violence, corruption and poverty. In such situations, it cannot be said that the employer/employee concepts are not relevant and of no use. It should be stressed that the opposite also applies. In such situations, the question is not the lack of modernity of the labour and social security law. It is the governance issue that must be solved first. This must be clear to lawyers who live in an environment with a rule of law and a system of industrial relations.

The complexity of legislation and how to implement it in a special context can be, in some situations, the reason for the lack of capacity to implement the basic concepts of labour and social security law. This can be especially true for Small and Medium-sized Enterprises (SMEs). From a sociological point of view, the definition of both employer and worker has to be considered in relation to the organisational and technical contexts. Procedural rules can be far more complex in big enterprises than in SMEs. The perception of labour law, and the way to implement it, is not the same if the employer is the owner of the enterprise or if he/she is the manager of the plant. The law has to help everyone find a sustainable way of solving the problems arising from concrete and daily labour relations. The sociological as well as the psychological context of the rules are of the greatest practical importance. Generally speaking, the specificities of the situations regarding SMEs have to be taken in account by legislators in many countries at both regional and international levels. The same basic principle can be expressed in different ways; the same result can be achieved by different rules, especially procedural rules. Technical alternatives are at the centre of any legal adaptation. But obviously, this goal is not always so easy to achieve politically or practically. The perception of the situation is frequently not the same from the employers' and the workers' points of view. The real reason not to take legal action, for example, can be of a very different nature, even if both sides agree on the lack of relevance of a labour tribunal's method of proceeding. When deciding how to take into account the full diversity of situations, it is not often easy to 'adapt' the rules, which were perhaps designed for big and mostly industrial enterprises. Nevertheless, in many countries, the social partners find appropriate ways of dealing with legal creativity, which is not always to the taste of lawyers.

2. THE DOGMATIC PERSPECTIVE

Taking results first, we need to take into account two goals, which are fundamentally linked to labour social security law: the need to make workers' rights effective (linking individual and collective rights) and the need to promote employment and enterprise. The linkage between individual situations and institutional perspectives is paramount, ie the basic issues of industrial relations, democracy at the workplace and in society are at the centre of the debate related to the definitions of employer and worker.

The basic goals of labour law have always been a matter of debate between experts, especially in Europe. The role of ideology has weighed heavily in this branch of law. Since the early nineteenth century, the meaning of 'worker' has differed sharply depending on the ideology. To a great extent, labour law was built and developed from the point of view of the class struggle, and concerned workers' rights, not employers' rights. This is a branch of law which is especially concerned with opposing capitalism. The ultimate goal, using labour law as a weapon, was to eliminate the employer, capitalist exploitation and capitalist organisation of society. Through legislation, the workers could oppose the power of the employer and impose their views. In this respect, the debate on collective autonomy was viewed as dangerous by both radicals and revolutionaries. Collective agreement could be seen as a betrayal, promoting collaboration with the class enemy. But the distinction between employer and worker does not feature such a radical objective. It has to be looked at more pragmatically. The goal is, not to eliminate, but to establish a more favourable balance of power on the workers' side. In fact, labour law has always featured a double intent. On one hand, it has to protect the worker against all kinds of abuses from the employer who holds capitalist power. On the other, labour law has to promote employment and organise the enterprise.[8] There is a will to structure individual relations as well as to institutionalise collective relations between employers and workers. The labour law coin has two sides: protection of the worker and promotion of the enterprise, through legislation and collective independence. Legitimacy, rights and duties are conferred to both sides: workers and employers. Such opposing views have not gone away, according to lawyers and non-lawyers debating the future of labour law.

In order to find alternatives to the radical opposition between employer and workers, many experiments have taken place on various sides and with contrasting ideologies. The question asked has always been the same: does labour law have the intent and/or can it help solve this radical dilemma? Could we use labour law in a different way, differently organising the relations between 'employer' and 'worker' for want of better legal definitions? The issue is one of finding a specific way to organise production and structure relations. The cooperative movement has always

---

[8] See E. Vinales, L. Greco, M. Angel Oliveros, F. Villamayor and R. Falchetti, *Derecho de los Empleadores. Estudio de Paises* (Santiago de Chile, OIT, 2002), 123; R. Falchetti, *La percepcion social del empresario, y sus derechos en la relacion labora* (Buenos Aires Paper of the OIT , 16 Sept. 2003), 30; H. Berg, *Rentabilidad de las Buenas Practicas Laborales* (Santiago de Chile, OIT-CPC, 2003), 64; A. Wisskirchen and C. Hess, *Employers' Handbook on ILO Standards-Related Activities* (Geneva, ACT/EMP, ILO, 2001), 141.

promoted new methods in organising labour relations and the rules related to these relations.[9] A new compromise could be struck between the need to promote employment and organise production, taking serious account of the need to protect workers. Do we need to implement special rules in order fully to take into account the cooperative philosophy and practice? Such special rules can deviate from classic labour law and have been adopted in many countries across the world. But there has been some discussion about the legitimacy of such derogation to the implementation of 'holistic' labour law protection for workers. Unions had to fight unfair use of the cooperative 'spirit' and special regulations that negated the protection established under general labour law. It could be a temptation for some employers to get round labour law and use the cooperative perspective in order to take advantage of exceptions, and of favourable state treatment, including less control by the labour inspectorate. In some countries, the cooperative philosophy could also be used to fight the right to unionise, or in a broader way freedom of association.

A debate of the same type has been initiated concerning enterprises with a special labour law situation due to their status as 'trend-setters'. The employer is considered a special case with a special confidential relationship with the workers. Not all countries have recognised this special situation for employers such as, for example, political parties, churches or non-governmental organisations. Legal experts have differing points of views on this issue. Some pragmatically accept the need to 'adapt', ie to derogate partly or broadly from the protection established in favour of the worker in a normal situation. The degree and the object of legal derogation (for individual as well as collective labour relations) depend on the level of confidence required by employers. Other experts stress the supremacy of labour law public order rules, especially those related to the protection of privacy and freedoms. Do labour laws or special rules limit those basic legal freedoms by taking into account the specificity of the employer? There are obviously very different ways of doing this. Judges have played a very important role in some countries on such issues. Some have tried to find a balanced and pragmatic way to heal the breach. Case law is not always easy to understand, especially from outside a country.[10] As often happens in labour law, there are very different technical ways to implement such a compromise. What judges can never allow is the intent to use such specificity of an

---

[9] See A.F. Pereira et al. (eds.), *Cooperativas: Mudanças, Oportunidades e Desafios* (Brasilia, OIT, 2001), 195.

[10] Comparative labour law is always a major challenge (i.e. Mission impossible). Who outside a country has a full understanding of its legislation, as well as its case law and collective agreements? The best we can do is to stress the main characteristics and trends, always linking them to those in the country who have a real knowledge of the situation. This is why the network between academics is of prime importance. The contribution of independent and respected lawyers is a condition for making comparative labour law and also for constantly improving any supervisory mechanism of international law (ILO included).

enterprise to get round labour laws and challenge basic rights and freedoms, such as the freedom of association and the basic individual freedom linked to the rule of law. If exceptions have to be admitted, it is always conditional on them being related and proportional to the specific goal laid down.

Lawyers are always facing problems related to the existence of a single concept with an abstract point of view, as well as to the complexity of reality, especially economic reality. This is not new, but globalisation and the emergence of a single market economy have created new technical and political challenges. Lawyers in many countries have challenged the limits of the very simple approach to the employer in labour law. They have also underlined the difference applied to the definition of worker, which is subject to the will to extend—or limit—the application of labour and social security law.[11]

From a technical point of view, the debate is far from easy. Among the questions to be considered by the lawyer, especially when appearing in court, is that of the employer. Who is the employer? Depending on the country and the industrial relations system, the answer given can have major consequences for the collective agreement to be implemented (or not), the competent tribunal, the authority with the right to dismiss the worker, the calculation of seniority rights, etc.

The law cannot take a limited view of any aspect of labour relations. When speaking of employers and workers, a great variety of contexts and relations are obviously included. The complexity of the situation of an enterprise has to be taken into account. The debate is far from new regarding the determination of the 'real' employer. The legal as well as the economic structure of the enterprise makes for a vast diversity of situations. Much case law is related to the necessity to find the employer who has the real power of decision and has to be declared responsible for the decisions taken relating to the individual as well as to collective rights and relations at plant level. With a far broader perspective and a philosophical point of view, the definition of 'indirect employer' has be considered as questioning the role of the state and its responsibility in implementing a policy favouring employment.[12]

Technically speaking, it is not easy to determine the direct impact on employment issues, especially in the public sector. In recent years, an important development has taken place around the world: states have privatised

---

[11] See G. Davidov, 'Who is a Worker?' (2005) 34 *Industrial Law Journal* 57.

[12] The Roman Catholic Church has underlined the importance and the duties of the 'indirect employer'. See Pontifical Council for Justice and Peace, *Compendium of the Social Doctrine of the Church* (Vatican City, Libreria Editrice Vaticana, 2004), especially 166, no 288). Indirect employers are 'those subjects—persons or institutions of various types—in a position to direct, at the national or international level, policies concerning labour and the economy' (*ibid.*).

many activities which were traditionally under their direct or indirect control and responsibility.[13] Such a move—from public to private employer—has had significant consequences on individual as well as on collective labour relations.

In some countries these changes have increased the scope of 'common' labour law (where public servants were not covered by the labour code, for instance). The distinction between 'private' and 'public' law—which is of such great importance in some legal systems—now seems to have far less importance in some countries. What are now the concrete and practical differences between a 'public' and a 'private' employer? From a managerial point of view, the 'public' side seems to implement many of the technical instruments used by the 'private' employer. The workers and their trade unions have pointed out how this move has the effect of reducing their rights and possibly of increasing stress at the workplace. This move from 'status' to 'contract' has introduced more flexibility in the management of the labour relations and also makes it more difficult for unions to organise due to the fact that not all workers have the same rights and tenure.

The diversification of the individual situations of workers and the development of precarious employment have had many consequences on industrial relations systems. But it would be wrong to say that this move—from status to contract—has had only a negative impact on workers' rights. In some countries it has strengthened the role of labour law:[14] workers are now demanding the implementation of the whole 'common' labour law, including, for example, the rules concerning health and safety and control by the labour inspectorate (which had been excluded on the grounds of state exception), and collective bargaining and the right to strike. This is also reflected in the way workers are asking courts to implement the law.[15] Clearly, there is no move which can be considered in a simplistic or unique way. The role of the state and the impact of the developments mentioned above seem to be far more complex, especially regarding the reciprocal influence between 'public' and 'private' employer.

It is not surprising in a globalised economy and a free market that the 'real' employer is not the one seen by the workers and the labour lawyer at

---

[13] There are no areas where such a move cannot take place. The move made by many states regarding the Armed Forces is an example. The privatisation of military activities has been carried out on a scale unthinkable some years ago, except by those who know their history (especially the 17th and 18th centuries). This development also has to be considered from a political as well as an ethical point of view, as to the role and the power of the state. There will undoubtedly be debate on public security and workers' rights relating to the military as well as to those working under a different status for the Armed Forces.

[14] Especially in countries where the distinction between 'status' and 'contract' divided the legal worlds for those working in public and private sector. Note that this distinction has never been as clear as legal experts would have wanted.

[15] This seems especially true for the Armed Forces. Actions in court are introduced on the basis of labour and social security law, even if there is special status. Actions are also based on common law rules and human rights regulations.

plant level. The question of 'who is' the owner of the enterprise is not simple. Is the 'real' employer in labour law the one with the right to decide, even indirectly, on the organisation and even the very existence of the enterprise? It is clearly a challenge for the unions and the workers' delegates to determine with whom they need or can have a dialogue (in a very broad sense[16]). The mobility of capital cannot be compared with that of the workers. Who is the employer today? Who will it be tomorrow? Recognition of the employer at international level has been a struggle for many trade unions, at regional and global level. The role of the law has also to be made clear, as well as the interaction between legislation and collective independence. The case of the European Union is important. The role of the European Works Council has to be considered very seriously and on a permanent basis. This is the place where workers can obtain direct information on the development of labour relations, and more importantly on the strategies of their 'real' employer, especially as regards employment and offshoring. It must not be forgotten that this experience is closely linked to the European 'social model' and to political and cultural contexts. Not all governments and enterprises seek to facilitate and promote regional or global dialogue, and some enterprises even reject the economic and managerial appropriateness of such dialogue, even attempting to do without workers' unions at all costs.

In today's world, it is vital to possess a deep understanding of the various and changing relationships between enterprises as well as between institutions, at national, regional and global level. Some (not to say the vast majority of) labour and social security lawyers have, if not a simplistic view of the employer, then at the very least a static one. The complex and changing links between enterprises are key to their existence and development. Obviously the legal linkage has to be understood within the economic and technical framework, as well as the financial strategies. Triangular employment relationships are now very common, but not always conducive to the implementation of the labour legislation and collective agreements. In many situations, coordination between several parties to the employment relationship must be established.[17] The employer is not the only one in charge of implementing labour legislation, especially that related to safety and health at work, wages and trade union rights. The role of the law is to find the best way to take account of the complexity and permanent changes of

---

[16] There cannot be social dialogue if full implementation of the freedom of association is absent.

[17] This is especially true for migrant workers. We know the complexity of the situation and how legal concepts can be used in the worst way, sometimes relating to criminal activities at national as well at global level (See the integrated approach implemented by the ILO concerning migrant workers, *Report VI: Towards a Fair Deal for Migrant Workers in the Global Economy* (International Labour Conference, 92nd Session, Geneva, International Labour Office, 2004), available at: http://www.ilo.org/public/english/standards/relm/ilc/ilc92/pdf/rep-vi.pdf.)

these links between employers and enterprises. Legislation and collective bargaining need to find flexible ways to handle these links. Establishing the right balance between security and dynamics has always been a necessity for labour and social security law. Promoting good practices and fighting the bad one is the goal of every lawyer who respects the rule of law and democracy. Creativity is needed to obtain such a result. And we know that it is not always easy for lawyers to find a way to link the diverging interests and be creative at the same time.[18]

In addition, the labour and social security lawyer cannot avoid the debate on the effectiveness of the rules and the efficiency of legal action. We all know the lack of seriousness of some distinguished colleagues in describing their well adapted rules in detail and their wonderful labour code in theory. But in practice, never ask the question: for whom are you in practice implementing legal instruments? We know the awful answer all around the world. In some regions and countries, 90 per cent at least of the active population works outside labour law rules and without social security protection. This situation, from an expert's point of view, is critical. Are we drafting laws for a very small minority of the active population? Are we omitting the vast majority of the population from our theories and arguments?

First and foremost, we have to be cautious about the general consideration of this situation. We need to facilitate open and deep discussion, especially with our economist colleagues. This includes fighting the very simplistic views resulting from very limited knowledge—or complete ignorance—of law in practice and what the rule of law means. At the same time, we also need to convince other lawyers that simplistic answers to legal points are impossible to put into practice, if not in total contradiction with the very legitimate goal they aim at. On one hand, it would be easy to say that the informal economy provides evidence of the lack of relevance of the rules, especially those on labour and social security. But from experience we all know that the lack of implementation of any rule does not automatically provide evidence of its lack of relevance or of the necessity to suppress or modify it. We never find complete and perfect implementation of any article of a law or collective agreement. Any legal rule—in a democracy

---

[18] For many reasons that are not all related to her/his 'conservatism'. Possibly, the lawyers in relations with employers and workers, are far more reluctant to change things, being aware of the strategies in using law. Those in relations with politicians are also aware of the relativity of the law. Nevertheless, law cannot be a pure instrument. It always expresses values, and of necessity involves ethics. Sometimes, however, we would expect more commitment to the rule of law, and a more modest approach by politicians. Deep and broad reflection on governance is needed. See S. Deakin, *Renewing Labour Market Institutions*, International Institute for Labour Studies, ILO Social Policy Lectures, Central European University, Budapest (Geneva, International Labour Office, 2004), 86. In this perspective, international labour law is of the greatest interest and valuable use.

at least—is always under debate and pressure, from its adoption to its implementation. Implementation can vary by state depending on the role played by the courts, the administration, and the social as well as civil actors. We always need to explain and make clear that there is no mechanical functioning of law. Because they are related to human beings—institutions never being separate from their members—the rules have a variety of ways of being implemented, at different levels. The informal economy cannot be looked at as simply a failure of the law or a revolt against it.

On the other hand, we need to be very cautious with those labour lawyers who stress that the way to fight the informal economy is to extend current definitions, categories and protections to the people concerned. There is evidence that this 'imperialistic' view does not provide the legal keys to solving the basic issues of working conditions and social security for those working in the black or grey areas of the economy. There is no legal panacea to the extension to all workers of 'classical' labour and social security law around the world, especially not to those who are in contact with reality or those not benefiting from the vast and diverse experience of the International Labour Office. The lesson to be learned is essentially one of pragmatic adaptation and progressive solutions, both socially and legally.[19] Obviously law alone cannot fight the many problems linked to the informal economy—poverty, corruption, violence, discrimination and exclusion. But labour and social security law, if linked to realities and deeply rooted in society, can be a great help. This is precisely why the International Labour Organisation is committed to facilitating consensus on the way it can provide the employer and worker with new, dynamic definitions. Both the ILO vision since 1919 and international labour law are a great help to this end.

3. ILO WORK

The International Labour Organisation is committed to putting into practice what is enshrined in its Constitution. We always need to keep in mind what the Philadelphia Declaration says[20] about the aims and purposes of the International Labour Organisation and of the principles which should inspire the policy of its members, reaffirming that the Organisation is based in particular on these principles. The first is: (a) '[l]abour is not a commodity'. This is of fundamental importance when considering the basic definition of employer and worker. Equally important is (b) the principle of freedom 'essential to sustained progress'. In addition, (c) 'poverty anywhere constitutes a danger to prosperity everywhere'. The fact that there is (d) a

---

[19] See K. Sankaran, 'Labour Standards and the Informal Economy in South Asia: Need for a Rights-Centered Approach' (2002) XXIV *Delhi Law Revue* 90.
[20] ILO Constitution, 22 ff.

'war against want', which can waged by the representatives of workers, employers and governments should also be stressed. The answers to the problems we are facing can be found only 'in free discussion and democratic decision with a view to the promotion of the common welfare'. Is there any word written in this Constitution that is not of critical importance at the beginning of a new millennium?

However, it must not be concluded from the problems encountered that the introduction of principles and definitions results in the non-relevance of a body of standards, any more than it would from a doctrinal construction.[21] It is quite sufficient to use the example of the difficulty in applying legal standards, especially in the field of labour. In the field of international labour law alone, it is the least hasty to proclaim that conventions are little ratified or that they have only limited effect. Rigorous and comparative analysis is required on the obstacles to the application of law. It is not enough to use generalities. The real impact of such standards on labour law in different countries has to be measured.[22] Leaving aside national or regional realities is indispensable in order to measure what is expected and perceived of the law.[23] From a technical point of view, and taking as an example issues of safety and health at work, or of labour inspection, it is obvious that the impact of international labour conventions is great and goes well beyond the number of ratifications obtained. Some international labour standards have such an influence on legislation that it is easy to forget them. They have become common and comparative law. Naturally, this is not the case for all conventions. It cannot be denied, however, that there is too little knowledge and use of international labour standards.

It must also be added that international labour law is part of a wider project: that of developing a state of law, without which there are no freedoms or rights for citizens. The prime target for international conventions remains the state, and this must continue to play a determining role both in the ratification and application of standards. It should be added that all regulatory modalities should be linked, without any one being able to replace another. The distinction between hard law and soft law must be the object of discussion and common appreciation.[24] This is the cause of countless

---

[21] See, more generally, the work of Professor Bob Hepple in 'Rights at Work: Discussion Paper' (Geneva, International Institute for Labour Studies, International Labour Office, DR/147/2003, 2003), 28 and in *Labour Laws and Global Trade* (Oxford, Hart Publishing, 2005), 302.

[22] See *The Impact of International Labour Conventions and Recommendations* (Geneva, International Labour Office, 1977). An update of this publication would be most welcome.

[23] See *Standards and Fundamental Principles and Rights at Work in Asia and the Pacific*, 13th Asian Regional Meeting, Bangkok, Aug. 2001 (Geneva, International Labour Office, 2001). R. Blanpain (ed.), *Labour Relations in the Asia-Pacific Countries* (The Hague, Kluwer, 2004), 159.

[24] See J.J. Kirton and M.J. Trebilcock (eds), *Hard Choices, Soft Law: Voluntary Standards in Global Trade, Environment and Social Governance* (Burlington, Vt, Ashgate, Global Environmental Governance Series, 2004), 372.

misunderstandings between lawyers from different systems and cultures. Is it not high time we noted how synergy between standards, whatever their degree of accuracy and the legal force, is born of a more extensive and diversified labour law, but is also more complex and uncertain than in the past? The regional dimension of the development of labour law, like the practice of comparative labour law, which is now practical and done on a daily basis, must also be highlighted.[25] It is obvious that on the international scene, new players seem to be taking a more important role, in the shape of multinational and transnational corporations whose economic power is enormous[26] or NGOs whose influence is felt in many areas, including in the legal field. But this has in no way jeopardised the importance of the legal status in any country. The multiplication of sources of law should not weaken the national laws of a state, but on the contrary strengthen them. Normative independence, whatever its source, can never claim to push aside state or international heteronomy. The plea for good world governance[27] implies close attention to the strengthening of legal status as well as a viable link between legal sources, irrespective of their degree of accuracy and legal force.

However, without bringing into question the foundations of a discipline, certain limits must nonetheless be discussed, as must certain definitions, as well as adaptations proposed and strengthening made in order to maintain the indispensable link between economic and social realities on the one hand and on national and international law on the other. In the field of human labour, we cannot speak of comparative law as if it were applicable only to a swimming pool or skiing. The development of labour law, like that of social security law, cannot be separated from current thinking and study of the human being at work, whose normative importance and differentiating function must not be underestimated. The ILO Constitution and its annexes express a vision that translates mainly into normative action, whose content can vary according to the period and the context. But primarily it is a question of who provides the historical meaning, social value and strong ethical content to labour law. The links established between various

---

[25] In Europe, it is useful to study the convergence and diversity of working conditions and employment (see D. Vaughan-Whitehead (ed.), *Working and Employment Conditions in New EU Member States: Convergence or Diversity?* (Geneva, European Commission, International Labour Office, 2005), 381. In the Americas, the social dimension of economic integration processes occupies many labour lawyers: see A. Ciudad Reynaud, *Labour Standards and the Integration Process in the Americas* (Lima, International Labour Office, 2001), 268; F. Walker Errazuriz, *La legislación laboral de los Estados Unidos de Norteamérica y Chile. Un análisis comparado* (Santiago de Chile, International Labour Office, 2003), 155.

[26] Mr Bill Gates's own opinions in his speech at the opening of the 58th Session of the World Health Assembly are of interest: available at: http://www.who.int/mediacentre/news/releases/2005/pr_wha02/en/.

[27] See the report of the World Commission on the Social Dimension of Globalisation, *A Fair Globalisation—Creating Opportunities for All* (Geneva, International Labour Law, 2004), available at: http://www.ilo.org/public/english/fairglobalization/report/index.htm.

elements of such a law, mainly at international level, are essential and cannot be separated or questioned. Without concrete application of the diversity of human labour situations and the necessity to promote protection and responsibility, adaptation and security, there is no labour law—in the consistent and sustainable meaning of the term—that cannot be developed in a sustainable and useful way. This is doubtless why rigorous study of obstacles to the application of national and international labour standards must be carried out based on realities. The scope of the danger must be measured: that of hasty generalisation, of a remote and simplistic doctrinal view, that of legal ignorance by the international community on issues of labour and employment. Each of us is aware of this danger in all places and situations. As lawyers we must propose definitions and institutions that will extend the indispensable legal protections to the human being at work and also promote economic activity without which there is no real social protection.

4. DECENT WORK PROMOTED THROUGH A CONVERGENCE OF KNOWLEDGE

In law, as in all disciplines, the specialist can dream of giving his or her field—which is naturally at the centre of the scientific world—all his/her independence in order to emancipate him/herself from the bondage that is an obstacle to its full achievement (does one ever escape from the temptation to incarnate one's discipline?). And yet all of us are convinced that such an aspiration to absolute independence of a discipline, in absolute terms, is scientific madness as well as a technical illusion. The indispensable particularities of the legal profession that relate to it can and must only be founded on human labour.

Labour law is one of those professions in which the different interests are organised and the actors (employers and workers) produce state and conventional standards. This is a structure that is rooted in a past that cannot be obliterated. Or, rather, this past must shape the present and even its potential versatility of the discipline. Discussion with some colleagues in law faculties leads us to think that intelligence, with its apparently boundless disciplinary space, cannot be accompanied by any kind of taking into account of reality, or, worse, knowledge of reality or the diversity of social and economic situations. Labour, and more generally social, law is born of realities, of the translation into legal terms of the special constraints of the human condition at work, and the different legal modalities for dealing with labour collectivities in both individual and collective relations. Such account taking has not been—and is still probably not—welcome or acceptable to certain lawyers. It is not unusual to hear, in universities or among magistrates and even beyond, strong voices raised against labour standards. Crassly and arrogantly, labour law is simply stated as not being law, or law of inferior scientific value. Teaching labour law and international labour law is held up as pointless. The claim is that common law or civil law is quite adequate to cope with the situation.[28]

The lawyer's task is to make all work decent. It is simply a matter of giving back its own dimension to work: that of women and men at work in all its dimensions. There is a new reason for labour lawyers to come together. This definition was developed by the ILO under the leadership of Juan Somavia, its Director-General.[29] This is an objective whose modalities for progressive implementation are highly variable, but which correspond to needs expressed by those who are working, regardless of their qualifications, workplace, age, sex, economic environment or legal labour modalities.[30] This is quite simply the basic aim of the ILO in times of globalisation: 'that each man and woman can have access to decent and productive work in conditions of freedom, equality, security and dignity'.[31] The aim of the ILO is clearly expressed: 'Decent work for all'. But this is only a beginning. This is a global problem of the human condition at work in a global perspective and with a progressive dynamic. It is not a slogan that ILO officials are supposed to proclaim at every opportunity as a means of bureaucratic conformity.[32] Decent work is part of a development strategy, which implies fully integrating all normative action in such an effort. Major contributions are expected from lawyers, both technically and doctrinally, and will be decisive. But the legal substance of decent work acquires its full meaning only when it is developed in a multidisciplinary perspective. Labour law is at the heart of strategies aiming to promote social justice, democracy and economic development. To be in such a situation, lawyers must contribute to creating permanent, appropriate and innovative links between fundamental standards and technical standards related to work.

---

[28] In some countries, there is a trend in law faculties to a reduction of or even doing away with teaching of labour law, as of industrial relations in general training courses, given the lack of interest in research and thesis writing in these fields. On the other hand, business and management schools seem to be developing teaching and research. Could it be that law (mainly labour law) is no longer the business of lawyers? There seems to be a clear message that law is being 'secularised' or even 'instrumentalised', which is a cause for rejoicing. However, the multiple implications of such a development have to be mulled over.

[29] See J. Somavia, *Perspectives on Decent Work* (Geneva, International Labour Office, 2000), 79.

[30] 'It's the way ordinary men and women express their needs. . . Work on which to meet the needs of their families in safety and health, educate their children, and offer them income security after retirement, work in which they are treated decently and their basic rights are respected. That is what decent work is about': *ibid.*, at 17.

[31] Report of the Director-General, *Decent Work* (International Labour Conference, 87th Session, Geneva, International Labour Law, 1999), 3, available at: http://www.ilo.org/public/english/standards/relm/ilc/ilc87/rep-i.htm.

[32] Care has to be taken not to turn a definition into a slogan by making it into a sort of mantra. If taken seriously, it requires restraint and deepening in its use. Hence the major philosophical and spiritual reflections on decent work: see K. Tapiola, 'Preface' in D. Peccoud (ed), *Philosophical and Spiritual Perspectives on Decent Work* (Geneva, International Labour Office, 2004).

Starting with what has been said on the subject, and in a progressive though limited fashion, lawyers have to determine the many embellishments and possible uses of decent work in their own field. Such an affirmation underlines the many dimensions of technical processing of situations that differ widely depending on the economic, political and social contexts. A legal discipline can make no claim to coherence by being smug, even less so by making even the most assured doctrinal declarations. In many countries, labour law has doubtless contributed to the opening up of the law to other disciplines. Sociology, like psychology and labour economics, is a key element in dealing with issues related to work. These disciplines are not imprisoned in conceptual problems. We have to consider the multitude of situations of women and men at work, without regard to the qualifications required by law—and not necessarily just labour law. By linking different disciplines, law can play its part fully. Concepts and institutions have to be nourished by permanent interaction and evolution. Labour law has created over time institutions and instruments of its own and that need to be considered in the current context. Though there are problems, and some technical adjustment is needed, it is nevertheless a fact that its achievements since its inception in the middle of the nineteenth century remain essentially among the most relevant.

Legal subordination like (economic) dependency can undergo change in the way it is expressed—strengthened or relaxed according to trade, enterprise, level of economic development—but remains the determining factor for the legal discipline that deals with it. The shifting of disciplinary frontiers clearly seems to be a prelude to a renewal of the dynamic of social law. It matters little what name has been given to such a body of law: labour law or professional activity law. Its basic aim is to link institutions and definitions in a same spirit and movement, that of decent work. Globalisation— the novelty of which must never be exaggerated—implies a new and continuous search for complementarity between different standards, whatever their source, degree of constraint and even formulation.

18

What Immortal Hand or Eye?—
Who will Redraw the Boundaries of
Labour Law?

HARRY W ARTHURS*

What immortal hand or eye/could frame thy dreadful symmetry?

William Blake, *The Tyger* (1794)

1. INTRODUCTION

THE UNIFYING THEME of the contributions to this volume, and of much fine academic writing, is that we have to redefine the familiar 'boundaries of protection' established for workers by labour and social legislation in advanced democracies.

This formulation implies that the present boundaries have shifted so that they no longer define the appropriate domain of labour law. This shift—it is assumed—results from: (a) the original sin of inept conceptualisation or poor drafting of labour laws and/or (b) a subsequent fall from grace occasioned by the emergence of new paradigms of work and/or (c) the deliberate retrenchment of boundaries under the influence of neo-liberal policies. In each case, the result is that traditional communities of workers who once aspired to or enjoyed protection no longer receive it, and that new communities with equally compelling claims to protection are likely to be denied it. If we could but redraw the boundaries—it is assumed—we would then re-establish the proper zone of protection.

* President Emeritus, University Professor of Law and Political Science Emeritus, York University, Toronto, Canada. The views expressed in this chapter are expressed in my personal and academic capacity. They do not represent the position of Human Resources and Skills Development Canada or of the Commission Reviewing the Canada Labour Code Part III, of which I am the commissioner. I am grateful for the research assistance of Claire Mummé.

Obviously there is something to be said for this formulation, at least as the predicate of short-term diagnosis and prescription. But—I will argue—it underestimates the complexity and open-endedness of the problem.

The appearance of new paradigms of work results from transformations of the material conditions and of the legal, political, cultural, social and technological logics which on the one hand constituted earlier categories of 'labour', 'employee' or 'worker' and, on the other, defined the types and degrees of 'protection' society was willing and able to provide. (I list in Appendix I some of the transformations which have produced the new paradigms.) If indeed something as radical as these transformations has occurred, whether we redefine terms such as 'worker' or 'employee' more expansively, or introduce a new category of 'persons in need of protection', leaves unanswered both normative and political questions—who ought to be entitled to how much protection, from which risks, at what cost to whom and with what potential benefits?—and questions of modalities—what institutions and processes of private and public governance must be involved in providing protection and how can they be coerced, tempted or persuaded into doing so?

The answers to these questions will vary from one epistemic or diagnostic perspective to another, one country to another, one employment context to another, one political era to another. However, I maintain, there can be no 'answers'—only contestations, no definitive 'redrawing' of 'boundaries'—only ongoing negotiations and tentative compromises. In that sense, perhaps we have launched ourselves on a project which we will not be able to bring to a successful conclusion.

Nonetheless, since we are all committed to a practical and positive approach, I propose to isolate one factor in the equation. As with any other project of public policy formation, formal responsibility for 'redrawing the boundary' is usually thought to reside with some ministry or group of ministries specifically charged with the task. In the fordist era, that ministry was typically the Department (or Ministry) of Labour, although other government agencies were often involved. However, responsibility for 'redrawing the boundary' has increasingly been disseminated upwards, downwards and laterally across many agencies and departments of government and beyond. Moreover, since this dissemination is attributable both to work-related transformations referred to above and to exogenous influences, we cannot be sure in advance what results we are likely to achieve by shifting the boundary amongst legal and regulatory regimes. In the face of such ambiguities, what is needed is a new conception of labour law and a new approach to the institutions which offer workers protection.

While I will refer in general terms to Canadian experience, I do so only in order to invite readers to provide comparisons with their own countries. Comparisons may enable us to detect widespread tendencies or trends, to propose a general interpretation of these trends, and perhaps even to suggest policy responses to them.

2. THE STRANGE DISAPPEARANCE OF THE DEPARTMENT OF LABOUR

Canada's Department of Labour was founded in 1900[1] and continued to lead a separate existence until 1993 when it disappeared into a large, hybrid department called Human Resource Development Canada. In 2004, HRDC was reorganised as Human Resources and Skills Development Canada (HRSDC),[2] one of whose ministers was assigned specific responsibility for the HRSDC's 'Labour Program', as well as other functions. What do these recent changes in the location, autonomy, size and functions of the Ministry of Labour tell us about the prospects for 'redefining the boundaries of protection'?

Possibly nothing. The changes may simply reflect a variety of concerns including: the rationalisation and consolidation of government functions to achieve (or appear to achieve) economies in government operation; improving linkages amongst related departments to achieve more coherent policy outcomes; aggregating (or disaggregating) functions to mark a change of emphasis or direction in government philosophy; and opportunistically eliminating or adding departments to accommodate particular personalities or political constituencies. To the extent that the Department of Labour's descent into the relative obscurity of 'Program' stems from such concerns, its fate resembles that of many other units of government.

But possibly a great deal. In Canada, as in most western democratic countries, the Labour Department came to be perceived to be a 'natural' or 'functional' division of administrative and legislative responsibility comparable to, say, the Departments of Education, Agriculture, Industry or Foreign Affairs. Moreover, the creation of a Labour Department was understood to have symbolic significance for working people, especially in an era when they had only recently acquired the franchise, when collective bargaining was in its infancy, when labour standards were threatened by a predatory form of capitalism and when 'the social

---

[1] Canada created its Department of Labour in 1900 to deal with industrial disputes, collect labour statistics and improve labour conditions in public works. W.L. Mackenzie King was the first deputy minister (1900–1908) and then the first Minister of Labour (1909–1911) to hold that portfolio as a separate cabinet responsibility. King, a well-known expert in industrial relations, later served as an advisor to the Rockefellers on that subject (1914–18), became leader of the Liberal Party of Canada (1919) and then Prime Minister (1921–1926, 1926–1930, 1935–1948). See: http://www.collectionscanada.ca/notices/index-e.html.

[2] HRSDC is a single department, but four Ministers are politically accountable for various aspects of its programmes: Social Development, Ministry of State for Families and Caregivers, Human Resources Development and Labour and Housing.

question'—the welfare state—still agitated most economically advanced democracies.[3] Its continued existence in later years conveyed to workers that 'their' department would serve 'their' needs and protect 'their' interests, and that 'their' minister (often someone with links to the union movement) would present 'their' point of view sympathetically when important political and economic decisions affecting workers were taken at the senior levels of government.

For various reasons, however, the Department of Labour is no longer viewed in quite the same way. The increasing influence of the business community on public policy, the widespread acceptance of market solutions to social problems, the shift from Keynesian to supply-side economics and the desire to de-regulate labour markets are some of the practical reasons Labour Departments have been reconfigured and their original functions redistributed, downgraded or abandoned. And the symbolic reassurance provided by the existence of a special Labour Department is no longer thought appropriate. Given the dissolution of working class solidarity (to the extent it ever existed), the decline of trade union membership and power, the changing character of work, and the rise of cross-cutting identities such as race, gender and geography, 'labour' has become a less descriptive, evocative or compelling signifier than it once was.

What happens to 'Labour Departments' when they are no longer 'Labour Departments'? Some jurisdictions have chosen to reorganise their traditional functions in order to emphasise labour's role in a productive economy. Canada, as noted, has created a federal Department of Human Resources Development; British Columbia has a Department of Employment and Investment; Germany and Austria have Ministries of Economics and Labour; Ireland has a Ministry of Enterprise, Trade and Employment; a number of American states have Departments of Labour and Workforce Development or Departments of Labour and Industry; in the United Kingdom, many of the functions of the Labour Ministry have been simply absorbed into the Department of Trade and Industry (DTI). By contrast, other jurisdictions seem to focus on integrating the traditional Labour Department mission into a broader social welfare agenda. France and Québec have Departments of Labour and Solidarity; Japan's Ministry is called Health, Labour and Welfare; Mexico has a Ministry of Labour and Social Security; the United Kingdom, in addition to the DTI, has a department called Work and Pensions.[4]

The significance of these new departmental names and mandates is that each potentially signals a conscious departure from the fordist appellation

---

[3] D.T. Rodgers, *Atlantic Crossings: Social Politics in a Progressive Age* (Cambridge, Mass, Harvard University Press, 1998).

[4] See University of Connecticut, Department of Economics, Directory of Ministries of Labor or Employment, available at: http://edric.repec.org/minlabor.html.

and agenda of the old Labour Department, a new approach to thinking about relations amongst the state, capital and labour. In the one case, 'labour' deserves attention because it is an important factor of production ('human resources' in the case of Canada, which also has a department of 'natural resources') whose 'development' will enhance national prosperity. In the other case, 'labour' deserves attention because it comprises a significant clientele of those potentially in need of protection, either materially in the form of social security or symbolically by way of social solidarity. In neither scenario, however, does 'labour' feature as a distinct and significant social and political constituency with rights and agency. This is rather different from the heyday of the post-war welfare state in which Labour Departments were centrally concerned with collective bargaining, employment standards, occupational health and safety, full employment strategies and the promotion of labour's participation in corporatist or tripartite policy formation (or, more cynically, with making unions feel that they were influential).

Of course, Labour Departments never had a monopoly over crucial decisions affecting the well-being of the working class. Other departments and agencies of government always played a role. What has become noteworthy, however, is the way in which the Labour Department's mandate has not only been embedded in more complex departmental structures, but redistributed horizontally, upwards and downwards to sites of governance where the Labour Minister (or equivalent) has little or no influence, where 'labour'—as an interest group or constituency of concern—has no voice, and where 'labour' issues are not even on the agenda as it is laid down by the dominant governmental actors. In such a context, the prospects for 'redefining the boundaries of protection' are not great.

3. RESPONSIBILITY FOR DEFINING THE BOUNDARIES OF PROTECTION: HORIZONTAL REDISTRIBUTION

In many countries, responsibility for labour-related policy-making and programme delivery has migrated away from Labour Departments and now resides with other state agencies and actors. The extent and pace of migration have accelerated during the era of the so-called Washington consensus, of neo-liberal globalisation.

Today, for example, autonomous central banks are expected to use their power to set interest rates, and their influence over credit and investment, deliberately to 'cool out' the economy to prevent wages from rising too rapidly. Ministries of Finance regularly initiate reductions in taxation, public expenditures and public employment with the declared objective of stimulating private sector investment and job creation. However, these reductions frequently take the form of cuts in social programmes, training schemes, pensions and unemployment insurance—thus engendering insecurity amongst workers (especially vulnerable workers) and shifting the balance of power in the labour market. In addition, they often result in lower levels of staffing in labour inspectorates and tribunals and therefore in lower levels of regulatory compliance with labour standards. Ministries of Foreign Affairs and International Trade negotiate comprehensive trade treaties whose predictable consequences include the restructuring of the economy, the redeployment (and often long-term unemployment) of significant elements of the workforce and the weakening of the communities and organisational structures from which labour draws its political and economic power. If Ministries of Labour are involved in trade negotiations, it is usually at a side table and without being able to assert much influence; labour organisations are seldom involved at all. Ministries of Justice, Human Rights or Minority Affairs tend to enrol the workers most 'in need of protection' as their own clientele, thus detaching them from the generality of 'labour' policy and from their primary relationship with the Labour Department, and linking their protection and social advancement instead to the vindication of their identities and rights as women, people of colour or disabled people.

Ministries of Immigration issue temporary work permits to 'guest workers'. Some of these—vulnerable domestic or agricultural workers—have need of special protections (which they sometimes do not receive), and their presence may adversely affect the labour market for workers who reside permanently in the jurisdiction. Others—technicians, professionals and business executives—by their very presence help to establish a global market for knowledge workers whose comings and goings may generate labour market policies designed to stem a 'brain drain' or encourage a 'brain gain'. Initiatives by ministries concerned with urban planning, social housing, public infrastructure, health, education, child care or transport may directly increase or reduce job opportunities in their respective domains. Equally importantly, they establish the social environment of life and work which facilitates or inhibits labour force participation by particular groups of workers. A shift in the source of funding for health care, pensions and job training from the state to employers and employees may make sense from the point of view of reducing government spending; but it will have a significant impact on unit costs of production and thus on the complexity and intensity of employer–employee negotiations. Public policies designed to promote competition in order to ensure consumers access to low cost goods and services may collide with efforts by unions to control the supply of labour in order to drive up wages.

Or, to take a final example: in Canada, as in many other countries, the Department of Justice is the 'government's law firm'. But while of course it consults 'client' departments, unlike most law firms, Justice generally makes decisions for them rather than simply following their instructions.

Consequently legal values and the organisational logic of the Justice Department, rather than the pragmatics of labour and employment policy, are likely to shape the outcome of litigation, the drafting and interpretation of legislation and even the evolution of policy. Whether Justice lawyers can be spared from other tasks for the enforcement of labour legislation, what stance the government should take when labour laws are challenged on federalism or Charter grounds, what degree of juridification ought to be introduced into adjudicative proceedings at what cost to the ability of unrepresented workers to participate: such questions are very likely to be resolved by the Department of Justice, not the Department of Labour.

In each instance, decisions taken in other ministries and agencies—responding to their distinctive missions, ideologies, clienteles and policy logics—are likely to have an important, even transformative, impact on labour policy and on workers even though Labour Departments are not directly or influentially involved. The competition amongst policy logics thus greatly complicates the task of 'redefining the boundaries of protection'.

4. RESPONSIBILITY FOR DEFINING THE BOUNDARIES OF PROTECTION: REDISTRIBUTION UPWARDS

Perhaps as a result of frustration over labour's diminished visibility on the public policy agenda, and its dwindling influence in the councils of state, some workers' organisations and advocates have shifted the focus of their efforts 'upwards', from the level of administrative and legislative lobbying to constitutional litigation as well as from national to trans-national forums.

A. Constitutional Litigation: Using Charters of Rights

Constitutional litigation with a view to 'redefining the boundaries of protection' has not been a conspicuous success for reasons suggested above—the potential incompatibility of labour—specific norms and norms of general application. In Canada, attempts to secure 'normal' collective bargaining rights for provincial public servants, police and agricultural workers by means of litigation based on the Charter of Rights and Freedoms finally resulted in a lofty declaration affirming their freedom to associate; however, they continue to be excluded from rights guaranteed by statute to other workers.[5] Attempts to protect the rights of workers to picket, as the

---

[5] *Reference re Public Service Employees Relations Act* [1987] 1 SCR 313; *Delisle v Canada* [1999] 2 SCR 989; *Dunmore v Ontario (Attorney General)* [2001] 3 SCR 1016.

exercise of freedom of expression under the Charter, likewise produced rhetorical victories and practical defeats.[6] Ironically, labour's most unequivocal Charter victories have benefited not so much workers in need of protection as workers already receiving it as members of relatively powerful civil service and building trades unions.[7]

Claims based on Charter guarantees of equality have produced somewhat more favourable outcomes. For example, female and homosexual workers have been held to be entitled to the same employment-related benefits as heterosexual males.[8] However, in general the labour market position of historically disadvantaged groups (part-time, women, disabled, low-skilled and visible minority workers) has changed only marginally, if at all.[9] Even when gains have been made under legislation, they have sometimes proved to be ephemeral. Thus, in one case, a provincial government repealed employment equity legislation altogether;[10] in another it delayed implementation of a pay equity award in favour of its female employees on grounds of financial exigency.[11] In neither case were these workers able to secure Charter protection of what were arguably their vested rights.

There seems to be little in the Canadian experience, then, to suggest that constitutionally-based strategies designed to protect vulnerable workers are likely to be successful. However, one scholar has argued that the Charter has had the unanticipated effect of making judges more sympathetic to workers, with the result that common law, rather than constitutional, doctrines have become more favourable to them.[12] On the other hand, as he also indicates, most vulnerable workers 'in need of protection' cannot afford to sue, so that ironically the prime beneficiaries of worker-friendly common law doctrines tend to be relatively affluent managerial, technical and professional employees.

Finally, the overall effect of these legal moves 'upward' is gradually to integrate labour law more thoroughly into the general legal system and, to

---

[6] *Retail, Wholesale and Department Store Union, Local 580 v Dolphin Delivery Ltd* [1986] 2 SCR 573; *Retail, Wholesale and Department Store Union, Local 558 v Pepsi-Cola Canada Beverages (West) Ltd* [2002] 1 SCR 156.

[7] *Lavigne v Ontario Public Service Employees Union* [1991] 2 SCR 211; *R v Advance Cutting & Coring Ltd* [2001] 3 SCR 209.

[8] *Brooks v Canada Safeway* [1989] 1 SCR 1219; *Egan v Canada* [1995] 2 SCR 213.

[9] H. Arthurs and B. Arnold, 'Does the Charter Matter?' (2005) 11 *Review of Constitutional Studies* 37.

[10] Employment Equity Act 1993, SO 1993, c 35, Repealed by SO 1995, c 4, effective 14 Dec. 1995.

[11] *Newfoundland (Treasury Board) v Newfoundland and Labrador Association of Public and Private Employees (NAPE)* [2004] 3 SCR 381.

[12] *McKinley v BC Tel* [2001] 2 SCR 161, and see G. England, 'The Impact of the Charter on Canadian Individual Employment Law: Reworking an Old Story' in M. Lynk and J. Craig (eds.), *The Charter at Work: Essays on Constitutionalism and Labour Law* (Toronto, University of Toronto Press, forthcoming).

that extent, to reduce its uniqueness and autonomy.[13] As the whole development of modern labour law was thought to depend on precisely the opposite tendency—the creation of distinctive substantive rules and specialised tribunals—integration could be seen as a retrograde move. Or, to phrase the matter differently, special 'boundaries of protection' were historically important precisely because they had the effect of removing workers from the inhospitable domain of general law and relocating them in a more friendly environment. The question is whether these boundaries continue to be important for the same reason, or whether they now are perceived to stand between workers and the protections available to all citizens under constitutional or other legal doctrines of general application.

B. Transnational Strategies: Labour Standards, Human Rights and Trade Regimes

Attempts to appeal beyond national courts and legislatures to universal human rights standards and internationally recognised labour norms have been equally unrewarding. As I have suggested elsewhere, Canadian courts and tribunals have barely conceded the existence of globalisation,[14] and Canadian lawyers (like their counterparts in many countries) seldom invoke transnational legal norms.[15] Canadian courts do occasionally cite ILO conventions and refer to the international declarations of human rights. But almost always these references are mere make-weights.[16] Nor is there any sign that Canada will apply its laws extraterritorially to protect foreign workers from abusive treatment at the hands of Canadian corporations. Nor have Canadian governments been particularly sensitive to allegations (and even rulings) that they have failed to adhere to international labour standards.[17]

---

[13] H. Arthurs, *The New Economy and the Demise of Industrial Citizenship* (Kingston, IRC Press, 1997), and 'The New Economy and the New Legality: Industrial Citizenship and the Future of Labour Arbitration' (1999) 7 *Canadian Employment & Labour Law Journal* 45; P. Verge and G. Vallée, *Un droit du travail? Essai sur la spécificité du droit du travail* (Cowansville, Les Editions Yvon Blais, 1997).

[14] H. Arthurs, 'Who's Afraid of Globalization? The Transformation of Canadian Labour Law' in J. Craig and M. Lynk (eds.), *Globalization and the Future of Labour Law* (Cambridge, Cambridge University Press, 2006) and H. Arthurs, 'The Administrative State Goes to Market (and cries wee, wee, wee all the way home)' (2005) 55 *University of Toronto Law Journal* 797.

[15] H. Arthurs, 'The Role of Global Law Firms in Constructing or Obstructing a Transnational Regime of Labour Law' in R.P. Appelbaum, W. Felstiner and V. Gessner (eds.), *Rules and Networks: The Legal Culture of Global Business Transactions* (Oxford, Hart Publishing, 2001), 273.

[16] B. Roy, 'An Empirical Survey of Foreign Jurisprudence and International Instruments in Charter Litigation' (2004) 62 *University of Toronto Faculty Law Review* 99.

[17] Canada, eg, has attracted more complaints that it has violated ILO freedom of association conventions than any other country. See Heenan Blakie LLP, 'Canada and the ILO: Freedom of Association Since 1982', available at: http://www.cec-cce.ca/research_other/article_one.htm.

The long-standing debate over the effects of globalisation on labour conditions in the first and third worlds has now been unfolding for some time. The arguments are complex; the evidence is mixed. But one thing is indisputable: so far governments have exhibited no appetite for conditioning access to world markets on respect for workers' rights and interests.

Worse yet: even those relatively rare trade-related agreements specifically designed to ensure adherence to core labour standards—including protection for vulnerable workers—have had little or no effect. Thus, the North American Agreement on Labour Cooperation, arguably an innovative attempt to embed the principle of respect for labour rights within the constitutional norms of trade regimes,[18] has produced disappointing outcomes. (In this case, the structure of Canadian federalism partly explains its failure: the national government, which signed the NAALC, has no right to bind provincial governments which have primary legislative authority over labour and employment matters.)

If transnational strategies hold any hope for vulnerable workers at home or abroad, it is in the sphere of political and social action, not in conventional legal forums. Canadians, like citizens of other advanced economies, have supported campaigns designed to help vulnerable workers by bringing pressure to bear on exploitative employers and repressive governments. But while such campaigns have sometimes borne fruit, they do not constitute a systematic, institutionalised process for addressing the problems of workers excluded from protection either at home or abroad. However, they may generate some long-term effects by promoting acceptance of 'soft law' concepts which will ultimately form part of the normative environment within which 'hard law'—state law—functions; they may prompt discussion amongst governments, employers and social movements leading to the adoption of voluntary codes of conduct or better employment practices; and they may stimulate academic reflection on how to create effective protections for workers of all kinds and countries in a globalised world where states, the traditional architects of such protections, are unwilling or unable to pursue their calling.

5. RESPONSIBILITY FOR DEFINING THE BOUNDARIES OF PROTECTION: REDISTRIBUTION DOWNWARDS

If attempts at upward redistribution of responsibility for defining the boundaries of protection have not produced tangible results, tendencies favouring downward distribution, always present, seem to be accelerating.

---

[18] See J.S. McKennirey, 'Labor in the International Economy' (1996) 22 *Canada–United States Law Journal* 183.

A. The Privatisation of Responsibility

Modern labour law presupposes the existence of a sustained, consensual relationship between the providers and recipients of services—whether called 'employment' or something else. It therefore concedes to those parties an indispensable role in defining who gets what degree of protection. True, the parties may be represented by proxies—a union, an employers' association, a referral service, a government agency; true, their relationship may be 'consensual' only in the most formal sense; and true, that relationship may be past, prospective or precarious. But in the absence of a work-related relationship established by the parties, the protections provided by labour law cannot be invoked.

Once that relationship is acknowledged, moreover, the parties are assigned considerable responsibility for defining the boundaries of protection. Collective bargaining partners are given relatively wide latitude to define who will be hired and under what terms and conditions of employment. They can construct their own 'web of rule' which confers greater protection on some employees and less on others. They can largely define the modalities of negotiation and—within stricter legal limits—choose their weapons of conflict, again with differential effects on different groups of workers. Individual workers and their employers are also allowed to negotiate the terms of individual contracts of employment so long as they avoid forbidden grounds of discrimination and operate above statutorily defined minimums. And finally, for their own purposes the parties are pretty much free to include or exclude anyone they wish as parties to 'employment' relationships, although this will not necessarily determine their eligibility for statutory protections.

Thus, even during the 'golden age' of postwar labour legislation the state allowed private actors (often in practice one private actor) to determine the scope of protection for workers. However, with a decline in union density, partial de-regulation of the labour market, and a shift in the balance of power between workers and employers, we can anticipate that buyers of labour will act increasingly unilaterally to ensure that fewer rather than more sellers of labour will be protected. We can already see developments tending in this direction. Employers, after all, invented and insisted on the new forms of non-standard employment which are becoming commonplace. Employers generally sought, and benefited from, the shift in the site of enforcement of labour standards and workers' rights from state to private tribunals[19] in which protection will almost certainly be retrenched rather than expanded. Employers have persuaded governments (and, often, social movements) that corporate self-regulation is preferable to state regulation,

---

[19] See, eg, Employment Standards Act, 2000, SO 2000, c 41, ss 84–89, s 97; Labour Relations Act, 1995, SO 1995, c 1, Sched A, s 114(1); *Weber v Ontario Hydro* [1995] 2 SCR 929; *Parry Sound (District) Social Services Administration Board v Ontario Public Service Employees Union, Local 324* [2003] SCC 42.

again with foreseeable consequences in terms of which workers ultimately receive how much protection. And finally, conservative think tanks, supported by employers, have taken the lead in urging governments seriously to consider the further privatisation of social risk—which is already considerable.[20] At the very least, these two, linked developments are unlikely to result in more workers receiving better protection.

B. Devolution of Constitutional Authority

Many commentaries on globalisation note that, in parallel to the upward drift of power to supra-national bodies, there is a downward drift to sub-national authorities. In the context of the present discussion, the peculiarities of Canadian federalism and the particular form which this downward movement takes in the Canadian context are not important in themselves. However, they may serve as a reminder that the project of redefining the boundaries of protection in the labour context may become enmeshed in the project of redefining the boundaries of power as amongst local, regional and national governments.

In Canada, as elsewhere, the assertion of regional, linguistic and ethnic identities is one of the primary forces driving the devolution of authority from the national government. Québec's continuing flirtation with secession, regional alienation in Alberta and British Columbia with their distinctive political cultures and economic profiles, the recrudescence of historic grievances in Newfoundland, claims for self-government by First Nations: these and other tensions have made the federal government wary of using any of its powers to the full. In the case of labour and employment matters, that power was radically curtailed by a series of somewhat bizarre decisions in the 1920s and 1930s, which left the federal government with authority over only 10 per cent of the national workforce—the balance of which is regulated by provincial governments.[21] Subsequent constitutional

---

[20] Coverage of Canada's Employment Insurance regime has declined from about 80% of the workforce to under 50%; expenditure on social housing and welfare has fallen precipitously; public schemes of old age security are being considered for partial or full privatisation; prospects for increased state expenditures on social reproduction—day care, for example—are at a low ebb, with negative results for women workers in particular. See generally J. Brodie, 'The Politics of Social Policy in the Twenty-First Century' in D. Broad and W. Anthony (eds), *Citizens or Consumers? Social Policy in a Market Society* (Halifax, Fernwood Publishing, 1999), 37; D. Broad and W. Anthony, 'Citizens or Consumers? Social Policy in a Market Society' in *ibid.*, 184; J. Fudge and B. Cossman, 'Introduction' in J. Fudge and B. Cossman (eds), *Privatization, Law and the Challenge to Feminism* (Toronto, University of Toronto Press, 2002), 3.

[21] *Toronto Electric Commissioners v Snider* (1925) 2 DLR 8 (PC); *AG Canada v AG Ontario* [1937] AC 326 (PC) (*Labour Conventions* case); R. Howse, 'The Labour Conventions Doctrine in an Era of Global Interdependence: Rethinking the Constitutional Dimensions of Canada's External Economic Relations' (1990) 16 *Canadian Business Law Journal* 160.

amendments gave the federal government power over unemployment insurance and old age pensions,[22] while several judicial decisions upheld federal power to intervene in labour market policy during wartime or in the context of a national economic crisis.[23] However, the fact remains that while Canada is a fully-integrated national economy over which the federal government is assigned control in many respects, it does not have the legislative right to redefine the boundaries of protection for most Canadian workers. Or rather: it does not clearly have that power. Arguably, it could seek to re-litigate the constitutional precedents which stripped away federal powers (as the United States did in the 1930s); or it could find new ways to use its existing powers and influence to take a more active role in promoting national labour policies.[24] But in the current context of Canadian federalism, it is most unlikely to do that.

The new political economy of North America reinforces these constitutional constraints on federal labour initiatives. Free trade with the United States, historically important to Canada and virtually doubled under NAFTA, has made it necessary for provinces to align their economies so as to take full advantage of their geographical proximity to huge US markets. Ontario, for example, has become dependent to an unhealthy degree on the auto mobile industry; Alberta has grown rich on exporting oil and gas; the export of electrical power is critical to Québec's economy. The result has been that international (primarily US) exports have become more important to most Canadian provinces than inter-provincial exports. The federal government therefore lacks not only constitutional control over the provinces but, increasingly, political and economic influence over them as well.

And the situation is more complicated yet. For many years following the war (during which labour policy was 'nationalised') inertia worked in favour of the provinces adhering to the federal model. This tendency was prolonged to some extent by innovative federal policies during the 1960s which influenced at least those provinces anxious to enact state-of-the-art legislation. But in recent years, provincial governments have tended to go

---

[22] Unemployment Insurance—Constitution Act, 1867, 30 & 31Vic, c 3 (UK) as amended by the Constitution Act, 1940, 3–4 Geo VI, c 36 (UK), (10 July, 1940), s 91(2)(a); Old Age Security—Constitution Act, 1867, 30 & 31 Vic, c 3 (UK), as amended by the Constitution Act, 1964, 12–13 Eliz II, c 73 (UK), as originally enacted by the British North America Act, 1951, 14–15 Geo VI, c 32 (UK), as repealed by the Constitution Act, 1982, s9 4(a).

[23] *Reference re: Application of Hours of Work Act to Metalliferous Mines* [1947] 1 WWR 841 (BCCA); *Reference re: Anti-Inflation Act (Canada)* [1976] 2 SCR 373.

[24] By way of example, the federal government has enacted employment equity legislation which, of course, does not legally bind employers under provincial jurisdiction. However, the legislation requires compliance by any corporation which has contractual relations with the federal government: Employment Equity Act, SC 1995, c 44, s 18. Similar use of its contracting power to deal with labour standards could conceivably extend the reach of federal labour power well beyond its present boundaries. In addition, the federal government has often used its constitutional power to tax and spend to lure provincial governments into social welfare schemes which are effectively national in scope, even though legislated and administered by the provinces.

their various ways, in accordance with their ideological predilections and what they perceived to be their economic interests. In several provinces at least, the result has been, if not a race to the bottom, then at least a stroll in that direction. In Ontario and British Columbia, for example, neo-conservative governments consciously adopted labour policies which would signal that these provinces were 'open for business'. The resulting retrenchment of labour rights not only exacerbated the difficulty of redrawing the boundaries of protection on a national basis; it initiated something like regulatory competition which may discourage otherwise progressive governments from attempting the task on their own.

The effect of devolution on Canadian labour policy may have no precise counterpart in other countries. However, in most countries there are regional, sectoral, ethnic and other constituencies—often not defined by their labour market role—which will argue that shifting the boundaries of protection in the labour sector harms or ignores their special interests and concerns. This is but one more example of how difficult it is to define either the population of protected workers or the modalities of protection in universal, or even national, terms. Without universal or national labour standards, and governance structures to make them effective—experience teaches—those most in need of protection are most likely to be denied it.

6. REGIME CHANGE: A CAVEAT ABOUT THE EFFECTS OF REDRAWING THE BOUNDARIES OF PROTECTION

An implicit assumption of the project of redrawing the boundaries of protection is that workers will thereby be transferred from one legal or regulatory regime to another—from the regime of private contract, say, to the regime of state regulation or to the regime of collective bargaining, or from the regime of employment to the regime of social welfare, of human rights or of entrepreneurship. These regime changes, which clearly do alter workers' legal entitlements, are also expected to alter their economic power, financial fortunes and personal autonomy and dignity. But is this necessarily so?

It has long been understood that legal regimes tend to emerge 'in the shadow of the law' as well as within its formal boundaries, and that these penumbral regimes sometimes subvert or distort the formal regimes alongside which they emerge.[25] For reasons I have discussed elsewhere, this is especially true of labour law.[26] It is therefore crucial when investigating the eligibility of particular workers for admission to particular legal regimes to ask two

---

[25] C. Albiston, 'Bargaining in the Shadow of Social Institutions: Competing Discourses and Social Change in the Workplace Mobilization of Civil Rights' (2005) 39 *Law and Society Review* 11.

[26] H. Arthurs, 'Labour Law without the State?' (1996) 46 *University of Toronto Law Journal* 1.

important questions. First, do workers subject to that regime in fact receive the protection it is supposed to provide, or are there practical obstacles which prevent them from asserting their rights and claiming their benefits? Secondly, even though a particular regime of state law affords them no protection, do workers in fact benefit from some alternative, non-state regime of workplace normativity, which provides at least a partial substitute?[27] There is no way of answering these questions in the abstract: each situation requires empirical investigation. However, this knowledge should make us at least a little wary of becoming over-invested in boundary-drawing.

7. CONCLUSION

The question which this chapter has addressed is not which workers are in need of protection, though that remains an important and controversial issue. Rather, it is how to deliver protection to any workers in the absence of an identifiable governmental champion, in the teeth of public policies which tend to assign low priority to workers' rights and interests, in a discursive universe where the very concepts of 'worker' and 'protection' no longer have the resonance they once did, in the context of structures of domestic and international political economy which are no longer congruent with labour markets and in the face of knowledge that shifting boundaries do not necessarily lead to transformations of empirical reality.

How, then, can we re-imagine the project of boundary definition so that it has the best chance of practical success?

As suggested earlier in this chapter, at this juncture in history it seems more likely that the domain of protection will contract rather than expand. However, if we can willingly suspend disbelief and imagine a more optimistic moment in which new categories of workers are being accommodated within newly-resuscitated regulatory and welfare regimes, the question arises whether 'boundaries' are any longer an appropriate metaphor. Boundaries are fixed for the long term; boundaries are binary in nature: one is either 'in' or 'out'; boundaries are clearly marked so that crossings occur or are prevented as a result of deliberate choice rather than by accident; and boundaries are consequential, in the sense that they trigger positive or negative

---

[27] H. Arthurs, 'Understanding Labour Law: The Debate Over Industrial Pluralism' (1985) 38 *Current Legal Problems* 83; L. Haiven, 'Past Practice and Custom and Practice: "Adjustment" and Industrial Conflict in North America and the United Kingdom' (1990–91) 12 *Comparative Labour Law Journal* 300; D.G. Taras, 'Portrait of Nonunion Employee Representation in Canada: History, Law, and Contemporary Plans' in B.E. Kaufman and D.G. Taras (eds), *Nonunion Employee Representation: History, Contemporary Practice and Policy* (Armonk, NY, ME Sharpe, 2000) 121; D.G. Taras, 'Alternative Forms of Employee Representation and Labour Policy' (2002) 28 *Canadian Public Policy* 121; C.J. Cranford, J. Fudge, E. Tucker and L.F. Vosko, *Self-Employed Workers Organize: Law, Policy and Unions* (Montreal/Kingston, McGill-Queens University Press, 2005).

outcomes for those who move from one side to the other. But none of these characteristics describes the likely future of work, workers or labour law.

Indeterminacy and informality, flexibility and fluidity are more likely to capture the future of our subject. Perhaps, then, a 'magnetic field' is a more appropriate metaphor for labour law—a zone within which opposing and attracting forces interact to produce calculable but not invariable outcomes. The metaphor of a magnetic field is widely used in the literature of legal pluralism (including studies of workplace normativity[28]) and it resonates with the work of Teubner, Bourdieu and other scholars whose focus is on the context-specific nature of legal regimes, their semi-autonomy, their reflexive character and especially their interaction with and adaptation to other regimes.[29] In such a vision of labour law, content and coverage may be less significant than the modalities and the direction of movement. The greatest gains for workers might perhaps come, not from securing access to a fixed array of legally enforceable protections and benefits, but from being regarded as an indispensable component of every calculus of public policy which might affect them.

In this new vision of labour law, the well-being of workers would not be simply the externality accidentally generated by deliberations convened for other purposes; rather it would be an explicit and important concern of all decision makers. This implies a new role for workers' representatives both within the enterprise and within the state; it implies therefore new means of identifying and empowering these representatives; and it implies new ways of harmonising the interests of workers, employers and other groups or of resolving inevitable conflicts amongst them which occur when those interests diverge. It also suggests that the role of the Ministry of Labour might evolve or expand so that the Ministry becomes an advocacy agency intervening with other public and private decision makers rather than, as now, primarily a deliverer of programmes and dispenser of services.

Or has disbelief been too easily suspended? If boundaries are not about to be drawn to expand the reach of labour law's protections, why would labour's voice and influence be enlarged? If labour does gain a voice of its own, would this alter any of the social or economic circumstances which have led to its present plight? If labour is to benefit from more effective advocacy by the Department of Labour, how will that advocacy come to prevail over other ministerial advocates with their own agendas and clients? And if, indeed, 'labour' and 'employment' and even 'worker' are terms which have been largely stripped of their significance, how are they to regain symbolic and practical heft?

---

[28] See, eg, S. Falk Moore, 'Law and Social Change: The Semi-autonomous Social Field as an Appropriate Subject of Study' (1973) 7 *Law and Society Review* 719.

[29] H. Arthurs, '"Landscape and Memory": Labour Law, Legal Pluralism and Globalization' in T. Wilthagen (ed.), *Advancing Theory in Labour Law and Industrial Relations in a Global Context* (Amsterdam, North Holland Press, 1998), 21.

APPENDIX

Shifts in Workplace Organisation and Activity

from manufacturing to service economy
from human power to machine power
from human intelligence to digital intelligence
from local to remote/global management

Shifts in Workplace Population and Worker Identities and Consciousness

from relatively homogenous to highly heterogeneous workplace populations
from an indisputably gendered and racialised to a contestably gendered and racialised division of labour
from working class collective identity to essentialised, individualised identities
from producer constituencies to consumer constituencies

Shifts in Workplace Governance

from security to flexibility
from rights to benefits
from managerial hierarchy to self/virtual management
from semi-tenured employment to affinity/relational contracts
from worker participation to passivity
from workplace conflict to cooperation/cooptation

Shifts in Public Governance and Discourse

from national to sub/transnational protection systems
from public governance to hybrid public/private governance
from generality to specificity of institutional arrangements
from specificity to generality of the language of protection
from justice/politics to efficiency/economics
from labour as a distinct policy domain to labour as a derivative of fiscal, trade, human rights, environmental, technology, welfare etc. policies

Index